Remembering Transitions

Media and Cultural Memory

Edited by
Astrid Erll · Ansgar Nünning

Volume 38

Remembering Transitions

Local Revisions and Global Crossings
in Culture and Media

Edited by
Ksenia Robbe

DE GRUYTER

ISBN 978-3-11-221372-8
e-ISBN (PDF) 978-3-11-070779-3
e-ISBN (EPUB) 978-3-11-070790-8
ISSN 1613-8961

Library of Congress Control Number: 2023939794

Bibliographic information published by the Deutsche Nationalbibliothek
The Deutsche Nationalbibliothek lists this publication in the Deutsche Nationalbibliografie;
detailed bibliographic data are available on the internet at http://dnb.dnb.de.

Cover image: Dane Gillett/iStock/Getty Images Plus
Typesetting: Integra Software Services Pvt. Ltd.
Printing and binding: CPI books GmbH, Leck

www.degruyter.com

Acknowledgments

This edited volume was long in the making and has benefitted from the input of many individuals and the support of several institutions. The idea for it originated during the editor's research stay at the Polish Institute of Advanced Studies (PIASt) in 2019, which was supported by the EURIAS Fellowship Program of the Europeam Commission (Marie-Sklodowska Curie Actions – COFUND Program – FP7). Many thanks to PIASt for hosting me as an associate researcher in January and February 2022 when I was preparing the draft manuscript for peer review; it was also gratifying to present the entire book at the place where it originated.

The volume's themes and approaches further crystallized during the conference panels in which several contributors took part: "The Politics, Ethics and Aesthetics of Post-Transitional Time" at the First Postsocalist and Comparative Memory Studies (PoSoCoMeS) Conference in 2020 and "Recalibrating the 1970–90s Transitions: Contested and Transforming Memoryscapes" at the Annual conference of the Memory Studies Association in 2021. I am grateful to all the contributors for their commitment, care, and understanding as they were working on their chapters in the midst of the COVID-19 pandemic in 2020–2021 and after Russia's full-scale invasion of Ukraine in 2022. My gratitude also goes to the anonymous reviewers for close engagement with the volume and helpful feedback. I appreciate the support of the Netherlands Institute of Advanced Studies (NIAS) where I am finalizing the manuscript.

Finally, my sincere thanks to the series editors, Astrid Erll and Ansgar Nünning, for their enthusiasm and support, and to Myrto Aspioti and Stella Diedrich at De Gruyter for their professionalism and attention.

https://doi.org/10.1515/9783110707793-202

Contents

Part I: Transitions' Working Memories

Part II: Reworking Memories of Transitions

Afterword

Ksenia Robbe

Introduction. Remembering Transitions: Approaching Memories in/of Crisis

Querying transitions

This volume probes the ambiguous meanings of the 1970–1990s political 'transitions' across postsocialist, postapartheid, and postdictatorship contexts. I begin the introduction to this collection by discussing two poems – one by South African poet Tumelo Khoza and the other by Russian/Ukrainian poet Galina Rymbu. Although they may seem an unlikely pair, these poems represent the entangled desires to forget, to recover, and to question the solidified or ignored meanings of the historical turning point of transition and the evolution of these meanings over time.

> There's a teenage boy / who presently chills at
> the corner / where the future intersects with our
> history, his name is Democracy / he's forever
> mumbling what sounds like poetry / forever
> high on a spliff of our dis(joint)ed society /
> forever sniffs on the stiff aroma of whiskey /
> counting how many governing bodies make the
> front page daily.

This stanza of Khoza's (2017) poem "Democracy" opens a collection showcasing the work of young spoken-word South African poets.[1] Speaking about the experiences of the so-called 'born free' generation – those born during or soon after South Africa's transition to democracy in the 1990s – the poems confront head-on the failure of the postapartheid state to improve the lives of the majority. Among the symptoms of the new generation's dis-ease with the contemporary moral economy, the poem mentions the elites' "revolutionary hypocrisy" and overall "obsess[ion] with the honey of money," which is underpinned by the routine "forget[ting]" of "what happens in the rural vicinity" and, more broadly, to all those who have no access to economic and cultural resources. This poem, like many in the collection, expresses the discontent of the time. It resounds with the student

---

1 I would like to thank Kylie Thomas for drawing my attention to this collection titled *Home is Where the Mic Is*.

Acknowledgments: I'm grateful to the colleagues who shared their thoughts and feedback on drafts of this chapter, especially Ioana Luca, Kylie Thomas, and Kevin Platt.

protests that took place across the country in 2015 and 2016, starting with action for decolonizing university campuses and curricula and then extending to resistance against the socioeconomic policies of universities, which included the lack of proper housing and the outsourcing of workers, and ultimately to protest against the state. The poem also signifies the despondency of a generation faced with the predicament of chronic unemployment and, more generally, at the resentment of the dispossessed, which may break out in violence.[2]

> [. . .] such leaves
> Democracy angry / it leaves him tearing his
> book of rhymes in fury / because no one wants
> to listen to him as he speaks whole-heatedly /
> so Democracy lights a ciggie and chills by his
> corner silently with his container of gasoline / he
> folds his country flag neatly / slowly takes a drag /
> pours the gas / lights another match and utters,
> "Phuck this man!" (Khoza 2017)

The extreme indifference and cynicism with regard to any talk about law or democracy is also the context reflected on by Rymbu (2020),[3] for instance in "The Law is Not in Force Here":

> The law is not in force here
> and constitution will not save us from pain
> or hatred. I have only two hours of free time
> to write this – from 5 to 7 am.
> The rest of the time doesn't belong me,
> just like the law. Constitution has never 'belong to me'
> Guaranteed safety
> For me or my family,
> We were hiding under a blanket every time something happened (85).[4]

These lines convey the enormous gap between appeals to constitutional rights and the reality of lives among the majority of people in Russia. They, and especially the underbelly sketched in this poem, do not encounter or perceive the Law, just like the Constitution does not recognize who these people are and how they live, since it does not acknowledge their daily pain and deprivation. The poem was part of a writing

---

2 The riots that broke out in July 2021 across South Africa, in response to the imprisonment of former president Jacob Zuma (for ignoring a corruption inquiry) and fueled by the economic crisis as a consequence of COVID-19, were a recent case. Having claimed over 300 lives, these riots were the most large-scale case of civil unrest in South Africa since the end of apartheid.
3 Born in 1990, Rymbu is of the same generation as Khoza.
4 My translation (KR).

project – a collective reflection on the event of introducing amendments to the Constitution in 2020 – which resulted in a series of texts titled *Constitution Passion*.[5] The amendments proposed by the Russian president and legitimized through a national referendum conducted in the midst of the COVID-19 pandemic included several conservative and populist positions – most importantly, the 'nullification' of the presidential terms served by Vladimir Putin, which, therefore, allows him to be elected again. This event, along with the intensified neo-traditionalism and violence of biopolitical power in Russia and the expulsion of oppositional voices, has generated a state of hopelessness; but it has also, as we see from the writing project that resulted in *Constitution Passion*, generated a wish to explore the meanings of the Constitution and, more particularly, its relationship to daily life. Passed into law in 1993, during the 'transition period,' the Constitution points to a time of hope for new, democratic beginnings[6] and, simultaneously, to the time when precisely this future appeared to be foreclosed as the then President Boris Yeltsin used military force to suppress opposition to his fast-paced economic reforms. The Constitution that was subsequently adopted, thus, already incorporated the fundamental contradiction between the rhetoric of democracy and the concentration of power in the hands of the president enshrined in this document.

Both poems are *writings in crisis*. From this viewpoint in the present, they re-envision the past of transition as a time of crisis too; this nurtures a dialectic of ends and beginnings, of hoped-for possibilities and their foreclosures, and of the institution and the subversion of democratic principles. The poems are also inter-related through their imagery and structures of affect. At the core of both is the complete disconnection between the states (and the elites) and the masses ('the people' who should be the subjects of democracy and constitutional protection). Instead of the more familiar voices of politicians or intellectuals speaking for or against transitions from public platforms, the poems speak with those who are unseen and unheard by the latter; their voices and gestures, rendered in this poetry of the everyday, are disconcerting and uncanny. These subjects hold the power to negate and destroy everything as they have nothing to lose; yet, they remain downtrodden and "beaten up again" (Rymbu 2020, 89). Other aspects that interconnect these poems are their tone of urgency and the perceived necessity of reckoning with the past of transitions, as well as the sharpness of their critique and the power of affect. But they also reach beyond "the politics of impatience"

---

5 The collection is based on the online platform *Bookmate*: https://ru.bookmate.com/series/ttKqwjrP.

6 As studies of public opinion in Russia indicate, before the 1993 crisis, ideas of liberal democracy and leaders associated with them (Mikhail Gorbachev, Boris Yeltsin) enjoyed popular support (Levinson 2007, Simonyan 2011).

(Mbembe 2015) as their insistent questioning does not merely mediate feelings of betrayal; it inquires into the subjectivity of those who feel betrayed, particularly among the dispossessed, and into the social conditioning of this being and feeling.

Such sensibilities, generationally specific or not, whether characterized by "cruel optimism" (Berlant 2011) or longing for a revolution, are global in their scope and resonance; they are the signs of our crisis-ridden, discontented, and seemingly future-less times. But they have a particular urgency, as this volume proposes and outlines through a variety of cases, in societies that underwent transitions from authoritarian regimes of different kinds during the late 1970s to the early 1990s (for example, state socialist governments, military dictatorships, colonial and apartheid regimes with variations, of course, within these categories). In these societies, the appeal to the moral narratives of overcoming the politics and legacies of repressive authoritarianism is especially strong as it is grounded in experiences and memories of the recent past, either directly or mediated through positive narratives of transformation in education, media, and cultural production. In other words, the ideals of democratic transformation in these societies (also in those cases where they have been seriously compromised from the very start of the transitions) are alive and serve as a meaningful reference point and cultural resource. Furthermore, through the narratives and practices of transitional justice, references to the transitions (particularly those framed as the success stories of Germany, Poland, or South Africa) have been circulating globally in recent decades as transitions have been carried out, or attempted, in places such as Rwanda, Bosnia, Cuba, Iraq, Tunisia, and Colombia. At the same time, scholars have increasingly questioned the idea of turning transition practices into templates and have contested the rather mechanistic use of these templates in other sociopolitical contexts (David 2020, Gabowitsch 2017).

These and similar tensions between the local and global aspects of transitions, the historical entanglement of various transitions, and the possibilities as well as limits of translatability, form the focus of this volume. After all, recent historical studies have demonstrated how globally mediatized transitions, which have often been proclaimed 'miraculous,' were undergirded by complex and long-term transactions between politicians, democracy experts, and economists from the Global South and North (Mark et al. 2019). While regime transformations that led to the end of the Cold War were interdependent,[7] it would be mistaken to assume that each of these processes took the same or even a similar direction. As

---

7 To cite an example elaborated by Chari and Verdery (2009), South Africa's transition through negotiation between the apartheid government and the ANC would not have been possible, at least in the form it took, had the Soviet bloc not collapsed in 1989–1991.

Monica Popescu (2003) has argued, drawing on South African writer Ivan Vladislavic's astute enquiry into the false analogies between transitions in South Africa and the USSR, these simultaneous processes are characterized by a wealth of both "mirrorings and reverse-mirrorings" (421). On the one hand, societies of Southern and Eastern Europe, Latin America, and East and Southeast Asia were all 'transitioning' from regimes characterized by authoritarian control, massive state-organized repressions, and intolerance to non-conformity; on the other hand, the economic structures and ideologies differed significantly and, in fact, even stood in opposition to each other: varieties of state socialism, on the one hand, and dictatorships underpinned by (neo-)liberal economies and racial capitalism, on the other. Hence the divergence between various critiques of transitions and conflicts in contemporary politics of remembering these pasts. This volume is an attempt to make sense of these diverging and converging imaginaries of transitions and their dynamics over the last few decades. It certainly is not able – and does not aim – to represent the entire variety of national contexts or practices that challenge and revise dominant narratives of transition. However, by placing selected cases from different regions in conversation, it highlights parallels and variations that are rarely reflected upon.

As will become clear from the set-up of this collection and each individual chapter, our use of the term 'transition' is informed by extant critiques of the teleological and Eurocentric imaginaries invested in this concept (Buden 2010, Chakrabarty 2000, Grunebaum 2011, Petrov 2014, Velikonja 2009). At the same time, political uses as well as critiques of this term serve to interconnect very different societies and regions; addressing the experiences of 'transition' as a way of understanding social processes is what makes the past of the 1970 to 1990s in several regions 'recognizable' to contemporary publics and what triggers memories, their transnational circulation, and transregional analysis. Due to the multivalency of remembering these periods and the specificity of local political and mnemonic processes that the chapters approach, the volume keeps open the temporal coordinates of when the remembering begins. In some societies, particularly those that experienced political transformation during the 1970s and 1980s, but also in Russia where states of indeterminacy during the 1990s were closed off by the beginning of Putin's presidency, 'transitions' are commonly associated with a finalized past. In other societies such as Romania, as the chapters that engage with this context suggest, 'transition' became a subject of intense public engagement only during the 2000s, and it is currently perceived as an ongoing process. Whatever the temporal perceptions of transitions are (which may also differ within societies), the common condition addressed by this volume is the unsettling presence of the social questions opened by or tackled during the transitions and their demand for reconsideration.

Memories of transitions and the role of the media

Particularly during the last decade, transitions have turned from a subject of 'cold' to a matter of 'hot memory,' to use the terms with which Charles Maier (2002) described the dynamics of memories of communism and fascism in Europe two decades ago. The mnemonic instrumentalization of transitions in political discourse takes diverging forms and directions, and it is propelled by different political actors, even within a single region of East-Central Europe (Bernhard and Kubik 2014). If we broaden the scope beyond the region, the directions become certainly more diverse or even opposing, although not incomparable. This is also the case when the same idiom is used in different contexts: think of the calls for completing or radicalizing 'unfinished' transitions. In East-Central European countries such as Hungary and Poland, this slogan, adopted by right-wing populist parties, refers to the insufficient decommunization during the 1990s and the need to reinvigorate traditionalist social norms as the 'forgotten' foundations of 'real Europeanness' (Dujisin 2021, Mark 2010); in countries of the Global South such as Chile or South Africa, critiques of unfinished transition often point to the ideals of social justice being compromised by neoliberal transformations (cf. Beresford 2014, Borzutsky and Perry 2021). In yet other contexts where no transitional justice processes have taken place, where no official apology for state-directed atrocities has been expressed, and where democratic principles have been delegitimized (Russia is an example of this tendency in the long term, but we can also think, for instance, of Brazil in the time of Bolsonaro (Schneider 2020)), oppositional movements perceive transitions as 'undone' or never properly initiated. At the same time, recent protests and revolutions that resulted in a change of government, as in post-Euromaidan Ukraine or post-Mugabe Zimbabwe, tend to refer to the ongoing or desired transitions as returning to the moments of independence and restarting processes of democratization.

Even this quick glance at some tendencies of recalling transitions in contemporary politics demonstrates the radically unsettling and highly contentious uses of memory. The latter are directly linked to contemporary social imaginaries of democracy and the declining role of future-orientations within them (Assmann 2013, Hartog 2015, Huyssen 2003). If the role of transitions as points of moral and political orientation has been discredited, what is there to rely on to counter cynical abuse of power? If promises of democratization and cosmopolitanism have been paired with neoliberal transformations from the start, can we even think about transitions outside of the contexts of predatory capitalism and globalization? The broad disillusionment in the promises of redistribution of access, socioeconomic opportunities, and social justice releases the energies that are easily appropriated by nationalist and populist leaders. This disillusionment also finds expression in 'left-wing melancholia,' Walter Benjamin's concept that has been used by cultural theorists more recently in critiques of contemporary closures of political horizons (Brown 1999, Traverso 2017). Between and beyond these trajectories lies a landscape of multiple variations on discontent, disappointment, and ambiguity (expressed in statements such as 'a transition was necessary, but this is not what we expected it to be'). The currency of these affects and their channeling into political projects have motivated recent intellectual reckoning with earlier ideals and frameworks of imagining transformation (Krastev and Holmes 2019).

To comprehend the variety and ambiguity of post-transitional feelings and memories, to make sense of their complexity beyond political (ab)uses, and to imagine productive ways of dealing with them, practices of cultural memory and mediation can be a particularly apt terrain: this is where reflection on personal and collective experiences and recollections of transitions is actively underway, incorporating new voices and subjectivities and shaping new social imaginaries. Certainly, mediations of memory also often involve practices of homogenizing, silencing, or obscuring memories that do not fit into frameworks of a 'usable past'. It is these tensions between the openings and closures of memory that contributions to this book closely examine. The volume approaches 'cultural' and 'media' processes in a broad sense, offering reflections on practices of literature, film, theater, photography, and social media along with critiques of post-transitional time and memory. With this focus, the collection begins to outline and theorize cultural memory perspectives on transitions and to engage with these perspectives' local and global dynamics. Since transitions often serve as points of narrative and visual orientation – of plot, identity, or temporal-spatial coordinates constructed through endings, beginnings, turning points, symbolic or historical visual references – close examination of these forms can yield a more nuanced understanding of how these pasts make up part of our cultural vocabularies. Scrutinizing cultural mediations of transitions can also help us to make sense of how our perceptions of historical time and the present are continuously 'haunted' by transitions: we keep demarcating our present as 'postcolonial,' 'postapartheid,' 'postsocialist,' or 'postdictatorship,' despite repeated attempts at introducing new terms or rethinking these periodizations. Indeed, as long as we use these terms to mark the beginning of the present, transitions hold sway of our sociohistorical imaginaries. Reading the texturing of these imaginaries in arts and media can facilitate our understanding of how they come into being.

The approach taken by this volume is two-fold. Chapters included in the first part examine the forms of memory and time that became hegemonic post-transition, with the focus on how they influence present-day memory cultures, as well as those forms that harbor alternative visions and counter-hegemonic potentialities. These chapters dialogue with recent studies into the new trajectories of post-transitional

memory as developed by postdictatorship, postapartheid, and postsocialist generations (Blejmar 2016, Gook 2015, Legott 2015, Ros 2012, Schwartz et al. 2020; Wale et al.
2020) as well as the research on the politics of time and time regimes initiated by
transitions (Barnard and Van der Vlies 2019, Bevernage and Lorenz 2013, Grunebaum
2011, Platt 2020, Van der Vlies 2017). The second part of the volume traces the ways in
which transitions come to be regarded as *pasts in their own right* (though undoubtedly, closely entwined with the 'before' and 'after'). The main focus of these chapters
is on the mnemonic forms of re-writing earlier temporalities and imaginaries of
transformations. By focusing on contemporary revisions of transitions, these readings bring into close scrutiny the chronotopes, as Kostis Kornetis points out in his
chapter, that current performances of memory form in relation – and often with explicit reference – to earlier practices of envisioning change.

In foregrounding transitions as objects of inquiry, the work of this collection
aligns with recent historical research into the intellectual trajectories (Kopeček
and Wciślik 2015) and global entanglements of the 1980–1990s transitions (Mark
et al. 2019) as well as the ways in which the processes and meanings of the transitions are being interrogated by activists and movements in the context of recent
crises (Cavallaro and Kornetis 2019), the latter coming close to the focus of our
inquiry on the present. The volume complements the focus of this research with
its inquiry into the (re)mediations of transitions and the forms that allow certain
aspects of these historical pasts to become memorable. Overall, with its focus on
the 'texturing' of transitions – of recollecting these pasts as turning points in stories of individuals and communities as well as spaces of experience and projection that resonate in the present – this volume makes a novel contribution to the
vast field of research on the (trans-)formations of memory in post-transitional
cultures.

With the transformation of political practices and outlooks (the demand for
direct democracy), with the financialization of markets and the growth of socioeconomic precarity, and with increasing nationalization and border closures (resulting in so-called 'migration crises'), the "horizons of expectation" established
by the 1970–1990s transitions do not meet contemporary "spaces of experience,"
to use Reinhart Koselleck's (2004) terms. Hence, this volume addresses the need
to re-examine the ideas and experiences of transitions through mnemonic constellations between the present and past as well as the many different pasts and
futures emerging and circulating in the present. re-framings of the transitional
past through experiential lenses have recently become the focus of studies into
the vernacular memories of transitions in East-Central Europe (Hilmar 2021,
Laczó and Wawryzniak 2017, Massino 2019, Wawrzyniak and Leyk 2020). The current volume, in turn, presents the first book-length examination of mediated

memories of transitions, charting a broad transnational field of locally specific and globally entangled practices.

To summarize, this volume, on the one hand, explores the practices and modes of recollecting transitional pasts which feature new voices, perspectives, and experiences; on the other hand, it examines the silences produced by established frameworks of memory and time and possibilities for intervening into these frameworks. Since cultural memory of these transitions (as a stabilized, institutionalized set of narratives) has not yet formed, in most contexts, the examined memories are ways of challenging dominant narratives and positing alternatives. They can, thus, be considered 'deterritorializing' practices that propose radical ambiguity (by considering multiple experiences, sites, resonances, or durations of crises) while also charting, by using related tropes and evoking similar affects, grounds for articulating new narratives and subjectivities.

Crisis in memory

Looking back at the rapid development and institutionalization of memory studies as an academic field alongside public memory work and memory activism, several scholars have observed a close interconnection between the 'memory boom' since the 1980s and the end of the Cold War. Andreas Huyssen points out the "emergence of memory as a key concern in Western societies, a turning toward the past that stands in stark contrast to the privileging of the future so characteristic of earlier decades of twentieth-century modernity" (2011, 21). Aleida Assmann (2013) further theorizes this development as the unfolding of a new 'time regime' which perceives the past as something that can be 'reversed' and re-made, rather than discarded, according to the ethical concerns of the present. This time regime is characterized by an emphasis on victimhood, recognition of trauma, 'politics of regret' (Olick 2007), and the ethics of human rights (Assmann 2013, 51–56). The discarded future-oriented paradigm involved, along with the grand narratives of progress, memories that combined a strong anti-fascist stance with anticolonial orientation (Forsdick et al. 2020, 2–3; Traverso 2017). In addition, more recent historical-theoretical reflections have emphasized the economic aspect of these transformations: in other words, the entwinement of the contemporary memory and time regime with the emergence of neoliberalism as a leading paradigm in the West during the 1970s and the globally extended model since the 1980s and especially post–1989 (Ghodsee and Orenstein 2021, Pehe and Wawrzyniak 2023). As Kristen Ghodsee (2017) has noted, "[if] the communist ideal had become tainted by its association with twentieth-century Eastern European regimes, today the democratic ideal was increasingly sullied by its links to neoliberal capitalism" (xv–xvi).

In recent years, the human rights-centered mnemonic regime has come under fire from both right- and left-wing actors, who have expressed their discontent with the normative aspects of 'cosmopolitan memory' (Levy and Sznaider 2002), although these critiques are dissimilar and are underpinned by vastly diverging ideals. In their introduction to a recent special collection tracing these dynamics, Forsdick, Mark, and Spišáková (2020) refer to this present condition of conflict between memory frameworks as "the global crisis in memory." The present volume traces the ways in which contemporary culture and media take part in shaping and responding to this crisis while also exploring the alternative, 'non-crisis' memory practices they advance. In other words, the chapters inquire into the different facets of *remembering transition 'in crisis'* (the current 'crisis in memory' as well as a plethora of other perceived and announced 'crises'). In what follows I outline the place of 'transitions' within the present-day shifts and conflicts between and within memory frameworks.

However diverse memory processes have been in countries 'transitioning' to democracy, "as a powerful ideal they were also linked [. . .] by a common idea that the defense of civic and human rights, and thus of liberal citizenship, required that we remember past atrocities and state violence" (Forsdick et al. 2020, 2). The powerful ethical claim of remembering victims served as a way of connecting the varied transformations and "stabilizing the 'transitions' to a politically liberal democratic and neoliberal economic order" (Forsdick et al. 2020, 5). However, employed within the standardized practices of a global memory industry (often linked to transitional justice mechanisms), this potentially empowering perspective turned out to carry with it colonial undertones and, eventually, to have counter-democratic effects. The instrumentalization of memory within human-rights initiatives has led to creating frameworks that ignore the complexity and incommensurability of mnemonic processes in different locations. "Securing the past" to make sure that everyone remembers in a correct way (Huyssen 2011, 621), as recent critical examinations have shown (David 2020, Gensburger and Lefranc 2020), erases locally or nationally specific histories of violence and invests even more power in those who have politically and financially benefitted from the transitions.

The gradual shift of perspective from international networks of resistance to national communities "removed a consciousness of structural interconnected violence from countries whose modernization had been attempted by dictatorships" (Forsdick et al. 2020, 6). On a broader scale, this was part of displacing the paradigm of politics and memory that centered on anticolonial and anti-fascist resistance and substituting it with the opposition between dictatorship and liberal democracy (Forsdick et al. 2020, 6). Finally, in adopting developmental perspectives, transition narratives framed all 'democratizing' societies as needing to 'catch up' and become re-educated in order to be admitted into the family of democratic nations (Buden 2010). To refer to Dipesh Chakrabarty's critique of similar tropes in colonial ideologies, the subject of transition narratives will always remain "grievously incomplete" (2000, 40). As this brief overview shows, the politics and ethics of past and future in globalized post-transitional memory involved a number of erasures as well as the foregrounding of categories, such as victimhood, that appeared to be open to essentialization and abuse.

Most critical reflections on how the mnemonic framework outlined here has been challenged and abused have focused on right-wing denouncements of Holocaust memory (for its alleged 'imposition' of a culture of guilt) as well as the politics of equating Nazism and Communism. Memory of transitions forms the flip side of this framework; although divergences and conflicts in these memories also cause serious tensions, they are often overlooked in memory studies scholarship. On the one hand, the currently authoritative framework based on Holocaust memory promotes the remembrance of victims of all totalitarianisms; on the other, it envisions democratic transitions as end-points of major atrocities (with celebrations of '1989' in Germany as an example). As memories of suffering have become the most accepted and powerful mnemonic template over the past decades – even employed by populists to create nationalist narratives of victimhood while contesting transnational memory projects (David 2020, Lim 2010) – memories of resistance and activism have lost their global appeal or institutional support (Rigney 2018). Activist memories or celebratory commemorations of '1989' have not shaped a European *lieu de mémoire* (Sierp 2017) or a template that would facilitate transregional connections and 'travelling' memory.[8] The reasons behind this are the vast diversity and fragmentation of meanings attached to the transitions in different national contexts and the (often politicized) controversies that these different interpretations cause within and across national borders (Kovács 2019, Laczó and Wawrzyniak 2017). However, as Della Porta et al. have argued in the context of Spain, "the weakness of a memory of conflict during the transition period may give more space for new frames and new memories to emerge, especially in a weak and relatively autonomous civil society" (2018, 28).

This volume starts from the premise that memories of transitions need to be approached in their complexity, contradictions, and global entanglements to yield more open, non-divisive, and social equality-oriented ways of remembering. To instrumentalize transitions as acts of overcoming totalitarianism obscures the historical realities which involved, along with new freedoms and re-established connections, much

---

8 For the concept of 'travelling memory' see Erll 2011.

conflict and even violence with present-day continuities and repercussions (Betts 2019, Kenney 2021, Marinovich 2019). Precisely in light of these controversies and the ongoing nationalist-populist appropriations of the symbolism and meanings of transitions (Iacob, Mark, and Rupprecht 2019), a closer look at the possible alternatives harbored in memories of these periods could make a valuable contribution to creating mnemonic frameworks that focus on both democracy *and* social justice. Certainly, remembrance of transitions can serve nationalist interests equally well. This has been the case, for instance, with conspiracy-inspired memories of the collapse of the Soviet Union, advanced since the 1990s (Oushakine 2009, Borenstein 2019) or narratives of the 'stolen transition' in Poland and Hungary (Kofta and Soral 2019, Krekó 2019), including literary mediations of this trope in alternate histories (Noordenbos 2016, Oziewicz 2011, Tabaszewska 2020). These narratives can also circulate and generate affect transnationally. This collection, however, zooms in on the narratives and performances of memory that address the complexity of transitions while shedding light on the structural omissions of transformation processes and experimenting with new mnemonic perspectives. With this focus, the volume contributes to research on memories that could counter right-wing populist mnemonics (De Cesari and Kaya 2020) and propose alternatives. In Astrid Erll's (2020) formulation, such memories should be based on the principles of 'truthfulness,' 'non-divisiveness,' and 'humane generativity' in order to help imagining a better future for all.

The structure of the book: Working and reworking memories

As already mentioned above, the contributions to this volume look in two directions – at the forms of time and modes of memory that were produced in the course of the transitions (having varied public presence and power today) and at the revisions of those forms and modes, particularly during the past decade. Hence, the book elaborates two complementary and entangled optics, which render the 'remembering' in its title as both an adjective and a gerund: on the one hand, the collection engages with how the transitions generated memories (which were focused on the earlier periods but, in the same breath, produced the structures of thinking about transitions as 'hinges' between the past and the future); on the other hand, it explores the practices of looking back at the transitions as turning points from the viewpoint of a new present. How do we make sense of such memories of a recent past that have not formed a stabilized and generally recognizable cultural memory (Assmann 2008) but have been actively mediated and remediated (Erll 2008)? In her book on the modes of remembering socialism at the time when socialist states and forms of organization were coming to an end during the 1980s and 1990s, Charity Scribner uses the term 'working memories':

> Metaphorically, working memory is that which remains 'in living memory.' In the lexicon of digital technology, however, it designates 'random-access memory,' or RAM: the space of temporary storage where programs are created, loaded, and run. Once a programmer has manipulated this data on the screen or desktop, he or she has the choice of writing it into the computer's hard drive. Our recollection of life under socialism now hovers at the same level as digital working memory. It remains to be determined how the second world's history might be recollected. Will it be permanently inscribed into Europe's collective memory or merely deleted from the disk? (2003, 17)

Now, two decades later, memories of socialism and their mediations have generated much research; yet, the subject remains riddled with ambiguities, which makes its inscription into Europe's collective memory an uneasy task. Memories of transitions, in turn, still await proper recognition as a subject of research and public remembrance. However, to make sense of their emergence, circulation and impact, this volume proposes to focus on their ongoing workings and reworkings before they become more solidified.

The first part, 'Transitions' Working Memories,' focuses on the forms of remembering and time-making that were developed during and in the aftermath of the political transformations. In their readings of these forms, the chapters explore how the 'break' between the past and the present has been imagined, what kind of subjecthood and values these imaginaries foreground, and how they are being questioned or reclaimed. Placing these memories in (trans)national political and aesthetic contexts, they reflect on the tenacity or ephemerality of these imaginaries. The section is framed by Florin Poenaru and Kylie Thomas' chapters that develop critiques of the dominant forms of time and modes of remembering in a postsocialist and a postcolonial context, in Romania and South Africa. The three middle chapters, in turn, provide critical perspectives on alternatives to hegemonic memory frameworks – in the re-readings of a play about the Spanish transition (Bonifacio Valdivia Milla and Pablo Valdivia Martin) and in forms of (post) postmodern writing in Hungary and Romania (Mónika Dánél) and in Taiwan (Darwin Tsen).

Florin Poenaru's chapter provides a critique of the damaging effects of transition narratives that involved an obsession with revealing the 'truth' about state violence in Romania. This obsession manifested itself in acts of searching though one's files in the Secret Police archives, in other words, relying on the very instruments of violence that manufactured lies about individuals during communist rule. Poenaru's reading of two 'file-memoirs' by the writer Herta Müller and anthropologist Katherine Verdery, distills how the authors remain confined to the subject positions of 'victimhood' by following the logic of traumatic repetition inherent in the archives. Mourning the loss of their past friendships makes them reevaluate their whole lives and eventually leaves them dispossessed of their agency: the past remains nothing but emptiness and defeat. This imaginary of loss associated with life under communism formed the dominant narrative of transition in Romania and other countries of Eastern Europe. Through the popularity of the 'file-memoirs' in the West, this narrative participated in the global mnemonic turn, which, as the argument goes, reinforced Orientalist visions of the European East as the realm of experience and orality.

Bonifacio Valdivia Milla and Pablo Valdivia Martin's re-reading of the play *Trampa para Pájaros* by José Luis Alonso de Santos, written and first staged in 1990, turns to the related questions of victimhood and perpetratorship and shows how more recent interpretations of the play by the director represent the conflicts of the transition with greater complexity than was afforded by the narratives of reconciliation and oblivion. This analysis reveals the play's transgression of the conceptual metaphor of the 'two Spains,' an imagined domain of 'victims' and 'perpetrators' under Francoism – a displacement that remained unarticulated by the playwright and the reviewers in the initial interpretations of the play. These early readings approached the play as a Manichean allegory of the struggle between good and evil. The chapter's re-reading based on a qualitative-quantitative analysis of the metaphorical structures in this play demonstrates 'multidirectional' and 'agonistic' memory at work, which "negotiates" between "the conflicting poles of reconciliation and oblivion," however, without addressing the questions of "justice and reparation."

The next three chapters focus on the productions of temporality in transition narratives and the ways in which dominant times and time-scapes are questioned, queered, and revised in practices of remembering. Mónika Dánél explores the figures of metalepsis and collage as devices that displace the linear temporality of transition and the concomitant forgetting of the many dissonances present during that time. Her reading of a Romanian novel and a Hungarian film from the mid-1990s,[9] juxtaposed with more contemporary memories in a photographic exhibition and a film,[10] demonstrates the continuous use of these devices for foregrounding the conflicts of world-views, perceptions, and ideologies, thereby contesting the scripts organized around 'resistance' vs. 'passivity,' 'revolution' vs. 'stagnancy,' and showing how the analyzed counter-scripts transcend national boundaries.

---

9 *Bolshe Vita* (1995) directed by Ibolya Fekete and *Hotel Europa* (1996) written by Dumitru Țepeneag.
10 The exhibition titled *Cluj 1989 21.12* with the focus on Răzvan Rotta's photographs and Corneliu Porumboiu's *12:08 East of Bucharest* (2006).

Darwin Tsen's chapter continues by examining the ways in which the poetics of post-postmodernist writing intervenes into the imaginaries of smooth and universal 'transitioning' during the 1980s–1990s in Taiwan. In his reading of two texts by the Taiwanese writer Luo Yijun (駱以軍), a short story "A Roll of Film" from the collection *The Red Ink Gang* (1993) and a novel *An Elegy* (2001), he traces the structures of 'dysrhythmia,' which at the level of style and of narrating generational affiliation pinpoint multiple tensions in relation to the official temporality of transition from dictatorship to 'progressive' capitalist society. Moving from the remembering of White Terror during the transition towards recollection of the transition itself, the chapter reads the forms and aesthetics of dysrhythmia as characteristics of post-postmodernism which has developed since the 1990s as a radicalization of (and in some ways, a counterpoint to) the postmodern sense of global synchronization.

Kylie Thomas concludes this section with a theorization of 'transitional time' in post–1994 South Africa – a structure that echoes the hegemonic temporalities of the Taiwanese and Romanian/Hungarian transitions. Her reading of postapartheid social amnesia (perpetuated despite the work of the Truth and Reconciliation Commission) shows how transitional time performed as 'common' is, in fact, characterized by 'radical dyssynchrony': while for some apartheid is a distant past with no connection to the now, for families of murdered activists knowing the past is a way to claim social justice in the present. Here we see temporal dissonance as a colonial structure of inequality which inheres within the time of transition and is facilitated by the global/local memorialization industry. At the same time, acts of foregrounding this dyssynchrony – like the uses of dysrhythmia or metalepsis – enable a critique of the mnemonic erasures that were/are constitutive of transitions.

The second part of the volume, 'Reworking memories of transitions,' engages with transformations and re-significations of earlier forms of memory and the emerging perspectives and modes. These discussions move from the scrutiny of contemporary activist memories of transitions, at the interfaces of politics and aesthetics, in Spain, Portugal, and Greece (Kostis Kornetis) as well as Russia (Andrei Zavadski) to an examination of aestheticized and commercialized memories of the 1990s on the Russian Instagram (Mykola Makhortykh). The last three chapters offer readings of mnemonic forms and practices in literary writing and focus on transnational and transregional constellations that these memories produce. These cases involve remediations of a popular Romanian novel for local and transnational audiences (Ioana Luca), the development of transnational imaginaries of remembering the end of dictatorships in Argentina and Uruguay (Cara Levey), and a comparative theorization of modes of remembering transitions in South African and Russian literatures (Ksenia Robbe).

Kostis Kornetis's contribution examines memories of political activism that led to the establishment of democracies in Portugal, Greece, and Spain during the 1970s. The chapter discusses how forty years later, during the Great Recession of the early 2010s, iconic songs, poems, and theater plays of the transitional period were re-performed and film scenes remediated in new productions, often by representatives of the younger generations with only childhood memories of the 1970s. Through the readings of such artifacts alongside interviews with young activists and reviews in the media, this study considers the political potential and limitations of these mnemonic performances. On the one hand, due to their mediations of affect, some of these artifacts facilitate involvement in political struggles; on the other, they tend to create entrapment in the past. Moreover, some of the productions involve commercialized nostalgia for the 1970s that aestheticizes the revolutions.

In the cases of activist remembering of transition in Russia, as analyzed by Andrei Zavadski – the projects organized by the independent Russian contemporary culture magazine *Colta.ru* – aesthetic practices and references to cultural innovation of the 1990s played an important role in shaping a 'mnemonic counterpublic.' The chapter develops this concept in the context of authoritarian power, focusing on activities and events that sought to develop a public memory of the first post-Soviet decade as vehicles that allowed for reaching wider publics, beyond the core community. In particular, it discusses the productive uses of nostalgia in this process. Together, these first chapters of the section scrutinize the workings of affect and nostalgia in mnemonic activism. In both instances, activist remembrance intersects with political protest and involves representatives of different generations (those who were adults and children during the transitions).

Mykola Makhortykh's discussion of (re)mediations of the 1990s on the social media platform Instagram in Russia inquires into the amalgamation of trauma and nostalgia that characterizes memories of the first post-Soviet decade. Such entwinement is clearly discernible in memories of the 1990s in Russia, although it is far less explored than the complexity of traumatic/nostalgic affect associated with the Stalinist period. The particular intensity of these affects, the analysis shows, is related to the multiple and unresolved traumas of the 1990s (related to massive impoverishment, criminality, and radical change of values) as well as the political instrumentalization of these traumas by representatives of the Russian state. However, while expressions of trauma do occur on Instagram (mainly in posts by male users), nostalgia represents the predominant mode. Commercial exploitation of nostalgic feelings does play a role; yet, as the chapter concludes, the nostalgic representations also challenge the hegemonic narrative about the 1990s as the time of misery and hardship.

By approaching the (trans)formations of remembering transition in Romanian cultural productions – more particularly, the novel *I'm an Old Commie!* by Dan Lungu, which was published in 2007 to much acclaim, and its more recent remediations as a film and a theater play – Ioana Luca's chapter develops a transnational lens that can capture multiscalar articulations of memory. Her readings of these mediations offers perspectives on how political democratization and the development of capitalist relations in Romania during the and 2000s have involved the production of social inequalities and the feelings of nostalgia as well as this nostalgia's commercialization and remediation in recent years. In addition to examining how these productions map the global entanglements of transition, the chapter traces the regional 'travelling' of Lungu's novel and the structures of 'minor transnationalism' that it creates. Like Poenaru's contribution on Romanian memory culture, Luca's readings argue that memories of transition have always been transnational, but this fact is obscured by the predominantly national frameworks applied in public and academic discourse. The elaboration of comparative and transnational optics on the transitions is, thus, an important next step for the scholarship on transitions and their memories, for which examinations of cultural and mediated memories can offer pertinent examples.

The following chapter by Cara Levey inquires into the new voices and associated spatio-temporal modalities of writing the 1980s transitions in the Southern Cone via its reading of autofictional texts by second-generation exiles, French-Argentine Laura Alcoba and Dutch-Uruguayan Carolina Trujillo. It outlines the ways in which the authors reflect on these historical processes from the displaced positions of growing up in Europe while feeling closely connected to their countries of birth. The detailed comparative reading demonstrates how these memories destabilize the myths of 'the Golden exile' which virtually excluded diasporic perspectives or experiences of the younger generations from narratives of transition. The chapter highlights how this transnational autofiction involves the displacement of teleological time-spaces and visions of victimhood that characterize those dominant narratives.

My own chapter continues explorations of the modes and genres of memory developed in literature by considering the possibilities of comparing temporal and mnemonic processes in contemporary Russian and South African writing. It suggests some pathways by beginning to conceptualize modes of remembering via which literary and film narratives engage with typically contradictory states, affects, and feelings that are associated with this time, such as trauma and hope, loss and aspiration, movement and stasis. The focus is on the modes that do not reduce or 'forget' this complexity but, instead, develop frameworks for mediating the 'transitional' crisis-pasts in response to the continuing and intensifying crises in the present. The chapter approaches memories of transition as a lens for developing intersectional postcolonial/postsocialist approaches. Comparisons across these contexts can elucidate how the decline of anticolonial and socialist imaginaries and the rise of nationalism and neoliberalism constitute points of mnemonic return and persistent social re-assembling across different parts of the post-Cold War world.

Across these explorations of subjectivity, affect, time, and mode, and the strategies used by a variety of mnemonic agents who produce these versions of the past (writers, film- and theater-makers, readers, social media users, and activists), the question about the extent and character of the transnational or global crossings indicated in this collection remains. Visions of transitions, from the very beginning of these historical processes, have developed between national and transnational framings. In each country, transitions were marked as symbolic points in nation-building processes; each nation had their own events and heroes to commemorate. At the same time, the events of transitions were closely interconnected through acts of politicians but also, not least, through the circulation of mobilizing images that would almost immediately become iconic. Some celebrations of '1989,' particularly in Germany, attempted to replicate this transnational interconnectedness as a mnemonic trope (Pearce 2014, 230). However, three decades after, national frameworks proved to be dominant. As Paul Betts (2019) has recently noted, "what is starting to become clear is that for eastern European countries 1989 was less a liberal story of re-internationalization than a tale of de-internationalization on the world stage" (300). Furthermore, as he and other historians confirm, "today's potent brew of nationalism, religious conservatism and racism in eastern Europe is hardly just a recent reaction to 1990s neoliberalism, but found overt expression in 1989 as well" (Betts 2019, 244; cf. Kovács 2019, Krapfl 2019). "The liberal story of re-internationalization" and the processes of de-internationalization that have become apparent more recently can be considered similar to the dynamics of de- and re-territorialization in the Global South which Jie-Hyun Lim and Eve Rosenhaft (2021) identify within appropriations of Holocaust memory. On the one hand, non-Western countries actively draw on the tropes of cosmopolitan (Holocaust-based) memory to create their own memoryscapes. On the other, "the global memory formation has contributed to re-territorializing the mnemoscape by providing a new frame for heightened competition among the parties to contending national memories," thus hampering the possibility of "mnemonic solidarity" (Lim and Rosenhaft 2021, 4).

The persistent national frameworks of remembering and making sense of the transitions which many of the chapters identify and discuss, testify to the limits of the internalization narratives that accompanied and framed the images of the 1970–1990s transformations. At the same time, some of the memories analyzed in this volume point to practices of alternative or 'minor' transnationalism – such as in Ioana Luca's reading of the 'communist biddy's reception across different countries of Eastern Europe'; or Mónika Dánél's outline of the transcultural effects in Hungarian and Romanian literary and film (re)mediations of the transitions; or my own identification of similarities in the transforming memory modes in post-Soviet and postapartheid literatures. Could memories that locate the beginning or intensification of neoliberal and neocolonial violence at the time of the 1970–1990s transitions build connections across the Global South and European East? For now, we do not see such mnemonic interconnections taking place, but we do witness a range of critical perspectives, expressions of discontent, or new subjectivities and modes of remembering transitions that appear in national or local (below the national) contexts and that sometime draw regional connections. All of them, as the chapters in this book elucidate, are in dialogue with global(ized) memory frameworks and practices, voicing critiques or performing alternatives. The task of this volume has been to chart some of these practices and place them in conversation with each other. Apart from the thematic conversations which structure this collection, the chapters inquire into the dialogues taking place on the regional and global scales.

As a whole, this collection puts in practice what Manuela Boatcă (2021) has called the method of 'counter-mapping.' She defines this method as a "relational perspective capable of revealing the constitutive entanglements through which a global capitalism grounded in colonial expansion interlinked all areas of the world," whereby the focus is on uncovering links between the regions "constructed as fixed and unrelated location on imperial maps" (246). In the context of remembering transitions, the 'disconnected,' national(ist) frameworks as well as the homogenizing global ones (usually, foregrounding historical processes in more 'Westernized' nations as normative) function as imperial maps. Seeing beyond and against them requires forging links across global peripheries and semi-peripheries (to use the language of world-system theory) as a form of solidarity (which may strategically reinvoke the 'forgotten' 'Second-'and 'Third-World' solidarities of the past). This suggests a perspective in memory studies involving intersections between perspectives of the Global South and the 'Global East' (including Eastern Europe and Eurasia). Particularly in the case of Eastern Europe, such mnemonic counter-mapping can be a method of counteracting strong Eurocentric sensibilities, articulated, quite prominently, through discourses about transitions. Such perspectives, grounded in 'Southern theory' (Connell 2007, Mbembe 2019), can provide a lens onto the intersections of (neo)imperial and neoliberal violence in the course of post-war, post-conflict, or regime change-related transformations. This volume is an invitation to begin such counter-mapping by tracing the critical reopening of transitions as sites of intersecting and continuing 'crises.'

Coda: Memories of crisis

This volume began with reflections on memories of transitions emerging in contemporary culture and media as responses to the lasting and erupting systemic crises, including the 'crisis in memory' – a notion that points to the limitations of available frameworks and languages of remembering in relation to the emerging practices and the political ends which they pursue. The chapters of this volume chart a diverse transnational field of memories and of critical perspectives on them that zero in on 'transitional' pasts and map these pasts beyond imaginaries of a gap or a void. Taken together, these readings open a field of multidirectional (Rothberg 2009) and agonistic (Bull and Hansen 2016) memories beyond the tropes of successful revolution or civilizational collapse, the zero-point time of ultimate beginning or end. If we would like a concept that represents these contradictions and conflicts, we could call this remembering of uncertainty, precarity, and potentialities *memories of crisis.*

Memory studies to date have been characterized by an overwhelming concentration on remembering atrocity: war, genocide, political repression, and state violence have been its privileged subjects. The main causes for remembering such pasts have been to praise the heroes or mourn the victims, ensuring that past violence is not repeated, or to motivate resistance and retaliation. More recent research has proposed theorizing the 'remembering of hope' (Rigney 2018) that revives past practices of activism and encourages activism in the present. These memories are activated to facilitate interconnections of "mourning and militancy" (Crimp 1989, Traverso 2017, 21), to create a consciousness of continuity between past and present injustice, and thus validate old and inspire new struggles. Memories of the 1970–1990s transitions do involve 'mourning' and 'militancy,' as singular modes and as an interconnection. But many of the examined memories involve something beyond these frameworks – the senses of disorientation, indeterminacy, disappointed hope, or permanent insecurity – that do not seamlessly translate into discourses of trauma or resistance. 'Crisis,' with its flexibility of use (and overuse in late modernity), multidirectionality ('crisis' can lead to both positive and negative turns), but also the urgency it generates regarding a situation (Boletsi et al. 2020), might be an apt term for conceptualizing contemporary memories of those sociopolitical and economic transformations that focus on processes, experiences, and social effects.

Approaching memories of transitions requires a new conceptual language due to the varied, highly uneven, but also interconnected workings of transformations on different levels, within societies and transnationally. In this context, the idiom of 'crisis' can be helpful for (re)thinking transition as "an array of temporal experiences and affective registers," as Rita Barnard (2019, 10) suggests in comparing the notions of 'transition' and 'crisis.' At the same time, as Janet Roitman (2014) has argued, crisis narratives are epistemological 'blind spots' and thus involve the regulative, normative function that is embedded in modern practices of history and memory. *Remembering* crisis, however, can, within some practices, cast a reflective perspective precisely on these blind spots of enunciated 'being in crisis' as it engages with processes in the past from viewpoints of the present. such remembering (especially when mediated as narratives) will also often involve an intentionality by putting a spotlight on what the remembering subjects perceive as having been erased, over-written, or made unrecognizable. In this regard, much depends on the dominant narratives of transitions within a society, against which counter-remembering takes place. In situations where transitions have been framed as catastrophic moments, re-framing them as 'crises' can imply the (recalled) possibility of positive transformation. In the contexts of dominant appraisal of transition, the crisis idiom can draw attention to the hardships that were experienced, with feasible effects in the now, if that past is seen as continuing in the present.

With regard to the emerging languages of remembering transitions as 'crises' which this volume begins to map, two initial observations can be made. One concerns the different and overlapping temporalities of transitions-as-crises. Interpretations of transitions as 'collapse'[11] of old regimes or 'turning points' (i.e., new beginnings) that were most common during those periods are characteristic of the time regime of modernity (Koselleck 2006). More recently, those transitions have come to be perceived – along the lines of contemporary invocations of crisis – as "a protracted historical and experiential condition," a chronic state rather than a "critical, decisive moment" (Roitman 2014, 2). As essays in this volume show, remembering the 1970–1990s transitions can involve both tropes – of *rupture and chronicity*. It can emphasize the unresolved, chronic social problems that were neglected, exacerbated, or, in some cases, generated by transition, thus pointing at transitions as a relay stage of a systemic and ongoing conflict.[12] But recalling transition can also create a rupture with or in the present by the very act of looking back and (re)telling stories of crisis.

---

11 The recent volume *Collapse of Memory – Memory of Collapse* brings together contributions reflecting on memories of war, terror, migration, environmental disaster as well as systemic collapse (such as the end of state socialism in Eastern Europe), and uses the terms 'collapse', 'disaster' and 'crisis' interchangeably. While such dialogue between studies of memory narratives that are usually discussed within narrower contextual fields (e.g., memories of World War II) can produce new insights, such broad clustering as well as the use of new concepts for it requires theorization.

12 See Robbe et al. 2021 for brief reflections on the temporalities that represent the 'chronicity' of crisis from critical perspectives.

The second point pertains to the contradictory and contested memories of transitions that reflect the uneven distribution of suffering and benefitting. With regard to Eastern Europe (including Russia and Eurasia), this characteristic has been highlighted, with the support of various data sets, in Kristen Ghodsee and Michael Orenstein's study. "In the average postsocialist country," they observe, "the transitional recent recession dwarfed the US Great Depression of the 1920s and 1930s, a truly epic crisis whose effects will be remembered for generations. [. . .] Maddison Project data show the postcommunist recessions to be the worst in modern history since 1870." (2021, 32) However, "the benefits of transition were divided so unequally that majorities of the population no longer support the transition paradigm" (2021, 15). Similar social consequences of transition are at the forefront of popular views on this period in South Africa, the country in which extreme inequality institutionalized under apartheid has not been remedied since its end (Gready 2010). Given the depth and duration of the crises, and the highly differential vulnerability of social actors, what modes, forms, and perspectives of remembering can capture these conditions? What is the politics and ethics of such remembering?

To remember the (often unresolved) conflicts and conundrums of the transitions in the present is to address the lives and perspectives that have been omitted from public histories and memories, the loss and suffering that have not been registered or that have been 'appropriated' in narratives of national trauma, but also practices of resistance and resilience that formed in response to these conditions. Such remembering may involve looking into the power relations that determined the underlying mechanisms of what was or is viewed as crises. To remember crisis is also to generate affinity with those who lived through it, to understand how they acted and re-constituted themselves as subjects in the contexts of rapidly changing values and increased knowledge about the suffering caused by repressive regimes.

While some highly mediatized images such as the fall of the Berlin Wall, the toppling of Lenin statues, or footage of Nelson Mandela walking out of prison, just like the popular narratives of transition, have become iconic and formed memoryscapes of '1989,' any simple celebratory memory does not do justice to those revolutionary processes. As Padraic Kenney (2021) has noted with regard to Eastern Europe,

> [a]ll of these highly visual moments imprinted themselves globally because they conveyed something true about the desires of Eastern Europeans to express themselves and to claim spaces of freedom. They are not false in any way. They do, however, give us an incomplete, and perhaps even distorted, story of the revolutions.

These spectacular events were characterized by what Ann Rigney calls "melodramatic memorability" which "means that some events are upstaged at the cost of others, or at the cost of failing to grasp the 'slow violence' of chronic injustice or the singularity of individual suffering" (2016, 92). The same can be said about the narratives of Truth Commissions (Cole 2009) or of reading Secret Police files (Poenaru, this volume).

What makes other, occluded events and experiences of transitions worth remembering today, as we observed in the poems quoted at the beginning of this introduction, is the moral outrage at the consequences of change (of the lack of it) and the sense of a crisis in the present. Both poems point to the transitions as crises in the double sense: as the moments when ideals of transformation were articulated and positive change was imagined as imminent (crisis of 'the old') and, in the same breath, the processes that compromised these ideals or the social sites where these ideals never had a chance to be realized (crisis of 'the new'). The transitional past is, then, framed as a point of conflict that planted seeds for the tragic, radical mismatching experienced in the present. Starting with expressions like these, the volume begins to inquire into the transformations of languages for thinking and recalling transition, with contributions examining the silences produced by transition narratives as well as the emerging alternatives that may become building blocks for new vocabularies that stem from the 'problem spaces' (Scott 2004) of the present.

∗∗∗

The chapters of this volume were written before the full-scale invasion of Ukraine by the Russian army in February 2022; however, in finalizing this book as the war continues devastating the country, the question must be raised about the immediate present and future of remembering transitions in Eastern Europe (as events that brought about the end of the Cold War) and globally. Zooming in on the 'uses' of the transitional past within political discourse in Russia, it can be clearly seen how the state and state-supported media have been mobilizing memories of perestroika and the 1990s as an epitome of 'the dark past' or the 'collective trauma' from which the national body has gradually recovered since the beginning of Vladimir Putin's presidency (Malinova 2021, Oushakine 2009, Sharafutdinova 2020). This discourse has intensified since the beginning of the war in Ukraine in 2014. In hindsight, the documentary *Russia. Recent History* [Rossiya. Noveishaya istoriya][13] produced by the state-sponsored Russia 1 channel and aired in December 2021 (as a gesture of commemorating thirty years since the break-up of the Soviet Union) can

---

13 The film is available here: https://www.youtube.com/watch?v=deRbBopd2LA&list=PLYP5VWdRJBSAUxQRutSnqUTFFyEwl55XW.

be seen as one of the key (media) events that legitimized the subsequent full-scale invasion of Ukraine, along with Putin's "On the Historical Unity of Russians and Ukrainians" published in July 2021 and the banning of Russia's leading human-rights organization Memorial in December 2021 (the institution whose establishment and achievements are firmly associated with the 1980–early 1990s political transformations). At the same time, as a reaction to this outright debunking of democratization during the first post-Soviet/postsocialist decade, political and memory actors in Eastern Europe foreground the achievements of the late 1980s and 1990s as a clear break from all things Soviet, strategically 'forgetting' the socioeconomic crises that the political change unleashed for many, with many inequalities persisting today (Ghodsee and Orenstein 2021).

Thus, the war has polarized memories of transitions in this region even more, and just like the terror and suffering in Ukraine are causing repercussions in the rest of the world, these mnemonic wars and competing nationalisms that they feed are likely to have global effects. This volume sets out to draw attention to memories of the late-twentieth century transitions as a field in which major conflicts and contestations of the past and present are taking place. More specifically, it has attempted to elucidate and critically examine the different modes and forms, cultural practices and media of memory that call into question the weaponized and manipulative uses of the transitional past. Whether these forms of memory will gain more traction and 'travel' or become restricted to archives is something to be seen. But at least being able to see these forms and understand their workings equips us with knowledge and, perhaps, hope.

Works cited

Assmann, Jan. "Communicative and Cultural Memory." *Cultural Memory Studies: An International and Interdisciplinary Handbook*. Ed. Astrid Erll and Ansgar Nünning. Berlin: De Gruyter, 2008. 109–118.

Assmann, Aleida. "Transformations of the Modern Time Regime." *Breaking Up Time: Negotiating the Borders between Present, Past and Future*. Ed. Chris Lorenz and Berber Bevernage. Göttingen: Vandenhoeck & Ruprecht, 2013. 39–56.

Barnard, Rita, and Andrew Van der Vlies, eds. *South African Writing in Transition*. London: Bloomsbury Academic, 2019.

Barnard, Rita. "Introduction." *South African Writing in Transition*. Ed. Rita Barnard and Andrew Van der Vlies. London: Bloomsbury Academic, 2019. 1–32.

Beresford, Alexander. "Nelson Mandela and the Politics of South Africa's Unfinished Liberation." *Review of African Political Economy* 41.140 (2014): 297–305.

Berlant, Lauren. *Cruel Optimism*. Durham: Duke University Press, 2011.

Bernhard, Michael, and Jan Kubik. *Twenty Years after Communism: The Politics of Memory and Commemoration*. Oxford: Oxford University Press, 2014.

Betts, Paul. "1989 at Thirty: A Recast Legacy." *Past and Present* 244 (August 2019): 271–305.

Bevernage, Berber, and Chris Lorenz, eds. *Breaking Up Time: Negotiating the Borders between Present, Past and Future*. Göttingen: Vandenhoeck & Ruprecht, 2013.

Blejmar, Jordana. *Playful Memories: The Autofictional Turn in Post-Dictatorship Argentina*. Basingstoke: Palgrave Macmillan, 2016.

Boatcă, Manuela. "Counter-Mapping as Method: Locating and Relating the (Semi-)Peripheral Self." *Historical Social Research* 46.2 (2021): 244–263.

Boletsi, Maria,Janna Houwen, and Liesbeth Minnaard. "Introduction: From Crisis to Critique." *Languages of Resistance, Transformation and Futurity in Mediterranean Crisis-Scapes: From Crisis to Critique*. Ed. Maria Boletsi, Janna Houwen, and Liesbeth Minnaard. Cham: Palgrave Macmillan, 2020. 1–24.

Borenstein, Eliot. *Plots against Russia: Conspiracy and Fantasy after Socialism*. Ithaca: Cornell University Press, 2019.

Borzutzky, Silvia, and Sarah Perry. "It Is Not about the 30 Pesos, It Is about the 30 Years: Chile's Elitist Democracy, Social Movements, and the October 18 Protests." *The Latin Americanist* 65.1 (2021): 207–232.

Brown, Wendy. "Resisting Left Melancholy." *Boundary* 26.3 (1999): 19–26.

Buden, Boris. "Children of Postcommunism." *Radical Philosophy* 159 (January/February 2010): 18–25.

Bull, Anna Cento, and Hans L. Hansen. "On Agonistic Memory." *Memory Studies* 9.4 (2016): 390–404.

Cavallaro, Maria E., and Kostis Kornetis, eds. *Rethinking Democratization in Spain, Greece and Portugal*. Cham: Palgrave Macmillan, 2019.

Chakrabarty, Dipesh. *Provincializing Europe: Postcolonial Thought and Historical Difference*. Princeton: Princeton University Press, 2000.

Chari, Sharad, and Katherine Verdery. "Thinking between the Posts: Postcolonialism, Postsocialism, and Ethnography after the Cold War." *Comparative Studies in Society and History* 51.1 (2009): 6–34.

Cole, Catherine M. *Performing South Africa's Truth Commission: Stages of Transition*. Bloomington: Indiana University Press, 2009.

Connell, Raewyn. *Southern Theory*. Cambridge: Polity, 2007.

Crimp, Douglas. "Mourning and Militancy." *October* 51 (Winter 1989): 3–18.

David, Lea. *The Past Can't Heal Us: The Dangers of Mandating Memory in the Name of Human Rights*. Cambridge: Cambridge University Press, 2020.

Della Porta, Donatella et al. "Transition Times in Memory." *Legacies and Memories in Movements: Justice and Democracy in Southern Europe*. Ed. Donatella Della Porta et al. Oxford: Oxford University Press, 2018: 1–29.

Drost, Alexander. "Collapse Makes Memory: An Introduction." *Collapse of Memory – Memory of Collapse: Narrating Past, Presence and Future about Periods of Crisis*. Ed. Alexander Drost, Olga Sasunkevich, Joachim Schiedermair, and Barbara Törnquist-Plewa. Cologne: Böhlau Verlag, 2019. 9–26.

Dujisin, Zoltan. "A History of Post-Communist Remembrance: From Memory Politics to the Emergence of a Field of Anticommunism." *Theory and Society* 50.6 (2020): 65–96.

Erll, Astrid. "Literature, Film and the Mediality of Cultural Memory." *Cultural Memory Studies: An International and Interdisciplinary Handbook*. Ed. Astrid Erll and Ansgar Nünning. Berlin: De Gruyter, 2008. 389–398.

Erll, Astrid. "Travelling Memory." *Parallax* 17.4 (2011): 4–18.

Forsdick, Charles, James Mark, and Eva Spišáková. "Introduction. From Populism to Decolonization: How We Remember in the Twenty-First Century." *Modern Languages Open* 1 (2020).

Gabowitsch, Mischa. "Replicating Atonement: The German Model and Beyond." *Replicating Atonement: Foreign Models in Commemoration of Atrocities*. Ed. Mischa Gabowitsch. Cham: Palgrave Macmillan, 2017. 1–21.

Gensburger, Sarah, and Sandrine Lefranc. *Beyond Memory: Can We Really Learn from the Past?* Cham: Palgrave Macmillan, 2020.

Ghodsee, Kristen. *Red Hangover: Legacies of Twentieth-Century Communism*. Durham: Duke University Press, 2017.

Ghodsee, Kristen, and Mitchell Orenstein. *Taking Stock of Shock: Social Consequences of the 1989 Revolutions*. Oxford: Oxford University Press, 2021.

Gook, Ben. *Divided Subjects, Invisible Borders: Re-unified Germany after 1989*. London: Rowman and Littlefield, 2015.

Gready, Paul. *The Era of Transitional Justice: The Aftermath of the Truth and Reconciliation Commission in South Africa and Beyond*. New York: Routledge, 2010.

Grunebaum, Heidi. *Memorializing the Past: Everyday Life in South Africa after the Truth and Reconciliation Commission*. New York: Transaction, 2011.

Hilmar, Till. "'Economic Memories' of the Aftermath of the 1989 Revolutions in East Germany and the Czech Republic." *East European Politics and Societies* 35.1 (2021): 89–112.

Huyssen, Andreas. "International Human Rights and the Politics of Memory: Limits and Challenges." *Criticism* 53.4 (2011): 607–624.

Huyssen, Andreas. *Present Pasts: Urban Palimpsests and the Politics of Memory*. Palo Alto: Stanford University Press, 2003.

Huyssen, Andreas. "International Human Rights and the Politics of Memory: Limits and Challenges." *Criticism* 53.4 (2011): 607–624.

Iacob, Bogdan, James Mark, and Tobias Rupprecht. "The Struggle over 1989: The Rise and Contestation of Eastern European Populism." *Eurozine* (September 3, 2019). https://www.euro zine.com/the-struggle-over-1989/ (Accessed April 3, 2023).

Kenney, Padraic. "Missing Pictures? Towards an Alternative Visual History of 1989." *Public History Weekly* (June 24, 2021). https://public-history-weekly.degruyter.com/9-2021-5/alternative-visual-history-1989/ (Accessed April 3, 2023).

Khoza, Tumelo. "Democracy." *Home Is Where the Mic Is*. Ed. Mandi P. Vundla and Alan K. Horwitz. Braamfontein: Botsotso Publishing, 2017. 10–11.

Kofta, Mirosław, and Wiktor Soral. "Belief in the Round Table Conspiracy and Political Division in Poland." *Social Psychological Bulletin* 14.4 (2019).

Kopeček, Michal, and Piotr Wciślik, eds. *Thinking Through Transition: Liberal Democracy, Authoritarian Pasts, and Intellectual History in East Central Europe After 1989*. Budapest: CEU Press, 2015.

Koselleck, Reinhart. "Crisis." Trans. Michaela W. Richter. *Journal of the History of Ideas* 67.2 (2006): 357–400.

Koselleck, Reinhart. *Futures Past: On the Semantics of Historical Time*. Trans. Keith Tribe. New York: Columbia University Press, 2004.

Kovács, Éva. "Talkin' 'bout a Revolution: On the Social Memory of 1989 in Hungary." *From Revolution to Uncertainty: The Year 1990 in Central and Eastern Europe*. Ed. Joachim von Puttkamer, Włodzimierz Borodziej, and Stanislav Holubec. New York: Routledge, 2019. 103–116.

Krapfl, James. "Czechoslovakia's Year of Decision: From the Socialist Revolution of 1989 to the 'Real' Revolution of 1990." *From Revolution to Uncertainty: The Year 1990 in Central and Eastern Europe*. Ed. Joachim von Puttkamer, Włodzimierz Borodziej, and Stanislav Holubec. New York: Routledge, 2019. 80–102.

Krastev, Ivan, and Stephen Holmes. *The Light that Failed: Why the West is Losing the Fight for Democracy*. London: Pegasus Books, 2019.

Krekó, Péter. "'The Stolen Transition': Conspiracy Theories in Post-Communist and Post-Democratic Hungary." *Social Psychological Bulletin* 14.4 (2019).

Laczó, Ferenc, and Joanna Wawrzyniak. "Memories of 1989 in Europe between Hope, Dismay, and Neglect." *East European Politics and Societies and Cultures* 31.3 (2017): 431–438.

Legott, Sarah. *Memory, War and Dictatorship in Recent Spanish Fiction by Women*. Lewisburg: Bucknell University Press, 2015.

Levinson, Alexei. "1990e i 1990i: soziologicheskie materialy" [The 1990s and 1990: Sociological Materials]. *Novoe literaturnoe obozrenie* 2 (2007). https://magazines.gorky.media/nlo/2007/2/1990-e-i-1990-j-socziologicheskie-materialy.html (Accessed April 3, 2023).

Levy, Daniel, and Natan Sznaider. "Memory Unbound: The Holocaust and the Formation of Cosmopolitan Memory." *European Journal of Social Theory* 5.1 (2002): 87–106.

Lim, Jie-Hyun. "Victimhood Nationalism: Mourning Nations and Global Accountability." Memory in a Global Age: Discourses, Practices and Trajectories. Ed. Aleida Assmann and Sebastian Conrad. Basingstoke: Palgrave Macmillan, 2010.138–162.

Lim, Jie-Hyun, and Eve Rosenhaft. "Introduction: Mnemonic Solidarity – Global Interventions." *Mnemonic Solidarity – Global Interventions*. Ed. Jie-Hyun Lim and Eve Rosenhaft. Cham: Palgrave Macmillan, 2021. 1–14.

Maier, Charles S. "Hot Memory . . . Cold Memory: On the Political Half-life of Fascist and Communist Memory." *Transit* 22 (2002).

Malinova, Olga. "Framing the Collective Memory of the 1990s as a Legitimation Tool for Putin's Regime." *Problems of Post-Communism*, 68.5 (2021): 429–441.

Mark, James. *The Unfinished Revolution: Making Sense of the Communist Past in Central-Eastern Europe*. New Haven: Yale University Press, 2010.

Mark, James, Bogdan C. Jacob, Tobias Rupprecht, and Ljubica Spaskovska, eds. *1989 after 1989: A Global History of Eastern Europe*. Cambridge: Cambridge University Press, 2019.

Massino, Jill. *Ambiguous Transitions: Gender, the State, and Everyday Life in Socialist and Postsocialist Romania*. New York: Berghahn Books, 2019.

Mbembe, Achille. "The State of South African Political Life." *Africa is a Country* (September 19, 2015). https://africasacountry.com/2015/09/achille-mbembe-on-the-state-of-south-african-politics (Accessed April 3, 2023).

Mbembe, Achille. *Necropolitics*. Trans. Steven Corcoran. Durham, NC: Duke University Press, 2019.

Mignolo, Walter. *Local Histories/Global Designs: Coloniality, Subaltern Knowledges and Border Thinking*. Princeton: Princeton University Press, 2000.

Moyn, Samuel. *Not Enough: Human Rights in an Unequal World*. Cambridge, MA: Belknap Press, 2018.

Noordenbos, Boris. *Post-Soviet Literature and the Search for a Russian Identity*. Basingstoke: Palgrave Macmillan, 2016.

Olick, Jeffrey K. *On Collective Memory and Historical Responsibility*. New York: Routledge, 2007.

Oushakine, Serguei A. *Patriotism of Despair: Nation, War and Loss in Russia*. Ithaca: Cornell University Press, 2009.

Oziewicz, Marek. "Coping with the Trauma of Allied Betrayal: Alternate Histories of Poland in Konrad T. Lewandowski's 'Noteka 2015' and Marcin Ciszewski's Major Trilogy." *Exploring the Benefits of the Alternate History Genre*. Ed. Zdzisław Wąsik, Marek Oziewicz, and Justyna Deszcz-Tryhubczak. Wrocław: Wydawnictwo *Wyższej Szkoły Folologicznej*, 2011. 113–126.

Pearce, Susan. "1989 as Collective Memory 'Refolution': East-Central Europe Confronts Memorial Silence." *Silence, Screen and Spectacle: Rethinking Social Memory in the Age of Information*. Ed. Lindsey Freeman et al. New York: Berghahn Books, 2014. 213–238.

Pehe, Veronika, andJoanna Wawrzyniak. "Introduction: Neoliberalism, Eastern Europe and Collective Memory." *Remembering the Neoliberal Turn: Economic Change and Collective Memory in Eastern Europe after 1989*. Ed. Veronika Pehe and Joanna Wawrzyniak. New York: Routledge, 2023 (forthcoming).

Petrov, Kristian. "The Concept of Transition in Transition: Comparing the Post-Communist Use of the Concept of Transition with That Found in Soviet Ideology." *Baltic Worlds* 7.1 (2014): 29–41.

Platt, Kevin M.F. "Commemorating the End of History: Timelessness and Power in Contemporary Russia." *Power and Time: Temporalities in Conflict and the Making of History*. Ed. Dan Edelstein, Stefanos Geroulanos, and Natasha Wheatley. Chicago: University of Chicago Press, 2020. 400–419.

Popescu, Monica. "Translations: Lenin's Statues, Post-Communism and Post-Apartheid." *The Yale Journal of Criticism* 16.2 (2003): 406–423.

Rigney, Ann. "Differential Memorability and Transnational Activism: Bloody Sunday, 1887–2016." *Australian Humanities Review* 59 (April/May 2016): 77–95.

Rigney, Ann. "Remembering Hope: Transnational Activism beyond the Traumatic." *Memory Studies* 11.3 (2018): 368–380.

Robbe, Ksenia, Kristina Gedgaudaite, Hanneke Stuit, Kylie Thomas, and Oxana Timofeeva. "In and out of Crisis: Chronotopes of Memory." *(Un)Timely Crises: Chronotopes and Critique*. Ed. Boletsi et al. Cham: Palgrave Macmillan, 2021. 51–76.

Robbins, Bruce. *The Beneficiary*. Durham: Duke University Press, 2017.

Roitman, Janet. *Anti-Crisis*. Durham: Duke University Press, 2014.

Ros, Ana. *The Post-Dictatorship Generation in Argentina, Chile and Uruguay: Collective Memory and Cultural Production*. Basingstoke: Palgrave Macmillan, 2012.

Rothberg, Michael. *Multidirectional Memory: Remembering the Holocaust in the Age of Decolonization*. Palo Alto: Stanford University Press, 2009.

Rothberg, Michael. *The Implicated Subject: Beyond Victims and Perpetrators*. Palo Alto: Stanford University Press, 2019.

Rymbu, Galina. "The Law Is Not in Force Here." *You Are the Future*. Moscow: Voznesensky Center, 2020. 85–89.

Schneider, Nina. "Bolsonaro in Power: Failed Memory Politics in Post-Authoritarian Brazil?" *Modern Languages Open* 1 (2020).

Schwartz, Matthias, Nina Weller, and Heike Winkel, eds. *After Memory: World War II in Contemporary Eastern European Literatures*. Berlin: De Gruyter, 2020.

Scott, David. *Conscripts of Modernity: The Tragedy of Colonial Enlightenment*. Durham: Duke University Press, 2004.

Scribner, Charity. *Requiem for Communism*. Cambridge: MIT Press, 2003.

Sharafutdinova, Gulnaz. *The Red Mirror: Putin's Leadership and Russia's Insecure Identity*. Oxford: Oxford University Press, 2020.

Sierp, Aline. "1989 versus 1939 – A Missed Opportunity to Create a European Lieu de Mémoire?" *East European Politics and Societies and Cultures* 31.3 (2017): 439–455.

Simonian, Renald. "Likhie ili slavnye devianostye?" [The turbulent or glorious 1990s?]. *Svobodnaia mysl'* 12 (2011): 159–174.

Tabaszewska, Justyna. "Memory of 'What Almost Was': Alternative Histories of the 1989 Polish Political Transformation." Paper presented at the annual Conference of the Memory Studies Association, Warsaw, 2020.

Traverso, Enzo. *Left-Wing Melancholia: Marxism, History, and Memory*. New York: Columbia University Press, 2017.

Van der Vlies, Andrew. *Present Imperfect: Contemporary South African Writing*. Oxford: Oxford University Press, 2017.

Velikonja, Mitja. "Lost in Transition: Nostalgia for Socialism in Post-Socialist Countries." *East European Politics and Societies and Cultures* 23.4 (2009): 535–551.

Wale, Kim, Pumla Gobodo-Madikizela, and Jeffrey Prager, eds. *Post-Conflict Hauntings: Transforming Memories of Historical Trauma*. Cham: Palgrave Macmillan, 2020.

Wawrzyniak, Joanna, and Alexandra Leyk. *Cięcia: Mówiona historia transformacji* [Cuts: An Oral History of Transformation]. Warsaw: Wydawnictwo Krytyki Politycznej, 2020.

Part I: **Transitions' Working Memories**

Florin Poenaru

Herta Müller and Katherine Verdery as *Spies*: File-Memoirs as Forms of Remembering *through* and *against* the Secret Police Archives

Abstract: The chapter analyzes a particular genre of the transition memory regime: file-memoirs, that is texts produced by people after reading their secret police files that sought to reestablish their auctorial voice. The opening of the secret
police archives was supposed to bring moral and historical clarity to the transition period. Instead, this chapter shows, it engendered a cult for the occult and
prolonged the performative power of the secret police into the present. Herta
Müller's and Katherine Verdery's reflections and actions upon reading their respective files are a case in point of this melodramatic reversal: the performative
power of the Securitate is so strong that it forces the subjects of the files to instan-
tiate its logic into the present. By reducing the communist experience to the secret
police – as institution and as archive – and by placing it at the core of the memory regime of the transition, postcommunist anticommunism paradoxically continued into the present the logic, the mystique, and the practices of the institution
such as the impetus for denunciation, the peddling of secrets and inside information, and the proclivity for spying the other while being suspicious of his/her past.
Moreover, this reinforced a perspective on socialism as being linked to the nation
state at the cost of erasing its global and internationalist character.

The archival turn

The archives of the secret police in former communist countries have received
ample public and scholarly attention, especially in the last decade.[1] Sheila Fitzpatrick even referred to a "quantum leap" in the historiography of state socialism
following easier access to the archives of the former regimes (2015, 377). Indeed,
there was an 'archival turn' in the study of the communist past at beginning with
the new millennium, and the archives of the former secret police featured prominently in this approach.

---

1 See especially Fitzpatrick 2013, Gokariksel 2019, Vatulescu 2010, and Verdery 2013.

https://doi.org/10.1515/9783110707793-002

However, the opening and incorporation as sources of history and memory of these secret files was neither uncontested nor unproblematic. They were intensely scrutinized, and their empirical status was highly debated, leading to the constitution of a contentious space regarding the past, history writing, memory, representation, voices and silences, justice and truth. They delineated a social arena fraught with contradictions, struggles and trauma, both before and after 1989. There has been a constant public and theoretical concern not only with what is in the archives but also with the archives themselves, as sources of fear, angst, and danger, or on the contrary, of truth, knowledge, and revelation. Hence, legacies of the past are intensely fought over in the present, shaping it, while the present has the power to retrospectively determine the past. Despite their ambiguous status, or, maybe, precisely because of this, these archives were central to the constitution of the memory regime of the transition period. The secret police became a synecdoche for communism.

For some anticommunist public figures, politicians, and historians, these archives were important sources for learning about the past. The underlining thinking was rooted in the belief that the documents of the former secret police have a special status among other archival sources because they can reveal the "truth" about the communist past, and more specifically about people's choices and moral standing. Symptomatically for this stance, in *Arrested Voices*, Russian writer and journalist Vitaly Shentalinsky wrote: "There, at the Lubyanka, is hidden the truth about the life and death of our best writers" (1996, 3). The impetus to open the files was often formulated in the jargon of Christian theology, pertaining to issues of 'guilt,' 'redemption,' 'confession,' 'sin,' 'moral rectitude,' 'forgiveness,' etc. It was hoped that the 'revelations' of the files would tell the truth about everyone's past. Put differently, people carried a different degree of fault in relation to the past, a different burden as it were, and this difference had to be inscribed into the new order of society. The files were vital in order to distinguish between victims, perpetrators, and various forms of collaboration with the repressive apparatuses of the former regimes. From this perspective, open and full access to the content of these files was deemed crucial (Glajar et al. 2016, 6–9).

Others, like Adam Michnick for example, were less inclined to trust these materials. After all, the information they contained was obtained through means of interrogation, forced confessions, surveillance, and testimonies from untrustworthy informants. Furthermore, the institutions that produced these files were well known for their disinformation techniques and conspiratorial ways of working. Therefore, it was better to leave them untouched, or at least to deny the pretense that they can have any sort of connection to 'the truth.' In addition, many documents from these files were destroyed or lost before they became available to the public (Funder 2003, Poenaru 2017b, Uitz 2008). It was impossible to reconstruct them in full and thus have a comprehensive view of their real scope and size.

Postcommunist countries adopted different strategies in relation to the opening of these archives (Stan 2009, 8–10). Despite the variety of legal arrangements – which entailed prolonged political and juridical battles – in all cases the access to these archives was linked to lustration goals. Ultimately, shedding light on the secret police files was supposed to perform a moral cleansing of postcommunist societies, not just simply to offer a glimpse into the inner workings of an infamous institution.

The cult of the occult

Following their opening, in a purely dialectical reversal, the truth and purification that access to the secret files was supposed to bring, led in fact to the proliferation of a climate of suspicion, fear, and denunciation. This was precisely what the former secret police was blamed for and what the lustration mechanisms were hoping to eliminate from the public life of postcommunism. Because of their equivocal character, these files became sources of public scandal and shaming, following revelations of their content. Being endowed with the capacity to reveal truth, the secret police files offered instead a vast spectacle of information and 'scandal' that played out on the front pages of the newspapers and on television, each time promising yet a bigger revelation and a more complex web of spies, hidden plots, and victims. From politicians to writers, from artists to sportsmen, from business people to poor scientists, few people escaped unscathed by this concoct of data, rumors, allusions, suggestions, and presuppositions, all extracted from the secret files. All of a sudden, and at regular intervals, everybody could potentially become a Stranger, somebody with a different identity, a different history, and a different past. Moreover, there was the suspicion that there must be something hidden, something unknown about every single individual. It was just a matter of time until things will come to light.

And indeed, they came. It is impossible to mention here all instances of such shattering revelations, but some stand out. The discovery in 2008 that Czech writer Milan Kundera was a secret police informant caused an international uproar and led to a deeply divisive struggle among Czech historians (Aviezer 2009). Previously, in 2006, historian Andras Gervai outed world-famous Hungarian film director Istvan Szabo as collaborator of the secret police. Szabo's demasking unfolded in a context in which lists of secret police collaborators flooded the social life of Hungary at the time (Uitz 2008) with traumatic social and personal consequences. Péter Esterházy discovered that his father was an informant (Esterházy 2002), while András Forgách learned about the extensive spying activities of his mother (Forgách 2018). In Germany, Christa Wolf's case encapsulated the paradox of simultaneously being a victim of Stasi and an I.M (*inoffizielle Mitarbeiter*). In Romania, Sorin Antohi, a prominent intellectual and at the time history professor at Central European University, Budapest, was exposed as having been an informer for the Securitate about the activities of his closest friends, a group of intellectual dissidents to which he was affiliated.

By inscribing these files as sites of truth about the past, postcommunism simply prolonged their inner logic into the present. One notable effect was the strengthening of a cult of the occult and secrecy, itself already an obsession of the former secret police and its main *raison d'etre*: finding secrets (held by enemies of the state, dissidents, etc.) and keeping secrets (through files, surveillance, and the like). When people could finally read their own files, they discovered their persona through the eyes of the secret police and also the names of the relatives, close friends, and neighbors who did the spying. This had the powerful traumatic effect of altering one's entire emotional and social universe. Things that had been taken for granted before were now shattered. Past certitudes were blown to pieces and social solidarities and networks were destroyed. These 'revelations' from the files had the capacity to alter the memory of the past significantly, or, to put it differently, to cast past memories that now gained new meaning in a different light. These particular social, mnemonic, and emotional consequences of opening the secret police files are the focus of this chapter.

The 'ex-files'

More specifically, I center on a particular and peculiar genre, (auto)biographical in nature and placed at the intersection of history and memory, that so far has remained unexplored. I refer to the writings that people produced after reading the files opened in their names (or related to them or their families) by the former secret police. I suggest calling these writings *file-memoirs*.[2] I was first drawn

---

2 Valentina Gajar suggested the term 'file stories' to designate these files because they contain fragments of lives and life stories that can be retrieved, relieved and remembered. I agree with her perspective, especially with the suggestion that they can be read as fiction, which destabilizes the official narrative of the creators of these files. What I have in mind though is something different: the actual process of coming to terms with, of reading and responding to the content of these files. Therefore *file-memoirs* are necessarily a metanarrative genre. (Gajar et al. 2016, 56).

to this topic when I researched the role secret police archives played in the anti-communist historiography of communism after 1989 and in shaping the memory of the transition period (Poenaru 2017b). I was impressed by the large number of people who told me that they were stunned by this encounter, that they needed to go out of the reading hall and take a deep breath, while they sat in utter shock and in silence. Then, after a period of time, most, if not all of them, felt the need to write, to offer their counter-narrative to what the file had to say about them and their past lives. I am interested in this mechanism of wanting to speak back to the archives of the secret police, of putting things right, of remembering through and against them. What kind of memory regime is created by and through these writings? What do these writings hope to achieve and to whom are they addressed? What is the relationship between these writings and the content of the police file? Also, I want to inquire who is the 'I' of these writings and whether a memory regime centered on the individual can form the basis of a mnemonic practice that can dislodge the performative power of the secret file.

There is a growing body of such file-memoirs in the Romanian context of my investigation.[3] Perhaps the extension of the Romanian secret police – the Securitate – to almost all spheres of life and its large network of informants and collaborators (estimated at half a million people) contributed to the proliferation of this genre during the transition period. Generally, the goal of these writings is to come to terms with the information offered by these files and to correct the composite image they construct about the subject writing the file-memoir. Contextualization is also an important purpose: the information presented by the files is brought back into the historical context in which it was produced and from which it was abstracted. The work of memory here is key for reconstructing the historical situation but, as most of the authors agree, it is also highly unreliable. Personal annotations, especially diaries, come in handy to supplement the weaknesses of remembering.

Unsurprisingly, professional writers and former dissidents are over-represented in this corpus (Stelian Tănase, Gabriel Andreescu, Dorin Tudoran, Bujor Nedelcovici, Luca Pițu, Herta Müller), and their file-memoirs necessarily contrast their fictional writings with the fictional constructions of the Securitate. In addition, the search for moral clarification and legitimation is also characteristic for these authors. Their scope is to neatly delineate between good and evil; the evil must be denounced and punished at least symbolically, in writing.

---

3 Some of the most prominent texts in this genre are: Tănase 2002, Nedelcovici 2003, Munteanu 2007, Andreescu 2009, Müller 2009, Tudoran 2010, Bugan 2012, Pițu 2012, Bos 2013, Liiceanu 2013, Stork 2013, Verdery 2018, Karnoouh 2020. Outside the Romanian context see especially Ash 1997, Esterhazy 2008, Marton 2009, Wolf 2011, Fitzpatrick 2013, Forgách 2018.

Anthropologists (Katherine Verdery) and ethnologists (Claude Karnoouh) tend to focus instead not just on the content of their files, but also on the broader and societal dimensions in which these files emerged. Karnoouh offers a scathing criticism of people informing on him, not because of their collaboration with the Securitate, but because of the poor quality of their reports which showed a modest understanding of social reality. Coen Stork, the Dutch Ambassador to Romania at the time of the fall of the regime, also narrativized the secret police file opened in his name but the goal of this file-memoir is to highlight the ambassador's support for the anticommunist circles. More interesting and insightful are the musings of Jan Willem Bos, a Dutch translator who lived in Romania intermittently in the late 1980s. Through the eyes of the secret agents following him around one can reconstruct the anodyne elements of everyday life in the latest stages of the regime. A special case is philosopher Gabriel Liiceanu file-memoir because it is structured as a (fictive) epistolary between him and the secret police operative in charge of his file. Thus, Liiceanu dramatizes the need of speaking back to the Securitate by staging an impossible conversation.

In this chapter, I engage closely with two key contributions to this genre. One is the piece the Romanian-born German author Herta Müller wrote after her encounter with her Securitate's file.[4] The other is Katherine Verdery's account of reading the file opened in her name by the same institution (Verdery 2018). The two texts and the two authors are significantly different to make any comparison tenuous. Herta Müller (born 1953) is the 2009 Nobel Prize winner for literature and her entire work is structured around the experience of the oppressive communist regime in Romania and her frequent encounters with the Securitate before 1989. The essay I discuss is inscribed into her oeuvre, but at the same time is distinct from it because of its non-fictional character. In it, following a series of events during a visit to Bucharest, she bemoans the fact that the secret police are still active in postcommunism despite its revamped institutional face. Large blame should be apportioned to local intellectuals who are not interested in such matters, Müller believes. She then describes the strenuous processes of getting access to her file and the painful intellectual and emotional labor of reading it.

Katherine Verdery (born 1948) is an American prized anthropologist who did fieldwork in Romania since the 1970s. Her book-length text describes her encounter with the Securitate right from the beginning of her study and her continued surveillance until the end of the regime. But the text is more composite than this

---

4 The German original is available here: http://www.zeit.de/2009/31/Securitate. For the English version from which I quote see: http://www.signandsight.com/features/1910.html. Accessed September 8, 2021.

autobiographical narrative first suggests. Excerpts from her Securitate files (both texts and photos) are interwoven with memories from the communist past and with contemporary diary entries that record Verdery's intellectual and emotional processing of her file. In addition, especially in the second part of the book, the text bounces between theoretical investigations of the secret police files – thus harking back to Verdery's previous work (Verdery 2013) – and personal reflections. In the end, taking a cue from Ash (1997) she tries to reach out to the officers in charge of her file in the hope of a reckoning.

However, despite these obvious differences, what the two accounts nonetheless share is confrontation with the performative power of the secret police files and the impossibility to transcend it. More generally, both texts bespeak the failure of the liberal paradigm that incorporated the secret police files as sources of truth and of historical data about particular individuals and their moral choices. In addition, both texts are symptomatic for seeking to confront in writing the version of oneself created by the secret police. Beyond their specificities, the two narratives are also indicative of the wider contradictions and dialectical reversals that fundamentally structure the attempts to remember through and against the secret police archives. Read together it becomes clear that for both authors the Cold War remains the unsurpassable ideological and temporal horizon of their thinking about the secret police files and of the regime that produced it. This is the case for most, if not all, productions in this genre. But because of Müller's and Verdery's influence in their respective fields, both texts contributed significantly more than others to the solidification of a type of transitional memory in which secret police officers and the spies play central roles.

Global networks

This juxtaposition brings together particular trajectories that originate in Romanian state socialism, but extend and overlap at a global scale. By way of the two examples discussed here I want to draw attention not only to various forms of confronting one's secret police file, but also to the fact that this preoccupation is not something confined to the peculiarities of postcommunist Eastern Europe. Rather, it is consonant with a 'global turn' in memory studies, which emphasizes connections and continuities beyond national borders, political regimes, and symbolic dates. But how is this turn to be conceptualized?

Kraenzle and Mayr (2017, 6) argued that taking seriously the history and memory of Eastern Europe following European integration opens a pathway to analyzing the ways in which European memories as a whole are transnationally structured and negotiated. Indeed, European memories surpass the boundaries of individual nation states and also those of Europe itself. Chiara de Cesari and Ann Rigney (2014, 1–2) also maintained that national frameworks are no longer satisfactory units of analysis to account for the formation of memories and histories, hence the suggestion to discard such seminal notions as *imagined communities* (Anderson 1983) and *places of memory* (Nora 1989) because of their attachment to the nation-state. Influenced by Arjun Appadurai's notion of globalization, Assmann and Conrad similarly argue that global mobility and movements have shifted the terrain of memory practices from the national to the transnational and the global, which becomes the defining arena for all actors involved (2010, 4–5). Pei-chen Liao rightfully noted that only a transnational paradigm could illuminate the multiplication of memory practices and fictional constructions after 9/11 (2020, 6). Fazil Moradi et al. in their investigation of genocides across the globe seek to trace the "plurality of memories beyond the eyewitness narratives and the border of the modern nation-state" (2017, 1), while Amy L. Hubbell et al. (2020) do the same in their examination of global places of traumatic memory.

Against the grain of this scholarly methodological optimism, the nation-state is still very much salient for shaping both local and transnational trajectories. Zoltan Dujisin rightfully noted the role of Central and Eastern European states like Czech Republic, Poland, Hungary and Romania in imposing a conservative anticommunist agenda at the EU level, while mobilizing in the process broader transnational networks of historians, politicians, think-tanks and museums (2021, 66). Aline Sierp (2021) sharply investigated the manner in which various EU initiatives and institutions replaced nation-states in promoting a continent-wide memory agenda focused around national socialism and Stalinism. At the same time, however, with the complicity of nation-states, the same EU institutions remained silent in relation to transcontinental and global memories of colonialism (Sierp 2021, 689). Rather than being displaced, nation-states are in fact even more active in modeling global memory regimes and commemorative practices. The opening of the secret police files is also a case in point: national legislations shaped the content of these archives and the rules granting access to them.

The conundrum surrounding the nation state seems to plague indelibly the quest for genuine global memories. The nation state always creeps in. Even de Cesari and Rigney's volume for example, despite its bold claims, is in fact structured around national states and the conversation only branches out from there. One solution to escape this deadlock is the one I suggest in this text: to look at mnemonic practices as being always-already globally constituted. Thus, 'transnational' and 'global' cease to be a question of scale (the one that transcends the local, which is usually defined as the nation-state), but one of *processes* unfolding at various scales, in different locales and temporalities. Hence, I subscribe to Blacker and Etkind's notion of *memory events*:

> acts of revisiting the past that create ruptures with its established cultural meanings. [. . .] These events are simultaneously acts and products of memory. They have their authors and agents – initiators and enthusiasts of memory – who lead the production of these collective events in the same way that film directors make their films. Memory also has its promoters, as surely as it has its censors and foes. Memory events are secondary to the historical events that they interpret, usually taking place years or decades later. Sometimes, a memory event attains the significance of a historical event, therefore, blurring the distinction between the two. (2013, 6)

The opening of the secret police files and especially the reaction to their content by those concerned represent such instances of memory events that are locally circumscribed, but are also global in nature and implication. They are 'slotted' as it were in a more general and trans-local framework. For example, the first time I encountered the notion of memory event was not in Blacker, Etkind and Fedor's edited volume, but in Bujor Nedelcovici book in which he describes his experience of reading his secret police file (2003, 28). Nedelcovici is a Romanian writer who emigrated to Paris in the late 1980s and, following the collapse of the regime, began addressing questions related to time, memory, and history in his writing. For him, reading the file and reflecting about it and about the manner in which it was produced, represents a painful "memory event." Nedelcovici's trajectory is indicative of the always-already global character of the mnemonic practices I describe here: as a Romanian émigré writer he was part of a larger anticommunist network, based in Paris but active around Europe, which enabled the intellectual and publishing space for such histories and memories of the secret police files to emerge.

Andreas Huyssen in *Twilight memories* wrote:

> My hypothesis . . . is that the current obsession with memory is not simply a function of the fin de siècle syndrome, another symptom of postmodern pastiche. Instead it is a sign of the crisis of that structure of temporality that marked the age of modernity with its celebration of the new as utopian, as radically and irreducibly other. (1995, 6)

The memory boom in postsocialism bespeaks the crisis Huyssen identifies, and enlarges it. Remember here the explosion of dissident memories and literature in the West immediately after 1989, telling horror stories from the other side of the divide.[5] Initially, postsocialist histories of communism were produced directly as personal memories, as stories of dissidents and victims, perfectly fitting the ideological expectation about the 'East.' The Easterners finally had a voice and a lot to reminisce about. But the point not to be missed here is that precisely this welcoming

---

5 To my mind, paradigmatic for this genre is Slavenka Drakulic's *How We Survived Communism and Even Laughed.*

attitude towards the harsh memories of Easterners prolonged in fact and entrenched the Orientalist tradition in which the West is the subject and creator of history and the East is the realm of memory, tradition and orality.[6]

Furthermore, what is characteristic to this obsession is that by highlighting memory it reduces knowledge to a process of revelation and illumination that in turn simply deems one's biography extraordinary and meaningful. The past is then accessible only to the initiated few, to the priests of the temple, who will act as promoters of a national pedagogy of memory. The past is strictly connected to direct (auto)biographical experience. It can be remembered, invoked and reworked but always within a subjective horizon. The individual hero of the mnemonic process is quintessential. In this sense file-memoirs are significant for the global turn in memory studies: not (necessarily) in the sense of transcending nation-state borders, but as symptoms of the crisis of (global) modernity.

This genre should not be confused with 'stories of the Soviet experience' of the type documented by Irina Paperno. In her work, Paperno (2009) analyzes memoirs, diaries, dreams and other materials published during the perestroika. These forms of expression depict the catastrophic life in the Soviet Union throughout the twentieth century and they are written from the perspective of a subject who managed to survive it. Moral pathos is their distinctive mark as one might expect. But what distinguishes these moral and intellectual productions is that they were encouraged by the Soviet state itself in the latter stages of its existence as part of a general attempt to reform the entire system, to understand what went wrong in the past in order to avoid the same mistakes in the present and in the future. Equally significant is the fact that the authors of these mnemonic productions are not tout court against the Soviet state or against communism. By contrast, the postcommunist authors of memoirs, diaries and file-memoirs are explicitly anti-Soviet and anticommunist and, in addition, they want to put to trial the entire system – at least symbolically, if not juridically. Hence the two genres are not similar and cannot be usefully compared. The postcommunist memory boom incorporates the perspective of the victors of the Cold War and it is addressed to them.

---

6 Johannes Fabian coined the term allochronism for the location in different temporalities (2011, 32–33).

The lure of the file

Approaching now the very act of reading one's file, it must be noted first that the confrontation with the secret police file is an attempt to regain control over one's life story, of getting hold, again, of one's persona, confiscated by the purview of the state and its secret agents.[7] More than a confession or memorialization, it represents the unbearable traumatic moment of confronting oneself as a Stranger, the proper image of the split subject.[8]

This aspect was magnified by the acknowledgment that what gave consistency to the claims of dissidence was the registration by the Securitate in its files of such acts, in keeping with its internal logic. Cristina Vatulescu showed that in the last part of Ceauşescu's regime the opening of surveillance file was not linked to indictment. Rather, the purpose of the file was to offer the legal framework by which to accumulate various details about one's life and biographical trajectory (2010, 32). Seen from this perspective, the Securitate archive appears to be the sum of various overlapping biographies and biographical details of the people under surveillance, and sometimes of the people doing the surveillance. Little wonder then that the practice of using the Securitate archives as (auto)biographical sources has been quite widespread in postcommunism and also led to the significant reconsideration of peoples' biographies and experiences.

For example, Timothy Garton Ash wrote:

> The Stasi's observation report, my diary entry: two versions of one day in a life. The 'object' described with the cold outward eye of the secret policeman and my own subjective allusive, emotional self-description. But what a gift to memory is a Stasi file. Far better than a madeleine. (1998, ix)

Gabriel Andreescu, a Romanian dissident and subsequently a scholar of the Securitate archive, made a similar point. He wrote that his Securitate file was a highly useful aid-memoire because it saved some elements or details that he could not possibly remember otherwise: the exact day and hour of his first arrest; the content of his pockets during one interrogation; some dialogues between him and his parents while being under home surveillance, etc. (Andreescu 2009, 228).

---

7 What I discuss here concerns the experience of opening up the archives of the secret police in postcommunist countries. But I hasten to add that the 'lure of the file' is not reducible to this time and context. In fact, recently, the secret files of such institutions as FBI, MI5 and MI6 have received intense scholarly attention. See Saunders 2015, Evans 2019, Caute 2022.

8 This is evident in the quite common practice of publishing one's file parallel to one's diary of the time. On the one hand the official version of the self, on the other the personal version. For a paradigmatic case, see Tănase 2002.

Also, many writers discovered in their files texts that they long lost, Securitate preserving their last copy.[9] The files act not only as sources of history, but also – and in fact primarily – as sources of memory. They turn into memory prosthesis, the external mechanism capable to record everything, and most importantly, to never forget.

Franco Moretti noted that despite the collapse of the Greco-Roman culture, the term 'narratio' – central to it – reappeared not in the literary domain but in the courts (1987, 211). The trial has a straightforward narrative structure that emphasized the simplicity of justice, but also its melodramatic character (the villain gets caught and punished). According to Moretti, in modernity the *Bildungsroman* exists as a genre only in so far as it is capable to replicate the structure of the trial. The novel is inseparable from the trial: in both senses of the term, judgment and going through obstacles.

This is the case in both Herta Müller's and Katherine Verdery respective texts depicting their experiences of reading their secret police file and the mnemonic mechanisms this reading triggers. They express in a crystalized form the problem of trauma in relation to the secret police archive and, more generally, in relation to the violence of the communist past.

Enter the doppelgänger

The essay entitled "Securitate in All but Name" was published in *Die Zeit* before Müller won the Nobel Prize. The beginning of the text assesses the uninterrupted activity of the Securitate in today's Romania, still engaged in spying activities. It also draws attention to the opacity and bureaucratically arbitrary nature of the activity of the CNSAS, the national council mandated to open and analyze the archive of the former secret police. However, the very last paragraph of the text makes the more remarkable observation that:

> In my file I am two different people. One is called 'Cristina' [Müller's code name in the Securitate file], who is being fought as an enemy of the state. To compromise this 'Cristina' the falsification workshop of Branch 'D' (disinformation) fabricated a doppelganger from all those ingredients that would harm me the most – party-faithful communist, unscrupulous

9 The representative case here is, of course, the discovery in the KGB archives of Bulgakov's diary. Following a police search, the diary was taken away with other incriminating writings. When some years later Bulgakov got his writings back, the first thing he did was to destroy his diary. However, a copy of it, the only one, survived in the secret police archive and was published after the regime change in 1991.

agent. Wherever I went, I had to live with this doppelganger. It was not only sent after me wherever I went, it also hurried ahead. Even though I have always and from the start, written only against the dictatorship, the doppelganger still continues on its own way. It has taken on a life of its own. Even though the dictatorship has been dead for 20 years, the doppelganger is still wandering about. For how much longer?

In the reading hall of the CNSAS, a veritable *lieu de mémoir* of the transition, people reading their files were confronted with their alternative biographies, with their secret selves, or better said, with their selves composed in secrecy. They encountered themselves as Others, dispossessed of their own subjectivity and auctorial powers over their life trajectories. Consequently, according to many reports, the first, immediate reaction to this confrontation is unspeakability – the very inability to speak. Deprived of its auctorial powers, the subject is left mute, unable to grasp this act of violent subjective dispossession.

After this initial shock and confrontation with the unspeakable, the immediate reaction is to fight back and reassume the power to write one's biography. In this transition from the impossibility to speak to the loquacity of the biographization two major issues are at stake: on the one hand, the subjects are fighting to recover their voices and auctorial powers from the Secret police by telling their own stories; on the other hand, the subjects are trying to regain the social trust to make credible their own self-narration. The doppelganger's claim to reality seems to be much stronger and much more real than any account the subjects can offer about them retrospectively. In a sense, the authentic subject engaged in writing its postcommunist biographization always seems fake, a pale copy of the subject created by the secret police file, as Müller's paragraph testifies.

Commenting on the aforementioned passage from Müller's text in the opening of her own reflection on the secret police file, Verdery also highlights the multiplicity of identities the secret police file creates and plays with:

> Our situations differ considerably, of course. Unlike me, Herta Müller is a world-renowned writer who was the direct target of Securitate harassment and persecution, meeting regularly with her oppressors face to face, as I did not. What joins us, however, is the experience of having been multiplied, turned into something we do not recognize as ourselves. We have been crafted, in a peculiar way, by an organization working presciently on the postmodern assumption that people's identities are unstable and do not unify us, but also on the modernist one that surface appearances are deceiving and reality must be sought beneath them. This combination gives the officers a number of powerful tools as they analyze the behavior of a target (their name for the people they follow) for signs of a hidden truth. (2018, 7)

The traumatic encounter with the doppelganger is further supplemented by its schematicism, by the type of selections the secret agents made in the subject's biography. It is not only that the Securitate managed to create a completely new double, very powerful and with a life of its own, but more importantly this double is the result of a series of selections from one's biography and also outright fabrications. What are missing are precisely the subjective humiliations, acts of violence, harassment and personal psychological discomfort the person under surveillance went through. While the file can performatively create an entire new subject,[10] it does not save the proper evidence for a realist retracing of the past. Put differently, while it can easily construe a subject in an incriminating fashion, it does not offer the possibility for a rebuttal based on evidence.

In Müller's case in particular, we encounter the very limits and paradoxes of the postcommunist politics of memory, especially regarding the calls for the full opening of the secret police files: it is not only that by opening these files the logic of the Securitate and its performative powers are prolonged into the present, but also that it is precisely the dissident and anticommunist intellectuals who are suffering as a result of this opening, not the former perpetrators. Their names are surrounded by doubt and their life trajectories lose the unconditional social trust that they claimed to have. As a result, they must engage in a lengthy self-referential literature defending themselves. In an almost tragic twist, the postcommunist accusers of the Securitate, through their very gesture of accusation, become themselves (again) accused by the Securitate and in need to defend and justify themselves.

At a more general level, what this mechanism espouses is the failure of the liberal paradigm of memory that seeks to approach the issue of guilt, punishment, and responsibility in moral terms. Also, it takes the perspective of the individual seen as a monadic actor, who struggles with internal turmoil while disregarding the social edifice, part of which were the interactions with the secret police. The very need for biographization that ensues after the reading of the Securitate files represents in effect a powerful reaffirmation of the collective and of society: not only as addressees of the autobiography, but also as a recognition that history happens in a collectivity and individual figures cannot be singled out *a priori* either as victims or as perpetrators. Ultimately, this need for biographization represents the failure of the idea of individual victimhood and/or heroism, especially during communism.

Verdery is "befuddled" by her encounter with her secret double. Again, what is at stake is identity and the destabilizing mechanism the information contained in the file has on one's current persona. This is a crucial point raised by Verdery as she begins to examine herself (and her profession) through the eyes of those writing the file: "When I read their descriptions of myself as a spy, I begin to won-

---

10 See also Tudoran 2010, when the very actions of Securitate lead to the creation of Tudoran as an anticommunist dissident, precisely the outcome the Securitate was trying to avoid in the first place.

der whether I really was one. How much of the practice of anthropologists resembles spying?" (2018, 7) Verdery also highlights how the many doubles in the file "unmoored her self-perception," a fact that is compounded by the messy nature of the file (8). The heap of documents is impenetrable from the perspective of an outsider. It needs to be organized first, to be put into *order* – precisely the order the reader of the file seeks between her many identities, as Verdery mentions.

The way Verdery reads her file and then decides to write about it is both typical and distinctive. First, she voraciously reads through the file in the CNSAS reading room. Absorbed by the experience, she skips lunch. When she finally takes a break, she steps outside and has the unnerving feeling that all the people around her are secret police spies; that they are there to get her. The logic of the file, and of the Securitate more generally, is already at work. The Other is a menace, somebody to be aware of and stay away from. But, perhaps by virtue of her position as an international scholar, Verdery is able to take a step back. She has her file copied – almost 3000 pages – and deposited in a box in her office where it sits for almost two years while she finishes other academic projects. This time lag is quite rare. Usually, those who have access to their file read it at once, with curiosity and trepidation. But when she does read it, Verdery is overwhelmed too by an assortment of emotions:

> outrage at seeing photos that a hidden camera had taken of me in my underwear; despair and anger at learning of people whom I had considered close friends yet who had given nasty informers' reports on me; terrible remorse at learning how I myself had delivered friends to the Securitate by being careless; amusement at how officers had garbled important facts; indignation at the ugly picture of me that surfaces in these pages (cold as ice, manipulative, scheming); and above all, like other readers of their files, astonishment at the remarkable extent of the surveillance – the sixteen-and eighteen-hour days of following me around, the intercepted correspondence, the eavesdropping and wiretaps. [. . .] My surveillance engaged the visual and the auditory almost equally, enriched by their interplay with the text and with my own sense-making efforts. I found the variety and force of the conflicting emotions all these aroused – along with the sensation that the Securitate knew absolutely everything, down to my most intimate thoughts – quite exhausting. (2018, 11)

The question becomes how to sift through these emotions, how to give them form and meaning for the person experiencing them, but also for a broader audience. In Verdery's case this takes the form of an attempt to understand the Romanian communist state and the experience of surveillance. The file then becomes a pretext for a broader academic endeavor that is already consonant with Verdery's previous work. While Müller seems to remain preoccupied with the emotionally destabilizing effect of the revelations in the file, Verdery's account seems to shift quickly from personal reaction to scholarly investigation. In addition, Verdery goes further in that she circumscribes the content of the file to the wider Cold War context of its formation. By seeing the world through the eyes of the secret police officers – which is what the file actually provides – Verdery tries to understand their perspective of her as a spy. After all she was an US academic doing fieldwork in a socialist country, taking field-notes, talking to people and then using the diplomatic service of the embassy to ship her notes back home. At the height of the Cold War this can only resemble spying and ultimately it seems that Verdery becomes convinced of the fact that there is substantial resemblance between the work of anthropologists and those of the secret police spies.[11]

The power of agents

Despite their divergent strategies, both Müller and Verdery nonetheless remain closely focused on the secret police officers they encounter in their files. The secret police agents become a scapegoating category. In his classic study René Girard noted that the function of the scapegoat is to bring a resolution to a crisis of which it was considered guilty through its ritual killing (1986, 139). The peace and harmony of society are restored. Nonetheless, this elevation of the secret police officers to the mythical status of sole bearers of responsibility for all the communist and postcommunist societal failures effectively precludes the possibility of grasping the structural mechanisms of a society that make individual actions possible, and also blocks a genuine act of introspection and of coming to terms with the past. In this transference mechanism, the blame is just shifted around. At this level there is an uncanny overlap between the discourse of the secret police officers prior to 1989, that justified their repressive actions against the dissidents as a need to defend the country, and the accusatory practices of the postcommunist dissidents, who support their claims to lustration as a patriotic duty to cleanse the social body.

In particular, Müller's text carries the melancholy that this purging has failed, that the former officers are still deeply ingrained in the nation's fabric, organizing its functioning from the background. Ultimately, this is also the structural problem with the law of lustration: far from being a mechanism for generating truth or justice, it simply tries to operate a bureaucratic cleansing of the nation by automatically conflating structural conditions with individual guilt. In this context, both Verdery and Müller's biographization brings to light another form of corruption and its subsequent moral dilemmas. When reading her file Müller is confronted with the bitter truth that one of her main spies was, of course, her best friend (Verdery experiences a similar situation):

---

11 See also Poenaru 2017a and Verdery 2013.

> This friendship, which meant so much to me, was ruined by her visit to Berlin, a terminally ill cancer patient lured into betrayal after chemotherapy. The copied key made it clear that Jenny had fulfilled her task behind our backs. I had to ask her to leave our Berlin flat at once. I had to chase my closest friend out in order to protect myself and Richard Wagner from her assignment. This tangle of love and betrayal was unavoidable. A thousand times I have turned her visit over in my mind, mourned our friendship, discovering to my disbelief that after my emigration, Jenny had a relationship with a Securitate officer. Today I am glad, for the file shows that our intimacy had grown naturally and had not been arranged by the secret service, and that Jenny didn't spy on me until after my emigration. You become grateful for small mercies, trawling through all the poison for a part that isn't contaminated, however small. That my file proves that the feelings between us were real, almost makes me happy now.

What Müller experiences here is the typical melodramatic reversal, the real secret of the secret files. Melodrama always involves some unexpected and excessive knowledge possessed not by the hero, but by the Other, a knowledge that the hero learns at the end. This stands in obvious contrast with the tragedy, which is based on a principle of misrecognition or structural ignorance (Žizek 2001, 12). What one finds upon reading the files in the archive is not some long repressed secret about him/herself, but something that the Other (the neighbor, the friend, etc.) knew all along, but kept silent. Consequently, the reading of the personal file represents in fact not only a tragic confrontation with one's individual self and past but also with a collective sociality. The question to be asked here is then: how does the whole subjective and emotional structure of a situation change when one gets to know that the Other (considered as friend, as neighbor, etc.) is in fact a Stranger or even an Enemy?

Laplanche and Pontalis defined trauma as a fragment from the past that cannot be meaningfully integrated in the symbolic universe of the self and becomes a hurtful point of fixation (1974, 13). But what Müller's and Verdery's narratives express is not the encounter with an element from the past that cannot be properly integrated, but on the contrary, an element from the present (the revelation of knowledge) that retrospectively changes the coordinates of the past. Contrary to the mainstream understanding, anxiety in the postcommunist East is not necessarily determined by the insecurity of the unpredictable future of the transition, but perhaps even more traumatic, by the uncertainty of the past. Here, it is not only that one's life can suddenly be deemed futile, useless, and immoral, but also one's life-time intellectual, emotional, and erotic attachments can be torn to pieces, or at least sunk into doubt by revelations from the secret police archive, as the texts discussed here vividly and emotionally demonstrate. In this highly volatile context, in which the next revelation might blow away today's certitudes, it is worth asking what does it mean to live a moral, just life? Is there truly a neat border between complicity and victimhood, between perpetrators and victims? In turn, these concerns repose the question of community and friendship: what is the degree of familiarity, intimacy, and tolerance that offers the substance of these collective forms of attachment?

A loss of memory – not as absence, but in substance

Müller notes in the fragment quoted above that after the revelation she was left mourning for her lost friendship. She might have known or suspected her friend's allegiances earlier. But the revelation from the file makes it official. She experiences two forms of dispossession at the hands of the Securitate: on the one hand she was dispossessed of her auctorial power, but also, in the process of mourning, of her subjectivity. She is being forced to re-evaluate her entire biography following the loss of her friend after the revelations from the archive. This loss of voice and of subjectivity defines postcommunist mourning.

Significantly this is not a loss in the present, but in the past: Müller is deprived of her own friendship in the past, of her own memories of her friends that now have to be rearticulated and recast in a different light. Freud wrote that when we lose someone, we don't know what it is *in* the person we lost (2005, 205). Something is hidden in the loss itself which generates a double anxiety: that of the loss itself, and that of not knowing what the loss actually is. This, I think, explains very well the condition Müller and Verdery try to articulate in their file – memoirs as a symptom of other similar conditions: while postcommunism was supposed to generate a confrontation with the past, a victory over the past humiliations, it is ultimately experienced as a defeat, as another form of dispossession and loss.

The dark irony implicit in this mechanism is that the only tenable moral position during communism was death: the real, true dissidents of communism were those killed by the regime. All those who made it out alive will always be haunted by the suspicion of compromise and moral failure. Müller herself was haunted by these suspicions both before her emigration (because she managed to publish a book in Romania and take part in the cultural industry of communism) and after her arrival in the West where she was suspected of being an informer. She writes in her final part of her text:

> The reasoning behind this lenience [of the Securitate], however, was malicious: instead of being considered a dissident among my colleagues at the school, as I had been until then, I was to be seen as profiteering from the regime and, in the West, suspected of espionage.

Therefore, can the situation of mourning offer an insight into new forms of normative politics of memory, guilt, and reconciliation in postcommunism? Can mourning for one's double loss and double dispossession actually articulate a new relationship that manages to leave behind the violence of the Securitate archive and its twin logic of punishment and denunciation? The failure of Herta Müller's moral stance appears precisely at this level: it is incapable of articulating a politics of memory beyond the register set by the Securitate. Following her suspicion that her friend was a spy for the Securitate, Müller goes on to clandestinely rummage through her luggage in search for clues and evidences in order to incriminate her friend, effectively transforming herself into a spy. The possibility of solidarity with the Other, the grounds for reconciliation, pardon, and love are annulled. Radical moralism, as an epitome of the postcommunist anticommunism quest for justice and reparation, seems completely incapable and ill equipped to offer the contours of a new community based on solidarity and trust.

It is important to recall here Christa Wolf's controversial suggestion that those who left their communist countries for the West were only interested in an easy life, acting cowardly and avoiding the harder, but more heroic task, of rebuilding communism (2013, 301–302). This opposition is structurally constitutive for Müller's case: she not only left Romania for a life in the Federal Republic of Germany, but in so doing, she also abandoned her socialist political and aesthetic conviction of her youth as member of the critical Aktionsgruppe Banat. From this perspective, one can recast the fundamental opposition of the communist regimes not as that between the former dissidents and the former communists, but between those who abandoned communism and those for whom communism remained the unsurpassable horizon after the experience of Nazism. This point becomes important after 1989 as well, when most of the former antit dissidents remained completely silent and oblivious to the transition injustices, preferring to continue to focus instead on the past as a worse alternative.

In *The Names of History*, Jacques Rancière wrote that only by rediscovering its 'literaturness' the historical writing can reassume the power of a discourse of truth that then could be politically mobilized for giving voice to the people (1994, 51–52). But the postcommunist experience I describe here, in which the literaturness of the historical writing was reassumed by the writings of the anticommunist literati to the extent that it was transformed into a new genre, points in fact to the opposite direction: the literatureness of the autobiographical writing leads to the enclosure of the historical discourse and historical investigation by a privileged few. The autobiographical focus of anticommunism, favoring the experiences and memories of the dissidents and intellectuals, also engenders a new regime of memory and memory politics which tends to dismiss the alternative memories and autobiographical practices, especially of the working classes, as 'nostalgic,' or as 'fake.' This framing, in turn, underpins the national pedagogy of memory: that is, a process in which the memory and experiences of the dissidents are elevated to the status of the history of communism. Alternative regimes of memory and memory practices both before and after 1989 are thus foreclosed.

Verdery's account lacks the moral undertone of Müller's. In fact, Verdery reflects on the manner in which her own presence among her Romanian friends and interlocutors brought them in trouble by allowing the secret police officers to come close and infiltrate in their lives. The relationship with the Securitate is never a one-way street in her reflection. However, in the end, Verdery too becomes a spy. Or, more precisely, she becomes a different kind of spy. She starts as a spy in the eyes of the secret police officers tasked to follow her around as a young US research student. In their eyes, by logic of their practice and ideology, she was already a spy, henceforth the need for her surveillance (Glaeser 2005, 335). Precisely by virtue of this surveillance Verdery becomes a spy in the eyes of all people she interacts with as well (Verdery 2018, 48). Following Timothy Ash, she tries to contact some of the secret police officers mentioned in her file. To be able to do so, she basically steps into their shoes: she makes connections, tries to find out their current addresses and phone numbers, calls them unexpectedly and pushes them for answers.

Surely, the circumstances changed and the finality of this process is radically different than was the case when the Securitate was a mighty force. But this only reinforces the fact that the performative power of the secret police file exceeds individual options and strategies. The logic of the file imprints itself onto the present and shapes the practices of those who try to remember through and against it. In the end, it cannot be domesticated and its narrative prevails. The initial impetus to write the file-memoir in order to counteract the power of the file seems to be lost and the doppelgänger triumphs. Müller's and Verdery's accounts fully express this melancholy, and with it, the contradictory nature of the memory practices that seek to remember through and against the secret police files.

Transitional memory, memory of transition

In her investigation of contemporary artistic practices that question the notion of the global transition(s) after 1989, Ksenia Robbe (2016) suggested to rethink these transformations through a poetics of failure. In this text I suggested that the file-memoirs also reflect a poetics (and politics) of failure, in a double sense. First, despite their attempt to dislodge the narrative construction of the secret police files and restore the truth, the file-memoirs only manage to affirm (or at least concede defeat to) the performative power of the secret institution. Herta Müller's and Katherine Verdery's complex reflections articulate this defeat.

Secondly, at a higher level of generality, the file-memoirs express the failure of a memory regime specific to the postcommunist transition period that was centered around the secret police and its employees and informers. This prolonged the logic and the mystique of the institution into the present and – not infrequently – its own detestable means, such as the practice of denunciation, the peddling of secrets and inside information, and the proclivity for spying the other while being suspicious of his/her past. Far from 'clearing the air of the transition' the importance awarded to these secret files managed in fact to darken the societal atmosphere. Just like before 1989, the information contained in these archives was still able to make or break one's life – even though circumstances changed. This is another paradox: the centrality of the secret police archives in postcommunism was achieved precisely through the hegemony of the anticommunist discourse. It was not an unintended consequence. It was inscribed in the very logic of anticommunist postcommunism.

What is lost in this reduction of communism to its secret police apparatus that the transition memory regime managed to inscribe in relation to the past? In a letter sent to a Romanian cultural weekly, Aurel Tudose – a former political prisoner in the 1950s – recalled how after a harsh interrogation, one of his fellow inmates told his interrogator that he will retract everything he had said and signed during his detention once he will be out and will tell the true story instead. To this, the police officer replied laughingly: "you bandit, you don't get it, do you? The history will be written based not on what you'll say but on our archives."[12] Tudose wrote this letter in order to show that the police officer was ultimately right: the communist past was being written based on the archives produced by the former regime, especially those of Securitate.

Ovidiu Ţichindeleanu (2010), offering a criticism of this memory regime, noted that anticommunism produced a perspective on communism from the point of view of the national state. Thus, the main subject of transition had not been the (socialist) world, but the nation – state. The genre of file-memoirs discussed here is a symptom of this fixation. What was lost in the memory regime of the transition period was exactly the global and internationalist character of socialism. With all its focus on 'remembering' and 'memory,' transition was in fact a vast mechanism of forgetting and of erasing the past. A critical reexamination of the memory regime of transition should bring to light this silencing.

---

12 Aurel Tudose, Placerea de a polemiza in vant, *Observator Cultural*, no. 460, February 2009. Text available here, http://www.observatorcultural.ro/PRIMIM-LA-REDACTIE.-Placerea-de-a-po lemiza-in-vint*articleID_21183-articles_details.html, accessed 13 March 2022.

Works cited

Anderson, Benedict R. *Imagined Communities: Reflections on the Origin and Spread of Nationalism.* London: Verso, 2006.

Andreescu, Gabriel. *L-am urât pe Ceaușescu: ani, aameni, disidență* [I hated Ceaușescu. Years, People, Dissidence]. Iași: Polirom, 2009.

Ash, Timothy. *The File: A Personal History.* New York: Vintage Books, 1998.

Assmann, Aleida, and Sebastian Conrad, eds. *Memory in a Global age. Discourses, Practices and Trajectories.* New York: Palgrave Macmillan, 2010.

Aviezer, Tucker. "Czech History Wars: The 'Milan Kundera Affair." *History Today* (March 1, 2009). https://www.thefreelibrary.com/Czech+History+wars%3A+the+%27Milan+Kundera+affair%27% 2C+in+which+the . . . -a0195323360 (Accessed October 11, 2022).

Blacker, Uilleam, Alexander Etkind, and Julie Feodor, eds. *Memory and Theory in Eastern Europe.* New York: Palgrave Macmillan, 2013.

Bos, Jan W. *Suspect. Dosarul meu de la Securitate.* Bucharest: Trei, 2013.

Bugan, Carmen. *Burying the Typewriter. A Memoir.* Minneapolis: Graywolf Press, 2012.

Caute, David. *Red List. MI5 and British Intellectuals in the Twentieth Century.* London: Verso, 2022.

De Cesari, Chiara, and Ann Rigney, eds. *Transnational Memory: Circulation, Articulation, Scales.* Berlin: De Gruyter, 2014.

Drakulic, Slavenka. *How We Survived Communism and Even Laughed.* New York: Harper Perennial, 2016.

Dujisin, Zoltan. "A History of Postcommunist Remembrance: From Memory Politics to the Emergence of a Field of Anticommunism." *Theory and Society* 50 (2021): 65–96.

Esterhazy, Peter. *Ediție revăzută.* Bucharest: Curtea Veche, 2008.

Evans, Richard J. *Eric Hobsbawm. A Life in History.* Oxford: Oxford University Press, 2019.

Fabian, Johannes. *Time and the Other. How Anthropology Makes its Object.* New York: Columbia University Press, 2011.

Fitzpatrick, Sheila. *A Spy in the Archives.* New York: I.B. Tauris, 2013.

Fitzpatrick, Sheila. "Impact of the Opening of Soviet Archives on Western Scholarship on Soviet Social History." *The Russian Review* 74 (2015): 377–400.

Forgách, András. *The Acts of My Mother.* London: Hamish Hamilton, 2018.

Freud, Sigmund. *On Murder, Mourning and Melancholia.* London: Penguin Books, 2005.

Funder, Anna. *Stasiland.* London: Granta, 2003.

Girard, René. *The Scapegoat.* Baltimore: Johns Hopkins University Press, 1986.

Glajar, Valentina, Alison Lewis, and Corina L. Petrescu. *Secret Police Files from the Eastern Bloc. Between Surveillance and Life Writing.* New York: Camden House, 2016.

Glaser, Andreas. *The Secret Police, the Opposition, and the End of East German Socialism.* Chicago: The University of Chicago Press, 2005.

Gokariksel, Saygun. "Facing History: Sovereignty and the Spectacles of Justice and Violence in Poland's Capitalist Democracy." *Comparative Studies in Society and History* 61.1 (2019): 111–144.

Hubbell, Amy L., Sol Rojas-Lizana, Natsuko Akagawa, and Annie Pohlman. *Places of Traumatic Memory: A Global Context.* London: Palgrave Macmillan, 2020.

Huyssen, Andreas. *Twilight Memories: Marking Time in a Culture of Amnesia.* London: Routledge, 1995.

Karnoouh, Claude. *Tribulațiile unui călător străin în România (1971–2017). Reflecții și amintiri.* Iași: Sedcom Libris, 2020.

Kraenzle, Christina, and Maria Mayr, eds. *The Changing Place of Europe in Global Memory Cultures: Usable Pasts and Futures*. Basingstoke: Palgrave Macmillan, 2017.

Laplache, Jean, and Jean-Bertrand Pontalis. *The Language of Psycho-Analysis*. New York: W.W. Norton, 1974.

Liao, Pei-chen. *Post-9/11 Historical Fiction and Alternate History Fiction. Transnational and Multidirectional Memory*. Cham: Palgrave Macmillan, 2020.

Liiceanu, Gabriel. *Dragul meu turnător*. Bucharest: Humanitas, 2013.

Marton, Kati. *Enemies of the People. My Family's Journey to America*. New York: Simon & Schuster, 2009.

Moradi, Fazil, Maria Six-Hohenbalken, and Ralph Buchenhorst, eds. *Memory and Genocide: On What Remains and the Possibility and Representation*. New York: Routledge, 2017.

Moretti, Franco. *The Way of the World: The Bildungsroman in European Culture*. London: Verso, 1987.

Munteanu, C. Nicolae. *Ultimii șapte ani de acasă. Un ziarist în dosarele Securității*. Bucharest: Curtea Veche, 2007.

Nedelcovici, Bujor. *Un tigru de hârtie*. Bucharest: Allfa, 2003.

Nora, Pierre. "Between Memory and History: Les Lieux de Mémoire." *Representations* 26 (Spring, 1989): 7–24.

Paperno, Irina. *Stories of the Soviet Experience. Memoirs, Diaries, Dreams*. Ithaca: Cornell University Press, 2009.

Pițu, Luca. *Documentele antume ale 'grupului din Iași'*. Iași: Opera Magna, 2012.

Poenaru, Florin. "The Knowledge of the Securitate: Secret Agents as Anthropologists." *Studia Universitatis Babes-Bolyai-Sociologia* 62.1 (2017a): 105–125.

Poenaru, Florin. *Locuri comune*. Cluj: Tact, 2017b.

Rancière, Jacques. *The Names of History: On the Poetics of Knowledge*. Minneapolis: University of Minnesota Press, 1994.

Robbe, Ksenia. "'Anything Is Possible': Rethinking the Politics of Transition through a Poetics of Failure in the Works of William Kentridge and Dmitry Gutov." *Third Text* 30.5–6 (2016): 403–419.

Saunders, Frances Stonor. "Stuck on the Flypaper." *London Review of Books* 37.7 (2015). https://www.lrb.co.uk/the-paper/v37/n07/frances-stonor-saunders/stuck-on-the-flypaper (Accessed April 6, 2023).

Sierp, Aline. "EU Memory Politics and Europe's Forgotten Colonial Past." *Interventions* 22.6 (2021): 686–702.

Shentalinskii, Vitali. *Arrested Voices: Resurrecting the Disappeared Writers of the Soviet Regime*. New York: Martin Kessler Books, Free Press, 1996.

Stan, Lavinia. *Transitional Justice in Eastern Europe and the Former Soviet Union*. New York: Routledge, 2009.

Stork, Coen. *Dosarul de Securitate al unui ambasador*. Bucharest: Humanitas, 2013.

Tănase, Stelian. *Acasă se vorbește în șoaptă. Dosar/Jurnal din anii târzii ai dictaturii*. Bucharest: Compania, 2002.

Tudoran, Dorin. *Eu, fiul Lor. Dosar de Securitate*. Iași: Polirom, 2010.

Țichindeleanu, Ovidiu. "Towards a Critical Theory of Postcommunism: Beyond Anticommunism in Romania." *Radical Philosophy* 159 (January/February 2010): 26–32.

Uitz, Renata. "The Duna-Gate Scandal in and Beyond the Hungarian Media." Ed. Oksana Sarkisova and Peter Apor. *Past for the Eyes. East European Representations of Communism in Cinema and Museums after 1989*. Budapest: Central European University Press, 2008. 57–80.

Vatulescu, Cristina. *Police Aesthetics: Literature, Film, and the Secret Police in Soviet Times*. Stanford: Stanford University Press, 2010.

Verdery, Katherine. *Secrets and Truths*. Budapest: Central European University, 2013.

Verdery, Katherine. *My Life as a Spy. Investigations in a Secret Police File*. North Carolina: Duke University Press, 2018.

Wolf, Christa. *City of Angels, or The Overcoat of Dr. Freud*. New York: Farrar, Straus and Giroux, 2013.

Žižek, Slavoj. *Did Somebody Say Totalitarianism?* London: Verso, 2001.

Bonifacio Valdivia Milla, Pablo Valdivia Martin

Conflictive Cultural Narratives in the Collective Memory of the Spanish Transition: The Case of *Trampa para Pájaros* by José Luis Alonso De Santos

Abstract: In this study, we explore three related research questions: a) how is the cultural narrative of the collective memory in the Spanish transition configured from a twofold perspective based on the theoretical notions of 'multidirectional memory' (Rothberg 2009, 2019) and 'agonistic memory' (Bull and Hansen 2016) in *Trampa para Pájaros*'s text; b) how the study of metaphoricity in *Trampa para Pájaros* contributes to understanding the conflictive complexity in the regimes of metaphor that have articulated the dominant conceptual architecture of the Spanish transition's memory; c) in which ways *Trampa para Pájaros* facilitates a re-thinking of mediations of the Spanish transition in the public discourse and how such insight can be transposed to other similar cases. Today, this play reads as a tragedy in which the humanity of all characters and situations brings to the fore the extraordinary density of angles and perspectives that were canceled by the dominant cultural narratives of the 'two Spains' and the oblivion. In this regard, it is possible to argue that *Trampa para pájaros* was foregrounding the principles of multidirectional memory and agonistic memory *avant la lettre* and was genuinely innovating in the field of not only the Spanish transition memory but also in the possibilities of re-engineering the democratic process in Spain and in its relation to the wave of the democratization that internationally took place in the 1990s.

Acknowledgments: We sincerely thank the documentation services provided by the workers at the Fundación Jorge Guillén y del Centro de Documentación de las Artes Escénicas y de la Música (CDAEM) under the difficult circumstances of the COVID-19 pandemic. We want to express our gratitude to Esther Andela and Alberto Godioli for their excellent comments and suggestions in preparing this study.

Note: This research was funded by the research project PGC2018093852-B-I00, awarded by the Ministry of Science and Innovation, the State Research Agency and the European Regional Development Fund of the European Union.

https://doi.org/10.1515/9783110707793-003

Research questions, key concepts, theoretical framework, and methodology

This study departs from three related research questions: a) how is the cultural narrative of the collective memory in the Spanish transition configured from a twofold perspective based on the theoretical notions of 'multidirectional memory' (Rothberg 2009, 2019) and 'agonistic memory' (Bull and Hansen 2016) in *Trampa para Pájaros*'s text; b) how the study of metaphoricity in *Trampa para Pájaros* contributes to understanding the conflictive complexity in the regimes of metaphor that have articulated the dominant conceptual architecture of the Spanish transition's memory; c) in which ways *Trampa para Pájaros* facilitates a rethinking of mediations of the Spanish transition in the public discourse and how such insight can be transposed to other similar cases. It is important to note that this study solely focuses on the conceptual architecture of the text and not on analyzing the various performances of this play, as such a task would go beyond our goal of shedding a new light on the underlying notional configuration of this play's text. Neither do we aim to conduct a systematic study of its reception, which would have involved a different methodological and theoretical approach; furthermore, such a study was substantially completed by César Oliva in 2004, as indicated in the relevant section of this chapter. However, essential information is provided for contextualization and analytical purposes in the section "Alonso de Santos and *Trampa para pájaros* in the theatrical context of the Spanish transition" of this chapter.

Trampa para Pájaros was performed for the first time in 1990. This play's critical reception and the public soon noted José Luis Alonso de Santos' work as a novel problematization of the Spanish political and cultural transitional memory. In *Trampa para Pájaros*, Mauro (a violent policeman and torturer during Franco's regime) takes refuge in the old attic of the family home, besieged by his former comrades because he tortured a detainee, now that the society and the laws have been changed. His brother Abel, a musician and bisexual, goes to this attic accompanied by Mari (Mauro's wife) to convince him to surrender to justice. Throughout the play, by appealing to the characters' personal and historical configurations and attributes, there is a struggle between the ideas and values that Mauro defends and those that constitute Abel's reply. These elements overlap with the score-settling of personal traumas that have accumulated since the family's past. This exemplary case operates, in the context of the Spanish transition to democracy, within two coordinates: as an artistic intervention in the configuration of the Spanish transitional memory and as a psychological exploration of the relationship between the facts that oriented the Spanish transition to democracy and, simultaneously, the memory of a family which epitomizes the contradictions and struggles of a multi-layered society that attempts to reconcile the repressive past with the construction of young and modern democratic social, political, and cultural structures. Such rich nuances and complexities are addressed in this chapter through the three above-mentioned research questions, which serve as an entry point to the study of the conceptual architecture of this play (see the section "Metaphoricity in Trampa para Pájaros").

To answer these questions, it is necessary – in the first place – to clarify the terminology we use and the exact delimitation of the qualitative and quantitative methodologies followed within this study of *Trampa para Pájaros*. In this sense, we shall take as a departure the definition proposed by Pablo Valdivia Martin (2019) regarding the concept of Cultural Narrative, which has been defined as the "moral and aesthetic coded symbolic matrix-in-the-making which orientates be-havior and signifies the imaginary relationship between an individual (and [vir-tual] community) and her (his/their) material conditions of existence in a given historical-spatial context." In short, a Cultural Narrative is a *dark matter* that es-tablishes the cognitive and performative grounds of social interactions, attach-ments, expectations, rationalities, and modes of becoming. Cultural narratives operate as cognitive and performative thresholds. They create meaning and ori-entate behavior in multidirectional ways. (2019, 16)

Regarding the metaphorical configuration of cultural narratives and how they operate in the field of public discourse, our study is sustained by the model, also established by Pablo Valdivia Martin, of the regime of metaphor and meta-phorical production (MELT model [Metaphor Field-Loop Theory], Figure 1), which describes how analogical modeling is processed and generated in a metaphorical field. In Valdivia's model, the regime constitutes "a key intermediate cognitive op-eration where metaphors are narratively enacted, made visible and experienced" (Valdivia Martin 2019, 293).

Following the above-proposed model, the metaphorical configuration (also known as *metaphoricity*) of a text, in any of its typologies and its mediations, is criti-cal in understanding the psycho-emotional activation – both individually and collec-tively – of a set of possibilities (*affordances*) of interpretation and of worldview orientations which operate under certain conditions (political, historical, social, amongst others).

In his above-mentioned work, Valdivia Martin offers the illustrative example of the primary metaphor 'EUROPE IS MOVEMENT,' which (as part of a bi-directionally powered and amplified system) constitutes, in turn, the condition of possibility for the conventionalized metaphor of 'THE EUROPEAN LOCOMOTIVE.' This convention-alized metaphor enables a metaphor scenario, 'the locomotive is progress,' that is hierarchically configured in a specific regime of metaphor comprised of four heg-

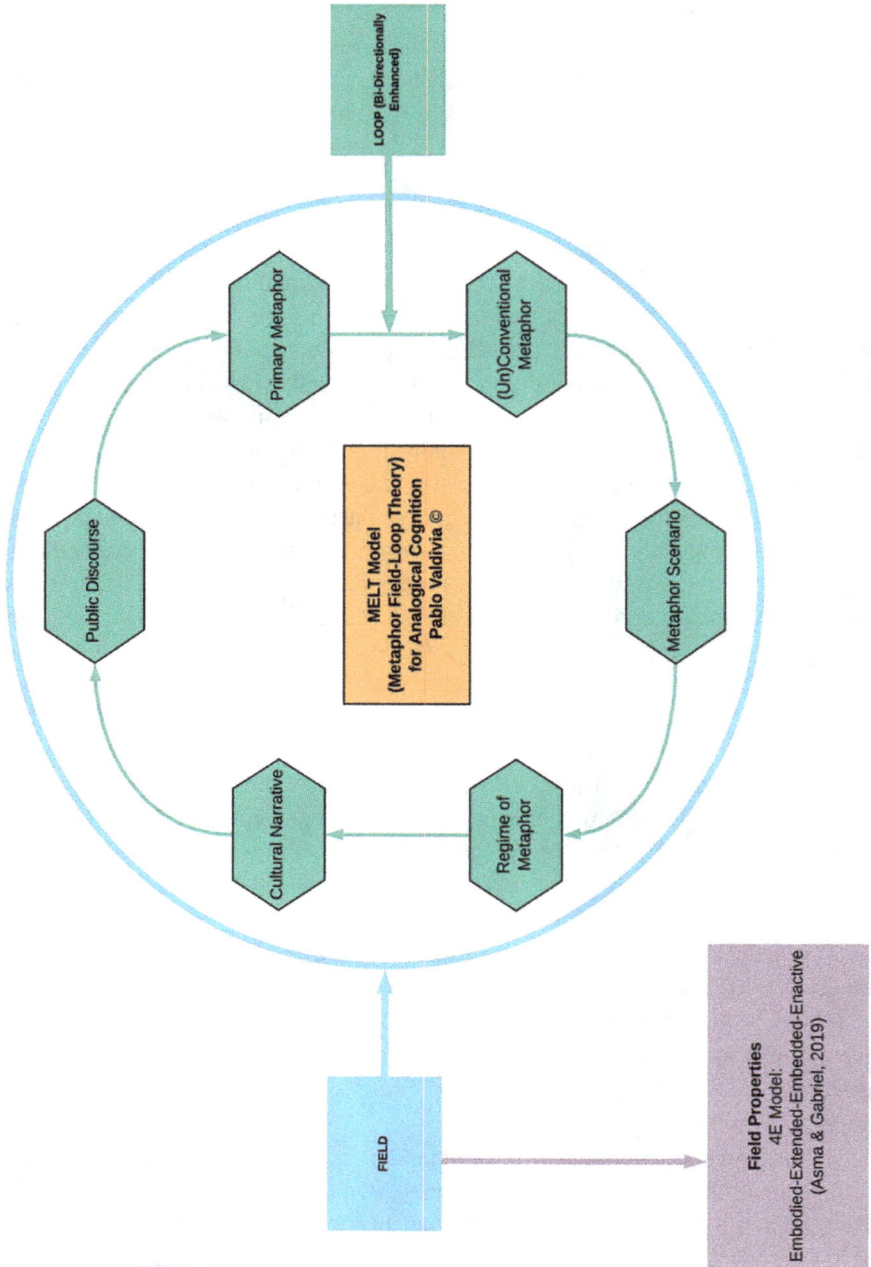

Figure 1: MELT Model © Pablo Valdivia Martin.

emonic metaphors: 'PROGRESS IS GOOD / PROGRESS IS ADVANCEMENT / PROGRESS IS FU-
TURE / PROGRESS IS SECURITY.' The regime of metaphor level is fundamental, according to the hypothesis of Valdivia Martin, because in this level, properties are
generated (shared or not shared with other metaphorical regimes) so that a cultural narrative – such as that of "building a Europe that protects" in the example
offered by Valdivia Martin – acquires the necessary cognitive validation to crys-
tallize in public discourse under multiple and simultaneous forms and means. In
his work, Valdivia Martin discussed the case study of the *White Paper for the Future of Europe and the Way Forward* (2017) published by the European Commission under the institutional target of building a public discussion for political,
economic, and cultural reflection to re-think the "possible Europe(s)" for 2025
(2019, 293–294).

Furthermore, as Asma and Gabriel (2019) explained, the *4e Model* (Embodied-
Extended-Embedded-Enactive), with which human cognition contributes to social
and behavioral engineering, demonstrates that all meaning processing, primarily
narrative, is evaluative, simulative, and experiential. Therefore, analogical cogni-
tion/modeling (the processing by which we put in relation elements that appear to
be unconnected or distant from each other) constitutes an essential mind mechanism for constructing fiction, crucial to all learning in any given communicative
situation and informational processing. Consequently, metaphor is a fundamental
analytical element in this research as one of the most complex and abstract mechanisms of analogical cognition/modeling.To avoid confusion, we want to make it
clear that when we speak of metaphor, we are referring to the critical notion of
Conceptual Metaphor that Cristina Soriano defines as "esquemas abstractos de pen-
samiento que se manifiestan de muchas formas, entre ellas el lenguaje" [abstract
thinking schemes that manifest themselves in many ways, including language]
(2012, 87). In her study, Soriano updates the Conceptual Metaphor Theory framework, whose first theoretical propositions are to be found in the classic works of
Lakoff and Johnson (1980a, 1980b, 1993) that have been expanded and enriched in
recent years, as Valdivia Martin explained in his article "Narrating Crises and Populism in Southern Europe: Regimes of Metaphor" (2019).

In terms of methodology, we integrated the NVivo software for the coding
(also called here *categorization*) of *Trampa para Pájaros*. In this research, we
have used the edition published by Ediciones Irreverentes in 2014. We took a
mixed or qualitative-quantitative methodology approach to avoid possible biases
of the observers and because it allowed us to trace both the metaphorical configuration of *Trampa para Pájaros* and the specific memory of transition that is mediated in it. This play presents a non-competitive memory that tries to overcome
binary oppositions between good and evil as much as it aspires to understand the
Spanish transition, not as a merely historical phenomenon but as an experiential

and complex fabric interconnected with the private and public spheres. For this reason, our qualitative-quantitative methodology draws upon Rothberg's insights, who, in his works of 2009 and 2019, convincingly asserted that International Law and any legal, political, and cultural perspective based on human rights principles should avoid traditional models of competitive memory that have customarily established hierarchies favoring some victims over others (2019, 4–5). In this vein, Rothberg suggests adopting a perspective based on 'multidirectional memory,' in which the actors of a conflict are not forced into stereotyping cultural narratives. Moreover, Rothberg argues that a multidirectional memory approach aims at revealing the radical complexity and contradictions present in any conflict (2019, 6).

Further developing this line of inquiry, Bull and Hansen have conceptualized the 'agonistic mode' of memory (in the positive sense of 'contestant' and 'conflictive'). This mode comprises seven fundamental elements:

> 1) Nature of conflict and violence depend on social circumstances, context and agency; 2) Learning from the memories/perspectives of victims, perpetrators and third-party witnesses; 3) Remembering historical context and socio-political struggles; 4) Reflexive, dialogic, multi-perspectivist; 5) Exposing the constructed nature of memory; 6) Open-endedly dialogic (in the Bakhtinian sense); 7) Passions oriented towards collective solidarity, preparing emotions for democratic institutions" (2016, 400).

In the case of *Trampa para Pájaros,* we find a productive overlapping of these seven elements which contribute to an 'agonistic' mode of remembering. According to Bull and Hansen, "in addition to exposing the socially constructed nature of collective memory and including the suffering of the 'Others'", this mode "would rely on a multiplicity of perspectives in order to bring to light the socio-political struggles of the past and reconstruct the historical context in ways which restore the importance of civic and political passions and address issues of individual and collective agency" (2016, 401). In this regard, *Trampa para Pájaros*, among its many achievements, activates a debate on the memory of the Spanish transition and situates it at the interface of the individual and the community. At the same time, it leaves aside the traditional mechanistic approach of micro – vs. macro-history principles based on dichotomic terms that featured the dominant cultural mediations of the 1990s around the so-called conflict between the 'two Spains [las dos Españas].'

In alignment with our line of inquiry, the analysis of *Trampa para Pájaros* offers, as an interpretative space, the nodes and categorizations indicated in the following scheme (Figure 2. Structural scheme *Trampa para Pájaros*), where the primary metaphor of COUNTRY / PLACE / SPAIN IS A FAMILY HOUSE illustrates the properties of the informational processes and the interpretative possibilities (*affordances*) of this theatrical piece. In this sense, all the action takes place in a physical space, in the attic of an old family home, which simultaneously operates as a conventionalized metaphor of the past and the social and personal history.

Within this space, two settings of the past are activated concerning the 1990s dominant cultural mediations: on the one hand, the *historical memory,* in which there is a clear operationalization of the conceptual network of the so-called 'two Spains' and, on the other hand, a *tessella* of family and personal memories in which the survival of the so-called 'two Spains' is seen in the mirror of the fratricidal confrontation starring the brothers Mauro and Abel. What is especially remarkable about *Trampa para Pájaros* is that the arguments woven within it are reflective, dialogical, and multi-perspectivist (in the sense of Rothberg and Bull and Hansen), as we will see later in our detailed analysis of the play. Such arguments place the reader-viewer before a complex psycho-emotional network that goes beyond any hint of sectarianism or political pamphlet.

Although Bull and Hansen do not refer to Rothberg's concept of multidirectional memory in their work, their critical approaches complement our perspective. As the scheme of our analysis of this play (Figure 2) shows, the conflicts that develop in the text are shaped under an 'agonistic' mode of memory: namely, in a constant multidirectional struggle. A similar conflictive configuration characterizes the relationship between the attributes of the 'past country' (Francoism, dictatorship, repression) and those of the 'desired country' (democracy, freedom, human rights); it is also to be found in the characters' actions. Regarding the latter, this play shows a gender bias since the only victim, Mari (Mauro's wife), occupies a secondary role: Mari is mistreated, confined to the household, and positioned on the boundaries of the main struggle between the brothers. However, Mari bears a triple burden comprising the heavy psychological weight of the family and personal memories, being the target and victim of the 'madness' attributes (Mauro: violent, sexist-abuser, policeman-torturer, gun) and being the recipient of the 'rationality' attributes (Abel: tolerant, bisexual, musician, piano). *Trampa para Pájaros* represents a complex symbolic constellation characterized by dialogic and multidirectional conflictive elements. Such complexity is a challenge for critical analysis, which we have empirically substantiated in the data collection and processing operationalized with NVivo 12.

In alignment with our qualitative-quantitative methodology and to achieve the highest levels of transparency in data collection, we transferred our structural codification scheme (Figure 2) to the following automatic coding mind map that was used for the automatic and manually refined categorization of *Trampa para Pájaros.*

Upon completing the automatic coding of these fundamental nodes (see Figure 3), we manually refined the categorization of the remaining personal

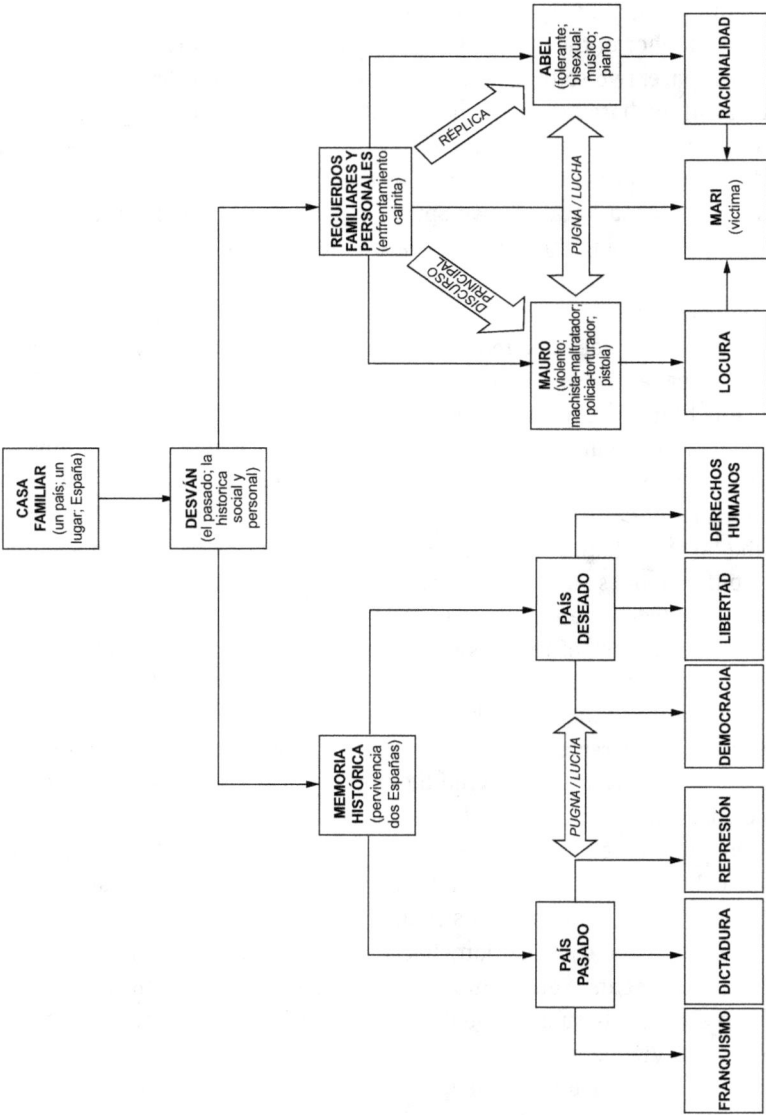

Figure 2: Structural scheme *Trampa para Pájaros* © Bonifacio Valdivia Milla and Pablo Valdivia Martin.[1]

---

1 Translation of the terms: Casa Familiar (un país; un lugar; España) = Family Home (a country; a place; Spain) / Desván (el pasado; la historia social y personal) = Attic (the past; the social and

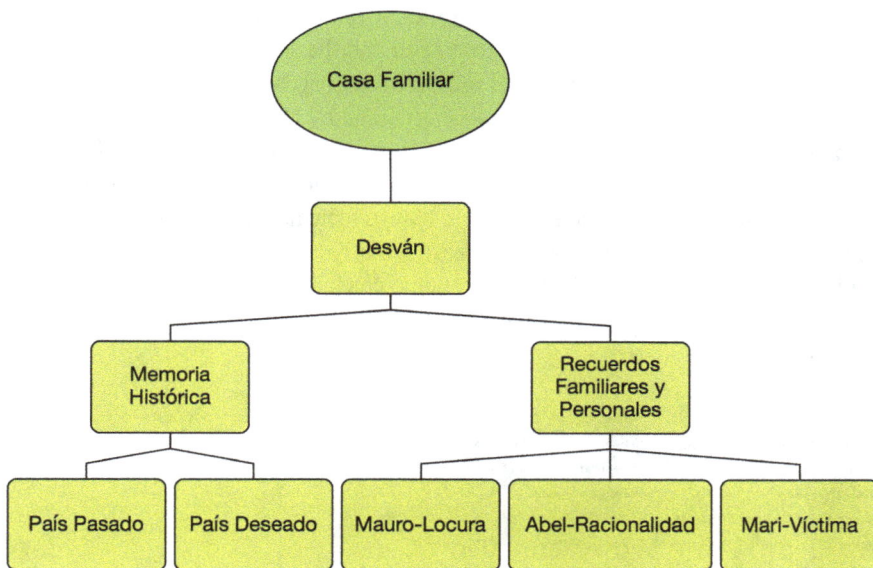

Figure 3: Automatic Coding Scheme *Trampa para Pájaros* © Bonifacio Valdivia Milla and Pablo Valdivia Martin.[2]

attributes and the imaginary representations of the two conceptual areas and characters in conflict. As a result, we encoded 30 nodes (a figure that includes the automatic and the manually refined encoding nodes), applying a targeting protocol to contextual and literal pervasive structural elements until we isolated 259 direct and specific references in the text.

One of the obtained results has had special significance in our qualitative interpretative analysis of this work. The data offered by NVivo reflect a greater prevalence of the categories related to the psycho-emotional states of the protagonists and to the attributes associated with the 'past country' than to those of the contex-

---

personal history) / Memoria Histórica (pervivencia dos Españas) = Historical Memory (survival of two Spains) / País Pasado = Past Country / Pugna-Lucha = Struggle / País Deseado = Desired Country / Franquismo = Francoism / Dictadura = Dictatorship / Repression = Repression / Democracia = Democracy / Libertad = Freedom / Derechos Humanos = Human Rights / Recuerdos Familiares y Personales (enfrentamiento cainita) = Family and Personal Memories (Cainite confrontation) / Discurso Principal = Main Discourse / Réplica = Reply / Mauro (violento, machista-maltratador, torturador-policía, pistola) = Mauro (violent, sexist-abuser, policeman-torturer, gun) / Abel (tolerante, bisexual, músico, piano) = Abel (tolerant, bisexual, musician, piano) / Locura = Madness / Mari (víctima) = Mari (victim) / Racionalidad = Rationality.

2 For a translation of terms see the previous footnote.

tual political setting that the general conflict of the work presents to us: namely, the survival of Francoism during the transition and the subsequent period.

As shown in Figure 4, the central prevalence of psychological elements against political-historical elements and the space occupied by Mauro and his attributes in *Trampa para Pájaros* both stand out with a more significant number of coding references than those (in)directly related to Abel. The latter confirms one of our initial working hypotheses (see Figure 2): Mauro articulates the main speech, and Abel gives his reply. Consequently, we argue, the rest of the characters, Mari and the infrequent appearance of Roque la Hiena, constitute the dialogic and multidirectional support regarding the structural narrative perspectivism, which contrib-

Trampa para pájaros

Nodes	Number of References by Codification
Nodos\\Casa Familiar\Desván\Memoria Familiar-Personal\Mauro-Locura	31
Nodos\\Casa Familiar\Desván\Memoria Familiar-Personal\Mauro-Locura\Violento	25
Nodos\\Casa Familiar\Desván\Memoria Familiar-Personal	23
Nodos\\Casa Familiar\Desván\Memoria Familiar-Personal\Mauro-Locura\Pistola	19
Nodos\\Casa Familiar\Desván\Memoria Histórica\País Pasado\Represión	15
Nodos\\Casa Familiar\Desván\Memoria Familiar-Personal\Mauro-Locura\Policia-Torturador	14
Nodos\\Casa Familiar\Desván\Memoria Histórica\País Pasado	12
Nodos\\Casa Familiar\Desván\Memoria Familiar-Personal\Mari-Víctima	10
Nodos\\Casa Familiar\Casa Familiar-Lugar	9
Nodos\\Casa Familiar\Desván\Memoria Familiar-Personal\Abel-Racionalidad	9
Nodos\\Casa Familiar\Desván\Memoria Familiar-Personal\Abel-Racionalidad\Música	8
Nodos\\Casa Familiar\Desván\Memoria Histórica\País Pasado\Franquismo	8
Nodos\\Casa Familiar\Casa Familiar-Refugio	7
Nodos\\Casa Familiar\Desván\Desván-Pasado	7
Nodos\\Casa Familiar\Desván\Desván-Personal	7
Nodos\\Casa Familiar\Desván\Memoria Familiar-Personal\Abel-Racionalidad\Piano	6
Nodos\\Casa Familiar\Desván\Memoria Familiar-Personal\Mauro-Locura\Machista-Maltratador	6
Nodos\\Casa Familiar\Casa Familiar-País	5
Nodos\\Casa Familiar\Desván\Desván-Historia Social	5
Nodos\\Casa Familiar\Desván\Memoria Histórica	5
Nodos\\Casa Familiar\Desván\Memoria Histórica\País Deseado	5
Nodos\\Casa Familiar\Desván\Memoria Histórica\País Deseado\Democracia	5
Nodos\\Casa Familiar\Desván\Memoria Histórica\País Deseado\Libertad	4
Nodos\\Casa Familiar\Desván\Memoria Histórica\País Pasado\Dictadura	4
Nodos\\Casa Familiar\Desván\Memoria Familiar-Personal\Abel-Racionalidad\Tolerante	3
Nodos\\Casa Familiar\Desván\Memoria Familiar-Personal\Abel-Racionalidad\Bisexual	2
Nodos\\Casa Familiar\Desván\Memoria Histórica\País Deseado\Derechos Humanos	2
Nodos\\Casa Familiar	1
Nodos\\Casa Familiar\Casa Familiar-España	1
Nodos\\Casa Familiar\Desván	1

Figure 4: *Trampa para Pájaros* Nodes and Coding. © Bonifacio Valdivia Milla and Pablo Valdivia Martin.[3]

3 See footnote 26 for a translation of the terms.

utes to consolidating a model of agonistic memory, as we will fully explain in the coming pages of this study:

To recapitulate, our study establishes how the cultural narrative of the Spanish transition (understood as a private space in conflict) is configured in *Trampa para Pájaros* from the primary conceptual metaphor COUNTRY / PLACE / SPAIN IS A FAMILY HOME (see Figure 1 MELT model). This primary metaphor simultaneously conveys conventionalized metaphors around the notions of violence, fratricidal struggle, cainism, and madness, which operates with a metaphorical scenario based on the narrative coordinates of the cage-trap of the policeman-torturer.

Thus, *Trampa para Pájaros* makes visible and validates a particular regime of metaphors HOME-MADNESS, HOME-TRAP, HOME-VIOLENCE, HOME-PAST, HOME-FRANCOISM, HOME-REPRESSION, HOME-REFUGE, interwoven within the shared space of the ATTIC-PAST that is populated by family memories also hybridized with the collective memory of a country in transition and on its way to a new society engendering democratic aspirations. In the following section of this study, we will situate the author, the play, and its staging in the context of the 'theater of the transition' and the Spanish democracy. Such contextualization complements the specific analysis of how *Trampa para Pájaros*' dialogical metaphoricity operates.

Alonso de Santos and *Trampa para pájaros* in the theatrical context of the Spanish transition

In a 1991 interview, José Luis Alonso de Santos stated: "Theater – this is a good definition – is human beings talking to other human beings about other human beings"[4] (Díez 1991, 20). From this perspective, it can be considered, as a working definition, that theater *per se* is the denial of silence in the public sphere. In fact, in the general social context of the late Francoism and the transition from Francoism to democracy, theater never assumed the "pacto de silencio" [pact of silence] tacitly consecrated by the consensus of the Amnesty Law (1977) in Spain (García Martínez 2016, 33–34).

In the transition and democracy,[5] there has always been a collective memory gap (more or less wide, of greater or lesser depth among the spectator/reader),

---

4 "El teatro – esta es una buena definición – son unos seres humanos hablando a otros seres humanos de otros seres humanos." Here and further on all translations from Spanish are ours.
5 For a general overview of the main features, authors and works of the theatrical panorama of this period, we suggest reading the informative chapters, 8, 9 and 10 of the volume *Teatro español del siglo XX* by César Oliva. Also, we find very useful the features and authors that Eduardo

regarding the meaning of the Civil War and Francoism. This gap was filled in theatrical texts earlier and with more profusion than in journalistic and, especially, political discourses. Regarding the latter, it is important to note that such a gap was partially filled as a late echo in the drafting and implementation of the Ley de Memoria Histórica [Law of Historical Memory] (2007). From our perspective, this was the case because of the particular nature of the dramatic text and the performative act as "theater (is) the ideal terrain for crisis and questioning, since it feeds on them, it takes up all the problems of this period, these conflicts, and builds up a basic dramatic material with them"[6] (Alonso de Santos 2000, 101).

These words of Alonso de Santos, delivered in the course of a talk he gave in 1999, referred to his conception of the craft of playwrighting in general at the end of the century. He pointed to the fundamental capacity of theater to productively engage with conflicts that mark an era. In the Spanish case, he connected his views to the theatrical practices that deal with the disputes related to the Civil War, Franco's regime, and its prolific and dramatic cultural legacy during the decades after Franco's death. In this regard, Anabel García Martínez has traced a total of more than 70 works (of theater) about the war and dictatorial past under what she calls a "pacto de memoria" [pact of memory] after Franco's death (García Martínez 2006, 2). Furthermore, thanks to Alison Guzmán's research, we have hard evidence on the number of plays that engage with or refer to the Civil War or Francoism. In total, figures reach 149 plays, 63 of them written between 1939 and 1969, and 86 plays between 1970 and 2009 (Guzmán 2012, 22–24). These figures sufficiently corroborate theater's contribution to the construction and configuration of Spain's collective and historical memory discourses.

In this regard, under the theatrical context of the transition and democracy in Spain, José Luis Alonso de Santos was one of its pivotal figures, not only because of the rich qualities of his writing but also because he was "a man of the theater" [un hombre de teatro]: namely, the author, adapter, actor, director, producer, teacher, researcher (Romera Castillo 2002, 2–3) who combined all these facets understanding that "theater is its theory and its practice, the instrument to know the world and a philosophy to engage with it"[7] (Monleón 1982, 39).

Pérez Rasilla compiles in pages 15–26 of his *Introducción* to the edition of *¡Ay, Carmela!* and *El lector por horas* by José Sanchis Sinisterra and in the *Presentación* and *Notas sobre la dramaturgia emergente en España* in the magazine *Don Galán*, issue 2, 2012.

6 ". . . el teatro [es] terreno ideal para la crisis y el cuestionamiento, ya que se alimenta de ellos, recoge toda esa problemática de esta época, de estos conflictos, construyendo con ellos un material dramático básico."

7 ". . . el teatro es su teoría, y su práctica, el instrumento para conocer el mundo y, también, la filosofía para insertarse en él."

Alonso de Santos's work spans the early 1960s to the present. The positive reception of his plays among professional companies and the audience is undeniable. Alonso de Santos acknowledged during the above-mentioned 1999 conference that in the six previous years, "in a list of about a hundred titles, we would find that the authors who have released more works in this period are: Francisco Nieva, Juan José Alonso Millán, Santiago Moncada, Jaime Salón, Albert Boadella, José Sanchís Sinisterra and the author who writes these lines"[8] (Alonso de Santos 2000, 102–103). We must emphasize this evidence to fully justify how Alonso de Santos texts' have managed to establish a pervasive power in shaping the cultural and political imaginaries of the spectators and the general public. In his own words

> [i]t is essential to try to connect with the spectators of our time, guessing this intimate task commissioned, communicating with them through today's language about modern day's problems; trying to bring vitality, energy, unity, and style to our work, to have a sincere and genuine dialogue with the audience within that credible conviction that is the theater, getting our hands in the mud of our time for creating characters, situations, and conflicts with it.[9] (Alonso de Santos 2000, 100)

Moreover, Alonso de Santos' previously discussed definition of what it means to write drama and how it should get into the mud of its time is directly connected to *Trampa para Pájaros*' original conception. As a follow-up to some general rehearsals carried out in Torrelodones on December 14 and 15, 1990, Alonso de Santos publicly meditated on some structural guidelines, which we believe serve as a good synopsis of this play:

> *Trampa para Pájaros* is a drama between two brothers, reflecting many of the antagonisms that can occur in a family situation. On the one hand, there is the eternal struggle between the two Spains – the Spain of the past and the Spain of the future. On the other hand, there is the struggle between Cain and Abel. Again, there is the struggle of arms and the arts represented by a gun and a piano. The firearm is represented by a policeman and the piano as a pianist. In order words, two completely different conceptions of life. It is a work that takes place in an attic, which is a bit like the memory of the past of a Spain that existed before the one we are living in and the conflictive situations of which allow me to talk about the present. As in all my works, the basic objective of this play is to attempt to get as close as possi-

---

8 ". . . en una lista de cerca de cien títulos encontraríamos que los autores que hemos estrenado mayor número de obras en este periodo somos: Francisco Nueva, Juan José Alonso Millán, Santiago Moncada, Jaime Salón, Albert Boadella, José Sanchís Sinisterra y el autor que escribe estas líneas."
9 "Es importante intentar conectar con el espectador de nuestra época, adivinando ese encargo íntimo, hablándole con lenguaje de hoy, de problemas de hoy, tratando de aportar vitalidad, energía, unidad y estilo a nuestro trabajo, para poder tener así un diálogo sincero y real con el público, dentro de esa convención creíble que es el teatro, metiendo las manos en el barro de nuestro tiempo para crear con él personajes, situaciones y conflictos."

ble to what has a resonance at this moment. This play allows me to touch on many topical issues; such as the police force under Franco and how it has adapted or has not adapted to the current democratic situation, the limitations of this democracy and this political system, the negative memories of the past; and the debate on police corruption, political effectiveness, on the marginalized in a given context.[10] (Castilla 1990, 20–21)

Trampa para Pájaros' text has been edited and performed on several occasions by several companies and theater groups both in Spain and abroad.[11] From the many performances produced so far, we would like to highlight two. The first one was the premiere by the company Pentación Producciones, directed by Gerardo Malla, on December 20, 1990, in Toledo's Teatro de Rojas. The second was staged by Metamorfosis Teatro on January 30, 2009, in the Teatro Alameda of Málaga as part of the program of the 16th Festival of Theater (the same production was performed later that year on Teatro Fernán Gómez of Madrid from May 7 to 17), directed by José Luis Alonso de Santos. This is particularly relevant as it manifests how this play evolved in connection to the author's close participation in the production. During the time-lapse between the two productions, Alonso de Santos made some public declarations where he alerted the audience to the final revisions of *Trampa para Pájaros*' text for the 2009 performance.

In this regard, it should also be pointed out that, as the author himself mentioned on various occasions, his works explicitly or implicitly include critical references to the concrete reality of Spain but, at the same time, they cannot just be included within the straitjacket of what is known as historical or political the-

---

10 "*Trampa para Pájaros* es un drama entre dos hermanos, en el que se reflejan muchos de los antagonismos que pueden vivir en una situación familiar: por un lado existe el eterno enfrentamiento entre las dos Españas – la España del pasado y la España del futuro –; por otro lado, está el enfrentamiento entre Caín y Abel; por otro, el enfrentamiento de las armas y las artes –una pistola y un piano, uno es un policía y el otro pianista –: es decir, dos concepciones de la vida completamente diferentes. [. . .] Es una obra que sucede en un desván – que es un poco el recuerdo del pasado de toda una España anterior a la que estamos viviendo – y en la que se crean unas situaciones dramáticas que me permiten hablar de la actualidad. El objetivo básico de esta obra, como en todas mis obras, es tratar de acercarme lo más posible a lo que tiene resonancias en este momento. Esta obra me permite tocar muchos temas candentes, como la Policía del franquismo y cómo se ha adaptado, o no, a la situación democrática actual, las limitaciones de esta democracia y de este sistema político, los recuerdos negativos del pasado y el debate sobre la corrupción policial, la eficacia política, sobre los marginados en un sistema determinado."
11 We refer to the next *Trampa para Pájaros*' editions: a) with a foreword by J. L. Alonso de Santos, Madrid, Marsó / Velasco, 1991; b) with a study by Eduardo Galán, in *Teatro realista de hoy*, Madrid, Edelvives, 1993; c) with a study by Eduardo Galán, Madrid, Sociedad General de Autores de España (SGAE), 1993; d) Madrid, Caos editorial, 2003; e) with a prologue by Miguel Ángel de Rus and note by the author, Madrid, Ediciones Irreverentes, 2014, which is the one we follow in this study.

ater *sensu stricto*. Alonso de Santos aims to transcend the local anecdote and reach any audiences with his drama writings. He makes a very clear point when, concerning *Trampa para Pájaros*, we read:

> Francoism as a theme does not interest me. It is a context for dealing with other issues. In *Trampa* . . . I raise the great theme around which tragedy and our theater of the Golden Age revolve, that of the battle that we humans maintain between sanity and madness. That of the responsibility of our acts. [. . .] We grow by entering and leaving our origins.[12] (Gente del Puerto 2009)

And more specifically, referring to Mauro, the main character:

> "He is a human being who discovers that he does not belong and believes that the best thing is to disappear," he explains. He defines a situation that does not refer to a country or period, such as post-Francoism, but is repeated all over the world. [. . .] It would be too easy, he declares, to criticize Franco, that is why he addresses 'the current francos.'[13] (Sotorrío 2009)

Indeed, after the premiere in December 1990, we can trace two constants in the ideas declared by the author in the press of the different places in which *Trampa para Pájaros* was performed: 1) Alonso de Santos attempts to establish the essential character of the dramatic conflict in "the struggle between two forces, one that lives anchored in the past and the other that wants to advance" ["la lucha entre dos fuerzas, una que vive anclada en el pasado y otra que quiere avanzar"], incarnated by the characters of the two brothers, in the Spanish society of the early 1990s. He describes this society as "the modified Francoist society" [la sociedad franquista modificada] in which "there beats, in the background, a very conservative feeling" [late, en el fondo, un sentir muy conservador]. However, if he can choose "between this society and the previous one, I have no doubt. If this society is bad, the other was terrible" [entre esta sociedad y la anterior, no tengo ninguna duda. Si esta sociedad es mala, la otra era terrible] (De Alzaga 1992). 2) Simultaneously, along with this reflection on social and historical issues, Alonso de Santos emphasized (throughout 1991 and 1992) the aim of his theater to focus on marginalized characters. He had already done so in works of great success, such as *La estanquera de Vallecas* (1982) and *Bajarse al moro* (1985). Alonso de

---

12 "A mí, el franquismo como tema no me interesa: es un contexto para tratar de otros asuntos. En Trampa . . . planteo el gran tema sobre el que gira la tragedia y nuestro teatro del Siglo de Oro, el de la batalla que mantenemos los humanos entre la cordura y la insensatez. El de la responsabilidad de nuestros actos. [. . .] Crecemos entrando y saliendo de nuestros orígenes".
13 "'Es un ser humano que descubre que ya no tiene hueco y cree que lo mejor es desaparecer', explica. Una situación, defiende, que no hace referencia a un país o época – como el postfranquismo – sino que se repite en todo el mundo. [. . .] Sería demasiado fácil, declara, criticar a Franco, por eso se dirige 'a los francos actuales.'".

Santos notes this in *La Nota del Autor* [The Author's Note] edition of the text (2014) which we are following in this study:

> I enter now with this work in the land of extraordinary outcasts: people who have been stuck in a dominant ideology of other times and rejected today by most citizens. Those who for so long have marginalized others are now marginalized by a new social order, in which they live with the anguish of the old dinosaurs, without possibilities of adapting to the environment, and therefore condemned to disappear.[14] (Alonso de Santos 2014, 13)

In short, what marked the presence of *Trampa para Pájaros* on the Spanish stage of the early 1990s is what Alonso de Santos recognizes, more or less explicitly on different occasions, and summarizes in this statement: *"Trampa para Pájaros* is my most political work. I describe a character that I hate, but I end up understanding him."[15] (Díez 1991, 20)

Trampa para Pájaros was broadly received by the press and toured all over Spain under the label of a 'political drama' until it arrived in Madrid on February 6, 1992. However, the drama critic Eduardo Haro Tecglen presented a dissenting voice as he did not perceive *Trampa para Pájaros'* political character nor the legacy of the Francoist's memory. In this regard, he noted on the pages of *El País*:

> The allusions to the past and to its time, the possibilities of the political legacy, are usually made by the author outside the stage; in hand programs or public statements. I do not see them in the play. The situation is rather Romanian, or Czech, or German. Anyhow, I do not see any political case, no matter how much effort I make. Neither the author's insistence that it is a timely topic nor that it [this topic] has been inherited from the previous power regime. [. . .] In any case, without seeing such a thing, without worrying about it, I am instead rather interested in this play about the human episode, the lockdown situation and the character's mixture of despair and hopelessness.[16] (Haro Tecglen)

---

14 "Entro ahora con esta obra en el terreno de unos marginales especiales: las personas que se han quedado estancadas en una ideología dominante de otros tiempos y rechazada hoy por la mayoría de los ciudadanos. Los que durante tanto tiempo han marginado a otros son ahora marginados por un nuevo orden social, que ellos viven con la angustia de los viejos dinosaurios, sin posibilidades de adaptación al medio, y condenados, por tanto, a desaparecer."

15 "*Trampa para pájaros* es mi obra más política. Describo a un personaje que odio, pero acabo entendiéndole."

16 "Las alusiones al tiempo pasado y a éste, las posibilidades de la herencia política, las suele hacer el autor fuera de escena; en programas o declaraciones. Yo no las veo. La situación es más bien rumana, o checa, o alemana. De todas formas, no veo caso político alguno, por mucho esfuerzo que haga – soy romo –; no la insistencia en que es una cuestión de ahora, ni de lo que ha heredado el régimen anterior. [. . .] En todo caso, sin ver tal cosa, sin preocuparme de ella, sino del episodio humano, de la situación de encierro y de la mezcla de desesperación y desesperanza del personaje, me interesa mucho más la obra."

In 2009, almost two decades later, since the first performance in Málaga directed by Alonso de Santos himself, the author highlights that his main focus of interest in *Trampa para Pájaros* was, on the one hand, the human archetypes represented by the characters connected to the historical and the social conflicts surrounding them. On the other hand, he claimed to search for the universal performative possibilities rather than describe the specific social situation of a country like Spain (Metamorphosis 2009, 8; Artezblai 2009). Opposed to what he declared in 1991, Alonso de Santos manifested in 2009 that *Trampa para Pájaros* was "perhaps my most psychological work" and it "speaks of human beings trying to get out of a dead-end"[17] (Bravo 2009).

Thus, we can conclude that, in the context of the transition to democracy and for both the audience and the readers of the text, Alonso de Santos' theatrical proposal in *Trampa para Pájaros* was received under the general framework of three key-terms: politics, psychology, and drama. Furthermore, it was received as the dramatic development of two unresolved conflicts: "*Trampa para Pájaros* is a political and a psychological drama. Its greatness lies in the strength with which it confronts us with the reality of a whole community through the lives of (some)"[18] (Metamorphosis 2009, 6).

Metaphoricity in *Trampa para Pájaros*

As we have just discussed, *Trampa para Pájaros* (see Figure 2) presents two main conflicts. The first one concerns two social positions, two conflicting and antagonistic general expectations about life – engaging with the Spanish historical memory – and perfectly transposable to any other historical and geographical area undergoing a process of transition departing from a repressive and dictatorial regime. The second conflict is related to two individuals, two brothers with physically, psychologically, and even sexually opposing characteristics. Such personal memories are in conflict too, and they intersect with life events connected to the family memory and the attic as Mauro says, "everything comes together, brother, everything comes together. Like dominoes. You push one and all fall over."[19] (Alonso de Santos 2014, 40)

---

17 "tal vez mi obra más psicológica,' que 'habla de seres humanos tratando de salir de un callejón sin salida."

18 "Trampa para pájaros es un drama político y un drama psicológico. Su grandeza reside en la contundencia con la que nos enfrenta a la realidad de un pueblo a través de la vida de unos individuos."

19 "Todo se junta, hermano, todo se junta. Como las fichas del dominó. Empujas una y caen todas."

These two conflicts, personal and political, are intimately interwoven in the play's dramaturgy (i.e., they are not developing in parallel) thanks to how the author builds into the text and the stage a set of conventionalized metaphors. A primary conceptual metaphor which identifies A COUNTRY with A FAMILY HOUSE is the gravitational point of this play. Consequently, the family – the ties with the parents and the relations among the siblings – is recognized metaphorically as the society formed inside such a social unit: namely, THE SOCIETY OF A COUNTRY IS A FAMILY. Thus, the personal references and the characters' particular experiences acquire a special significance both as characters and as transposable references and frames of thinking for the general public.

Therefore, in the Spanish context, the reading/performance of *Trampa para Pájaros* directly engages with the dramatic conflict and metaphoric framing between Mauro and Abel going on at the stage: SPAIN IS A FAMILY HOME.[20] Such metaphorical frame inscribes itself into the general conceptualization of the so-called 'two Spains' that are pervasively present in the general conceptualization of the country's history.

In the context of the Francoist past, Mauro's attitude as a violent policeman and torturer is discursively justified by the need to obey the dictatorship's law and the death penalty. In the social sphere of the transition to democracy, the SPAIN OF THE PAST has a present and potential future projection due to the persistence of its old problems: terrorism, corruption, and the active survival of most of its actors and political leaders. (Alonso de Santos 2014, 19–22, 26–27)

In open conflict and opposition to the Spain epitomized by Mauro, the SPAIN DESIRED represented by Abel is the Spain of Democracy. In this regard, Abel outlines, in his responses to his brother's speech, a country that fights for freedom and consolidates fundamental human rights in the social sphere; meanwhile, he promotes individual responsibility and tolerance in the private realm. The SPAIN OF THE PAST coexists, and clashes with the SPAIN DESIRED in this COUNTRY IS A FAMILY HOME. The above-mentioned are the central metaphorical tensions underlying the conceptual framing of the dialogic social conflict in *Trampa para Pájaros*.

We also find a whole set of inferences of meaning (affordances). In the play, there is no direct literal reference to the Spanish Civil War, but the notion of the

---

20 This metaphoric framing can relate to any country. As the author himself notes "this play has been received in different ways depending on which country it was performed: they were Videla's policemen in Argentina, communist police forces in Eastern Europe or Francoist at the first performances of this play around 1990." [la obra ha sido vista de forma muy diferente según el país donde se representaba: eran policías de Videla en Argentina, de servicios policiales comunistas en los países del Este de Europa o franquista en la primeras representaciones de la obra, allá por 1990.] (Artezblai 2009).

family home that is Spain, in which two possible countries (the 'two Spains') fight, is perfectly coherent with the cultural imaginary of a 'fratricidal struggle.' The rivalry and struggle between brothers and sisters in the family refer to the image of cainism, that is, to the metaphor of a personal confrontation that is fundamentally triggered by envy and jealousy. This is how Alonso de Santos develops the other conflict that runs through this work: two human beings and a family's fate are intrinsically linked to the social and historical context. The metaphor of cainism is explicitly used by the author in *Trampa para Pájaros* and not only thanks to the affordances produced by Abel's name, which converts Mauro into an image of Cain, but also from a clear statement in the first paragraphs of the play: "MAURO.– (Hidden) You are the good one here, brother, not me. I am the evil one, as it was then."[21] (Alonso de Santos 2014, 16) The score-settling is maintained throughout the work: "ABEL.– You and I have never agreed on anything. We are not going to agree now. Since you were a child, you always liked to solve everything with punches . . ."[22] (Alonso de Santos 2014, 22)

The two brothers' physical and moral description also builds their images in this particular cainism under a remarkably metaphorical character. Mauro is the older brother, the strong and violent one since childhood. He is a brutal, obtuse, bald, homophobic, and pathological macho policeman who presents "the image of a defeated and crazy man" [la imagen de un hombre derrotado y enloquecido] (Alonso de Santos 2014, 17) who carries a gun. Abel, the youngest brother, "goes elegantly dressed and is in every way his opposite image" [va elegantemente vestido y es en todo su imagen contraria] (Alonso de Santos 2014, 17). As a child, Abel suffered his brother's violence and was protected by his mother. Abel is a bisexual musician who plays the piano for a living. The portrait of the first one is a metaphor for the irrationality of the large force treasured since Franco's time; the other represents a metaphor for the hope of the future freely conquered.

Bearing this in mind, it is essential to note that the two conflicting positions do not fall into an oversimplifying Manichaeism (Medina Vicario 1992, 99) in a staging space that shares similar metaphorical values: the ATTIC OF THE HOUSE IS THE ATTIC OF MEMORY (social and historical, particular and personal). Mauro has taken refuge in this space, which means putting into play a division of the previous metaphor into two subsidiary metaphors: THE PHYSICAL ATTIC IS A REFUGE FROM ASSAULT; and MEMORY IS A REFUGE OF THE FAMILY GHOSTS, FAMILY TRAUMAS, & A REFUGE FROM THE HISTORY OF THE COUNTRY. Abel, who was invited by the police force to act

---

21 "MAURO.– (Escondido) Tú eres el bueno aquí, hermano, no yo. Yo soy el malo, como entonces."
22 "ABEL.– Tú y yo nunca hemos estado de acuerdo en nada. No vamos a estarlo ahora. Desde pequeño siempre te gustó resolverlo todo a golpes . . .".

as a mediator, goes into this converging space (thus allowing 'the old wounds to be reopened,' which is another metaphor inferred by that of the conceptual 'fratricidal struggle') of the memories that are associated on stage with a certain set of metaphorical cues. These cues also carry affordances with their own symbolic value: the portraits of the parents, the old sewing machine, the mannequins, the cardboard horse, and the old piano. Alonso de Santos uses such cues to bring to the stage each of the particular themes that populate Mauro's discourse and can be summarized under the conceptual nodes of envy, jealousy, homophobia, and almost pathological chauvinism.

The conventional metaphor of 'old wounds' has been present since before the beginning of the Spanish transition until today within the cultural and political narratives associated with the 'reconciliation' as the only possibility of healing the past in contrast to the public requirements of 'reparation and justice.' In the attic of the country's historical memory, Alonso de Santos outlines Abel's final desire for the possibility of social reconciliation. The overcoming of Francoism interests him not so much from a dramatic point of view. As we argued before, the main engine of this play's dramatic conflicts is found in the attic of personal and family memories: Mauro's struggle against Abel constitutes it. In this struggle, Abel powerfully proclaims the need for 'reconciliation,' which will end conflicts in general and their struggles in particular (Alonso de Santos 2014, 43). Abel advocates living in peace and tries to find "another way to fix this, but we do not see it" [otra forma de arreglar esto, lo que pasa es que no la vemos] (Alonso de Santos 2014, 51).

However, in *Trampa para Pájaros*, the old rivalry between brothers, the metaphor of the 'fratricidal struggle' is maintained until the end of the play when another socially primary metaphor comes into play, namely the vanishing recognized as death: TO DIE IS TO DISAPPEAR and vice versa. From Mauro's perspective, before the family ghosts of his parents and Mari's presence as a testimony of the primary victim of his continued mistreatment, he believes that the only possible solution is his physical disappearance, together with all the baggage of what he represents. According to Mauro's inner logic, his death does not translate into the victorious image of Abel and his world: "ABEL (. . .) goes to the door and comes out, wrecked" [ABEL [. . .] va hacia la Puerta y sale, hundido], the author points out in the final note (Alonso de Santos, 2014, 57). Alonso de Santos has consistently and publicly expressed the need for Mauro's disappearance and the metaphorical meaning of his figure (namely, the disappearance of the past executioners who are now 'out of joint' and lost in democratic times) while, at the same time, emphasizing the dramatic interest that these characters hold for him. According to Alonso de Santos:

> There are too many of them, and they know it. Those who were executioners for so long, resist the role of the victim. Therefore, they are protagonists of the constant conflict that the

forces of progress and return originate in their path. That is why they deserve to live their scenic journey as misfits who fabricated their misfortune.[23] (2014, 13)

Finally, we should note that, in the metaphorical system (conceptual architecture) that structures the text of *Trampas para Pájaros*, there is a final element of ambivalence: madness. References to madness are used metaphorically with the broad meaning of irrationality and literally to designate the pathological state in which Mauro finds himself. In the author's explanatory note mentioned above, Alonso de Santos refers to Mauro as one of the "maladjusted beings who fabricated their misfortune" [seres inadaptados que fabricaron su propia desgracia] and as "a special outcast" [un marginado especial] (Alonso de Santos 2014, 13). Nevertheless, Mauro is profiled from the beginning of the work as a 'misfit.' Still, his figure is also much more complex and irrational than the social convention he represents. From the initial allusion to Mauro's state of madness in the first speech of the characters, or in the author's note ("a defeated and insane man" [un hombre derrotado y enloquecido]) (Alonso de Santos 2014, 16–17) until the final unraveling, we find throughout the text more than a dozen of references to madness. Not all of these references are used with metaphorical meaning. However, when the author uses them with this value, he is alluding to both a social and a personal evil (MADNESS IS VIOLENCE, MADNESS IS IRRATIONALITY) that comes from the regime of metaphor: THE HISTORY OF THE FAMILY is THE HISTORY OF A COUNTRY. At one point in the play, Mauro comments, referring to his state of "hallucination": "[. . .] You see everything that has been stored [both material and abstract memories]. And not only yours. You also see father's and grandfather's and everyone else's who was here before you."[24] (Alonso de Santos 2014, 50)

Indeed, the complex metaphorical system with which *Trampa para Pájaros* is constructed eludes a Manichean approach in the narrative as it structurally allows the author to load the characters' statements, especially those of Mauro, with arguments that constitute the necessary explanation and justification of his attitude and behavior in life: "someone has to do the dirty work" [alguien tiene que hacer las tareas sucias] (Alonso de Santos 2014, 19); "I followed orders! Do you understand? In this bloody life there are people who command and people

---

23 "Sobran y lo saben. Y los que fueron verdugos tanto tiempo se resisten al papel de las víctimas. Son protagonistas, por tanto, del conflicto constante que las fuerzas en pugna del progreso y el retorno originan en su camino. Por eso merecen vivir su peripecia escénica como seres inadaptados que fabricaron su propia desgracia."
24 "Ves todo lo guardado. Y no solo lo tuyo. También lo de papa, y lo del abuelo, y lo de todos los que estuvieron aquí antes."

who obey"[25] (19–20); "the death penalty is what this country needs to put an end to everyone, as they do to those whom they get"[26] (20); "and those who command me, you command them . . . Guys like you who never get involved in anything, who are very civilized and understanding, but who want their streets to be full of peace so that they can enjoy life at the expense of others"[27] (22); "Yes! Whatever you want, but it was unlike now that we are all equal and free . . . Some live like kings and others . . . Moreover, lies and lies covering everything up"[28] (26); "They are all the same . . . Aren't they stealing everything they can? . . . They steal, brother, they steal"[29] (26). These examples, among some other less explicit, are the main features of a discourse and they are constructed as paradigmatic of what the character represents. They are a whole set of expressions full of tropes and, amongst them, outstanding pervasive metaphors of everyday use in Spanish.

As an unavoidable counterpoint, Abel's replies serve to frame the terms of the debate on Spain's social situation at the time of the transition in struggle and as an adversary force to the Francoist era. Also, they contribute to finally settle the old Cainite conflict that his brother is maintaining. Abel appeals to the individual responsibility of one's actions: "So if I did what I wanted to do, you could have done the same. Enough of justifying yourself, neither for father, nor for the era in which you had to live, nor for anything else! I have lived it too, as have many others, and we did not just sit there, complaining about everything, surrounded by ghosts and with a gun in your hands which you do not know well who to use against!"[30] (Alonso de Santos 2014, 44) Later on in the play, Abel advocates getting out of the attic of the historical, family, and personal memory: "To get out to live! We have to live, like the people live and try to make sense of it, of

---

25 "¡Cumplía órdenes! ¿Comprendes? En esta puñetera vida hay gente que manda y gente que obedece."

26 " la pena de muerte es lo que hacía falta en este país para acabar con todos, como hacen ellos con los que cogen".

27 "y a los que a mí me mandan se lo mandáis vosotros. [. . .] los tipos como tú que nunca se meten en nada, que son muy civilizados y comprensivos, pero que quieren sus calles llenas de paz para poder disfrutar a gusto de la vida que se pegan a costa de los demás".

28 "¡Sí! lo que tú quieras, pero por lo menos no se decía como ahora que todos somos iguales y libres . . . Unos viviendo como reyes y otros . . . [. . .] Y mentiras y mentiras tapándolo todo."

29 "Son todos iguales . . . ¿No están robando todo lo que pueden? . . . Roba, hermano, roban."

30 "Así que si yo hice lo que quería hacer, lo mismo podías haber hecho tú. ¡Ya está bien de justificarte, ni por papá, ni por la época que te tocó vivir, ni por nada! También yo la he vivido, y muchos otros, y no nos hemos quedado ahí sentados, quejándonos de todo, rodeados de fantasmas y con una pistola en las manos que no sabes bien contra quién usar."

every morning, to wake up and walk on the street among everyone else"[31] (Alonso de Santos 2014, 51). The public is left wondering which are the possible options for the resolution of this conflict: reconciliation and/or oblivion? We clarify this point in the coming lines of our study.

Conclusions

At the beginning of this study, we posed three fundamental research questions: a) how is the cultural narrative of the collective memory in the Spanish transition configured from a twofold perspective based on the theoretical notion of 'multidirectional memory' (Rothberg 2009, 2019) and 'agonistic memory' (Bull and Hansen 2016) in the text of *Trampa para Pájaros*; b) how the study of metaphoricity in *Trampa para Pájaros* contributes to understanding the conflictive complexity in the regimes of metaphor that have articulated the dominant conceptual architecture of the Spanish Transition's memory; c) in which ways *Trampa para Pájaros* facilitates a re-thinking of mediations of the Spanish transition in the public discourse and how such insight can be transposed to other similar cases.

Concerning question a), we believe we have sufficiently demonstrated that *Trampa para Pájaros* constructs a cultural narrative of the Spanish transition's memory that goes beyond the logic of 'us versus them.' Instead, this play delves into the psycho-emotional setting of the propositional concepts that the characters dialogically present. Therefore, this play is situated, *avant la lettre*, in the field defined by the theoretical principles of multidirectional memory and agonistic memory. There is no moral victory or resolution of a competitive process in this play, but rather the polyhedral revelation of a complex process of overlapping conflicts that ends in tragedy for all its participants at different levels: Mauro allegedly dies, Abel suffers the loss of his brother as he fails to convince him to turn himself in to the police and Mari becomes a victim without prospects of reparative justice. Thus, *Trampa para Pájaros*' sense-making/cognitive/analogical modeling network is built upon the conceptual metaphor of the COUNTRY IS A FAMILY HOME, and the transition features as a cultural narrative that negotiates (without finding a clear and all-encompassing response) the conflicting poles of reconciliation and oblivion, which are alien to those of justice and reparation.

As for question b), we can affirm that the above-mentioned singularity of *Trampa para Pájaros* as a mediation of transitional memory, without competitive

---

31 "¡Salir para vivir! ¡Tenemos que vivir, como vive la gente que trata de encontrarle un sentido, cada mañana, a levantarse y a caminar por la calle entre los demás!".

resolution but rather a multidirectional and agonistic representation, is based on a particular construction of its metaphoricity and on how the dominant regime of metaphor HOME-MADNESS, HOME-TRAP, HOME-VIOLENCE, HOME-PAST, HOME-FRANCOISM, HOME-REPRESSION, HOME-REFUGE, activates, makes visible, validates, and orientates the cultural narrative of negotiation between terms of reconciliation and oblivion. One of the most interesting findings offered by this qualitative-quantitative research is to better understand how a work that presents personal psychoemotional conflicts reaches a high degree of universality, to the point of not only allowing its constituent principles to be transposable upon the particular context of Spanish transition memory but also to other negotiation processes in post-repressive transitional contexts.

Finally, concerning question c), in this vein, we consider that our methodology and the data collected can not only enrich a more significant and more systematic inquiry with regards to the memory of the Spanish transition but also the study of metaphoricity in a vast corpus of works that can illuminate existing conceptual complexities under a similar selection of criteria. The methodology deployed in this study of *Trampa para Pájaros'* conceptual architecture may be applied to other transitional memories, in which the performing arts significantly function as an object of cognitive mapping of post-repressive conflicts.

The metaphorical universe constructed and developed in this play allows Alonso de Santos to convey "how nothing is left behind. We are what we seed, and each of our acts marks our destiny" [cómo nada queda atrás. Somos lo que sembramos y cada uno de nuestros actos marca nuestro destino] (Bravo). Additionally, Alonso de Santos enunciates a valuable reflection: "Those defenders of totalitarian ideologies sometimes seem to us already distant and without any sense, although they have filled with suffering and sadness most of the past, and they still are hidden in the folds of our present"[32] (Alonso de Santos 2014, 13).

The logic of Mauro's discourse holds and hides an ethic that remains encapsulated when the fundamental conditions of historical changes are not favorable. However, his discourse reactivates as soon as it finds a situation that allows it to leave its hibernation until it reaches the state of shameless dissemination and, secondly, of vindication and defense. This occurs in the face of today's democratic societies, without any need to return to the authoritarian or dictatorial political forms of the twentieth century, such as, among others, those of Franco's regime.

---

32 "Esos defensores de ideologías totalitarias nos parecen a veces algo ya lejano y sin sentido, aunque han llenado de sufrimiento y tristeza la mayor parte del pasado, y aún andan escondidos en los pliegues de nuestro presente."

It is possible to apply the concepts of multidirectional memory and agonistic memory to the question of whether this play is a political pamphlet or a more complex representation. Our study attests that *Trampa para pájaros* is a complex mediation that prepares and opens up for democratic renewal and political citizens' participation. In the 1990s, this play presented an innovative typology of memory that overcame the typical dominant representations of the Spanish transition. However, more than a decade after, *Trampa para pájaros* became more than just the byproduct of a particular historical moment. Still, it reads as a psychological drama that attempted to understand more than to judge the complexities related to the characters featured in this play. Today, this play reads as a tragedy in which the humanity of all characters and situations brings to the fore the extraordinary density of angles and perspectives that were canceled by the dominant cultural narratives of the 'two Spains' and the oblivion. In this regard, it is possible to argue that *Trampa para pájaros* was foregrounding the principles of multidirectional memory and agonistic memory *avant la lettre* and was genuinely innovating in the field of not only the Spanish transition memory but also in the possibilities of re-engineering the democratic process in Spain and in its relation to the wave of the democratization that internationally took place in the 1990s. Therefore, our future research's objective will be to better understand how analogical modeling mechanisms operate to activate repressive and violent psycho-emotional states under certain given conceptual architectures. *Trampa para Pájaros* suggests that memory of the past is an extension of the present. It just requires some specific factors (we still need a better understanding of how they operate and function) to activate hatred and domination mechanisms.

Works cited

Agirre, Joxean. "Dos Espectáculos Musicales Y Un Drama Abren La Feria En Donostia." *Egin* (January 20, 1991).

Alonso De Santos, José L. "José Luis Alonso De Santos, Autor Teatral Que Estrenará En Torrelodones, Con Exclusiva Nacional, Su Última Obra *Trampa Para Pájaros*." Interview by J. L. Castilla. *Torrelodones, Revista de Información Municipal* (November 1990): 20–21.

Alonso De Santos, José L. "Un Dramaturgo Es Un Espía." Interview by Gontzal Díez. *La Verdad* (May 5, 1991).

Alonso De Santos, José L. "Vivimos En La Sociedad Franquista Modificada." Interview by Cristina De Alzaga. *El Mundo* (February 1, 1992a).

Alonso De Santos, José L. "El Arte Siempre Ha Sido Hermano De Nuestras Instituciones De Poder." Interview by Héctor A. De Los Ríos. *El Norte de Castilla* (February 8, 1992b).

Alonso De Santos, José L. "El Autor Español En El Fin De Siglo." *Signa, Revista de la Asociación Española de Semiótica* 9 (2000). http://www.cervantesvirtual.com/obra-visor/signa-revista-de-la-

asociacion-espanola-de-semiotica-8/html/dcd931cc-2dc6-11e2-b417-000475f5bda5_23.html#I_
15_ (Accessed April 3, 2023).

Alonso De Santos, José L. "La Estructura Dramática." *Las Puertas del Drama: Revista de la Asociación de Autores de Teatro* 10 (2002).

Alonso De Santos, José L. "El Autor Y Su Obra." *Poética y Teatro* (May 12, 2009). https://www.march.es/actos/22591/ (Accessed April 3, 2023).

Alonso De Santos, José L. "Trampa Para Pájaros. Notas a La Puesta En Escena." *ADE-Teatro* 125 (2009).

Alonso De Santos, José L. *Trampa Para Pájaros.* In *Colección Teatro.* Madrid: Ediciones Irreverentes, 2014.

Alonso De Santos, José L. "Ver El Abismo En Los Otros. Teatro Para Gozar." Interview by Beatriz Velilla. *Las Puertas del Drama: Revista de la Asociación de Autores de Teatro* (2018). http://www.aat.es/elkioscoteatral/las-puertas-del-drama/drama-50/ (Accessed April 3, 2023).

Armengol, Jaime. "Trampa Para Pájaros, Cuando Las Viejas Ideas Ya No Sirven." *El Periódico de Aragón* (January 17, 1992).

Bassiouny Rizk, and Ihab Youssef. "Los Marginados En El Teatro Finisecular (1990–2000) De José Luis Alonso De Santos." PhD dissertation. Madrid: Autonomous University of Madrid, 2011.

Berenguer, Ángel. *El Diálogo Político Del Teatro Español Contemporáneo, En Teoría Y Crítica Del Teatro. Estudios Sobre Teoría Y Crítica Teatral.* Alcalá de Henares: Servicio de Publicaciones de la Universidad de Alcalá de Henares, 1991.

Bravo, Julio. "Trampa En El Desván." *ABC* (May 8, 2009).

Bull, Anna Cento, and Hans L. Hansen. "On Agonistic Memory." *Memory Studies* 9.4 (2016): 390–404.

Campos, Rafael. "Drama De Intensos Perfiles." *El Heraldo de Aragón* (January 18, 1992).

Canut, Carles. "En La Última Obra De Alonso De Santos." *La Vanguardia* (December 21, 1990).

Del Teso, Begoña. "Guía Poco Formal Para No Perderse (En) La Feria." *Deia* (January 30, 1991).

Duffy, Sarah E. "The Role of Cultural Artifacts in the Interpretation of Metaphorical Expressions about Time." *Metaphor and Symbol* 29.2 (2014): 94–112.

"El Teatro Alfil Abre De Nuevo Sus Puertas." *Villa de Madrid* (January 1992).

García Martínez, Isabel. *El Telón De La Memoria: La Guerra Civil Y El Franquismo En El Teatro Español.* Hildesheim: Georg Olms Verlag, 2016.

Guzmán, Alison. "La Memoria De La Guerra Civil En El Teatro Español: 1939–2009." PhD dissertation. Salamanca: University of Salamanca, 2012.

Haro Tecglen, Eduardo. "Hombre Encerrado." *El País* (February 8, 1992). https://elpais.com/diario/1992/02/08/cultura/697503609_850215.html (Accessed April 3, 2023).

"José Luis Alonso De Santos. El Teatro Y El Puerto." *Gente del Puerto* (August 28, 2009). http://www.gentedelpuerto.com/2009/08/28/387-jose-luis-alonso-de-santos-el-teatro-y-el-puerto/ (Accessed April 3, 2023).

"José Luis Alonso De Santos, Trampa Para Pájaros." *Espectáculos de Madrid* 1 (October 1990).

Lakoff, George, and Mark Johnson. "Conceptual Metaphor in Everyday Language." *Journal of Philosophy* 77.8 (1980a): 453–486.

Lakoff, George, and Mark Johnson. *Metaphors We Live By.* Chicago: Chicago University Press, 1980b.

Lakoff, George. "The Contemporary Theory of Metaphor." *Metaphor and Thought.* Ed. Andrew Ortony. Cambridge: Cambridge University Press, 1993. 202–251.

Medina Vicario, Miguel. "La Poética De Alonso De Santos. A Propósito De 'Trampa Para Pájaros'." *Primer Acto* 243 (1992).

Medina Vicario, Miguel. *Veinticinco Años De Teatro Español (1973–2000).* Madrid: Fundamentos, 2003.

Monleón, José. "J.L. Alonso De Santos: Imagen De Un Hombre De Teatro." *Primer Acto* 194 (1992). 39–40.

Moreno, Aurora. "Trampa Para Pájaros Arriba a Catalunya Amb 16 Mesos De Retard." *Diari de Barcelona* 22 (April 1992).

Nienass, Benjamin, and Ross Poole. "The Limits of Memory." *International Social Science Journal* 62.203–204 (2011): 89–102.

Oliva, César. *Teatro Español Del Siglo XX*. Madrid: Síntesis, 2004.

Patiño, Juan. "Siempre Estrenaría En El Rojas." *El Día de Toledo* (December 20, 1990).

Pérez Rasilla, Eduardo. "Introducción." *¡Ay, Carmela! Y El Lector Por Horas De José Sanchis Sinisterra*. Madrid: Espasa Calpe, 2011.

Pérez Rasilla, Eduardo. "Notas Sobre La Dramaturgia Emergente En España." *Don Galán* 2 (2012). http://teatro.es/contenidos/donGalan/donGalanNum2/ (Accessed April 3, 2023).

Pérez Rasilla, Eduardo. "Presentación." *Don Galán* 2 (2012). http://teatro.es/contenidos/donGalan/donGalanNum2/ (Accessed April 3, 2023).

Piñero, Margarita. "El Buscón, Versión De J.L. Alonso De Santos. Narrativa Y Teatralidad." *Acotaciones. Revista de investigación y creación teatral* 13 (2004). https://www.google.com/url?sa=t&rct=j&q=&esrc=s&source=web&cd=2&ved=2ahUKEwj44uHn1pXpAhV-A2MBHepWBPEQFjABegQIBRAB&url=http%3A%2F%2Fwww.resad.es%2Facotaciones%2Facotaciones13%2F13pinero.pdf&usg=AOvVaw0sWnx7mZDNR5uK57o8uWE7 (Accessed April 3, 2023).

Rodríguez Richart, José. *Teatro Español e Hispánico: Siglo XX*. Arganda, Madrid: Verbum, 2012.

Romera Castillo, José. "El Teatro De José Luis Alonso De Santos Y Sus Versiones De Plauto." *Mis Versiones De Plauto. 'Anfitrión', 'La Dulce Cásina' Y 'Miles Gloriosus'*. Madrid: UNED, 2002.

Rothberg, Michael. *Multidirectional Memory: Remembering the Holocaust in the Age of Decolonization*. Redwood City: Stanford University Press, 2009.

Rothberg, Michael. *The Implicated Subject: Beyond Victims and Perpetrators*. Redwood City: Stanford University Press, 2019.

"Sherezade Apuesta Por 'Trampa De Pájaros' De Alonso De Santos." *Premios Max* (Fundación SGAE). www.premiosmax.com/estreno/878/sherezade-apuesta-por-trampa-de-pajaros-de-alonso-de-santos/ (Accessed April 3, 2023).

Sorela, Pedro. "José Luis Alonso De Santos Estrena En Madrid 'Trampa Para Pájaros'." *El País* (February 6, 1992). https://elpais.com/diario/1992/02/06/cultura/697330809_850215.html (Accessed April 3, 2023).

Soriano Salinas, Cristina. "La Metáfora Conceptual." *Lingüística Cognitiva*. Ed. J. Valenzuela Ibarretxe-Antuñano. Barcelona: Anthropos, 2012. 87–109.

Sotorrío, Regina. "Alonso De Santos Estrena En El Alameda 'Trampa Para Pájaros', Una Obra Con El Latido De Hoy." *Diario Sur* (January 30, 2009). https://www.diariosur.es/20090130/cultura/alonso-santos-estrena-alameda-20090130.html (Accessed April 3, 2023).

Torres Monreal, Francisco. "Aniversario Con Clásicos." *Diario* (February 16, 1991).

"Trampa Para Pájaros. Apasionante Porción De Actualidad." *Revista Reseña* (May 1991).

"Trampa Para Pájaros." *El Correo Gallego* (April 10, 1991).

"Trampa Para Pájaros." Gómez, Metamorfosis Producciones Teatrales y Teatro Fernán (2009). https://www.teatrofernangomez.es/prensa/trampa-para-pajaros (Accessed April 3, 2023).

"Trampa Para Pájaros." *Pentación Espectáculos* (1990). https://pentacion.com/obras-en-archivo/trampa-para-pajaros/ (Accessed April 3, 2023).

"'Trampa Para Pájaros' De Alonso De Santos Se Estrena En El Festival De Málaga." *Artezblai* (January 2009). http://www.artezblai.com/artezblai/trampa-para-pajaros-de-alonso-de-santos-se-estrena-en-el-festival-de-malaga.html (Accessed April 3, 2023).

"Trampa Para Pájaros, Una Obra Del Pasado Revisada Con La Fuerza Del Presente." *Diario Crítico* (May 05, 2009).

"Una Obra Que Habla De Problemas Cotidianos." *Lanza* (December 20, 1990).
Valdivia, Pablo. "Narrating Crises and Populism in Southern Europe: Regimes of Metaphor." *Journal of European Studies* 49.3–4 (2019): 282–301.
Velasco, Beatriz. "Hoy El Mundo Es La Crisis Y La Gripe, Lo De Más Es Decimonónico." *Europa Press* (2009). https://www.europapress.es/cultura/exposiciones-00131/noticia-hoy-mundo-crisis-gripe-demas-decimononico-20090505162237.html (Accessed April 3, 2023).

Mónika Dánél

Lost in Transition? Understanding Hungarian and Romanian 1989 Regime Change through Metalepsis and Collage

Abstract: This chapter analyzes how the mobile and decomposing devices of collage and metalepsis create mnemonic forms for representing and rethinking the historical legacies of the 1989 regime change. It does so through a comparative reading of a Hungarian and a Romanian early post-transition text – the film *Bolshe Vita* (directed by Ibolya Fekete, 1995) and Dumitru Ţepeneag's novel *Hotel Europa* (1996). Considering collage and metalepsis as visual and narrative poetic modes for depicting 1989 regime change and transition, I outline the insights we can gain from conceptualizing the simultaneity of disparate temporalities. Through their poetics, the analyzed artworks perform the co-temporality of the non-opposing, diverse temporalities and incommensurable differences. As memory media they perform the regime change as a constant negotiating process of folding narratives, an overlapping of different political systems, and a constant transgression between past memories, social attitudes, habits, and imaginary futures. Therefore, they create an alternative, layered, nonlinear vision, a temporal structure, and a memory form for the regime change and transition in postsocialist societies. Perceiving the postsocialist societies through this doubled lens, simultaneously framed by teleological narratives and interrupted by juxtaposition of multiple coexisting temporalities, even the revival of the authoritarian regimes and nationalistic narratives in our present acquires a denser historical context. The 'backlash' processes manifest how the juxtaposing aspect was obscured in teleological narratives, how people who found themselves 'stuck' between regimes were 'forgotten,' and how they are addressed by new totalitarian grand narratives.

Acknowledgments: I would like to express my gratitude to Ksenia Robbe for her unlimited support of this chapter and, above all, her patience. I also wish to thank Stijn Vervaet for his helpful reading and for the opportunity to participate as a postdoctoral researcher in the project "Probing the Boundaries of the (Trans)National: Imperial Legacies, Transnational Literary Networks, and Multilingualism in East-Central Europe" at the University of Oslo. Finally, I am grateful to Professor Răzvan Rotta, who authorized the publication of the details of his archival photographs, and shared with me his personal memories about the moments captured with his camera in 1989 in Cluj-Napoca.

Note: Research for this article was supported by the Research Council of Norway Grant "Probing the Boundaries of the (Trans)National: Imperial Legacies, Transnational Literary Networks, and Multilingualism in East-Central Europe" (275981).

https://doi.org/10.1515/9783110707793-004

Introduction: Photographs as irregular collages

The conceptual exhibition *Cluj 1989 21.12* commemorates the thirtieth anniversary of the 1989 revolution in Romania.[1] Răzvan Rotta's photographs, shot on the Union Square in Cluj-Napoca on December 21, 1989, constitute a part of this exhibition, which consists of smaller projects. Rotta's blow-up images, capturing tragic acts, were exhibited in two rooms.[2] Documenting the historical events that happened on that day, these photos testify that soldiers fired at civilians in the streets.[3] On the one hand, through images we can witness the very moment at which people were shot, since they show the (still) living and dead people on the square. On the other hand – and I will focus on this type of image – we can see several similar photographs, in which a man stands with naked chest in front of soldiers' weapons (Figures 1–3). These individuals can be seen from the back (as such they also serve as a 'shield' for the photographer) or in profile, and the soldiers' faces are visible from close up. These individual scenes are in the foreground of the images, and in the background, we can detect groups of people reacting, in different ways, to the scenes that are happening in front of their eyes. The shocking aspect of the photographs is rooted, on the one hand, in the captivating nature of an extraordinary event (victims just before and after they were shot); on the other hand, it is related precisely to the micro 'scenes' happening in the background of the images. The pho-

---

1 The exhibition opened on November 21, 2019, in the National Museum of Transylvanian History, Cluj-Napoca. According to the exhibition concept, "[i]t does not wish to narrate events or testimonies, nor to interpret the events of December 1989, but it desires to focus, in a subjective, sober, and decent manner, on personal drama, stimulating critical thinking, and stirring inner debates on the topic of civic duty during the contemporary period" ("Cluj 1989 21.12" 2019, 6).
2 Răzvan Rotta's photographs can be viewed online here: https://ro.wikibooks.org/wiki/Revolu%C8%9Bia_Rom%C3%A2n%C4%83_de_la_Cluj_%C3%AEn_imagini.
3 The special, controversial nature of the 1989 events in Romania is summarized as follows: "In 1989, the year of revolutions, the country broke ranks. [. . .] To this day, there is no consensus among historians about the precise events in Romania in late 1989. The removal of a Hungarian priest triggered protests against Nicolae Ceaușescu [. . .] Ceaușescu did not hesitate to use force but the greater part of the toll of more than 1,100 casualties did not occur until after his execution. It is still unclear who was responsible for these. Was the civil war like the regime change in favor of the politically well-connected Ion Iliescu a fake revolution aided and abetted by the media? Was it a genuine coup? Iliescu initially embarked on a course that seemed to speak the language of change – appointment of the National Salvation Front Council, endorsement of perestroika [. . .] and other exercises in democratic window dressing. These pronouncements were shown up for what they were worth in June 1990, when the Iliescu clan arranged for fanaticized Romanian miners to be trucked to Bucharest, where they battered the nascent opposition. The anti-Communist resistance against Iliescu was bloodily suppressed and the West turned its back on Romania." (Pavlenko and Ruggenthaler 2015, 143–144).

tographer's position, usually behind an individual in the foreground, has the effect that the viewer of the images – in a self-reflective mirror structure – sees the soldiers' faces in the front plane and, after that, in the back plane, the viewers/spectators positioned in the background. Therefore, these photos could be seen as concentrated juxtapositions of the multiple and disparate layers of regime change. As a result of the specificity of the medium,[4] the photographs 'freeze' the onlooking group's faces, positions, and postures in the background, depicting them as common bystanders of the individual tragic scenes happening in front of them. Except for the woman praying on her knees (Figure 2), people are mostly watching in different postures, some with pocketed hands (Figure 3), others even comfortably resting, leaning against a tree (Figure 1). The singular bodies in front of the soldiers' guns are extraordinary, and because of the contrast with them, the different postures of the common witnesses as spectators in the background, their bodily everydayness seems to be exceptional, too. Their waiting, everyday postures[5] look extraordinary in such an extreme situation. As a result of using the medium of photography, they are frozen in everydayness, in contrast to the solitary heroic acts in the foreground.[6] As "partial visions" (Barthes 1981 [1980], 57), these photographs document collective spectatorship.[7]

---

4 See Barthes (1981 [1980], 57): "When we define the Photograph as a motionless image, this does not mean only that the figures it represents do not move; it means that they do not *emerge*, do not *leave*: they are anesthetized and fastened down, like butterflies".

5 These waiting postures were developed throughout the 40 years of state socialism, during which people were socialized for/by waiting – in long queues for food, rations and goods; to do administration; at bus or train stations; or, during the 1980s, at home in darkness since electricity was used for building the monstrous Palace of the Parliament (People's House) in Bucharest.

6 According to the personal recollection of the photographer, Răzvan Rotta, at the very beginning of the events no one – including him – was imagining that the soldiers would use live ammunition (Personal communication, 2022).

7 Spectatorship is a key term in relation to the Romanian Revolution as the first televized revolution. Television was a medium that influenced the events – and thus its historicity appears as a media event. Analyzing re-enactment strategies in one of my previous articles (Dánél 2017), I argued for the determinative role of the television and demonstrated how the process of the occurrences was contradictory and manipulated, and how different narrative versions and political strategies were layered upon each other. Re-enactments revolving around embodiment try to recapture the realness of the events, which were 'fictionalized' via several contradictory (political) narratives, manipulations, and simulations.

Figure 1: Răzvan Rotta, enlarged photo detail, reproduced courtesy of the photographer.

Figure 2: Răzvan Rotta, enlarged photo detail, reproduced courtesy of the photographer.

Figure 3: Răzvan Rotta, enlarged photo detail, reproduced courtesy of the photographer.

Through contradictory bodily presences in the two planes of the images – on the one hand, the heroic, self-sacrificing individual acts, and the different postures of 'spectatorship' on the other – different temporalities are juxtaposed. This simultaneity of disparate bodily actions has a *collage effect*. As "a mode of juxtapositions" that "always involves the transfer of materials from one context to another," (Perloff 1998) collage, I argue, offers a highly relevant theoretical and artistic 'frame' to arrive at a nuanced understanding of the complexity of the events of 1989 in Romania. Because of the ambiguous relation between them, both planes of the images and their layers look liminal and extraordinary, and they do so for different reasons. The simultaneity of the incommensurable postures, attitudes, and acts could be palpably perceived as layers of a collage – if we focus on the exceptionally heroic scenes in the foreground of the images, the resting, watching postures look as if 'transferred' from another (social) context.

According to Susan Stanford Friedman, the goal of collage (originating in Dadaism) is "to defamiliarize and recontextualize what seemed familiar, to create startling new insights through an aesthetics of radical rupture and juxtaposition" (Friedman 2012, 516). The familiar everydayness of a man leaning to a tree, and of yet another one standing comfortably (with his legs astride), both with one hand in their pocket, feels uncanny, particularly when taking into account the context. The different social and individual behaviors emerge as a political act that, in response to an extraordinary event, creates rupture and juxtaposition. Those who are in the front plane open up, pioneer a different temporality for a possible (new) future narrative with their own bodies, and their individual acts do not only confront the soldiers as signifiers of an authoritarian power structure, but also their fellow citizens as the community standing at the back as spectators. The photos' tension is rooted in this dispersed and temporally differently contextualized bodily presence. As a result of the specificity of the medium, we cannot decide whether the spectators, with their automated postures, will follow the solitary individuals acting in front of them, whether they will join them. The images' *mise-en-scène* simultaneously displays continuity and a break with continuity. The viewers' postures, with almost empty plastic bags in their hands, signal the mental, bodily, and social continuity of a regime that condemned people to waiting. Bodies facing weapons perform a political act that creates a fissure in the regime. Consequently, the two planes of the images perform two different temporalities and two diegetic levels that, however, belong together. Analyzing the photos through the lens of non-hierarchical juxtaposition, such as in a collage, can allow us to see the different layers of people's reactions to crisis, without creating moral hierarchies.

The disparate, multilayered aspect of the photos as the visual structure of incommensurable but connected realities recalls the narratological concept of *metalepsis*, which unites two different diegetic levels in the same spatiotemporal world. Between these two frozen, disparate planes, the metaleptic transgression as "the very act of breaching the boundary between the diegetic levels" (Hanebeck 2017, 24) is performed by the viewer of the photographs, who oscillates between the layers of the pictures. Through the lens of metalepsis, we can detect the separate, non-identical directions of the disparate temporalities performed by bodily actions and postures, which condense the antecedents and even the consequences of the historical event in Romania.

After more than thirty years of experiencing the long processes of democratization in Romania and in other postsocialist countries, the divergent postures on the photos, as enactors of a heterogeneous and conflicted society, could suggest a new vision and memory pattern for understanding the regime change and transitions in Eastern Europe. These photos are irregular collages that register and preserve the clashes and conflicts of contrasting worldviews. At the time when the photos were shot, it was not predictable which 'posture' would be dominant in the future, and which would remain passive but still present in the background. The contemporary re-authoritarianization processes in postsocialist societies make us aware that the juxtaposed, collaged aspect was not just a characteristic of the historical event that seemed to perform "the synchronicity of the non-synchronous" ("die Gleichzeitigkeit des Ungleichzeitigen," Koselleck 1972, xxi); this aspect remained constantly present in these societies, and it depends on political framing which layer is being enhanced.

As theorizing modes, collage and metalepsis help us to understand the 1989 regime change as a constant negotiating process of folding narratives, an overlapping of different political systems, and a constant transgression between past memories, social attitudes, habits, and imaginary futures. Through the artistic conceptualizations analyzed below, they create an alternative, layered, non-linear vision and temporal structure for the regime change and for the transition in postsocialist societies, which could balance and nuance the concept of a 'genealogical turn.' Focusing on collage and metalepsis enables us to understand how the 'from . . . to' grand turn and teleological narratives – e.g., from socialism to capitalism, from dictatorial regimes to democratic societies – are saturated and undermined by multiple non-linear, stratified, and divergent coexistent temporalities. If we can see the postsocialist societies through this doubled lens, simultaneously framed by teleological narratives and interrupted by juxtaposition of multiple coexisting temporalities, even the revival of the authoritarian regimes and nationalistic narratives in our present acquire a denser historical context. The 'backlash' processes manifest how the juxtaposing aspect was obscured in teleological narratives, how people who found themselves 'stuck' between regimes were 'forgotten' and how they can be manipulated by new grand narratives. In this chapter, I argue that for a better understanding of the major historical transformations in contemporary

Eastern Europe (and globally), it is important to keep in mind the visual logic – the simultaneity of the non-synchronicity – of collage as a conceptual mode. Thinking through the lens of collage turns the persistent, stratified asynchronicities of Eastern European societies as mobile backgrounds for different (ideological and manipulative) narratives into a visible, societal legacy and condition.[8]

The Hungarian and Romanian artworks analyzed below represent Eastern European societies in the early 1990s as deeply saturated with patterns of state socialism. The Hungarian movie *Bolshe Vita* (1995), directed by Ibolya Fekete, and the Romanian novel *Hotel Europa* (1996), written by the emigrant Franco-Romanian writer and translator Dumitru [Tsepeneag] Țepeneag, perform and enact the regime change as a long, transitional oscillation process between state-socialist and democratic conditions. Combining the picaresque and road movie genres and figures, and staging characters from different postsocialist states (Russians, Hungarians, Romanians) on the road, both works (re)create the period of the early 1990s as an unbounded movement of mingling languages and different postsocialist accents.

Considering the film and the novel as media of cultural memory, I argue that through their use of collage as a visual trope and of metalepsis in multi-diegetic narration they enable a possible alternative memorial configuration for regime change and transition beyond the prevailing teleological patterns. Through their specific poetics, they create conditions for "dialogic memory" (Assmann 2015, 208, 210) in Eastern Europe as a shared territory. According to Astrid Erll, "through the operation of selection, literature can create new, surprising, and otherwise inaccessible archives of cultural memory: Elements from various memory systems and things remembered and forgotten by different groups are brought together in the literary text" (2011 [2005], 153). Collage and metalepsis as transnational poetics and memory forms highlight the "synchronicity of the non-synchronous," the co-temporality of the incommensurable differences – the aspects that persist and even dominate contemporary local and global fragmented perceptions of politics and culture.

---

8 Such stratified asynhcronicities are mobilized, for example, in contemporary Russia, "where 'official' strategies of memorialization have been actively redirecting nostalgia for the Soviet towards state-supported nationalist projects," "a strategy that seemingly annuls the rupture of 1991 and establishes continuities between the Soviet and the post-Soviet period" (Boele at al. 2020, 11–12).

In-between genres, narratives, and political systems: Eastern European figures of displacement

Through the displaced, transborder, Eastern European figures – picaros, drifters, tricksters, shifters – who interweave different cultures, languages, accents, and memories, *Bolshe Vita* and *Hotel Europa* explore the regime change of 1989 as a conglomerate of multiple spaces and of differently imagined futures. In both works, collage and metalepsis appear as a dominant narrative and visual trope. The 1989 events in Eastern Europe, narrated and visualized by metalepsis and collage in Ţepeneag's novel and Fekete's movie, not only make the rupture between systems detectable, but consequently, in this rupture, the juxtapositions of the systems and mentalities become palpable. Creating juxtaposed, layered temporal structures, both artworks enable such memory configurations by which Eastern European regime change could be understood as a conflicting coexistence of two different imaginations of a beginning: on the one hand, a teleological one, rooted in metaphors of break and replacement; on the other hand, a – more nuanced and detailed – 'collaged' one, based on juxtaposition and stratification. The film and the novel create visions for a non-teleological spatial simultaneity of disparate temporalities, for a coexistence of the state-socialist and capitalist conditions and habits. In this way, also the teleological vision is included as a layer or strata in regime change represented through collage and metalepsis.

According to the avant-garde definition of the collage,

> each cited element breaks the continuity or the linearity of the discourse and leads necessarily to a double reading: that of the fragment perceived in relation to its text of origin; that of the same fragment as incorporated into a new whole, a different totality. The trick of collage consists also of never entirely suppressing the alterity of these elements reunited in a temporary composition. (Group Mu: Manifesto, 1978 qt. in Perloff 2003 [1986], 47)

According to Marjorie Perloff, the avant-garde collage is a way or an act "of undermining the authority of the individual self" which "in the late twentieth-century, [became] an important mode of theorizing and model building as well as art-making" (1998). Correspondingly, Friedman defines collage as a comparative reading strategy: "collage stages a juxtaposition that foregrounds the tension – the dialogic – pull between commensurability and incommensurability" (2012, 517).

Metalepsis is also a subversive, 'frame-breaking' narrative mode, which blurs the ontological boundaries of the diegetic, as Gérard Genette defines it: the "sacred frontier between two worlds, the world in which one tells, [and] the world of which one tells" (1980 [1972], 236). Furthermore, it is "a grabbing gesture that reaches across levels and ignores boundaries, bringing to the bottom what belongs to the top or vice versa" (Ryan 2004, 441). Collage and metalepsis could be both defined as tropes of de-hierarchization, of "radical rupture and juxtaposition" (Friedman 2012, 516). In collage, "[w]hat is missing is an ordering system, a set of guidelines that might tell us to subordinate" (Perloff 2003 [1986], 63). "The word *collage* thus becomes itself an emblem of the systematic 'play of difference', the *mise en question* of representation that is inherent in its verbal-visual structure" (Perloff 2003 [1986], 51). Furthermore, metaleptic shifts between different diegetic levels implicate different narrative temporalities, which through subversive transgression are juxtaposed. Consequently, when, in an artwork, collage is combined with metalepsis, the temporal aspect of the collage becomes more detectable. As a mode of juxtaposition, a collage composition "always involves the transfer of materials from one context to another, even as the original context cannot be erased" (Perloff 2003 [1986], 47), which also means a juxtaposition of different temporalities. The historical event – in itself a temporary constellation – incorporates and overlaps different temporalities, levels and layers, and – using again the collage vocabulary – this process "undermines coherence and unity" (Perloff 2003 [1986], 72).

In *Bolshe Vita*, six characters search for a future in Budapest.[9] Two Western girls, Maggie from Wales and Susan from the USA, seem unimaginably unencumbered and free from the viewpoint of Eastern European people of that time. Both are disillusioned with capitalism, and they are searching for Eastern European 'human contacts.' Yura, Vadim, and Sergey come from the former Soviet Union and Erzsi is a Hungarian inhabitant in Budapest, an ex-Russian teacher, who rents her flat out to Russian people. Since she learns English from Maggie, her house is a

---

9 In the film, the historical context is narrated as follows: "It's hard to remember how you felt while things were changing. When the impossible became reality overnight. Ultimately, our story started when Hungary opened its Western borders. Then everything we hadn't even dreamt of happened. It came in a flash and it went just as fast. We had a short but memorable period when Eastern Europe was happy. [. . .] And on top of everything the Russians went home. They returned shortly, with many others and a new era began while all of Eastern Europe tried to get to the West via Hungary." The process of the regime change in Hungary differs from the Romanian one. The historical role of Hungary in Eastern European regime changes was the dismantling of the Iron Curtain between Hungary and Austria, which "was not a once-off momentous event but a long drawn-out process. [. . .] The symbolic and media appropriate mise-en-scène of dismantling the Iron Curtain by Hungary's and Austria's foreign ministers, Gyula Horn and Alois Mock, in late June 1989 took place at a time when hardly any of it was still left. Not that this event was purely symbolic. In summer 1989 no one could be sure how far the reforms of the Eastern bloc would go or would be allowed to go." (Pavlenko and Ruggenthaler 2015, 145).

meeting point. She is a translator, a mediator between languages, cultures, and systems. She is open toward new phenomena and new experiences, but she cannot adopt dominant mottos of the time, which tell people that they are free ("go ahead, go!"), and encourage them to "throw away" their previous life like rubbish. She cannot throw away her life lived under communism. Her attitude shows that it is impossible to jump from one system to another in everyday life practices. There is a long period of transition and of overlapping mental strata. The tension between the newly found freedom as a new life condition and the inner/mental preconditions is developed in Sergey's tragic character: "They all shout the world opened up. I thought I might become cosmopolitan or something, to live the way I want to and where I want to."

Sergey's attitude could be characterized as 'false expectations,' an important term through which the Croatian (Berlin-based) philosopher Boris Buden (2009) nuances and criticizes the conceptualization of Eastern European transition period as a "catching up" revolution. The latter term was introduced by Jürgen Habermas in his 1990 book *Die nachholende Revolution* [The Catching-up Revolution]. Buden critiques it as framing the revolutions in Eastern Europe as attempts to catch up with 'the West,' which, as such, betrays a logic of belatedness.[10] Illusionary expectations and realistic continuity are juxtaposed in Sergey and Erzsi's relationship as a couple. Even though they have Russian as a common language, their relationship remains a 'temporary composition' because of their different attitude vis-à-vis the new events and developments. The relationship of Susan and Vadim also remains temporary because of the linguistic barriers and social and cultural differences. Through their more intimate, English–Russian mixed language, it is only Maggie and Jura who can create fragile visions for a new, interpersonal relationship that helps them overcome the (historical) differences between East and West.

In *Bolshe Vita*, we can see only heterotopias as transient meeting points of the different, parallel life fragments: the port, the border zone, the cemetery, the postsocialist market (the COMECON market), open flats, and an underground, international ruin pub called Bolshe Vita. As Michel Foucault defines it, "the heterotopia has the power of juxtaposing in a single real place different spaces and locations that are incompatible with each other. [. . .] Heterotopias always pre-

---

10 "Not only the end of totalitarian dictatorship was promised in the beginning . . . There was the expectation that democracy and capitalism would be able to bring growth and an improvement on all levels of human life. Nobody believed that social welfare should be dismantled. People believed naively that they can preserve their social systems and have freedom, a functioning market economy, and being integrated into the world. But this is not possible." (Buden and Genova 2018) Also see Buden 2009 and Kiossev 2008.

suppose a system of opening and closing that isolates them and makes them penetrable at one and the same time." (1997 [1967], 335–336) In *Bolshe Vita*, this aspect of the heterotopia is connected with the poetic collage and multiple accents and languages of the film.

The historical uniqueness of Budapest (and of Hungary) is evoked in the film as a political, cultural, interpersonal contact zone; it is created as a heterotopic space in which nomads and traffickers from East and West meet temporarily. Budapest as a metropolis is composed through the juxtaposition of physical spaces, the materiality of these spaces, on the one hand (for example, Soviet architecture appears as shards of an existing legacy), and the imaginary space of the travelers' inner images, fantasies, memories, and hopes, on the other. It is both a real and an imaginary space, a place for the articulation of identity, a big open market for exchanging memorial shards and imagined futures. The Russian characters look like a moving cultural texture with quotes and allusions to (Soviet) Russian culture, literature, and music that are difficult to understand for the Western girls. Using the collage vocabulary, each can be seen "as an element displaced from its habitual meaning into another meaning" (Perloff 2003 [1986], 69). In these intercultural, interlingual interactions with the girls, they look like oscillating, accented human fragments, who as signifiers "refer to a presence that is consistently absent" (Perloff 2003 [1986], 63) – their pasts become absent, their own lives lived under state socialism as well as their imagined futures appear absent.[11]

The multilingual title of the film (*bolshe* in Russian means 'more' or 'bigger'; *vita* in Latin means 'life') recalls Federico Fellini's film *La dolce vita*, and it can be seen as an 'Eastern' reconceptualization of Fellini's metropolis as an artistic, non-linear, living representation of the city shaped by accidental interactions, but in very different social and mental circumstances. In this title, the word *bolshevik* can be heard as a subtext/subsound, referencing the Russian equivalent of the So-

---

11 This figure of absence of the previous life returns in most contemporary works. For example, it is developed in Noé Tibor Kiss's Hungarian novel *You Ought to Sleep* (Aludnod kellene; 2014). This figure has gendered characteristics. As a result of the deterioration of state agriculture in an isolated community, the downfall and the hopelessness is embodied by male inhabitants, who remain without future and past and live like ghosts. The dysfunctional father character with state-socialist skills appears also in the Romanian movie *First of All, Felicia.* (2009) In contrast with displaced post-Soviet male figures in Dan Lungu's Romanian novel *I'm an Old Commie!* (2017 [2007]) and in its adaptation with the title *I'm an Old Communist Hag* (dir. Stere Gulea, 2013), the mother character proudly and nostalgically undertakes her Communist worker-legacy. In both Romanian films, the communist legacy appears as a marker of the conflicting relation between an old generation living in Romania and the daughters who emigrated onto the West. (See Ioana Luca's chapter in this volume for a more detailed discussion of the latter novel and its adaptations.)

viet communist person. Metaphorically, we can say that the film positions the characters in this sounding collage zone between *bolshe vita* and *bolshevik*. *Bolshe vita* differs from *bolshevik*, but it incorporates the word as an audible allusion and legacy.

The film positions itself as an artwork collaged by allusions and layers. For example, Sergey arrives at Keleti (Eastern) train station in Budapest, and his whole route in the streets and squares is a big collage that provokes our tactile sensibility: various elements of Hungarian culture (songs, pictures, posters) and of the city are layered acoustically, visually, and haptically in these scenes (Figure 4).

Figure 4: Sergey's arrival in collage-like Budapest. Screenshot from *Bolshe Vita*.

His arrival also has a comic layer, an allusion to an iconic satiric film by Péter Bacsó: *The Witness* (1969), a parody of socialist production (subsequently banned for ten years in the communist regime). In Bacsó's film, following the example of Soviet accelerated production, the Hungarian socialist party also wants 'to produce' oranges. And when the one single orange that has been produced in Orange Research Institute disappears, it is substituted with a lemon, and it is offered for tasting for the visiting Soviet general as the so-called Hungarian orange: "A little bit yellow, a little bit sour, but it is ours!" In *Bolshe Vita*, Sergey, after a long hesitation in a shop, finally picks a bottle of lemon concentrate without knowing what it is, or mistaking it for lemonade. Sergey arrives in a city that has a Hungarian orange *taste* both in a concrete/real and in a figurative/cultural sense. But he is very resolute: he drinks the lemon concentrate. The rich cultural allusions and layers make the film itself seem *as a collage* of visible and non-visible material, memorial and imaginary folded shards.

In the poetic method of the film, one can recognize the practice and lifestyle of transborder figures as being in a *constant process of folding cultures* into each other and as *living in constant translation*; this way metalepsis becomes the dominant figure of the film. *Bolshe Vita* is based on a documentary film – *Children of Apocalypse I–II* (1992), made by Ibolya Fekete herself – and documentarism, as a layer, appears in several ways in the film. The metaleptic trans-bordering between real and fictional space is created through the inner documentary frames made up of archive images. At the beginning of the film, we see iconic archive images depicting the atmosphere of the 1989 events: streets, squares, people, destroyed idols, defaced, demolished Soviet symbols (Figure 5). At the end of the film, we see archival documentary images of the Yugoslav war: streets, squares, destroyed buildings, and human bodies. On the one hand, this inner documentary frames the film historically, while on the other hand, it becomes a really strange loop – as Douglas Hofstadter (1979) defined metalepsis – belonging to another level of diegesis. Through documentary strata, the film positions the other levels *as fictional*, but dead bodies, as trans-borders between different levels, show how documentary images 'infect' the fictional level. On the fictional level, Sergey is killed by the (post-)Soviet mafia. His corpse looks like a dehumanized shard within the ruins. According to Rosalind Krauss "eradication of the original surface and the reconstitution of it through the figure of its own absence [. . .] is the master term of the entire condition of collage as a system of signifiers" (1981, 19). Sergey's corpse, as eradicated and reconstituted through his absence, collaged in the ruined landscape, appears a 'badge' of the demystified real world, where new beginnings, expectations, and hopes seem illusory. The metaleptic strategy between documentary, found footage, and fiction in Ibolya Fekete's film can be interpreted as a visual and conceptual negotiation with the layered reality of that period. The film's collage poetics can be seen as an expressive, tactile method for the overlapping of different and incompatible mental realities, incommensurable temporalities which characterize the period of the 1990s, and a characteristic that was partially covered and overwritten by later teleological linear narratives.

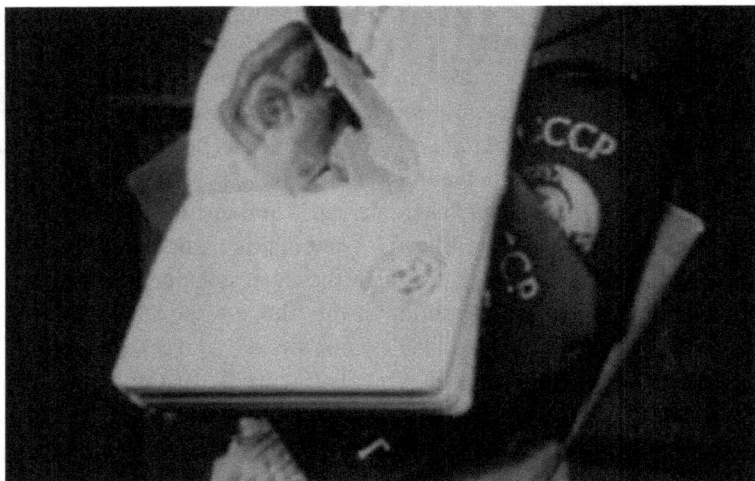

Figure 5: Archive images of the collaged Soviet passports in the opening documentary sequences depicting the atmosphere of 1989. Screenshot from *Bolshe Vita*.

From today's perspective, it is thought-provoking how certain artworks in the early 1990s represented Eastern European societies as deeply saturated with the legacy of state socialism: the characters cannot simply jump into or be replaced by a new system. (Erzsi's character also represents this on a personal level.) The teleological narratives of Eastern European transitions seem to forget or place into the background this contradictory aspect, which is nowadays sharpened with the backlash of new nationalistic and authoritarian systems. These systems mobilize the already existing perspective, that of discontent with the teleologies of regime change, fueled by visions of frustrated belatedness. The film represents the complexity of transitions through the non-hierarchical overlapping perspectives and temporalities. It emphasizes the legacy of the simultaneity of asynchronicities, which, as a mobile and fragile structure, can be re-framed within different narratives.[12]

The novel *Hotel Europa* (1996), written by Dumitru Țepeneag,[13] could be considered one of the first fictional literary works related to the 1989 events in Roma-

---

[12] This concerns, for instance, the strategic uses of nostalgia and appropriations of the shared (post)socialist memories by new nationalistic and restorative patriotic narratives, in which "[r]eappropriating the cultural forms of the past [. . .] should not necessarily be equated to re-imposing the ideology, which they once conveyed" (Boele at al. 2020, 6).

[13] In 1975, the Romanian Communist regime stripped him of his citizenship. He settled down in Paris, where he was a leading figure of the Romanian exile and one of the most important Romanian translators of French literature and philosophy (authors such as Alain Robbe-Grillet, Robert

nia[14] that perform the condition of the Eastern European regime transformations in terms of juxtaposition and overlapping. The novel[15] combines elements of the *Bildungsroman* and picaresque genre with nouveau roman auto-reflexive principles. Alluding to Hayden White, Astrid Erll observes that "the choice of plot structure already pre-forms the meaning given to an historical event." (2011 [2005], 148) Taking this assumption further, it can be pointed out that through juxtaposing different genre structures, *Hotel Europa* negotiates between contrasting, pre-formed (genre) meanings given to the 1989 events. The novel creates a hybrid and subversive postmodern composition,[16] in which metalepsis enacts irony and decentralization. Through the metaleptic narration of the novel, the level of diegesis of the self-referential bilingual writer, who wanders between French and Romanian linguistic worlds, is continuously transgressed by the fragmented journey-narrative of a Romanian young adult (Ion Valea), who, after the 1989 changes in Romania, travels to the West – first to Budapest, then to Vienna, Munich, Strasbourg, Metz, Paris, and Bretagne. The France-based writer's auto-poetic level of diegesis is crossed by Ion's journey as a fragmented picaresque plot formed by

---

Pinget, Albert Béguin, Jacques Derrida, and Alexandre Kojève). See: https://romanianliterature. fandom.com/wiki/Dumitru_%C8%9Aepeneag.

14 Other Romanian and Hungarian novels related to the 1989 events in Romania are, among others: Andrea Tompa's *A hóhér háza* (2010; The Hangman's House, translated by Bernard Adams, 2021); Bogdan Suceavă's *Noaptea când cineva a murit pentru tine* (2010; The Night when Somebody Died for You); Zsigmond Sándor Pap's *Semmi kis életek* (2011; Insignificant Lives); Zsolt Láng's *Bestiarium Transylvaniae. A föld állatai* (2011; Bestiarium Transylvaniae: The Animals of Earth); György Dragomán's *Máglya* (2014; The Bone Fire, translated by Ottilie Mulzet, 2020); Radu Pavel Gheo's *Disco Titanic* (2016); Gábor Vida's *Egy dadogás története* (2017; Story of a Stammer, translated by Jozefina Komporaly, 2022); Farkas Király's *Sortűz* (2018; Barrage). The listed Romanian and Hungarian authors were born in Romania in the 1970s. These novels can be understood as narratives of decomposition and transformation of the Communist/state-socialist ideological conditionings and inscribed fantasies, and as a search for (generational) self-expression through language. (Dánél 2021, 14–15).

15 *Hotel Europa* is part of a trilogy, which also contains the novels *Pont des Arts* (1999) and *Maramureş* (2001).

16 This poetic can also be connected to following the principles of dreams as text 'structure' in aesthetic oneirism. The author is also known as a founder of aesthetic oneirism, a movement in Romanian literature of the 1960s generation, which formed "as a reaction to Romanian Surrealism and to socialist realism" ("Aesthetic oneirism"). For oneiric literature, according to Ţepeneag, "the dream is not source/reference nor matter of study, but a criteria. The difference is fundamental: I am not transcribing/telling a dream [. . .] I am trying to build a reality analogue to the one of dream. [. . .] The Surrealists also tried to detect these strange elements of reality [. . .] but they were like some kind of reporters looking for the unusual, without the will to build with these elements a different world, one that is parallel to the world of dreams." (Dumitru Ţepeneag, *În căutarea unei definiţii* [In Search of a Definition], 1968, qt. in "Aesthetic oneirism").

the (Socialist) realism and surrealism of the Eastern European conditions. Similar to the post-Soviet figures in *Bolshe Vita,* Ion's figure could be interpreted as an expressive type of a disintegrated social order after the 1989 changes – a student who, after the fall of the marathon protest organized on the University Square in Bucharest in the spring of 1990 as a freedom-occurrence, wants to experience the Western world, and whose journey is also fueled by the disappointment in Romanian regime (non-)change.[17] Through metaleptic narration, the picaresque journey, created through border crossings, becomes a poetic experience, too. Narrative metalepsis, a frame-breaking trope of decentralization, itself marks a (crossed) boundary. Even if the fortuitous, dreamlike metaleptic transgressions between diegetic levels perform uncontrolled text processes, these transgressions combined with a picaresque plot (a journey from Eastern to Western Europe) make the frames and borders more detectable, 'structuring' this journey.

At the beginning of the novel, the diegetic levels are almost clearly separated by chapters. In the first chapter, the plot scene is placed in Paris, in the apartment of a married couple, where the first-person narrator (the bilingual emigrant writer) and his French wife Marianne start a usual day with morning preparations. As a forecast/projected reference of the other diegetic level appears the following sentence in parentheses: "(The same song, somewhat modified, was performed by the young people I met in Bucharest. One was called Mihai, another Ion. I can't remember the rest of the names; I should make an effort, but I'm not capable of it now. And what does it matter! Ion and Mihai promised they would write to me.)" (Tsepeneag 2010, 6) Narrated by a heterodiegetic narrator, the second chapter's plot starts in Bucharest, in Piața Rosetti, where Ion and Mihai meet. Then the narration goes forward by the unsignaled alternation of the plot levels:

> Mihai was almost running now, yet was managing to keep up the dialogue with his friend. It's easier like that, when you imagine it in your head, than it is in reality. And it's even easier when you're in the bath – even if the water's getting cold and you have to sit up and turn on the hot tap. [. . .]
>
> Mihai no longer had any reason to run. He could already see the Hotel Intercontinental. There were more people than usual on the sidewalk. The traffic seemed to be blocked on University Square: neither cars nor buses were moving. A truck covered with tarpaulin had come to a standstill, surrounded by an excited crowd. A police car was honking like crazy to clear a way through.
>
> Something's happened! Maybe a flying saucer landed . . .

---

17 For the historical context see: "On 22 April 1990, Bucharest's University Square saw the birth of a marathon protest against the team of neo-communists that had come to power immediately after the revolution of 1989. The marathon was to last until the dawn of 13 June, when the last protesters were violently evicted, brutalized and abused by the police and, subsequently, by the miners who had been summoned to Bucharest by President Ion Iliescu." (Cesereanu 2015, 181).

Mihai slowed down and put both hands in his raincoat pocket. He stopped. Someone's banging on the door, louder and louder. Marianne has woken up and is furious that it's locked. (Tsepeneag 2010, 11)

At this point in the novel, it seems to be clear "which narrative structure is hierarchically superior, which subordinate" (McHale 1987, 120). The scenes in Bucharest are placed in the self-ironic, first-person, embodied[18] narrator's imagination or remembrance. Right here – even if the abrupt shifting of the registers is close to the avant-garde cutting up-method – we can follow the logical structure of the text. A second, imaginary or memorial diegetic level is embedded in the first-person homodiegetic narrative. The embedded diegetic level itself looks multilayered: near the concrete, named places in Bucharest the appearance of a 'flying saucer' (in Romanian 'farfurie zburătoare'; Țepeneag 1996, 13) as an unconventional text-fragment seems to be a signal of another narrative register. With other elements in the novel, this register transforms the 'products' of Socialist Realism into comic surrealism. Later in the novel there also appears one Yuri Gagarin, the Soviet pilot and cosmonaut, the first human to journey into outer space, whom the writer paints "as a gang leader, a little Mafia godfather" (Tsepeneag 2010, 269), shifting the Soviet idol toward a more mundane role. As in Péter Bacsó's film *The Witness,* the real and alleged Soviet scientific invention and production appear as parts of the surrealistic dimension of the novel, but they also 'return' with the atmosphere of a controlling system. The surveillance and control, re-shaped as a haunting system, return in a new form. On the one hand, the Eastern European mafia-like organization 'follows' Ion's journey as an organic root/network. On the other hand, Ion's father, who remained in Romania, is interrogated by the police – described in the novel as a still operating, re-shaped Securitate. The interrogation signals that traveling abroad is still not perceived and accepted as a private, free activity. In this context of surveillance and control, *the mobile poetics* of the novel, performed by the metaleptic shifts and by the characters gradually emancipated from the authorial gaze and from the narrator's authority, can also be interpreted as a subversion of the controlled (narratorial) system.

The first passage between two distinct spatiotemporal levels – between "the world in which one tells" (scenes in Paris) and "the world of which one tells" (scenes in Bucharest), to use Gérard Genette's terms[19] – is created by the truck described in

---

18 The author–narrator reflects on his own corporeality (e.g., on his impotence and sciatica).

19 See: "All these games, by the intensity of their effects, demonstrate the importance of the boundary they tax their ingenuity to overstep, in defiance of verisimilitude – a boundary *that is precisely the narrating (or the performance) itself*: a shifting but sacred frontier between two worlds, the world in which one tells, the world of which one tells. [. . .] The most troubling thing about metalepsis indeed lies in this unacceptable and insistent hypothesis, that the extradiegetic

the Bucharest scenes, which actually is the truck with which the writer–narrator returned from Paris to Romania. He returned as a "Journey to the East" (Tsepeneag 2010, 37; "Voyage en Orient!" Țepeneag 1996, 41) with a truck relief consignment in Bucharest "at the height of the 'events'".[20] Appearing in both spatiotemporal levels, the truck, as a rhetorical metalepsis itself, travels/transgresses the textual diegetic levels. Furthermore, in the Paris scenes Marianne, the writer's wife, reads Marguerite Duras's *Le Camion* (1977), a book about a lady's journey on a truck. *Le Camion* itself is a passage between text/script and film.[21] Through this allusion, the biographical auto-referentiality – transgressive transformations between author–director–character–actress roles, performed by Duras – contextualizes Țepeneag's novel in a kind of transfigurative poetics of mutation and remediation.

How does the postmodern poetic as a textual vortex (e.g., multidirectional passages, intertextual mobility, multiple interruptions of the primary diegesis, intrusive characters, shifting registers) performed by the novel interact with the 1989 Eastern European events? How is the regime change (re-)created, (re-)imagined and (re-)understood by the poetics of transgressions? How can the oneiric poetic of the anti-(Socialist)-realism created by Țepeneag return and touch historical events? With the first line of this mobile poetic, the novel highlights the fictional aspect of the events; the real Romanian events were themselves fictionalized by fake news and the fake realities created by secret service powers (Securitate) in Romania.[22]

---

is perhaps always diegetic, and that the narrator and his narratees? – you and I – perhaps belong to some narrative." (Genette 1980 [1972], 236).

20 See the following description in the novel: "I feel like writing the novel that I've been thinking about ever since that trip I made in the truck. I hadn't been able to stop myself from going, even at the height of the 'events.' The truck, chartered by *Médecins sans frontières*, was carrying food and medicine. We crossed the Danube into Romania at Giurgiu, having driven through southern France, northern Italy, Yugoslavia, and Bulgaria. We avoided the route via Timișoara because we were afraid of the 'terrorists'; we were simply terrified of them. By the time we reached Bucharest, there no longer seemed to be any danger. It was days after the Ceausescus were executed." (Tsepeneag 2010, 29).

21 In the experimental film *Le Camion* (1977), directed by Marguerite Duras, the text is read/acted by Duras herself. The film is related to Duras' disillusionment with Marxism.

22 The controversial mediated nature of the Romanian Revolution has been discussed in several studies. One of the most recent and notable books, titled *Trăgători și mistificatori. Contrarevoluția Securității în decembrie 1989* (2019; Shooters and Dissemblers. The Securitate Counterrevolution of December 1989), was written by Andrei Ursu and Roland O. Thomasson in collaboration with Mădălin Hodor. Based on archival research, the book outlines the key role of the Securitate (Department of State Security), whose invisible power through coded messages controlled the 1989 events in Romania. They created chaos and a fake reality of phantom 'terrorist phenomena' that resulted in many deaths.

The metafictional postmodern composition is probably the most apt medium for a reflexive capturing of such a controversial, phantomized real event as the 'first televised' Romanian Revolution, during which the Securitate, using radio technology and simulation, created fictive (foreign) terrorists, through which it diverted and controlled the real revolutionary events (cf. Ursu et al. 2019). On the metaphorical level, the textual vortex as a medium of uncontrolled meanings and textual processes in *Hotel Europa* could also be seen as a 'free' poetics deployed against the Socialist-realist aesthetics and didactics.

The process of imagining[23] and then writing a novel (the narrator–author travels from Paris to Bretagne and there starts the writing of the novel) contains several reflexive and metafictional elements. On the one hand, by revealing how the world of the story is constructed, "[m]etafictional deconstruction has not only provided novelists and their readers with a better understanding of the fundamental structures of narrative; it has also offered extremely accurate models for understanding the contemporary experience of the world as a construction, an artifice, a web of interdependent semiotic systems." (Waugh 2001 [1984], 9) On the other hand, following Paul Ricoeur's conceptualization of mimesis in *Time and Narrative*, Astrid Erll states: "literary world-making rests on a dynamic transformation process [. . .] literature appears as an active, constructive process, in which cultural systems of meaning, narrative operations, and reception participate equally, and in which reality is not merely reflected, but in fact 'poetically refigured' ([Ricoeur 1984,] xi) and 'iconically augmented' ([Ricoeur 1984,] 81). Text and contexts, the symbolic order of extratextual reality and the fictional worlds created within the medium of literature, enter into a relationship of mutual influence and change." (Erll 2011 [2005], 152) Through the self-ironic, metafictional poetic, Ţepeneag's novel, as a construction, creates an imaginary frame in which the fictionalization and mystification (resulting in real deaths[24]) of the 1989 events by a controlling system could be seen as a postmodern-like method. The novel creates self-reflexive poetic forms by which the orchestrated fictionalization of the 1989 events in Romania could be understood through the lens of postmodern poetics. The paradoxical loop performed by metalepsis between the ontological lev-

---

23 See for example: "even before Marianne started hammering at the bathroom door like a woman possessed, I had thought of having Ion meet Petrişor that same morning, the Petrişor who had news fresh from Timişoara and knew of a demonstration due to take place in Bucharest itself" (Tsepeneag 2010, 14).

24 According to Ursu et al. (2019, 343), between December 17 and 21,1989, 177 persons were killed. After the fall of Ceauşescu and the dictator couple's escape by helicopter on 22 December at 12:08 p.m., 129 persons died on the same day, 428 persons on 23 December, and 247 persons on 24 December.

els of the 'real' and the 'fictional,' re-territorializes the border between the poetic imagination and the framework for understanding the real historical event.

Metaleptic disruptions as narrative strategy, firstly, shed light on the functioning of a text as fiction and underline its constructed character. Secondly, "the use of metalepsis paradoxically increases the power and credibility of the entire narrative" (Prince 2006, 627). As Monika Fludernik states, "imaginative transgression of narrative levels occurs in a pause of the story, as a narratorial insertion corresponding to no action on the plot level. The term 'transgression,' actually, is quite inadequate to the effect of these passages since they tend to enhance the realistic illusion of storyworld representations, aiding the narratee's (as well as the reader's) imaginative immersion into the story rather than foregrounding the metafictional and transgressive (nonrealistic) properties of such an imaginative stepping into the story world." (2003, 382–383) According to Sylvia Pantaleo, "metalepsis is one narrative device that increases narrative complexity by obscuring or collapsing the boundaries between reality and fiction" (2010, 14). It has, William Nelles adds, the "paradoxical effect of producing the illusion of a more profound realism [. . .] but also of undercutting that illusion at the same time" (2002, 349). Consequently, because of transgressions between diegetic levels, between fictionality and realistic illusion, metalepsis implies a split mental state. This is why it could be seen as an expressive trope for liminal experiences and events. As a result of transgressions, the levels are 'infected' and saturated by each other.[25]

Through emancipated characters and their metaleptic transgressions in *Hotel Europa*, the authorial self and authority are gradually decentered. As a gradually built ontological metalepsis,[26] the characters transgress from represented level to representing level – first, when they (Ion, Ana, and Mihai) call the writer or his

---

25 In this sense a very expressive example is the movie *Good bye, Lenin!* (2003), directed by Wolfgang Becker, which represents the re-collected, re-enacted socialist past for the amnesiac mother as a still present reality. It is not a simple material reconstruction, but one that is saturated by newly arrived capitalist experiences, both 'good' and 'bad.'

26 Marie-Laure Ryan distinguishes between rhetorical metalepsis (following Genette, who later re-conceptualized this rhetorical figure as a narratological concept) and ontological metalepsis: "Rhetorical metalepsis interrupts the representation of the current level through a voice that originates in or addresses a lower level, but without popping the top level from the stack. [. . .] Whereas rhetorical metalepsis maintains the levels of the stack distinct from each other, ontological metalepsis opens a passage between levels that results in their interpenetration, or mutual contamination. These levels, needless to say, must be separated by the type of boundary that I call ontological: a switch between two radically distinct worlds, such as 'the real' and 'the imaginary', or the world of 'normal' (or lucid) mental activity from the worlds of dream or hallucination." (2004, 441–442).

wife on the phone and send them letters, and later, when they arrive at the same spatiotemporal level, where the writer writes the novel.[27] This aspect is essential not just from the narratological perspective, but also from the ethical aspect regarding the novel's (decentralized) surveillance conceptualization. By offering a framework for understanding the real historical events, the postmodern poetics – as a kind of "mutual influence and change" (Erll 2011 [2005], 152) – become interconnected with the fictionalization techniques of the Romanian Securitate. However, how does it distinguish itself from the techniques used by the Securitate? By continuous interaction and negotiation between the represented and representing levels, the novel as a decentralization process evokes the illusion of an uncertain, fragmented world created by a writer and his characters in a co-authorship.[28] Connecting this aspect with the uncertain, chaotic world of the Romanian Revolution staged by the Securitate, the novel's poetic is demarcated from the latter by its deconstruction of the authorial self and the de-hierarchization of the controlling structure that was essential to the operation of the Securitate.

The metaleptical narration enables the representation and understanding of a historical event and its effects from different and divergent simultaneous perspectives as relational and collective without a universal consensus, whereby "as an instance of metalepsis" (Effe 2017, 261) the reader's participation turns into an extended responsibility.[29] The metalepsis preserves the ontological difference. The incommensurable difference appears in several layers in the novel. According to Erll, "literature actualizes elements which previously were not – or could not be – perceived, articulated, and remembered in the social sphere. Through the operation of selection, literature can create new, surprising, and otherwise inaccessible archives of cultural memory: Elements from various memory systems and things remembered and forgotten by different groups are brought together in the literary text." (2011, 153) In Țepeneag's novel, the mediated, realistic level of the Romanian 1989 events is, on the one hand, based on the writer's remembrance about his journey to Bucharest, and on Western media sources, such as TV news and news-

---

27 Even on the writer's diegetic level, his authority is consistently contested by his French wife and by their Siamese cat's expressed opinion.

28 Laura Pavel, in her monograph about Țepeneag's oeuvre, also interconnects the poetics of transgression with the vulnerability of the author/narrator position: "In Tsepeneag's novels, the frames of the various fictional and hybrid, referentially intermediate worlds are constantly being transgressed. [. . .] the author/narrator is more often than not *vulnerable*. Or else he displays a circumspect and ingeniously mimicked vulnerability in front of his characters." (Pavel 2011 [2007], 100).

29 See: "Metalepsis makes it possible to represent self and world without claiming to tell truth, to render the authorial self accountable for the act of writing, but also to extend responsibility to readers" (Effe 2017, 262).

paper fragments, on the other. The latter are narrated and reflected on by the narrator[30] or appear in the text as a news-collage quoted from different sources. The news-collage is an explicit method of reflecting on the "mediatedness of memory" (Erll and Rigney 2009, 5) within the writer's diegetic level. The novel depicts the appearance of such contrasting news, about which historians of that time were not able to write due to the absence of documented evidence:

> The French press concentrated only on the trial of the presidential couple. One psychoanalyst-journalist (or vice versa) wrote, under the title 'Romanian Hypnosis': 'There is no resemblance between the man on the balcony and the stubborn amnesiac peasant [in the courtroom] who looks at his watch and signals for his wife to keep quiet. What happened to the promised secrets, to the revelations we were expecting to hear? It was pointless shouting that the film footage had been stolen from us. The truth is that the Ruler only exists on the horizon of our imagination. Cut open his pot belly and you will find nothing inside. He is his own tomb.' [. . .]

> The *Libération* journalist goes on: 'Who can rationally believe that this dictatorship, protected for years and years by an inextricable web of security forces, could have collapsed unless elements within those forces, even leading elements, had colluded with opponents working to bring down the regime? Of course, this is not to deny the importance of the popular revolt, without which nothing would have been possible . . . But, in short, if there was a revolution on Christmas Eve, it was because some revolted and others plotted.' [. . .]

> The Front is keeping to the story that there was a revolution. Brucan said as much at a press conference. Of course they need a popular, revolutionary legitimacy.

> My eyes are beginning to close.

> László Rajk: '. . . that the Romanian-Hungarian frontier should no longer be any more than a line on the map . . .' (Tsepeneag 2010, 56–57)

By contrasting news fragments, the novel places the plot within the context of the contemporary social and media conditions, thus creating a mediated textual documentary level (similar to the archival images in *Bolshe Vita*).[31] On the other hand, as we can detect in the above quoted fragment, this collaged juxtaposition also

---

30 "Even the Paris papers, and especially French television, were quite alarmist: they quoted figures that now seem off the wall, but at the time, in the heat of the moment, we'd all lost our critical faculties. Logical thinking only served to make the horrors more plausible. The climax came when the TV news showed pictures of the bodies dug up in Timişoara: the abnormally pale infant on its mother's sallow belly, the corpses, all sewn up with wire, or so it seemed to me . . . Really harrowing." (Tsepeneag 2010, 14–15).

31 Silviu Brucan, a communist politician, was a member of the newly formed National Salvation Front, a party lead by Ion Iliescu that won the 1990 election in Romania. László Rajk Jr. was a prominent Hungarian intellectual, architect designer, and political activist, who in the 1980s was

highlights "the horizon of imagination" (in the original "la orizontul fantasmei" (Ţe-peneag 1996, 62)) and the "plotted" aspect of the events ('complot' in Romanian, "re-volta unora s-a 'încrucişat' cu complotul altora" (Ţepeneag 1996, 63)). The news-collage stages the interplay between the real and the phantasmatic, between an oc-curred and an orchestrated event.[32] Through a translated French journal article (which may or may not have existed) Ţepeneag's novel uses the fictional frame to communicate to Romanian readers of that time the assumptions that are later turned into historical evidence. The 'plotted' aspect of the events, as hypothesized in the news-collage in the novel written in 1996, turns into historical evidence in the above-mentioned historical work by Ursu, Thomasson, and Hodor, published in 2019. The French article quoted in the novel also nuances how the earlier system and its figures (e.g Silviu Brucan), in re-framed positions, spread over and saturate the new one. As in *Bolshe Vita*, where the displaced post-Soviet characters embody the juxtaposition of the habits and conditions of different regimes, *Hotel Europa* suggests that even the controlling systems were not changed, but just re-named and re-shaped. In *Bolshe Vita*, as a *mise en abyme* for stratification of the control-ling systems, the post-Soviet (Russians, Ukrainians, Chechen) mafia groups alternate the supervision and armed control of the COMECON market in Budapest. On a small scale, the movie shows the returned and intensified control in a documentary style. In Ţepeneag's novel, the surreal omnipresence of Gagarin as "a little Mafia godfather" and of a post-Soviet, mafia-like organization that follows and orches-trates Ion's journey could be seen as an ironic transfiguration of the similar phe-nomenon of control and surveillance.

Another whole chapter contains daily news fragments depicting different countries.[33] The collaged news as material for contemporary historical, social, and

---

co-founder of the underground samizdat publishing in Hungary and, after the free elections in 1990, served six years in the Hungarian Parliament as a liberal politician.

32 The ambiguous nature of the Romanian Revolution signaled in the novel later turns into a title of Corneliu Porumboiu's film *12:08 East of Bucharest* (2006), which transforms the positivist historical documentarism into a parody. The Romanian title literally means "Was there, or was there not?" (*A fost sau n-a fost?*), which is the shortened version of the question asked in the film "Was there or was there not a revolution in our town?".

33 See: "I copy out some of the press cutting from the scrapbook where I stuck them in with Scotch tape,

[. . .] In West Germany, in 1990, 270 racially motivated attacks were committed. After unifica-tion, the number rose to 2,280.

Romania:

The Association of Independent Journalists had accused Romanian President Ion Iliescu of molesting and insulting journalist at an election rally on Saturday in Constanţa. Following his example, bodyguards attacked another ten reporters who where on the scene. [. . .]

mental conditions 'maps' the East–West differences through news types. The fragment as a *mise en abyme* shows the use of collage as a writing method for layered, ambiguous textual fragments, for decomposed representations. Ion's journey to the West is paralleled by writer's wife Marianne's travel to Moscow. This mirroring structure captures the similar surface of experiencing otherness through traveling. Even if Ion experiences, in a picaresque way, different countries and places, he mostly comes in contact with emigrants from Romania (in Budapest he lives in the house of a Hungarian woman from Romania, in Munich he sleeps in the flat of a German emigrant from Romania, in Strasbourg he stays in the 'hotel' of a beggar named Gypsy) and with people in public spaces (streets, squares, cafes, train stations), who call him a 'Gypsy' ('cigány' in Budapest, 'Zigeuner' in Austria and Germany). At the same time, as I mentioned earlier, he is followed by a multilingual, mafia-like network constituted by shifters and prostitutes speaking in discordant post-Soviet accents. Marianne's East-experience is reduced to a hotel in Moscow. The title of the book also juxtaposes their journeys' directions. 'Hotel Europa' suggests, on the one hand, a singular, non-divided Europe and, on the other hand, the hotel as a common metaphor and place for Europe ironically determines the vision

---

Former Yugoslavia:
A new wave of violence erupted this Monday in Sarajevo and the rest of Bosnia. The commander of the Serbian forces in Bosnia, General Ratko Mladić, threatened to shoot down planes carrying humanitarian aid, on the grounds that – in his opinion – they were parachuting in weapons for the Muslim Bosniacs. The leader of the Bosnian Serbs, Radovan Karadzić, proposed the closure of a 'number of detention centers.' In Bonn, the interior minister announced that Germany would not accept any more refugees, as 'it is time for other countries to make similar commitments.'
Britain:
Three people were wounded on Friday by booby-trapped parcels delivered in several towns. [. . .]
An American woman has lost five hundred pounds in six months: [. . .]
Germany:
The German Justice Department is investigating links between local right-wing extremists and the American Ku Klux Klan [. . .].
Russia:
The Russian Justice Department opened an investigation on Tuesday evening following the death of a Zimbabwean student, who was killed by a policeman in front of Lumumba University.
Japan:
Maininchi reports that a forty-year-old fisherman arrested on Wednesday in the west of Japan has been charged with using his wife as shark bait. [. . .]
Romania:
A total of fifty-four skeletons dating from the 1950s have been on the grounds of former Securitate headquarters near Bucharest. Many of them bore marks of a violent death." (Tsepeneag 2010, 308–312).

of a newly reunited Europe as a "non-place," which, according to Marc Augé, "creates neither singular identity nor relations; only solitude and similitude" (Augé 1995 [1992], 103). In Budapest Hotel Europa is a hotel where post-Soviet, multilingual shifters and gangsters meet, in Strasbourg it names a place of emigrant beggars, and in Moscow a surveilled hotel, where Marianne stays with her friend during her travels to 'the East.'

A final important aspect that *Bolshe Vita* and *Hotel Europa* have in common is that they also constitute a sounding collage. They provide diverging visions of Eastern European transitions through the role of language accents, too. The accent preserves the sounding memory of another language, makes it audibly present. In *Bolshe Vita* the accent appears as an audible medium of the interaction, of the connection between figures from the East and West. Their accents 'embody' their newly found or hoped-for freedom and challenges. (The English Maggie learns Russian and starts to speak it with an English accent; the Russian male characters learn some Hungarian and English; Erzsi speaks Russian with a Hungarian accent and starts to learn English too.) The sounding collage created by discordant accents in *Bolshe Vita* stages a non-hierarchical interplay between languages, cultures, and mentalities, between East and West. Ibolya Fekete's film, according to its title, creates Europe – for a short period – as an interacted and connected audible. In Țepeneag's novel, various post-Soviet accents as specific attributes of the Eastern European mobile underworld intensify and confirm the East–West dichotomy. In this novel, accents turn into a medium of stigmatization.

In a more contemporary Romanian film, Corneliu Porumboiu's *12:08 East of Bucharest* (2006), collage and metalepsis as mnemonic forms for imagining transition remain relevant. Focusing on memorial acts in Romanian society, Porumboiu's film (re-)enacts the 1989 events in a commemorating live show staged 16 years later in an unnamed town in Romania. By juxtaposing different and contested personal memories, the talk show as a medium of remembrance creates "mnemonic multiperspectivity" (Erll 2011 [2005], 151) in a grotesque way. Porumboiu's film stages the tension between the revolution as a media event and as an event of one's personal past. Through juxtaposing handheld and fixed camera use, through oscillating between the diegetic levels of live transmission and broadcast preparations in the studio, and through creating metaleptic shifts between them, the participants of the show are framed, visually and plot-wise, as stuck between the past and the present. Furthermore, because of the visibility of the camera and its different uses, the viewers are kept "on the surface of medial representations, thus creating an experience of the medium (rather than of the past) and drawing attention to the mediatedness of memory" (Erll and Rigney 2009, 5). The live show, performing the clashes of worldviews, perceptions, and ideologies, in remembering through parody, transforms television – an "agenda-setting organization" (Erll and Rigney 2009, 9) in social memory processes – into a real site of conflicting memories.

This recent Romanian film enforces the poetics of juxtaposing, analyzed within the early post-transition works in this chapter, and highlights the relevance of such poetic conceptualization regarding the diversity and multi-temporality of Eastern European societies.[34] If we look through the lens of the collage poetics and metaleptical narration in these works, the mediatedness of the regime change events and of the memory processes becomes evident. But most importantly, through such mediated memory configurations, these narratives enable a more nuanced understanding of postsocialist societies. In these societies, as my reading suggests, the juxtaposition of divergent temporalities and worldviews was never definitively transformed into a 'catching up' linear and teleological temporality. For a period of time, the latter was in the foreground as a vision of an (unequal) united Europe, but today we experience its enmeshing with new (authoritarian) nationalisms and populisms and its being pushed back into the background. If we adapt the non-hierarchical collage "as a system of signifiers" (Krauss 1981, 19) for understanding our global contemporary conditions as multi-tiered incommensurable realities, we still have the open chance – incorporated within the collage-condition – to reconstruct the eradicated "through the figure of its own absence" (Krauss 1981, 19).

Conclusions

Considering collage and metalepsis as visual and narrative poetic modes for depicting the 1989 regime change and transition, I outlined the insights we can gain from conceptualizing the simultaneity of disparate temporalities. From today's perspective, teleological visions of '1989' as a synchronic moment in Eastern and Western Europe are questioned. Through their poetics, the analyzed artworks perform the co-temporality of the non-opposing diverse temporalities. Thus, as early mediums of remembering transitions, they highlight the essential role of temporal asynchronicities in contemporary (Eastern) Europe.[35]

The accidental picaresque journey and the road movie narration underline how the newly mobilized figures migrate without strategic future visions, em-

---

34 For further analysis of the film, see Dánél 2017.

35 In his analysis of literary representations of the Taiwanese transitions in this volume, Darwin H. Tsen also outlines the temporal asynchronicity performed by dysrhythmia, which he reads as "a signifier for the unevenness of time and injustice" (p.121 this volume).

bodying the stratification of differences; how they oscillate between worlds, systems, and languages. Through the poetics of collage and metalepsis *Bolshe Vita* and *Hotel Europa* created mobile and layered visual and textual worlds, which enable an understanding of the early postsocialist period in Eastern Europe as a permanent oscillation between simultaneously present and juxtaposed conflicting systems.

The novel stratifies the Western local (upper and middle class) living standards and immigrant way of life with the Romanian revolutionary events and, as a result of them, the Eastern vagabond life experience. The unity of such different worlds coexisting in the novel is part of a postmodernist poetics that mixes the real and the imaginary through the use of metaleptical leaps and a surrealist ending. By metalepsis the postmodern ironical composition itself indicates the ontological imperviousness, the gaps between the different layers. This postmodernist poetics, foregrounding an ironic interpretation *ab ovo*, can be re-read *now* as a poetic manifestation of trying to interconnect incommensurable worlds.

By representing multidirectional traveling between East and West, the film and the novel perform the transition period as a spatiotemporal, transnational contact zone. Countering nation-state container thinking, they depict regime change as a mobilizing legacy. Traveling without a concrete strategy and vision in both directions stresses the journey as a medium for transnational and accented experiences without economic reason. Today, grand nationalist narratives juxtapose the freedom performed in idle transnational journeys with the inability of many people to travel, for economic reasons, and mobilize this opposition for their ends. In contrast, the analyzed artworks generate solidarity for people being on the road by creating conceptual and poetic frameworks for our contemporary perception.

In one of the last documentary-style Yugoslavian war pictures in *Bolshe Vita*, a refugee woman begs to the camera: "Don't send us back, you are our Europe!" These words may remind us that our own place is not created only by our own imagination, it is also (re)localized and imagined by others. This woman's plea reflects that living in a place in Europe means also living in the imaginary place of the people without their own places.

Works cited

12:08 East of Bucharest. Dir. Corneliu Porumboiu. 42 Km Film, 2006.
"Aesthetic Oneirism." *Romanian Literature Wiki*. https://romanianliterature.fandom.com/wiki/Aes
    thetic_oneirism (Accessed November 29, 2022).
Assmann, Aleida. "Dialogic Memory." *Dialogue as a Trans-Disciplinary Concept*. Ed. Paul Mendes-Flohr.
    Berlin: Walter De Gruyter, 2015. 199–214.

Augé, Marc. *Non-Places: An Introduction to Supermodernity*. Trans. John Howe. London: Verso, 1995 [1992].

Barthes, Roland. *Camera Lucida. Reflections on Photography*. Trans. Richard Howard. New York: Hill and Wang, 1981 [1980].

Boele, Otto,Boris Noordenbos, and Ksenia Robbe. "Introduction: The Many Practices of Post-Soviet Nostalgia: Affect, Appropriation, Contestation." *Post-Soviet Nostalgia. Confronting the Empire's Legacies*. Ed. Otto Boele, Boris Noordenbos, and Ksenia Robbe. New York: Routledge, 2020. 1–17.

Bolshe Vita. Dir. Ibolya Fekete. Mozgókép Innovációs Társulás és Alapítvány, Zweites Deutsches Fernsehen, 1995.

Buden, Boris. "Das Elend des Nachholens." *Zone des Übergangs: Vom Ende des Postkommunismus*. Frankfurt: Suhrkamp, 2009. 52–73.

Buden, Boris, and Neda Genova. "A Better Past is Still Possible." Interview with Boris Buden. *Novinite* (August 10, 2018). https://www.novinite.com/articles/191590/%E2%80%98A+BETTER+PAST+IS +STILL+POSSIBLE%E2%80%99.+INTERVIEW+WITH+BORIS+BUDEN (Accessed November 29, 2022).

Cesereanu, Ruxandra. "Romania after Communism: Queries, Challenges and Mythifications. The Proclamation of Timișoara and the Marathon Protest from Bucharest's University Square in 1990." *Caietele Echinox* 28 (2015): 179–184.

Children of Apocalypse I–II. Dir. Ibolya Fekete. Hunnia Filmstúdió Vállalat, Magyar Dokumentum Műhely, MTV 1, 1992.

Cluj 1989 21.12. Conceptual Exhibition. Muzeul Naţional de Istorie a Transilvaniei. Curator: PhD. Ioana Gruiţă. Cluj-Napoca: IDEA Design & Print, 2019.

Dánél, Mónika. "Multiple Revolutions. Remediating and Re-Enacting the Romanian Events of 1989." *Acta Universitatis Sapientiae. Film and Media Studies* 14 (2017): 95–131. http://www.acta.sapientia. ro/acta-film/C14/film14-05.pdf (Accessed November 29, 2022).

Dánél, Mónika. "Accents and Locality: Hungarian Literature as a Medium of Multilingual Cultural Memory." *Studi Finno-Ugrici, N.S.* 1 (2021): 1–38 (Accessed November 29, 2022).

Effe, Alexandra. "Coetzee's *Summertime* as a Metaleptic Conversation." *Journal of Narrative Theory* 47.2 (2017): 252–275.

Erll, Astrid, andAnn Rigney. "Introduction: Cultural Memory and Its Dynamics." *Meditation, Remediation, and the Dynamics of Cultural Memory*. Ed. Astrid Erll and Ann Rigney. Berlin: Walter de Gruyter, 2009. 1–11.

Erll, Astrid. *Memory in Culture*. Trans. Sara B. Young. London: Palgrave Macmillan, 2011 [2005].

First of All, Felicia. Dir. Melissa de Raaf, Răzvan Rădulescu. HI Film Productions, 2009.

Fludernik, Monika. "Scene Shift, Metalepsis, and the Metaleptic Mode." *Style* 37.4 (2003): 382–400.

Foucault, Michel. "Of Other Spaces: Utopias and Heterotopias." *Rethinking Architecture: A Reader in Cultural Theory*. Ed. Neil Leach. London: Routledge, 1997 [1967]. 330–336.

Friedman, Susan S. "World Modernisms, World Literature, and Comparativity." *The Oxford Handbook of Global Modernisms*. Ed. Mark Wollaeger and Matt Eatough. Oxford: Oxford University Press, 2012. 499–525.

Genette, Gérard. *Narrative Discourse: An Essay in Method*. Trans. Jane E. Lewin. Ithaca: Cornell University Press, 1980 [1972].

Good Bye, Lenin! Dir. Wolfgang Becker. X-Filme Creative Pool, 2003.

Hanebeck, Julian. *Understanding Metalepsis: The Hermeneutics of Narrative Transgression*. Berlin: Walter de Gruyter, 2017.

Hofstadter, Douglas R. *Gödel, Escher, Bach: An Eternal Golden Braid*. Hassocks, Sussex: Harvester Press, 1979.

I'm an Old Communist Hag. Dir. Stere Gulea. MediaPro Pictures, 2013.

Kiossev, Alexander. "The Self-Colonization Metaphor." *Atlas of Transformation* (2008). http://monumenttotransformation.org/atlas-of-transformation/html/s/self-colonization/the-self -colonizing-metaphor-alexander-kiossev.html (Accessed November 29, 2022).

Kiss, Tibor N. *Aludnod kellene* [You Ought to Sleep]. Budapest: Magvető, 2014.

Koselleck, Reinhart. "Einleitung." *Geschichtliche Grundbegriffe. Historisches Lexikon zur politisch-sozialen Sprache in Deutschland*. Volume 1. Ed. Otto Brunner, Werner Conze, and Reinhart Koselleck. Stuttgart: Klett-Cotta, 1972. xiii–xxvii.

Krauss, Rosalind. "In the Name of Picasso." *October* 16 (Spring 1981): 5–22.

La dolce vita. Dir. Federico Fellini. Riama Film, 1960.

Le Camion. Dir. Marguerite Duras. Auditel, 1977.

Lungu, Dan. *I'm an Old Commie!* [Sunt o babă comunistă]. Trans. Alistair I. Bluth. London: Dalkey Archive Press, 2017 [2007].

McHale, Brian. *Postmodernist Fiction*. London: Routledge, 1987.

Nelles, William. "Stories within Stories: Narrative Levels and Embedded Narratives." *Narrative Dynamics: Essays on Time, Plot, Closure, and Frames*. Ed. Brian Richardson. Columbus, OH: The Ohio State University Press, 2002. 339–353.

Pantaleo, Sylvia. "Mutinous Fiction: Narrative and Illustrative Metalepsis in Three Postmodern Picturebooks." *Children's Literature in Education* 41 (2010): 12–27.

Pavel, Laura. *Dumitru Tsepeneag and the Canon of Alternative Literature*. Trans. Alistair I. Blyth. London: Dalkey Archive Press, 2011 [2007].

Pavlenko, Olga, and Peter Ruggenthaler. "Recent Studies on the 1989 Revolutions in Eastern Europe and on the Demise of the Soviet Union." *Contemporary European History* 24.1 (2015): 139–150 (Accessed November 29, 2022).

Perloff, Marjorie. "Collage and Poetry." *Encyclopedia of Aesthetics*. Volume 1. Ed. Michael Kelly. New York: Oxford University Press, 1998. 384–387.

Perloff, Marjorie. *The Futurist Moment: Avant-Garde, Avant-Guerre, and the Language of Rupture*. Chicago: The University of Chicago Press, 2003 [1986].

Prince, Gerald. "Disturbing Frames." *Poetics Today* 27.3 (2006): 625–630.

Ryan, Marie-Laure. "Metaleptic Machines." *Semiotica* 150.1 (2004): 439–469.

Țepeneag, Dumitru. *Hotel Europa*. Bucharest: Editura Albatros, 1996.

The Witness. Dir. Péter Bacsó. Mafilm, 1969.

Tsepeneag, Dumitru. *Hotel Europa*. Trans. Patrick Camiller. London: Dalkey Archive Press, 2010.

Ursu, Andrei, and Roland O. Thomasson, in collaboration with Mădălin Hodor. *Trăgători și mistificatori. Contrarevoluția Securității în decembrie 1989*. Iași: Editura Polirom, 2019.

Waugh, Patricia. *Metafiction: The Theory and Practice of Self-Conscious Fiction*. London: Routledge, 2001 [1984].

Darwin H. Tsen

Transition as Dysrhythmia: Luo Yijun, Generational Logic, and Taiwanese Post-postmodernism

Abstract: Amongst the world's political and social transitions in the twentieth century, the island nation of Taiwan (Republic of China) is often held up as a model example of a transition from an authoritarian state to a liberal democracy. Yet transitions are never 'finished' on the ground as they persist in memories, social contradictions, and unfinished calls for justice. This chapter examines how the Taiwanese author Luo Yijun's short story collection *The Red Ink Gang* (1993) and full-length novel *An Elegy* (2001) challenge and complicate the teleological narrative of Taiwan's democratic transition by presenting generational memories and aesthetic styles as counter-narratives. I argue that Luo Yijun's aesthetic approach to the transition can be best described with the concept of *dysrhythmia*: a temporal disturbance in the biological clock that points to an individual or collective feeling of unease, of being left behind, or the perception that a society is out of joint with its ideological and material developments. Taiwan's conditions described by dysrhythmia, then, draws it into the spheres of kinship with other postsocialist, postcommunist, and postdictatorship locales and regions. Finally, Luo Yijun's work positions itself as a critical corrective to the prevailing aesthetic that emerged during Taiwan's historical moment of transition – postmodernist literature and culture. Luo's writing can thus be seen to embody the inchoate category of 'post-postmodernism,' a placeholder for the yet un-periodizable and diverse aesthetics that appeared in Taiwan and the world after the late twentieth-century transitions coasted towards its caesurae.

Taiwan: A seemingly smooth transition

As literary and cultural scholars, the concepts and theories we mobilize from other fields are numerous to the point that a distinction between what is 'native' and what isn't often amounts to an exercise in futility. Throughout the twentieth

Acknowledgments: I want to give heartfelt thanks to Ioana Luca for her mentorship, guidance, and last but not least: her active bridging of Eastern Europe and East Asia, two post-transitional worlds that are so close, yet so far.

https://doi.org/10.1515/9783110707793-005

century to the beginning of the twenty-first, we have appropriated and learned from linguistics, history, philosophy, and even ecology. But one such distinction should be made for the volume's theme: the 'transition period.' Political scientists focus on two systems in transition: the economic and the political. Discussing the former Eastern Bloc, Annette N. Brown claims a transition period ends when "productive structure has been transformed from its inherited organization to a structure that continues to change only slowly with the evolution of the economy" (1999, 10). Juan José Linz and Alfred Stepan's definition of democratic political transition involved the formation of a directly and freely elected government whose executive, legislative, and judicial powers are not beholden to other political bodies (1996, 3). From this perspective, the island nation of Taiwan (Republic of China) off the coast of Southeast China appears as a classic example of a positive transition. Taiwan's shift from a one-party republic to a liberal democracy started in 1987, as then president Ching-kuo Chiang lifted Martial Law and paved the way;[1] this transition progressed with the 1996 direct presidential elections and the Democratic Progressive Party's first presidential victory over the ruling Nationalist Party (Kuomindang) in 2000.

Yet what presents itself as a clean transition is always complicated by its cultural representations. In this chapter, I discuss how Taiwanese writer Luo Yijun's (駱以軍) work complicates the ways in which Taiwan experienced the transition period both as a sequence of events and a supposedly finished teleology. Situated at two crucial moments in Taiwan's transition between 1987 and 2008, I look at how Luo Yijun's short story collection *The Red Ink Gang* (1993) and full-length novel *An Elegy* (2001) – which respectively narrate memories of post-WWII Martial Law and the social, political, and cultural changes of the 1990s – challenge the master narrative of Taiwan's transitional 'break' by mobilizing the concepts of generations and aesthetic style as counter-narratives. The lessons of Luo's work culminate into what I term a theory of 'dysrhythmia' in post-transition states. More commonly known as arrhythmia, a serious condition that occurs when "the heart's electrical system is out of synch and disorganized,"[2] dysrhythmia refers to a biological clock that's been disturbed after traveling across time zones. Luo's 'dysrhythmia' (*shicha*, 時差) adopts the latter sense and points to an individual or collective feeling of unease, of being left behind, or the perception that a society is out of joint with its ideological and material developments. As a descriptive concept for structures of feeling, I argue that dysrhythmia in Luo Yijun's work pinpoints the tensions be-

---

1 Regarding how Taiwan's transition was inadvertently helped by certain habits of the Nationalist's one-party state, see Mattlin 2011.
2 This information comes from Johns Hopkins University's Heart and Vascular Institute website.

tween the cultural, social, and individual forms of temporality and experience generated against its official counterparts, especially when we reevaluate cultures of
transition through the optics of generations and modernist/postmodernist aesthetics. Additionally, dysrhythmia's ability to highlight unevenness in the temporal
experiences of transitions can find resonance in the examination of the memories
of other transitions, namely those of the postdictatorship, postsocialist/communist,
or postcolonial. The concept shares a particular kinship to what Mónika Dánél calls
collage and metalepsis in her contribution to this volume: by showing how diegetic
layers interrupt and overlap and how contradictory images coexist, metalepsis and
collage reveal how Hungarian and Romanian films and novels about their transition periods are actually "saturated and undermined by non-linear stratified and
divergent co-existent multiple temporalities." Following Jacques Derrida, then: it is
precisely just what is out of joint in the times of (post)transition that collage, metalepsis, and dysrhythmia aim to excavate (1994, 61).

But before the analysis, some historical context. At a first glance, Taiwan's
transition from a single-party dictatorship to a liberal democracy finds its only
analogue in South Korea, another Cold War ally of the United States in East Asia
with a very similar economy and strongmen leaders.[3] When scrutinized from a
longitudinal perspective, Taiwan shares many commonalities with the greater
family of transitions throughout the last century, from its settler-colonial origins
in the premodern era to its transformation under colonial modernity, and finally
to its involvement in the schisms between nationalist-bourgeois and socialist/com-
munist political parties during the age of decolonization.[4]

As a settler-colony of many powers and peoples, Taiwan has not been a
stranger to transitions of the premodern sort.[5] Its modern tale of transitions
began with Japan's defeat in World War II in 1945: after five decades of Japanese
colonial rule[6] Taiwan was returned to the Republic of China (ROC), which then
swiftly fell into a civil war between the Communists led by Mao Zedong and the

---

3 One reason Chiang Kai-Shek's Taiwan flourished in the post-WWII developmentalist paradigm
was that it had a few capable technocrats. Educated elites like Sun Yunxuan and Li Guoding
were instrumental in Taiwan's state–directed capitalism for at least three decades. For a brief
overview of their influence, see Morita and Chen (2010, 295–405).
4 Mark T. Berger's *The Battle for Asia: From Decolonization to Globalization* contains a detailed
account of how competing theories of development, capitalism and socialism got caught up with
the nation–state (2004, 38–63).
5 For a recent analysis of Taiwan's indigenous history through the lenses of settler colonialism,
see Hirano, Veracini, and Roy 2018.
6 Leo T.S. Ching's *Becoming Japanese: Colonial Taiwan and the Politics of Identity Formation* is
one of the most comprehensive studies on the intersections of colonialism, modernity, and identity in Taiwan to date.

Nationalists led by Chiang Kai-shek. By 1949 the defeated Nationalists had re-treated to Taiwan, with Chiang establishing military rule and the infamous White Terror with U.S. support.[7] After Mao and Chiang's deaths in 1976/77, gradual rap-prochement began in 1987 with the lifting of martial law and visitation of rela-tives in China. The political liberalization of Taiwan followed with direct elections for the national assembly in 1991, direct presidential elections in 1996, and a change of the ruling party in 2000. With the Nationalist candidate Ma Ying-jeou's (馬英九) presidential victory in 2008, Taiwan settled into a two-party system simi-lar to other liberal democracies. From the view of neoliberalism's teleology, we could say that Taiwan's modern transition period concluded here.

Luo Yijun, writers' generations, and the post-postmodernist question

Let's turn our attention to Taiwan in the 1970s and the 1980s, where intense deba-tes concerning the literary aesthetics of modernism and postmodernism occurred. A quick foray will provide insight into why I deem the awkward term 'post-postmodernism' a necessary placeholder for Luo Yijun's generation. It goes without saying that Taiwan's literary postmodernism blossomed in the political, intellectual, and cultural conditions of the 1980s. Politically, the Taiwanese 1980s witnessed the passing of Chiang Ching-Kuo, son of Chiang Kai-Shek, the end of Martial Law, and the native Teng-hui Lee succeeding as president. Lee's political style was, in Ping-hui Liao's words, conducive to "doubts and uncertainty in the psychosocial struc-ture of identification," which catalyzed intense debates, discussions, and disputes regarding issues of national identity, ethnicity, and gender (1997, 56). Intellectually, Liao reminds us that in 1987, critics and theorists of postmodernism were intro-duced into Taiwan through academic institutions and conferences, the most nota-ble instance being Fredric Jameson's keynote at the Aesthetics and Literary Studies Conference organized by National Tsinghua University (1997, 42–43). In proximity to such shifts, writers like Zhu Tianwen, Zhong Mingde and Lin Yaode mixed "metafiction with journalism, romance with magic realism, literary discourse with post-identity politics, and localized pastiches with globalized ones" (1997, 43–44). Their appropriation of postmodernism was both a response to Taiwan's transfor-

---

7 Taiwan's White Terror refers to the Nationalist Party's long-term suppression of political dissi-dence. It coincides with the four decades of Martial Law after the Chinese Civil War (1949–1987). For an in-depth study on the cultural representations of White Terror, see Li-chun Lin 2007.

mations, and an intensification of the unresolved issues in the Nativist Literary Debate (鄉土文學論戰, *xiangtu wenxue lunzhan*) of the 1970s.[8] For Chang, the Nativist Literary Debate "stigmatized Modernism as a byproduct of postwar American cultural imperialism, initiating a collective search for 'subjectivity' that gripped cultural activities for the next few decades" (142). As the debate came to an impasse, the 1980s writers embraced postmodernism to circumvent the Realism-Modernism dichotomy from the Debate while continuing to explore the issues it generated. In retrospect, the postmodernists of this era – especially Zhang Dachun and Zhu Tianwen – misrecognized the budding Taiwanese nationalist sentiment as the prelude to a right-populist or even fascist rule, and instead defended the *ancien régime* of the Nationalist party. Regardless of its attitudes towards the transition itself, one could say that Taiwan's prevailing aesthetic regime during the transition *par excellence* was indeed, postmodernism.

Looming democratization; further integration into global capitalism; a developing Taiwanese nationalist consciousness: these issues entered the 1990s with renewed vigor, and a new generation of writers emerged. Luo Yijun first appears as an acolyte of postmodernism; many studies understood him as an heir to the postmodernist 1980s.[9] Yet copy, pastiche, and recirculation were never the only forte of postmodernism. Jacob Edmund has reframed Lu Xun's rewriting of Nikolai Gogol's *Diary of a Madman* (1835) into *A Madman's Diary* (1918) to show that modernism itself was as much a movement of periphery-to-periphery influences rather than a movement based on center-periphery transmission (2016, 138–139), and in that sense Luo Yijun and his peers' active consumption of foreign texts – from both centers and peripheries – adhere to this pattern. Jeffrey T. Nealon argues that what comes after postmodernism is not the end of it, but rather a "movement of intensification and spread [. . .] by the infelicitous phrasing of post-postmodern" (8). Post-postmodernism thus has the advantage of pointing to – with exigency and ugliness – postmodernism's fated mutation in Luo Yijun's generation.

It becomes apparent, then, that what we understood as postmodernism in the Euro-American sense – as a global aesthetic, cultural, and philosophical movement – was more a component of a period's transitional *Zeitgeist* instead of a full

---

8 Xiaobing Tang (1999) observes that the issues unresolved in the 1970s Nativist Literary debate re-emerged in Taiwanese literary discourse of the 1980s and 1990s. For a more comprehensive account of the Nativist debate, see Chang 1993.
9 Sung-sheng Chang sees Luo as a member of the 1990s generation, who have nonetheless "followed closely conventions established by baby-boom generation authors, such as the witty and playful portrayal of the yuppie culture" (2004, 203).

historical epoch that necessarily follows the establishment of modernism.[10] This mood had many names: the end of the Cold War, 'the End of History', and the triumph of global capitalism. If postmodernism was the dominant aesthetic regime during the transition, post-postmodernism appears as the placeholder and corrective for the yet un-periodizable and aesthetically diverse literature that appeared after postmodernism in Taiwan and elsewhere. This post-postmodernist literature is in a sense World Literature by default[11] – it thrives on the literary circulation made possible by the market and the internet, but also works in competition with other cultural mediums for attention. Post-postmodernist literature is thus a subsequent response to and continuous engagement with Taiwan's transition period.

For many readers, Luo Yijun's dense and often introspective prose obscures his insight regarding the role generational difference played during Taiwan's transitional period. On the contrary, by looking at his aesthetic form carefully, we can tease out how Luo's work is attuned to Taiwan and the contemporary world, with a particular feel for history's entwinement with the generational logic of history. For Luo, whose father is a 1949 refugee from mainland China, and whose mother is native Taiwanese, generational experience is already bifurcated across the categories of ethnicity and political history. As a member of the 'fifth grader' generation (1961–1969)[12] Luo Yijun grew up during the latter half of the Cold War: he also began to enjoy the fruits of Taiwan's capitalist developments and as an adult he experienced notable events in the country's political liberalization.

But how does one account for the differences between the ideologies, memories, and experiences between generations while registering the material changes during a transition? Perhaps one does not, but rather finds a method to hold together the ambivalences: for Luo Yijun, this is captured in his concept of dysrhythmia. Dysrhythmia takes on two forms in the pieces examined here: the strange sensation that past taboos have ironically become harder to access in a new era in "A Roll of Ink," and a metonymy for the separation of the living/dead, the prosperous/poor, as well as post-millennial security and gloom in *An Elegy*. A labile concept, my formulation of Luo's dysrhythmia is inspired by Svetlana Alexievich's *Secondhand Time*, a chroni-

---

10 This is also Fredric Jameson's argument in *Postmodernism; or, The Cultural Logic of Late Capitalism*.

11 Here I am thinking of David Damrosch's definition of World Literature as a 'mode of circulation' in *What is World Literature?*

12 This is generational slang based on the fact that Taiwan runs on two calendars: Republic of China Calendar (starting at 1911) and the Gregorian. Each 'grade' designates a decade of the Republic calendar in which one was born: 'fourth graders' (1951–1960) corresponds with the global 'baby-boomer' generation; fifth graders (1961–1969); sixth – and seventh – graders (1971–1980, 1981–1990) etc.

cle of Soviet loyalists' lives after the Soviet Union. In *Secondhand Time*, Alexievich implicitly advances the sense that any postsocialist or postcommunist condition is one where time is experienced unevenly amongst individuals, within generations, and alongside the rest of the world. One population's hopeful socialism or market reform is another's nostalgia or nightmare which they have already experienced decades earlier. Alexievich captures this temporal unevenness best when describing Vladimir Putin's Russia, a country featuring the strange return of Communist-style authoritarianism combined with hyper-marketization: "Now, a hundred years [after the October Revolution], the future is, once again, not where it ought to be. Our time comes to us secondhand." (16) If firsthand time is the dimension where teleology ought to have taken us, secondhand time is the concrete, profane reality that obliges us to live with varying degrees of cognitive dissonance. Extending this sense of 'secondhand time' to Taiwan and other transitions, dysrhythmia thus becomes a signifier for the unevenness of time and injustice in the contemporary neoliberal/postsocialist[13] condition, a disruptive *chronos* that refuses any simple closure of the transition period. Luo Yijun kicks off his career by tackling the secondhand time of terror.

Transitioning through white terror

Following Taiwan's elections for the National Assembly in 1991, Luo Yijun published his debut short story collection *The Red Ink Gang* in 1993. "A Roll of Film", one of the collection's six pieces, immediately deals with a major ghost haunting the transition: how to approach Chiang Kai-shek's White Terror regime aesthetically. For all of Luo's future work, "A Roll of Film" establishes a connection between generational difference, the aesthetic conflict between postmodernism and post-postmodernism, as well as the sense of temporal and spatial disjuncture Luo calls 'dysrhythmia,' a result of navigating the paradoxes in Taiwan's transition period. The short story features a young generation of writers struggling under an established writer, who teaches them the craft in university. The story contains two parallel but intertwined threads. The first is about aesthetics and writing: the students in the creative writing class are each given a photo made by the professor and tasked to investigate it by writing a piece of fiction. Presented with the photo of a pony-tailed man wearing a basketball jersey, the narrator conducts a city-wide search in Taipei. Throughout the futile search, the narrator begins to

---

13 I find Shu-mei Shih's elaborations on how the postsocialist and neoliberal conditions are mirror inverses very helpful: to grasp the totality formed by this, one must approach it from a "non-unitary perspective" (2012, 29).

reminisce about middle-school, where he clashed with a friend, and how his teacher suffered an emotional breakdown after witnessing an arrest. These flashbacks form the second thread of "A Roll of Film," which thematizes the shadows of Taiwan's White Terror lurking in the narrator's life.

The narrator starts searching for story material from elementary school. He remembers/fictionalizes how a classmate, Xu Da-bo (徐大伯), was shaken after he accused him of harboring communists at home, when Xu merely wanted to conceal his family's poverty (1993, 100–101). A more powerful example surfaces when "A Roll of Film" shows the narrator's middle-school teacher collapse under White Terror's power. The readers are introduced to the narrator's nineth grade teacher, 'Wu Dalang.'[14] A panic occurs when the narrator and Wu Dalang sees, from their classroom window, plainclothes agents escorting another teacher down the hall. The teacher was arrested because she allegedly studied Marx. Passing by the narrator's class, she "abruptly turned her head and stared straight at our teacher. Although she was staring intently, there was no apparent change on her facial expression" (107).[15] After the woman and the agents left the class's field of view, Wu Dalang "buried his face in his hands, and began sobbing silently in front of the entire class" (108). Did the teacher inform on his colleague? What was their relationship? These questions are left open. The examples of Xu Da-bo and Wu Dalang not only demonstrate the extent to which the memories of White Terror dominated the narrator's imagination, but also the malleability such trauma lends to writing fiction.

As riveting as these tales of White Terror are, they are merely reminiscences conjured for the purpose of finishing the narrator's homework. As the narrator inches closer to the deadline, a curious power shift occurs between the main storyline and the White Terror memories: the flashbacks in the narrator's middle-school years were initially just a distraction against the professor's request in the main plot, but as the deadline looms, the content of his flashbacks slowly morph into materials for the assignment. From this point on, a "A Roll of Film" focuses on how the narrator's generation of writers re-converge under their teacher, whose postmodernist aesthetic, political, and cultural sensibilities are dominant.

Confounded by the possibilities that abound in the narratives constructed from his memories and fantasies, the narrator relapses into the desire for a singular truth in order to complete his assignment. He returns to an advertisement featuring a lingerie model who, throughout the story, had replaced the photo's

---

14 *Wu Dalang* (武大郎) is an oft-ridiculed character from the Chinese classical novel, *The Water Margin: Outlaws of the Marsh.*

15 All translations of this short story are my own.

original subject and triggered the narrator's memories. In this moment, the imaginative elements for the flashbacks cross over to the present narrative in magical-realist fashion. He pleads to the model: "Tell me the final truth!" as he "stood knee-deep in a murky pool of plot fragments, desperate" (1993, 109). Responding, the model speaks: "Who are you?" asked the light-browed woman as she used one hand to cover her groin, and the other to cover her breasts. Her empty face that once swallowed all sorts of plot fragments began to crumble, twisted by a strong sense of fear and hostility: "Why'd you come into my private bathroom? Somebody, help, there's a pervert" (110). Startled by and ashamed of this turn of events, the narrator throws his "plot fragments" at the model and sprints off; his serious plea for truth – an aesthetic choice contradicting the teacher's postmodernist doctrine – was thoroughly rejected.

The finale of "A Roll of Film" arrives when the students submit their work. Unable to conceive of alternatives, the narrator and his classmates created photos that matched the stories, glued the picture to their scripts and called it a day. The narrator surprisingly discovered that "almost everyone else in the class did the same thing" (1993, 110). Greater surprise arrives when the teacher, instead of reprimanding them, gives praise: "Well done, kids! The only way to forcefully gaze at and explore the truth of life, is through tireless fabrication and *sui generis* creation" (111). The teacher is satisfied because while the students thought they broke the rules, they behaved according to plan: the initial photos given to the students were the product of the teacher's own "*sui generis* creation"; by partaking in such creation, the students faithfully followed his idea that truth exists only in relation to the endless act of "fabrication." The narrator's realization therefore signaled a generation-making moment: the students' collective disobedience towards their teacher was precisely that which unified them under his aesthetic regime. The teacher's statement converts their disobedience into obedience, successfully making them into a writerly generation of his.

Luo Yijun's "A Roll of Film" ends with these words: *sui generis creation* (不懈的虛構和無中生有). The teacher's aesthetic vision triumphed, but the allegories of White Terror that occupy most of the narrator's flashbacks, while fictitious, stem from a collectively shared history. Here the teacher's postmodernism stands at a tense counterpoint with the question concerning White Terror in Taiwan's transition era: for the younger writers, how is it possible to do aesthetic justice to a subject that was, for the most part of their adolescence, a taboo? This counterpoint therefore discloses how Luo Yijun narrates the discrepancies between generations, ideologies, and temporal experience in Taiwan's culture of transition. While the teacher in "A Roll of Film" may be satisfied by thinking of White Terror stories as just another genus of *sui generis* creation, the students cannot but feel drawn in by White Terror's largesse, horror, and ghostly persistence. Herein lies the short story's form of dysrhythmia: the students in the piece, who are less directly conditioned by the trauma and memories of White Terror than the teacher's generation, perceive that while Taiwan's political liberalization has finally allocated space to discuss the past, the proliferation of discourses simultaneously present obstacles in approaching it; in a time of enlightenment, one finds re-enchantment everywhere.[16]

Beyond "A Roll of Film," such dysrhythmia also discloses a symptomatic relationship between historical trauma and postmodernist aesthetic forms in transitional contexts:[17] one's inability or unwillingness to narrate or conceptualize said trauma in a linear, totalized fashion and the reluctant or eager embrace of epistemic unknowability and relativity is part and parcel of how the lingering effects of trauma emerge in culture – always belatedly as there is too much that has been repressed for too long.[18] But for another transitioning postcolony like Taiwan,[19] the writing and overcoming of trauma and terror need not fall into a "melancholic vocabulary [. . .] marked by notions of absence, deferral, crises of meanings, unknowing, and dissociation [. . .] precluding any possibility for healing for individuals or entire nations," as Ewald Mengel and Michela Borzaga argued within the South African context (2012, xii). Literature can, perhaps, perform what Kelly Oliver deems the "paradox of bearing witness": one's subjective narrative of a traumatic event may differ from official accounts, and it may be impossible to fully close the gap between these two positions (2001, 86). Nevertheless, it is with this 'impossible distance' that a subject constructs a relationship to the

---

16 While Morris Berman's *The Reenchantment of the World* describes a movement to end alienation, what I term re-enchantment here refers to the mystification, reification, and obfuscation of social issues by consumerism.

17 This dysrhythmia also illustrates how the synchronizing tendencies of capital directly thrusts supposedly belated locales, whether in terms of development or transition, into contact with the latest technological and cultural products and trends. In *Postsocialism and Cultural Politics*, Xu-dong Zhang discusses how postmodernism as a cultural form – supposedly correlating to the late capitalist formations of the so-called First World – becomes entangled with China's postsocialist socioeconomic transitions after the 1980s and 1990s (2008, 9).

18 As important as it is to explore the formal affinities between (post)postmodernism and trauma, Sylvia Li-chun Lin reminds us that there is a material substrate to the trauma, and behind fictional narratives are "real, actual victims" who only posit in "an analogous way [that] the recollection of Taiwan's past mirrors the symptoms of a trauma patient" (2007, 8).

19 Like South Africa, soon after direct elections became available in the 1990s, Taiwan initiated a Truth and Reconciliation process over the February 28 incident of 1947 as a synecdoche to the injustices that occurred during White Terror. An NGO, The Memorial Foundation of 228 was formed in 1995, but formal legislation establishing a Truth and Reconciliation Commission did not materialize until 2016.

trauma to heal and move on. Therefore, for Luo Yijun, the aesthetico-political transition must go on to supersede postmodernism – and it does.

Mourning the generation in transition

Three years after *The Red Ink Gang*, Taiwan had its first presidential election in 1996; another four years later, Shui-bian Chen, a former attorney for the defendants of the 1979 Kaohsiung Incident – where the government cracked down on mass protests held in the city of Kaoshiung on Human Rights Day that year – became Taiwan's first president from the opposition party.[20] Luo Yijun spent these seven years developing an aesthetics that would differentiate him from the postmodernism of his teacher at the Chinese Culture University, the writer Zhang Dachun (張大春)[21] – who also is the model of the instructor in "A Roll of Film".[22] As Zhang's influence peaked in post-Martial Law Taiwan, the marketization of the literary field of production, according to Sung-sheng Yvonne Chang, also resulted in "greater differentiation and professionalization [. . .] greater autonomy [. . .], and individual agents have become more conscious of [the field's] changing operational laws" (190). As a local writer in a marketplace with a growing interest in world literature, Luo closely read and imitated the Japanese 'I-Novel' by writers like Osamu Taizai, Shusaku Endo and Haruki Murakami, as well as the metafiction of European and South American writers such as Italo Calvino and Jorge Luis Borges.[23] Luo's intense study of non-Taiwanese/Chinese writers would bring him into the orbit of a peer in his generation.

Published in 2001, Luo Yijun's fourth novel *An Elegy* builds on the stylistic and thematic concerns of "A Roll of Film," namely the intersections between complex form and its (in)ability to engage with sociopolitical memories. *An Elegy* features a post-transition Taiwan in which members of Luo Yijun's writerly generation are now in their thirties and saddled with mundane duties of the petite-bourgeoisie.

---

20 A detailed and accessible study of this pivotal event in English can be found in J. Bruce Jacobs' *The Kaoshiung Incident in Taiwan and Memoirs of a Foreign Big Bear*.

21 Zhang was widely considered as *the* poster-boy of Taiwan's postmodernist generation. As a novelist, Zhang Dachun is best known for his works such as *The Lying Disciple* (撒謊的信徒) 1996, and *The City Gangs* (城邦暴力團) 1999.

22 Li-hua Ying states that while Luo Yijun "studied under several established writers," it was Zhang Dachun, whose "postmodern style of writing had a strong impact on the budding writer" (2010, 128–129).

23 The I-Novel (*shishousetsu*) is an introspective literary genre that emerged in Japan in the early twentieth century.

Yet one peer did not live to this age. *An Elegy* is structured around a series of 'dreams' and 'letters' that engages with *Last Words from Montmartre,* the posthumous epistolary novel by the lesbian writer Qiu Miaojin (邱妙津) who committed suicide in 1995.[24] *An Elegy*'s engagement with Qiu highlights the uncertainties that pervaded post-*fin de siècle* Taiwan: the ecstasy over Chen Shui-bian's victory had passed; 9/11 threw into doubt the possibility of peace in the new millennium. During all this, Luo Yijun was enjoying an upward arc in his personal and professional life, with a rising career and two children. But Luo's happiness co-existed with the deaths around him, from departed friends to family members. Living in this dysrhythmia of happiness and loss, *An Elegy* represents his attempts to understand the temporal chasm between the living and the dead, the hope and despair of the new millennium through Qiu's last work.[25]

Instead of mapping Taiwan's late capitalist consumer society, the literary postmodernism of Zhang Dachun and Zhu sisters, Zhu Tian-xin and Zhu Tian-wen, resulted in a largely reactive project that captured the nostalgia, trauma, and chaos that appeared after the dissolution of Nationalist ideological hegemony. Where does one go after yet another end of modernism, when the end of history has ended – again? For Luo Yijun and Qiu Miaojin's generation, the deliberate rejection of their predecessors' postmodernism comes in the form of a creative infidelity to the chronology of global pre-modern and modern aesthetic movements. As I have discussed earlier, Luo's generation both competed *with* and benefitted *from* the literary market, as they sought to discuss critical issues of Taiwan's transition period while rejecting predefined parameters. Their post-postmodernism is thus defiant or even indifferent to the practices of periodization in literary history. Hence, I want to demonstrate that *An Elegy* is not only Luo's tribute to a deceased member of his generation but a statement about the difficulty of aesthetic choice in a post-transition world: should one follow/abandon their postmodernist Taiwanese forerunners such as Zhang and the Zhu sisters, or chase after foreign canonical greats whose translations are just becoming available? Or does any act of abandoning simply constitute a following-in-reverse? Going one step further, in a gesture that questions the stability of generational logic in Taiwanese literary studies: I argue

---

24 Qiu Miaojin was born in Taiwan's Zhanghua County. A graduate of National Taiwan University, Qiu worked as a suicide hotline counselor and magazine reporter before moving to Paris to study clinical psychology and feminism at the University of Paris VIII. Her major works include *Notes of a Crocodile,* published in 1994, and *Last Words from Montmartre,* posthumously published in 1996.

25 David Wang (2001, 24) interprets *An Elegy* as Luo Yijun's attempt to narrate his *own* death through a dialogue with *Last Words,* an effort that is hampered by the different subject positions Luo and Miaojin inhabit.

that Luo's novel suggests that approaching transitional cultures through 'genera-tions' means one will always be caught in the dysrhythmia of temporality, space, ideology, and memory, thus making generational logic a paradoxical and deceptive yet alluring lens for thinking through the experience of historical change. After all, members from different so-called generations are not really segregated from the diachronic and synchronic ebbs and flows of history and hence cut off from mutual commensurability; they are marked as generations – and hence become meaning-ful as generations – because of the different and similar ways through which they relate to specific historical conditions, events, and institutional formations, and thus each define themselves *with* and *against* other generations.[26] The paradoxes of the 'generation' don't end here: the idea of a generation always runs the risk of becoming ungeneralizable due to its members' specificities, or too solidly generaliz-able because of what the members share. But as Eric Hayot argues, since "every instance is also a generality, and every generality a potential instance" (2012, 16), generations become generative as a literary and cultural heuristic because they snugly inhabit the fuzzy conceptual space between the general and the specific – generations are generalities that do not exclude its instances. Hence the tempta-tions of the generational.

The conundrum of representing transition through generations first appears in *An Elegy*'s Fifth Letter, which opens with a metafictional moment: the narrator, sitting in a cafe located in the lobby of a fancy hotel, describes his surroundings as he writes to *Nin* (the novel's stand-in for Qiu Miaojin), letters which comprise the text itself. Armed with notebooks, water, and cigarettes, the narrator sits in the cafe for an entire afternoon as he corresponds with the deceased Qiu. After a while, the narrator's mind drifts, entering a stream of consciousness that leads him to ponder – with *Nin* – what it means to write about one's generation:

> I once thought that maybe I should write about 'our' generation, and that might make you open your eyes . . . Yeah. What happened then? In the years after you hit the stop button, what was going on with those of us (survivors) who continued to play the tape? It's like a cascade of broken faces coming from the other side of the street towards us. Like the way a

---

26 This is why, I think, that a politics based on generations – national or transnational – is ulti-mately untenable as it tends to slip into *ressentiment*. However, as a loose collectivity, inquiries about (inter)generations can provide rich insights into the ideological, historical, and affective bases that subtend them. For an account of how examining generations can elucidate the failures of decolonization, the residual structures of the colonial past, and even point to future reconcilia-tion in Taiwan and East Asia, see Leo T.S. Ching's *Anti-Japan*, chapters 4 (80–97) and 6 (115–131) specifically. Alissa G. Karl's recent essay "Toward a Labor Theory of Generation X" likewise ex-amines generational logic through the cultural *Zeitgeist* and on-the-grounds stakes of working under neoliberal capitalism of the U.S. 1980s and 1990s.

solitary, drifting wild goose exiled on the wasteland of time, gazes with immense jealousy at whole flocks of geese who could easily find their way back to their packs, just because they were branded with clear generational markings: they identify, with ambivalent ebullience, the secret markings on each other: the February 28 incident, 1949, the Kaohsiung Incident, the Sixties, "Starry Starry Night" . . . Such is our generation . . . But later I felt like that was really just like compressing a bunch of stuff onto a floppy disk or CD-ROM for you.[27] (2001, 108–109)

Three metaphors in this passage convey the sense that attempting to write about one's own generation is a ludicrous idea. First, the metaphor of the members of one's generation as a "cascade of broken faces" swarming towards the narrator and *Nin* imply an us-and-them distinction: the "broken faces" are indistinct and unidentifiable, positioned against the collective 'us.' The second metaphor sustains the impression that the narrator considers himself and *Nin* as separate from their generation: the unit of two is transfigured into the figure of the lone goose who jealously gazes at other flocks of geese who share generational markers. First presented with three traumatic and formative historical events (the February 28 incident, 1949, and the Kaohsuing Incident) that define Taiwanese generations, the markers become more ambiguous and fragmented (popular American music from the 1960 and 1970s, of which "Starry Starry Night," the opening line from Don McLean's "Vincent" is representative) in this metaphor, hinting at a decreasing unity in generations. It is as if history is becoming more and more fragmented, descending from clearly dated events to rough periods and then to cultural commodities. The narrator's third metaphor directly compares the act of writing about his generation to *Nin* to data compression on disks and CDs, highlighting the hastiness in attempting to narrate a generation as a totality. Positioning the narrator and *Nin* outside and against the wall of indistinguishable faces and docile flock of birds that metaphorize their generation, *An Elegy* questions and ridicules the very idea of the generation.

Repudiating the idea of the generation not only requires positioning a different grouping against it – that which consists of the narrator and *Nin* – but also disavowing one's membership within it. Earlier in the Fifth Letter, in the middle of another flashback that strikes the narrator while he writes to *Nin* in the hotel lobby cafe, he exclaims:

I always say: 'our generation.' But how the hell am I in the same generation as those people? [. . .] Like an elementary student who's mobilized to donate blood, the whole queue of them kids snaking out of the door of the blood donation vehicle. I would always detach myself from the line, go near the classmates who just stepped off the vehicle [. . .] and ask with trepidation: 'What's going on inside?' 'Does it hurt?' 'Does it last long?' They would always

---

27 This translation and all that follow are my own.

answer me, with an air of inexplicable mystery from a prideful distance: 'you'll know when you get in.' (2001, 105)

In this example, the narrator, who explains his generational outsider-status (to both *Nin* and the reader), transforms memories of elementary school into a metaphor of his alienation. After the second sentence of the passage, the third sentence enacts the transformation of memories into a metaphor of his outsiderness, with "like" signaling the beginning of the metaphor and "younger self" securing the link between the flashback and its metaphorical quality. This episode about the narrator's experience of donating blood thus simultaneously functions as a flashback and a metaphor, as blood donation is a fertile signifier for the making of generational memory.[28] The donation from elementary schoolchildren represents a voluntary spirit towards their society; united through the needle's penetration, the students' collectivity is consolidated. The narrator's apprehension towards the needle and his anxious questions amount to a desire to defer his induction into the generation; it prompts disdain from those who have already completed their rite of passage. Their cold shoulder towards the narrator is described as having an "air of inexplicable mystery": a snub given to outsiders, a gesture that completes the metaphor of the narrator's self-exclusion from his generation. By using memories of blood donation as a metaphor of his generational alienation, the narrator relinquishes his membership. In the context of the novel, then, this gesture casts doubts on whether a generation is a meaningful concept that one can write about, commemorate, and bond with others over.

External to the narrator's anxieties towards finding belonging and re-evaluating historical memories through the generation, *An Elegy* captures the way in which Luo Yijun confronts the cognitive dissonance of living in a transition period – with its political instabilities and doubts – while enjoying consumerist wealth. Many of Luo's peers are now part of the petite-bourgeoisie through their labor, age, and an economy that continued to prosper after the new millennium. In the chapter titled "Marijuana," Luo describes how membership in his generation, expressed through the prosperity they acquired through the economic booms of the 1980–1990s, appears as a segregating marker in late-capitalist Taiwan. The narrator, looking to acquire marijuana cigarettes, visits an acquaintance's home. The host, an amateur chef who studied in Italy, serves him a marijuana-seasoned course. Rather than finding what he came for, the narrator was "penetrated" by

---

28 Blood donation's worst-case scenario, the outbreak of an AIDS epidemic, is a symbolic reservoir where communities are put to the harshest test. For a fictional account of AIDS and its effect on the collective, see Yan Lianke, *Dream of Ding Village*, and Phaswane Mpe's *Welcome to Our Hillbrow: A Novel of Postapartheid South Africa.*

the chef's food, causing him to enter a state of cannabis-induced high, in which he realizes the truth of his generation:

> Living in this generation feels like being soaked in a luxurious happiness that trembles (like completely developed erogeneous zones across one's body). As if a honeyed ointment is seeping into us through the crevasses that sew together the ice-like cracks of fragments. Those whose lonely noble tastes and fine appreciations are unrelated to the ugly underbelly and various vices of this entire city. It's like being suddenly inundated by a blinding light in the subway of a foreign country . . . Like living in a temporal dysrhythmia smuggled past the international date line. (2001, 300)

The narrator's verdict on his generation is thus laid bare: living as a member of it means one can enjoy an unprecedented amount of sensory and material pleasure, akin to constant sexual arousal that suffuses one's body. Such enjoyment is pre- mised upon *class* lines, given the way the narrator describes the generation's mem- bers with "lonely noble tastes" and "fine appreciations" who are separated from the city's "ugly underbelly" and "various vices." With pleasure seeping through the "crevasses" of their fragmented bodies segregated across class in post-millennium Taiwan, for the narrator, the lifestyle of his generation now resembles "a temporal dysrhythmia." Dysrhythmia, a descriptor of the separation of life and death in *An Elegy*,[29] now reveals another side: the physical experience of dysrhythmia is a priv- ilege for those who can fly past the international date line, or those who can afford to be hit by "a blinding light in the subway of a foreign country"; a temporal phe- nomenon hence becomes the expression for class. By accumulating images and terms associated with the Taiwanese petite-bourgeoisie, this passage shows that for the narrator and in extension Luo Yijun, the generation is a discriminating concept, unavoidably and unconsciously inflected through class. But the idea of the genera- tion is still appealing, with its nostalgic invocations of belonging.

To identify with and think in generational terms thus means to become plagued by dysrhythmia in a post-transition world. *An Elegy*'s skepticism towards the generation's ability to document the memories of transition nevertheless co- incides with the fact that the book stands as Luo Yijun's generational statement in relation to his postmodernist teachers and the literary market. The novel's con- nections with Tang poetry and French symbolism,[30] its ubiquitous mentions of

---

29 Kai-lin Yang sees death as Luo's extended metaphor for the act of writing itself: "on the one hand, writing cleaves apart the "dysrhythmia" between the time of the dead and the time of the still–living . . . on the other hand, writing attempts to shorten the distance between life and death, delaying for as long as possible the true arrival of death" (2015, 151–152).
30 The novel's title is a reference to a triptych of poems by the Tang dynasty poet Yuan Zhen, *An Elegy I-III* (遣悲懷三首), as well as the Chinese translation of André Gide's 1951 *Et Nunc Manet in Te* (*Madeleine* in English).

popular culture in Taiwan, Hollywood and Japan along with the near complete absence of Taiwanese and Chinese writers point to the author's determination to avoid his immediate context. Yet Luo chose Qiu Miaojin's *Last Words from Montmartre* as the novel's partner, suggesting that other than invoking Qiu as a cipher through which to discuss time, death, and sexuality, there is another way to use the generation productively. Right before the narrator reminisces about his outing with *Nin* to a lesbian bar in the Fourth Letter, he comments on their shared interest in Osamu Taizai: "For our generation's enlightenment, too many old-timers committed suicide before our eyes [. . .] Those scenes were lifelike dreams and fantasies. Because of their verisimilitude we always mistakenly thought that we were there in person a long time ago, witnessing those performances of death in slow motion" (2001, 90). The narrator goes on to say that these writers' influence upon their generation was so strong, that they developed a sense of proximity, thinking that they "were there in person a long time ago" to witness their deaths. This intimacy comes from careful and repeated reading, since the dead writers mentioned are Yukio Mishima, Yasunori Kawabata, and Osamu Taizai, all canonical Japanese modernists. What the narrator implies is that one can form an aesthetic bond with a generational peer through these texts, while simultaneously forming intertextual links with those texts through their work. Generations don't have to be discarded, from the perspective of intertextuality: they serve as a starting point for one to develop horizontal connections, or intertextual connections exceeding the generation itself.

Spring soil for the flowers

On May 20, 2015, the supplemental section of Taiwan's *United Daily News* unveiled an online literary feature. Ambitiously titled "Our Generation," they invited over thirty famous Taiwanese and Sinophone writers to explicate what their generation meant. Luo Yijun started off by writing about his generation in January 2016 with a piece titled "To Become Spring Soil for the Flowers" (化作春泥更護花).[31] Luo concludes the piece in bullet points, mulling over what the literary achievements of his generation meant for their successors. One, because of the international influences incorporated in the works of his generation, Luo sees their work as "becoming a sort of gift that you can mold into more genetically complex, flashier and livelier

---

[31] This refers to a line of poetry written by a late-Qing intellectual, Gong Zizhen. It comes from the "Fifth Poem" of the *Yi Hai Miscellaneous Poems* (己亥雜詩), a collection of poems written in 1839.

linguistic building materials, in comparison to other species" (2016). Two, given Taiwan's size and circumstances, even though it may be difficult for writers to attain the commercial and critical heights of their counterparts in Japan, China, and the U.S., there is always happiness in reaching an understanding with the writings of others: "Once you traverse a date line whose scenery you fully understand (過了一道你理解全景的換日線), a mysterious reverberating buzz will naturally arise in your heart, and you'll say to yourself: to become the spring soil for the flowers" (2016). In the end, Luo wishes that his generation – a flower dropping its petals in the ground – would become nourishing soil for writers to come. As the boundary of the earth's arbitrary temporal system, for Luo Yijun, the International Date Line represents the polyvalent concept of dysrhythmia – the temporal and qualitative differences between the self and the other, between life and death, between different classes, and the disparity between one generation and the next. Written during Tsai Ying-wen's historic 2016 presidential victory and the Democratic Progressive Party's return to power, Luo's piece shows that the work of transitions cannot be conceived solely within the sociopolitical: it continues, slowly and messily, in the ground of the cultural.

Therefore, as a normative political concept, the 'transition period' necessarily contains four implicit meanings which may in turn be posited as questions. First, in terms of periodicity, transitions must be situated in the modern/contemporary era; whenever we speak of a 'transition,' it seldom if ever refers to regime changes or political shifts in the premodern era. Second, a 'transition period' is a shorter interim contrasted against longer periods where stability, growth, and/or repression coincide, which leads to my third point: 'transition periods' are not neutral categories – they are deeply tied to Cold War geopolitical sensibilities and the dominant ways in which we remember the period itself.[32] Hence a 'transition period' – even from our *ex post facto* temporal position – is usually conceptualized as a one-way street, a teleological progression from a seemingly less desirable system to the so-called model of liberal democracy and capitalism, but rarely the other way around – one seldom hears about a 'transition' to fascism, or to a dictatorship that does not include amongst its ruling class the 'proletariat.' Fourth and finally, the temporal and political timestamp of the 'post' in any post-transition shares valences with the 'post' in the postcolonial: as Alfred J. Lopez proclaims, the postcolonial is "certainly a response to the brute facts of colonization; but beyond that it also represents an analysis of its own relation to colonialism, a reckoning or coming-to-terms with what has happened (and is happening)

---

[32] Film and literature are always tasked to complicate and perhaps revise our ways of remembering the transition. For an example in South America, see Jessica Stites Mor (2012).

under the banner of the colonial" (3). The 'post-' therefore does not signal a clean break from the colonial, but its persistence, mutation, and resistances to it, just like how post-postmodernism gestures towards greater messiness and intensities.

This messiness of the 'post-' is precisely what characterizes Taiwan's memories of transition in Luo Yijun's work. From the 1993 short story "A Roll of Film" to the 2001 *An Elegy* published a year after Taiwan's first presidential victory of the Democratic Progressive Party, Luo's trajectory as a writer represents the qualitative difference between writing *in* the heat of the transition to writing back *on* the transition. While "A Roll of Film" directly depicts the generational conflict between the aesthetics of postmodernism and post-postmodernism alongside the sociopolitical struggles regarding the legacies of the White Terror, *An Elegy* provides a retrospective look on these clashes as memories of Taiwan's transitional times. Mediated through a dialogue with the deceased, Luo Yijun's novel shows through the concept of dysrhythmia that both the material aftermaths and the memories of Taiwan's transition era – which include the ambivalences of the cultural politics of generationality and the aesthetic debates over (post)postmodernism – proliferate in a myriad of ways that contest, complement, and contradict one another without clear resolutions. Luo's two works examined here thus provide us with a necessary reminder of literature and culture's importance towards conceptualizing periods of transitions and its memories. Post-postmodernism therefore functions as a corrective to the ironic and glib attitude postmodernism took towards the transition, since it takes the passions, ambiguities, and uncertainties of the transition in earnest, even when it refuses to produce clear-cut answers.

In this chapter, I have advanced the idea that the strongest work from or about a transition period necessarily produces aesthetic, political, and social questions regarding the very concept of transition. Luo Yijun's fiction questions the fundamental validity in which generational logic can lay claim to memories in a transition period: his works do not provide definitive answers to 'what' the transitions were, but rather, they lay out an affective roadmap to the paradoxes, contradictions, and pathways forward in the nebulous landscapes of transition and post-transition periods. Luo's writing, with its carefully captured ambivalence, its daring formal expansiveness, and its strong mixture of playfulness and melancholy deserve a place on the shelves of non-Chinese reading audiences everywhere.[33] But until that happens, we all have to live patiently with the dys-

---

33 As of 2017, Luo Yijun's 2008 *Tangut Inn* was translated into English by National Taiwan University professor Ku Ping-ta, and has won a Pen Presents award, but definite publication dates remain unclear.

rhythmia comprising the temporal gap between any original literary work and its translated offshoots.

Works cited

Berger, Mark T. *The Battle for Asia: From Decolonization to Globalization*. London: Routledge, 2004.

Brown, Annette N., et al. *When Is Transition Over?* Kalamazoo: Upjohn Institute, 1999.

Chang, Yvonne Sung-sheng. *Modernism and the Nativist Resistance: Contemporary Chinese Fiction from Taiwan*. Durham: Duke University Press, 1993.

Chang, Yvonne Sung-sheng. *Literary Culture in Taiwan: Martial Law to Market Law*. New York: Columbia University Press, 2004.

Ching, Leo. *Becoming Japanese: Colonial Taiwan and the Politics of Identity Formation*. Berkeley: University of California Press, 2001.

Ching, Leo. *Anti-Japan: The Politics of Sentiment in Postcolonial East Asia*. Durham: Duke University Press, 2019.

Derrida, Jacques. *Specters of Marx*. Trans. Peggy Kamuf. New York: Routledge, 1994.

Edmund, Jacob. "Translating Theory: Bei Dao, Pasternak, and Russian Formalism." *Chinese Poetry and Translation: Rights and Wrongs*. Ed. Maghiel van Crevel and Lucas Klein. Amsterdam: Amsterdam University Press, 2016. 135–158.

Hayot, Eric. *On Literary Worlds*. New York: Oxford University Press, 2012.

Hayot, Eric, and Rebecca L. Walkowitz. *A New Vocabulary for Global Modernism*. New York: Columbia University Press, 2016.

"Heart Rhythm and Arrythmias." *Johns Hopkins University Heart & Vascular Institute*. Johns Hopkins Medicine. https://www.hopkinsmedicine.org/heart_vascular_institute/cardiovascular_research/heart_rhythm_and_arrythmias.html (Accessed October 31, 2021).

Hirano, Katsuya, Lorenzo Veracini, and Toulouse-Antonin Roy. "Vanishing Natives and Taiwan's Settler-Colonial Unconsciousness." *Critical Asian Studies* 50.2 (2018): 196–218.

Karl, Alissa G. "Toward a Labor Theory of Generation X." *LA Review of Books* (December 9, 2020). https://lareviewofbooks.org/article/toward-a-labor-theory-of-generation-x/ (Accessed October 31, 2021).

Liao, Ping-Hui. "Postmodern Literary Discourse and Contemporary Public Culture in Taiwan." *Boundary 2* 24.3 (1997): 41–63.

Lin, Sylvia Li-chun. *Representing Atrocity in Taiwan: The 2/28 Incident and White Terror in Fiction and Film*. New York: Columbia University Press. 2007.

Linz, Juan José, and Alfred Stepan. *Problems of Democratic Transition and Consolidation*. Baltimore: Johns Hopkins University Press, 1996.

Lopez, Alfred J. *Posts and Pasts: A Theory of Postcolonialism*. Albany: SUNY Press, 2001.

Luo, Yijun. *Hongzituan* 紅字團 [The Red Ink Gang]. Taipei: Unitas, 1993.

Luo, Yijun. *Qianbeihuai* 遣悲懷 [An Elegy]. Taipei: Rye Field Publishing, 2001.

Luo, Yijun. "To Become Spring Soil for the Flowers." *Two Forgettings* (兩) https://emmasha.pixnet.net/blog/post/442855193-%E6%88%91%E5%80%91%E9%80%99%E4%B8%80%E4%BB%A3%EF%BC%9A%E4%BA%94%E5%B9%B4%E7%B4%9A%E4%BD%9C%E5%AE%B6%EF%BC%88%E4%B9%8B%E4%B8%80%EF%BC%89%E5%8C%96%E4%BD%9C%E6%98%A5%E6%B3%A5%E6%9B%B4 (Accessed October 31, 2021).

Mattlin, Mikael. *Politicized Society: The Long Shadow of Taiwan's One-Party Legacy*. Copenhagen: NIAS Press, 2011.

Mengel, Ewald, and Michela Borzaga. *Trauma, Memory, and Narrative in the Contemporary South African Novel: Essays*. Amsterdam: Brill/Rodopi, 2012.

Memorial Foundation of 228. https://www.228.org.tw/index.php (Accessed October 31, 2021).

Morita, Ken, and Yun Chen. *Transition, Regional Development and Globalization: China and Central Europe*. New Jersey: World Scientific Publishing, 2010.

Nealon, Jeffrey T. *Post-Postmodernism: Or, The Cultural Logic of Just-in-Time Capitalism*. Palo Alto: Stanford University Press, 2012.

Oliver, Kelly. *Witnessing: Beyond Recognition*. Minneapolis: University of Minnesota Press, 2001.

Shih, Shu-mei. "Is the Post- in Postsocialism the Post- in Posthumanism?" *Social Text* 30 (*China and the Human*) 110.1 (2012): 27–50.

Stites Mor, Jessica. *Transition Cinema: Political Filmmaking and the Argentine Left Since 1968*. Pittsburgh: University of Pittsburgh Press, 2012.

Qiu, Miaojin. 邱妙津. *Mengmate Yishu* 蒙馬特遺書. Taipei: Unitas, 1996.

Qiu, Miaojin. *Last Words from Montmartre*. Trans. Ari L. Heinrich. New York: New York Review of Books, 2014.

Tang, Xiaobing. "On the Concept of Taiwan Literature." *Modern China* 25.2 (1999): 379–422.

Wang, David Der-wei. "My Decadent Obscenity and Sadness: Luo Yijun's Death Narration." In *Qianbeihuai* 遺悲懷 (*An Elegy*). Taipei: Rye Field Publishing, 2001.

Wang, Han-ping, and Jonathan Chin. "Tangut Inn Translation Praised." *Taipei Times* (June 29, 2017). https://www.taipeitimes.com/News/taiwan/archives/2017/06/29/2003673531 (Accessed October 31, 2021).

Yang, Kai-lin. 楊凱麟. *Shuxie Yu Ying Xiang: Faguo Si Xiang, Zai Di Shi jian* 書寫與影像：法國思想, 在地實踐 (*Écriture et Image)*. Taipei: Lianjing Publishing, 2015.

Ying, Li-hua. *Historical Dictionary of Modern Chinese Literature*. Lanham: The Scarecrow Press, 2010.

Zhang, Xudong. *Postsocialism and Cultural Politics: China in the Last Decade of the Twentieth Century*. Durham: Duke University Press, 2008.

Kylie Thomas

Refusing Transitional Time: Re-opening the Unresolved Truth and Reconciliation Commission Cases and the Future of Memory in Postapartheid South Africa

Abstract: This chapter focuses on the South African Truth and Reconciliation Commission (TRC) and its aftermath, in particular, on the ongoing struggle to prosecute apartheid-era perpetrators who either did not testify before the Commission or who were not granted amnesty. Since 2003, when the final TRC report was released, none of the perpetrators responsible for gross violations of human rights committed during apartheid has been held to account. The unresolved cases of activists who were detained, tortured, and murdered by the Security Police have been systematically suppressed for political reasons. In 2017, as a result of campaigning by civil society organizations and family members of those who were killed, the inquest into the death of anti-apartheid activist, Ahmed Timol, was re-opened. The verdict in the 2017 inquest found that Timol, who allegedly committed suicide while held in police detention in 1971, was in fact tortured and murdered by the Security Police. The finding in this case not only opens the possibility for prosecutions in cases of gross violations of human rights, but provides a critical opportunity to recalibrate what I term 'postapartheid transitional time.' The re-opening of the unresolved TRC cases has the potential to radically shift how people think about what apartheid was, how it continues to affect the present, and how people experience and understand impunity and injustice.

Introduction

> only the ignorant
> think that the martyrs are dead
> (Mphutlane wa Bofelo 2018)

The South African Truth and Reconciliation Commission process, which aimed to shed light on the violence committed during apartheid and to bring about a process

Acknowledgments: I am grateful to Imtiaz Cajee and the Ahmed Timol Family Trust for allowing me to reproduce images from their collection. Thanks to Ksenia Robbe, Emile Engel, Özgür Atlagan, and Alastair, Sophie and Jemma Douglas. This research has been supported by the KNAW Academy Institutes Fund.

of national reconciliation, has been widely regarded as a model to be adapted and used in other places where there have been violations of human rights committed on a large scale. The Truth and Reconciliation Commission (TRC) convened public hearings between 1996 and 1998 and investigated human rights abuses perpetrated between March 1, 1960 and December 31, 1993.[1] The Commission made it possible for many South Africans to speak about their experiences, to hear the testimonies of victims, and to learn the painful details about some of the traumatic events of the past.

One of the most controversial aspects of the Commission's work was a clause known as 'Amnesty for Truth.' Those perpetrators who came forward to testify before the Commission and who disclosed the full truth about their deeds, could be granted amnesty from prosecution. As a safeguard against future impunity, those who were denied amnesty, or who did not present themselves to testify before the Commission, would be liable for prosecution. However, since 2003, when the final TRC report was released, none of the perpetrators responsible for crimes committed during apartheid has been held to account. The unresolved cases of activists who were detained, tortured, and murdered by the Security Police have been systematically suppressed for political reasons. In 2015, the reasons for the state's failure to pursue the TRC cases were exposed, when Thembi Nkadimeng sought to compel the National Prosecuting Authority (NPA) to prosecute the Security Branch officers accused of torturing and murdering her sister, Nokuthula Simelane, an anti-apartheid activist who was abducted in 1983.[2] Although the family of Simelane had been told on numerous occasions that the case was being investigated, it emerged that 'political interference' ensured that the matter was blocked. The advocates responsible for the case were dismissed from their posts.[3]

On February 5, 2019, ten of the commissioners who served on the South African Truth and Reconciliation Commission wrote a letter to Cyril Ramaphosa, the President of South Africa, calling for a Commission of Inquiry to be established to

---

1 As Madeleine Fullard (2004) notes, the decision to use the date of the Sharpeville Massacre, which took place on March 21, 1960, rather than 1948 – the date of the founding of the apartheid state, to delineate the timeframe for the hearings signalled that the focus of the TRC was on physical rather than structural forms of violence. This meant that for the most part, the TRC did not engage with the policy of apartheid itself as a crime against humanity. On the establishment of the TRC, see Sachs 1999.

2 For further details about this case, see Sarkin 2015.

3 The affidavits submitted by Advocates Vusi Pikoli and Anton Ackerman as part of the Simelane case describe how they were prevented from pursuing these cases and were dismissed from their posts by former President Thabo Mbeki: http://www.southernafricalitigationcentre.org/wp-content/uploads/2017/08/Vusi-Pikoli-Affidavit-Simelane.pdf and http://www.southernafricalitigationcentre.org/wp-content/uploads/2017/08/Anton-Ackermann-Affidavit.pdf.

investigate why the more than 300 cases of gross violations of human rights committed under apartheid that were meant to be investigated after the TRC drew to a close, have not been pursued. "Post the TRC," they argue, "the story of post-apartheid justice in South Africa is a shameful story of terrible neglect. Both the SAPS [South Africa Police Service] and the NPA [National Prosecuting Authority] colluded with political forces to ensure the deliberate suppression of the bulk of apartheid era cases." (Sooka and Ntsebeza 2019) In their letter, the former TRC Commissioners argue that:

> The failure to investigate and prosecute those who were not amnestied represents a deep betrayal of all those who participated in good faith in the TRC process. It completely undermines the very basis of South Africa's historic transition. The failure stands as a betrayal of victims who have been waiting for the criminal justice process to take its course and has added considerably to their trauma. Indeed, the policy or approach to allow perpetrators to escape justice adds insult to the suffering endured by victims.
>
> Above all, the failure stands as a betrayal of all South Africans who embraced the spirit of truth and reconciliation in order to move beyond the bitterness of the past. The failure is wholly inconsistent with the spirit and purpose of South Africa's constitutional and statutory design in dealing with crimes of the past. (Sooka and Ntsebeza 2019)

The Commissioners' letter serves as a reminder that the findings of the TRC were intended as the beginning rather than as the end-point of engaging with the history of apartheid in pursuit of justice. At the time the TRC hearings drew to a close, no-one could have anticipated that it would take so long for the investigations into cases of torture, murder and enforced disappearances to begin, nor that justice itself would be perpetually deferred. The letter, sent 16 years after the final TRC report was completed, also raises the question of why a response to the failure of the state to prosecute these cases has been so slow to emerge.

In this chapter, I seek to trace the implications of this time delay for what I term, 'political time' and how this affects the meaning of justice in South Africa in the aftermath of apartheid. I focus in particular on the murder of anti-apartheid activist Ahmed Timol on October 27, 1971, the inquest into his death conducted in 1972, and the landmark judgment in the re-opened inquiry delivered on October 12, 2017. I argue that the re-opening of the inquest into the murder of Ahmed Timol interrupts 'transitional time' (the suspended time after the past and before the future), and returns us to political time (the time of action), making it possible to chart a different course in the present.

The 2017 verdict delivered by Judge Mothle overturned the findings of the 1972 inquest that found that no one was to blame for Timol's death and affirmed what the Timol family had maintained all along – that Ahmed Timol did not commit suicide but was murdered by members of the Security Branch of the South African

Police after being interrogated and tortured.[4] The Timol family waited for justice for precisely as many years (1971–2017) that the apartheid regime held power (1948–1994). It took 46 years for the truth regarding Timol's murder to be recognized in a court of law, and what is perhaps most difficult to comprehend is how it was possible that 23 of those years were passed *after* apartheid's legislative end.

Post-traumatic transitional time

The re-opening of the inquest into the Timol case, and the return of the events surrounding his murder in the present, fractures the hegemony of postapartheid transitional time. The teleological ideal implicit in the notion of transition is undone, as the re-opening of the case demands that we recognize the relation between the time of Timol's murder in the 1970s, the time of the TRC in the 1990s, and the current time. In this way, the case exposes what I am terming the 'dysynchrony' of South African society post-apartheid, literally a place where time does not operate in a synchronous way and metaphorically, adapting the medical term, a place where the activation of different parts of the heart are improperly synchronized and where auditory stimuli are not processed synchronously. A country that, were it a human body, could be diagnosed with both a neurological and cardiological condition that impairs its ability to listen and to feel, one ear stone-deaf and the other filled with the ceaseless voices of the dead.

In December 2014, newspaper reports revealed that an auction house in South Africa was offering the autopsy records of murdered anti-apartheid activists, Steve Biko and Ahmed Timol, up for sale (Whittles 2014). The opening bidding price was to be R70000-R100000 for the Biko records and R20000 for the Timol records. In the 1980s, the forensic pathologist who had been hired by the Timol and Biko families, Dr Jonathan Gluckman, handed the autopsy records to his private secretary, Maureen Steele, for safekeeping. Steele died in 2011, and the documents were being sold on behalf of her children, Clive and Susan Steele, who apparently had not thought of what the sale of these records would mean to the Biko and Timol families, nor about who really owned them and whether they had the right to sell them. In fact, after the Timol and Biko families won their case to interdict the sale of the documents, the Steele's went so far as to insist that Biko's

---

4 The judgment delivered by Judge Mothle can be accessed in full here: https://www.ahmedti mol.co.za/wp-content/uploads/2019/01/Judgment-THE-RE-OPENED-INQUEST-INTO-THE-DEATH-OF-AHMED-ESSOP-TIMOL.pdf.

son, Nkosinathi Biko, apologize to them for insinuating that the autopsy records had been stolen (Pillay 2014).

The failure on the part of the Steele's to understand not only the symbolic weight of the autopsy records but also their significance in a juridical sense reveals something of the dyssynchrony that characterizes the transitional postapartheid state. In the minds of the white children of an elderly woman who died a natural death, the autopsy records of people who had been killed more than thirty years before, belonged to a time long past. In a mercenary sense, they were clearly aware of the value of the documents, and sought to profit from their sale. For them apartheid clearly is no more, a closed chapter that is safely behind them, and it is for this reason that the auction house could describe Biko's autopsy record as "a unique document of the Struggle era of great historical importance" ("High Court Halts Auction" 2014). For the families of the murdered activists, the value of the autopsy records far exceeds their historical significance, for although Biko and Timol were murdered more than forty years ago, no one has been held to account for their deaths, and the cases remain unresolved. In the press release issued by the Steve Biko Foundation on behalf of the Biko and Timol families after they learned that the Steele's refused to return the autopsy records to the family members, Timol's nephew, Imtiaz Cajee, states:

> We believe that this is a matter that is not only of relevance to our respective families, but one which has a bearing on all South Africans. The Timol Family is united with the Biko Family and the Steve Biko Foundation to ensure that Clive and Susan Steele hand these documents over to us. In life, both Ahmed Timol and Steve Biko suffered indignities that were gross violations of their rights. Together, we will ensure that these indignities do not continue in death. (Cajee 2014).

For the Timol and Biko families the murders that took place in the 1970s are not situated in the distant past but continue to determine the shape of the present.

On October 27, 1971 the parents of anti-apartheid activist Ahmed Timol were informed that their son had committed suicide by throwing himself out of the window of room 1026 of what was then known as John Vorster Square, the police headquarters in central Johannesburg. Timol was a member of the South African Communist Party and a well-loved teacher who worked at Roodepoort Indian High School, not far from Johannesburg. Timol's family were convinced that he was murdered by the Security Police and this view was widely accepted by everyone who opposed the apartheid state at the time. Writing under his pen-name 'Frank Talk,' the Black Consciousness Movement activist and political thinker, Steve Biko, expressed his disdain for the patently fabricated claims made by the Security Police about the events that led to Timol's death while in police custody: "The late Ahmed Timol was "prevented from 'dashing' through the door but it was found impossible to stop him from 'jumping', through the 10th floor window of Vorster Square to his death." (Biko [Frank Talk] 1972).[5] Biko's article appeared in the widely-circulated newsletter of the South African Students Organization in early 1972, just a short while before the African National Congress (ANC) submitted a memorandum to the decolonization committee of the United Nations calling for South Africa's expulsion from the organization and for the denunciation of apartheid as a crime against humanity. The memorandum asserts what was common knowledge at the time – Timol's death was not the result of suicide but of murder: "The murder of Ahmed Timol at the hands of the Security Police on the now notorious 10th Floor of John Vorster Square Police Headquarters is still fresh in our minds" (African National Congress, 3). A short time later, at the inquest held in 1972, Magistrate JJL De Villiers ruled that no one was responsible for Timol's death.

In spite of the certainty of Timol's family that he was tortured and killed in detention, and although this view was shared by many South Africans, not one of the Security Police officers involved in his arrest and interrogation came forward to offer information about the case after the end of apartheid when the Truth and Reconciliation Commission proceedings began. Nor did anyone ask for amnesty for their part in Timol's murder, who, in 1971, was the twenty-second person to die in detention at the hands of the Security Police since the introduction of detention without trial, and the seventh person to have allegedly committed suicide while in police custody.[6]

The Timol family's lengthy quest for justice is the subject of Enver Samuel's documentary film, *Someone to Blame: The Ahmed Timol Inquest – A 46 Year Wait for the Truth* (2018), which begins with a black and white image of a row of closed doors along an empty corridor. The camera moves into one of the rooms and focuses on the metal instruments used to perform autopsies, and the figure of a person wearing a facemask and lab coat is shown leaving the room, closing the door. The effect is that the viewer is left behind inside the mortuary, one that represents the room where the autopsy on Ahmed Timol's tortured body was per-

---

5 Steve Biko was arrested and detained in August 1977 and tortured and murdered by the Security Police on 12 September 1977. The police claimed that Biko died as a result of head injuries sustained during what they described as a 'scuffle', and no one was held accountable for his murder.
6 In 1961, the General Laws Amendment Act made it possible for the police to detain people for up to 12 days without trial. In 1963, a law was passed that made provision for 90-days detention and this was doubled in 1965 when the Criminal Procedure Amendment Act, commonly known as the '180-day law,' was passed. In 1967, the Terrorism Act was enacted and allowed for indefinite detention without trial.

formed. The voiceover, which is spoken in English, inflected with the Afrikaans accent of the judge who presided over the 1972 inquest, narrates the findings of the case:

> The identity of the deceased is Ahmed Essop Timol, an Asian male, 29 years old, a born South African, teacher by profession. Date of death, 27 October 1971. Cause or probable cause of death: the deceased died because of serious brain damage and loss of blood when he jumped out of the window of room 1026 of John Vorster Square and fell to the ground on the Southern side of the building. He committed suicide. No living person is responsible for his death. Murder, in view of the testimony given, and even considering it, is ludicrous. – Findings of Magistrate J.J.L. De Villiers, at the 1972 inquest into the death of Ahmed Timol, Johannesburg Magistrate's Court. (*Someone to Blame*)

Watching this chilling opening sequence, one can imagine Imtiaz Cajee, keeping vigil over the body of his uncle, unable to exit this horrifying place, trapped in time. For the Timol family, liberation did not come in 1994, nor did it come at the TRC hearings, where Hawa Timol testified about her son's murder. At that time, Cajee vowed to seek justice for his family and in spite of the challenges he has faced, has not given up. Cajee has refused to allow the event of his uncle's murder to be assimilated into the chronology of postapartheid transitional time within which the past progressively recedes from the present. He has effected this not only by assembling all the materials that constitute the memory of Ahmed Timol – photographs, testimonies, news reports, legal documents – but through his own embodied memory and his physical presence in legal proceedings as representative of the Timol family.

Through his extensive research, Cajee has collected a large number of documents and newspaper articles relating to his uncle's murder, all of which he has made available online, and has also published two books about the long struggle his family has faced.[7] As Noha Aboueldahab notes, "this landmark case illustrates the significant impact of both documentation and advocacy in challenging so-called established truths, even more than four decades later" (2018, 9).

Someone to Blame traces the events that led up to the re-opening of the inquest, and through interviews and footage of the 2017 court proceedings, conveys the magnitude of this event for the Timol family. Cajee is shown on his way to the re-opened inquest, and driving between Pretoria and Johannesburg, he describes how he was trying to visualize the day in April 1972 when his maternal grandparents went to the first inquest, just four months after the murder of their son. As he relives their journey to the court to attend the inquest in 2017, Cajee quite literally re-members the pain of his grandparents. Like many trauma survivors for

---

7 See Cajee 2005 and Cajee 2020. See also http://www.ahmedtimol.co.za.

whom the present is overdetermined by the past and who seek a way to heal from what they have endured, Cajee sought to go back in time and to change the past. In psychoanalytic terms, this process of renarrativization takes place within the psyche and enacts a form of symbolic repair. In Cajee's case, the immense effort he has expended in resisting the paralysis of transitional time has resulted in a historic return.

Writing of the way in which the memory of the Nakba is mobilized in Israel/Palestine, Nadim Rouhana and Areej Sabbagh-Khoury develop the concept of the 'return of history,' which, they argue, "is not merely a process in which people simply "re/discover" historical "truths," facts, or evidence and reconstruct them within the present context, as they do with collective memory. It is also a process in which historical memories – those that were silenced but never forgotten – are transformed into political assets" (2019, 3).[8] The significance of the court's findings in 2017 for the Timol family cannot be overstated – Cajee has devoted his life to the pursuit of justice and in many ways, it is a deeply personal quest. At the same time, the finding in the Timol matter and the possibility that those responsible for human rights violations under apartheid will be tried in criminal courts is of enormous significance for the country as a whole. Through his refusal to allow the murder of his uncle to be consigned to the past, Cajee has tied a knot in time and has 're-turned history,' recalibrating political time. In this sense, the Ahmed Timol case is a great victory for all those who suffered under apartheid and who had given up hope of ever attaining justice.

As I argue below, the re-opening of the Timol case restores the names and experiences of people who were detained and tortured to public memory. At the same time, the case serves as an important reminder of the lengthy time-span of impunity in South Africa and raises questions not only about the past but about the present. The re-opening of the case returns us not only to the 1970s but to the beginning of the negotiated transition and to the time of the TRC. Through the re-opening of the case, the names and faces of people who committed atrocities under apartheid have also re-emerged, and with them a reminder of how so many people responsible for terrible deeds were reabsorbed into society, as if they had never done anything wrong at all. This re-opens the contentious matter of amnesty and all those who seemingly disappeared at the end of apartheid, all those who refused to tell the truth at the TRC or who refused to come forward and be held accountable for their crimes. Judge Mothle ordered that Joao 'Jan' Rodrigues be charged with Timol's murder and with defeating and/ or obstructing the administration of justice. In response, Rodrigues sought a permanent stay of

---

8 For my own articulation of the concept of re-turning history, see Thomas 2018.

prosecution that, if it were granted, would apply not only to him, but to all former Security Branch and former state agents who would effectively be exempted from being held to account for their actions in the future. Following the perverse logic that can characterize legal procedures, Rodrigues' defense argued that a trial against him would be unfair due to the time that has lapsed since Timol's murder. In an article about Rodrigues' attempt to evade being tried in court, Cajee is cited as saying, "[. . .] when Rodrigues faces the court on Thursday for a permanent stay of prosecution, he will be carrying on his shoulders the hopes and fears of hundreds or thousands of surviving policemen, soldiers and politicians who have until now not been held accountable for apartheid crimes" (Venter 2019). At a political moment in which the hope of justice seemed less possible than ever, the recognition of apartheid not only as a series of violations of human rights but as a crime against humanity has returned to public debate.[9]

This is one of the important outcomes of the re-opening of the Timol case – it deepens public knowledge and understanding of the many cases of people who were tortured and murdered under apartheid, and it serves as a reminder that those responsible for committing atrocities have almost without exception evaded responsibility and have never been held accountable for their crimes.[10] More than this, in most cases, those who perpetrated these acts have never been publicly identified, nor have they been subject to the scrutiny and censure one would expect in the aftermath of historical injustice. In a similar way to those who committed crimes as part of the National Socialist regime in Germany, almost all of the apartheid-era perpetrators have been absorbed into civilian life and have not been punished. The re-opening of the TRC cases and the possibility that perpetrators will be tried for committing crimes against humanity has the potential to radically shift how people think about what apartheid was, how it continues to affect the present, and how people experience and understand impunity and injustice.

---

9 See Yates 2018, York 2019, Smith 2020.

10 In 1996 former colonel in the South African Police Force and commander of the death squad based at Vlakplaas, Eugene de Kock, was denied amnesty and sentenced to 212 years in prison. He was released on parole in 2015. Adriaan Vlok, the former minister of law and order received a ten-year suspended sentence for ordering the Security Police to murder Reverend Frank Chikane in 2007. These are the only two convictions of apartheid-era perpetrators that have taken place.

Remembering the monster

> My cousin-brother Matthews Marwale Mabelane died at the hands of the police at the John Vorster Square Police Headquarters in February 1977. It was claimed that he jumped from the notorious tenth floor of the building and died instantly. Seeing that the stories of the 10th floor jumps were never and will not be true, we want to know why the killers are not coming out and apologise for their deeds. Such tricks by the perpetrators of those atrocities are really infuriating because these killers will only start talking about these things immediately they are exposed – otherwise they will keep quiet. Do they really think that their victims will just forget about the hardships they caused them? Or do they think that the people are still afraid of them hence talking about their deeds would cause them some more troubles like in the past? The family and relatives are very upset about the silence of the killers of Matthews. Time is running out now. Let them come out and tell the story. We also want to see them, how they look like, whether they are real human beings and have families, children, relatives and friends. (Entry by Mr K.C. Mabelane in the TRC Register of Reconciliation, September 10, 1998)

"Time is running out now," Mr K. C. Mabelane wrote in an entry, four years after the legislative end of apartheid, in the Register of Reconciliation, an initiative that that invited people who did not testify at the TRC to share their stories as well as to apologize for the wrongs of apartheid. The register indicates that the timespan for collective reckoning and atonement was brief – it begins in December 1997 and the final entry is dated December 2000.[11] Matthews Marwale Mabelane was 22 years old when he was detained by the Security Police. He was held in detention for 25 days and the police claimed that he climbed onto a window ledge and fell to his death from the tenth floor of John Vorster Square on February 15, 1977. The case remains unresolved, and is one of the cases that may be re-opened in the wake of the findings of the 2017 Timol inquest.

The testimony of anti-apartheid activists who were detained by the Security Police at the same time as Timol, and whose descriptions of the torture they suffered provided evidence of the routine practices used in interrogations at that time, were pivotal in the re-opening of the Timol case. The experiences of Salim Essop and of Dilshad Jhetam were used to cast light on what Timol himself must have endured, and their testimonies, which were not heard at the TRC, were told for the first time in court as a result of the re-opening of the Timol case.

It was as a result of the new evidence presented through the testimony of Essop, who had been arrested with Ahmed Timol in 1971, that the case was re-opened by the National Prosecuting Authority. The torture Essop was subjected to

---

11 The collection of statements forms part of the website of the Truth and Reconciliation Commission and can be accessed here: http://www.justice.gov.za/trc/ror/page16.htm.

was so severe that after being assaulted for four days he was close to death and he was incarcerated for months in a prison hospital. Deeply traumatized by his experiences at the hands of the Security Branch, Essop did not appear before the TRC. Convinced by Imtiaz Cajee of the importance of his testimony, his account proved critical in the re-opening of the Timol case: "My story had to be told so that in a way my story would mirror what he had experienced", Essop explains. Essop described in court how the Security Police perceived torture to be like a sport, and explained that they kicked him and shocked him on his thigh until his hair began to fall out, "tufts of my hair were coming out, I could see my hair on the ground . . .". In his testimony, Essop described having seen Ahmed Timol, who could not stand on his own, being dragged along a passageway by members of the Security Branch (Tolsi 2017).

The testimony of people who were detained and tortured leads not only to the names of perpetrators and provides evidence of the human rights abuses for which individual members of the Security Police are responsible, but also to the names and stories of other political activists.[12] The claims made by Security Police officers regarding detainees who allegedly jumped to their deaths through the windows of the tenth floor of John Vorster Square have been proved untrue by the testimonies of people who survived being tortured. Anti-apartheid activist Abdulhay Jassat relates how, after he was tortured by Security Policemen, they asked him if he wanted to escape and then seized him and took him to a window:

> They lifted me by my shoulders and pushed me head first out of the window. All you see is concrete. There is no one around at that time as it was about 2am. They then put two chairs next to me, a police officer on each one, and they pushed me out and held me by my ankles. Every now and again, they would ask if I was going to speak, but you can't speak, you're dangling there and all you see is concrete. Then the one guy would let go of your ankle, and you think that you're gone. And while he makes a grab for your ankle again, the other one let's go. This went on for quite a while. Now if they miscalculate, you're gone, you fall three floors down. That is what they did to Babla Saloojee at Grey's Building . . . as they did with (Ahmed) Timol, who they threw from the tenth floor of John Vorster Square." (qtd. in Vadi 2018, 12)

Jassat's account reveals how his own experience was affected by his knowledge of how Saloojee and Timol were murdered and his own experience serves as evidence of what they endured. The testimonies of detainees like Essop, Jhetam and Jassat provide evidence of how the memory of what they suffered is retained in their bodies. Their detailed accounts expose the sharp contrast between those

---

12 For further information about people detained and tortured at John Vorster Square see https://artsandculture.google.com/exhibit/detention-without-trial-in-john-vorstersquare/gQ-1o9MM.

who were tortured and who, try as they might, can never forget, and those who tortured them, who claim not to remember anything at all.

The re-opening of the Timol case provided an opportunity for those Security Branch officers implicated in the murder of Ahmed Timol to disclose the truth about what had happened more than 40 years before. The failure on the part of apartheid-era perpetrators to come forward and testify at the TRC significantly undermined the work of the Commission:

> It is the view of the Truth and Reconciliation Commission (the Commission) that the spirit of generosity and reconciliation enshrined in the founding Act was not matched by those at whom it was mainly directed. Despite amnesty provisions extending to criminal and civil charges, the white community often seemed either indifferent or plainly hostile to the work of the Commission, and certain media appear to have actively sought to sustain this indifference and hostility. With rare individual exceptions, the response of the former state, its leaders, institutions and the predominant organs of civil society of that era, was to hedge and obfuscate. Few grasped the olive branch of full disclosure. (TRC Report 1999)

In 2017, several of the men who interrogated Timol had already died and only three remaining Security Branch members could be traced, Joao 'Jan' Rodrigues, Neville Els and Seth Sons. The hope that they would tell the truth in order, as Howard Varney put it to Neville Els in his questions to him at the re-opened inquest, to "help the Timol family to find closure" was clearly misplaced. "I cannot remember that, I cannot recall" was the refrain that ran through the responses of both Els and Sons, a criminal amnesia that alone should indict them (Masilela 2017).

In 2017, the Security Branch officers chose to remain in 1972 and stuck to the fabricated version of events that was put before the apartheid-era inquest. Two versions of the same image that form part of the archive of materials Imtiaz Cajee has collected in support of the case against the Security Branch officers responsible for the death of Timol provide a concise visual record of the lie they constructed about how Timol was killed – at one and the same time pathetic and horrifying (Figures 1 and 2).

The photograph of the man standing at the window from which the Security Police alleged Ahmed Timol fell to his death was published in the newspaper *Die Transvaler* and included alongside an article entitled "Laste Ure van Timol Beskryf" Description of Timol's Final Hours (*Die Transvaler*, 1972b). The article cites Captain Johannes Hendrik Gloy, who is at pains to assert that Timol was well-treated by the Security police: "He made some requests that we met, for instance to brush his teeth and to go and wash." The reporter goes on to write that, "Die middag van sy dood het hy nog n koppie koffie saam met sy ondervragers geniet" [On the afternoon of his death he enjoyed another cup of coffee with his interrogators] (*Die Transvaler*, 1972b).

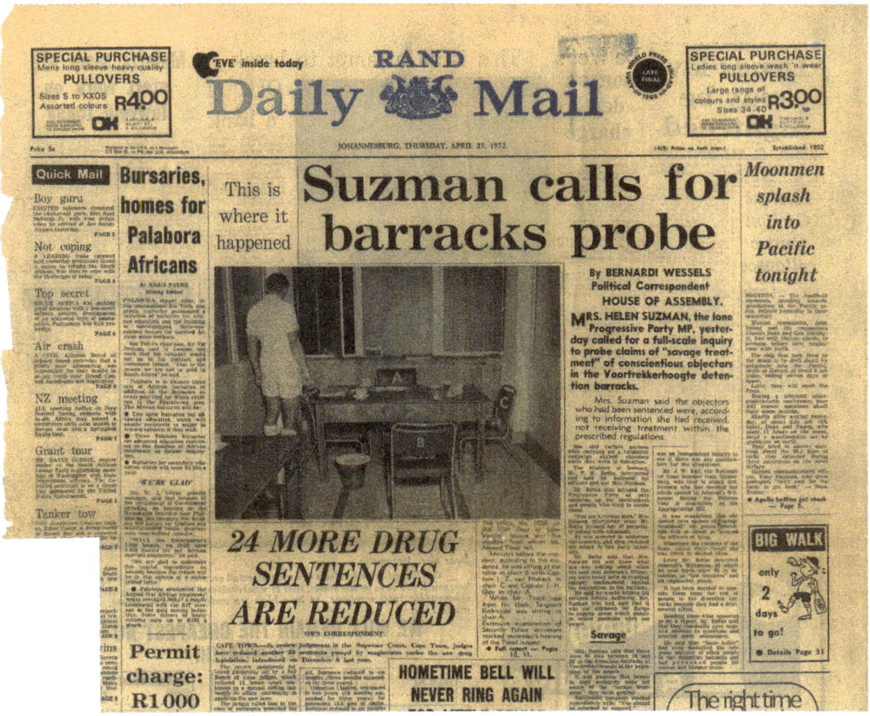

SPECIAL PURCHASE
Mens long sleeve heavy quality
PULLOVERS
Sizes S to XXOS
Assorted colours R4.00
OK

'EVE' inside today

RAND
Daily Mail

SPECIAL PURCHASE
Ladies long sleeve wash 'n wear
PULLOVERS
Large range of colours and styles R3.00
Sizes 34-40
OK

JOHANNESBURG, THURSDAY, APRIL 27, 1972.

Quick Mail

Boy guru

Not coping

Top secret

Air crash

NZ meeting

Grant tour

Tanker tow

Bursaries, homes for Palabora Africans

This is where it happened

Suzman calls for barracks probe

By BERNARDI WESSELS
Political Correspondent
HOUSE OF ASSEMBLY.

MRS. HELEN SUZMAN, the lone Progressive Party MP, yesterday called for a full-scale inquiry to probe claims of "savage treatment" of conscientious objectors in the Voortrekkerhoogte detention barracks.

Mrs. Suzman said the objectors who had been sentenced were, according to information she had received, not receiving treatment within the prescribed regulations.

Savage

Moonmen splash into Pacific tonight

24 MORE DRUG SENTENCES ARE REDUCED

Permit charge: R1 000

HOMETIME BELL WILL NEVER RING AGAIN

BIG WALK
only 2 days to go!

The right time

Figure 1: The caption included with the image reads: "This Is Where It Happened. The office No. 1026 on the 10th floor of John Vorster Square and the window from which Mr Ahmed Timol fell. Minutes before the incident, according to the evidence, he was sitting at the table in chair B with Captain J.Z van Niekerk in chair C and Captain J.H Gloy in chair A. When Mr Timol rose from his chair, Sergeant Rodrigues was sitting in chair A. Extensive examination of Security Police witnesses marked yesterday's hearing of the Timol inquest." (*Rand Daily Mail*, 1972). Image courtesy of the Ahmed Timol Family Trust.

The three cups of coffee Rodrigues ostensibly brought in on a tray and served to Timol and his interrogators in Room 1026 are visible on the table and desk. The man looking out of the window is Rodrigues himself, pictured from behind, looking at the open window, as if in disbelief at the dramatic scene he has just witnessed. This photograph was used to assert the veracity of the account given by the Security Branch, an image that so deliberately seeks to conceal evidence of torture that it inadvertently depicts what Arendt terms 'the banality of evil' (Arendt, [1963], 2006).

In the reopened inquest the lies told by the Security Police were finally accepted as untrue, and although this served to confirm what was already widely

'n Foto van die kantoor op die tiende verdieping van John Vorsterplein waar die man na die foto kyk, is die venster waardeur Timol na bewering gespring het. Timol het op stoel B gesit terwyl

Figure 2: A second version of the same image appeared in *Die Transvaler*, Thursday, April 27, 1972. The caption, written in Afrikaans, translates as follows: "A photograph of the office on the 10th floor of John Vorster Square from where Timol fell to his death. The open window at which the man in the photo is looking, is the window through which Timol allegedly jumped. Timol sat on chair B while . . ." (*Die Transvaler*, 1972a). Image courtesy of the Ahmed Timol Family Trust.

known, the validation by the court and the possibility that those implicated in the murder would be tried, constitutes one of the most significant moments in South African history. The withholding of the truth in the many other cases of violations of human rights committed under apartheid continues to have considerable force, a force that goes beyond the need for closure in each individual case. The Timol case makes it possible to recognize the connection between the lies told by the Security Branch officers in service to the apartheid state and the grand lie of apartheid itself, the claim to white supremacy and the legitimation of a system that was itself a crime against humanity. That those who know most about the torture and murder that took place under apartheid continue to lie about these events exposes the radical dyssynchrony of the postapartheid state. Postapartheid transitional time insists that we are all occupy the time of transition that has a blurry beginning and no precise end, a time before the time of true liberation in which everyone would not only be free, but in which there would be houses, security and comfort for all. Between the two points of transition and liberation is the continuous present, a time in which time is on endless repeat and the possibility of addressing the challenges bequeathed to us by the past have come to seem insurmountable, their enormity serving as a useful excuse for inaction in the present. In order for there to be justice, the erasures effected by transitional time have to cease. In the South African context, it is impunity that keeps the hands of transitional time ticking, and at the same time, locked in place.

Apartheid: Crime against humanity

The landmark verdict in the Timol case can be understood as an act that restores something of the deep loss of faith in the law South Africans suffered under apartheid. At the same time, this case raises the question not only of why it has taken so long for justice to be served, but of what justice in the aftermath of apartheid means. This is to ask not only about the timeframe within which justice should or can be done but about what form justice should take. In indicting Rodrigues for the murder of Timol, the court recognizes individual wrongdoing, but fails to indict the system of which the Security Police formed part. Recognising apartheid as a crime against humanity would mean indicting those who enforced the system itself and not only those directly implicated in individual violations of human rights. As Suren Pillay argues:

> If we wish to think beyond the individualizing move that the TRC makes, we would need to reconsider this violence in relation to apartheid. We will need to think about how this violence relates to the law itself since apartheid was a legal regime. And we would need to think about how this violence – orphaned by both law and the official political narrative – relates to the constitution of political community in a society with a colonial genealogy. (2011, 44)

One of the features of the apartheid state, was the significant place accorded to the judicial system and the 'rule of law'. In a similar way to the passing of the Nuremberg Laws in Nazi Germany, apartheid was brought into being through a slew of legislation. The apartheid system operated through the fetishization of the law and a simultaneous disregard for justice (under apartheid the courts were used to enforce the oppressive rule of the state while at the same time insisting that there was no pretence involved, and that events like the Treason Trial, The Rivonia Trial and inquests into the deaths of people who died in detention were all conducted within the bounds of the law). At the same time, and as the TRC report reveals, "Evidence placed before the Commission indicates, however, that from the late 1970s, senior politicians – as well as police, national intelligence and defense force leaders – developed a strategy to deal with opposition to the government. This entailed, among other actions, the unlawful killing, within and beyond South Africa, of people whom they perceived as posing a significant challenge to the state's authority" (TRC Report 1998, 213). The report goes on to state that "Killing is the most extreme human rights violation. Any legally constituted state that executes people outside of its own existing legal framework enters the realm of criminality and must, from that point on, be regarded as unlawful" (1998, 213). Framed in this way, it is extra-judicial killings that constitute the illegality of apartheid and that serve to render the state 'unlawful.' However, what the Timol case shows is how the apparatus of the law was manipulated to ensure that in spite of the widespread recognition that the apartheid state was a criminal state, there was effectively no outside of apartheid's 'existing legal framework' and no matter what atrocities were committed, these could be integrated into the system.

"Can we apply the same principle that is applied to a governmental apparatus in which crime and violence are exceptions and borderline cases to a political order in which crime is legal and the rule?", Hannah Arendt writes in relation to Germany under National Socialism (Arendt, [1963], 2003, 382). Under apartheid torture and impunity did not merely infest the criminal justice system, they were integral to the workings of the system of apartheid as a whole. Understanding apartheid as a crime against humanity is to recognize the injustice and systemic violence of apartheid itself, rather than reducing fifty-years of state-sanctioned racist hatred to a series of corrupt and criminal acts perpetrated within a system that was otherwise just. In their submission to the court in opposition to Rodrigues' bid for a stay of prosecution, advocates Salim Nakhjavani and Bonita Meyersfeld of the Southern Africa Litigation Center (SALC) argue that:

> Timol was killed as a result of a system that committed acts of racial discrimination, mass violence and that murdered in the name of protecting minority interests. This makes the murder of Ahmed Timol one of the most serious crimes that can be prosecuted in domestic and international law. Therefore, the submission by SALC seeks a legal characterisation that includes the particular social and political context which requires an indictment for crimes against humanity. (Kisla 2019)

SALC's submission demonstrated that apartheid was recognized as a crime against humanity by the United Nations in 1971. Meyersfeld notes: "There has never been any prosecution of apartheid crimes and if we cannot prosecute this, it does indeed make an ass of the law" (Kisla 2019). The inclusion of amnesty as part of the methodology of the TRC, which was intended to encourage those who were responsible for human rights abuses under apartheid to come forward to testify at the commission and to further the ends of national reconciliation, provided a way for the new order to operate on a continuum with the old.

Apartheid and traumatic repetition

A historical materialist cannot do without the notion of a present which is not a transition, but in which time stands still and has come to a stop. (Benjamin 2003 [1940], 396)

One way to understand the far-reaching consequences and significance of Judge Mothle's verdict in the Timol case is to read his findings in the light of recent events in the country, and in particular in relation to impunity in relation to state-sponsored violence. On August 16, 2012, almost twenty years after apartheid officially came to an end, a massacre took place at Lonmin Platinum Mine in Rustenberg, an area approximately 40 kilometers outside of Johannesburg. Hundreds of miners were injured and 34 miners were shot dead by the police. The outcome of the Commission of Inquiry into the events that took place at Marikana, which exculpated the state, the police and the Lonmin Mining Company, evokes the title of advocate George Bizos' book, *No One to Blame*, and reveals that the impunity that characterized the apartheid state has not been expunged.

In their letter to the President regarding the suppression of the TRC cases the former commissioners take note of the disturbing fact that the investigating officers appointed to investigate cases of human rights violations that took place under apartheid were themselves former members of the Security Branch:

> Emboldened by the outcome of the reopened Timol Inquest, human rights activists placed 20 more cases (including the Cradock 4 and Pebco 3 murders) before the NPA and the Hawks in January 2018. Although the Hawks appointed investigating officers it was subsequently discovered that the officers leading the investigations were former Security Branch (SB) or associated with the SB. The most senior investigator had been implicated in the torture of a political detainee in the 1980s. This detainee, together with his wife, were subsequently shot dead by the SB, after he sued the SAP for damages. Although the two officers have since been removed from these investigations following complaints, it is hardly surprising that no progress has been made in any of these 20 cases. As recent as 2018 it is still business as usual with the TRC cases ultimately controlled by forces from the past. (Sooka and Ntsebeza 2019)

The 'forces from the past' that continue to control the present can be understood as both structural and psychic. The terrible events that took place at Marikana expose the economic and political continuities between the past and the present. That the Commission of Inquiry into the massacre that took place in 2012 found 'no one to blame' makes clear that a deeply engrained societal acceptance of impunity for the gravest violations of human rights has not been overcome.[13]

---

13 "The Marikana Commission of Inquiry: Report on Matters of Public, National and International Concern Arising out of the Tragic Incidents at the Lonmin Mine in Marikana, in the North

The psychic state that has defined the national consciousness in the aftermath of apartheid has been a form of paralytic amnesia punctuated by bursts of rage and violence and underwritten by despair. Like melancholy somnambulists picking through the ruins of what has preceded us in a feverish sleep, we seem unable either to rest or to wake up and act in the present. An acute sense of living in a time *after time*, ostensibly moving towards a future that is always beyond reach but in actuality compulsively circling around the past that cannot be left behind, but that, as Moishe Postone writes, "has always been in tow", has come to define the transitional state (1980, 100). "It sounds paradoxical," Sami Khatib argues, "from a historical perspective, the past is still ahead of us. The task is not to rewrite the past from the perspective of the present but to destabilize the seemingly solid ground of the present through the past" (2017, 12).

In his remarks to the court, Howard Varney, counsel for the Timol family at the re-opened 2017 inquest into Timol's death, notes the immense struggle Cajee undertook when he sought to reopen the case and asks: "Why did the Timol family have to move heaven and earth to get this inquest off the ground?" (Smith 2017). The answer to this question lies in the enormity of what has been overturned along with the findings of the 1972 inquest. Imtiaz Cajee has, through a colossal effort and with the support of others, like advocate George Bizos, who was present at both the first and second inquest into the death of Timol, refused the relentless, amnesiac rushing of transitional time and called instead for a slow reversal, a painful return to the time when Timol was tortured and his body was thrown from the tenth floor of the police headquarters. Cajee's determination wrenched Joao 'Jan' Rodrigues from anaesthetized retirement in peaceful obscurity and thrust him back into the time of the murder. Judge Mothle's finding, that Timol did not commit suicide but that he was murdered, and that those responsible for his death should be put on trial in a criminal court, brings an event that took place 47 years ago into the present. While this bears a close resemblance to the re-emergence of traumatic memories that plague those who were tortured, it is also different in an important way – Mothle's judgment means that the victims of human rights violations, such as Salim Essop, are not forced to relive the events of the past only to have their torturers lies affirmed, but what they have suffered is recognized by law. On the day that the verdict was delivered and the truth about Timol's murder was recognized, a silence fell in the courtroom, Imtiaz Cajee began to cry, and a voice called out "Long Live Ahmed Timol! Long Live!"

West Province," 2015, can be accessed online at http://www.justice.gov.za/comm-mrk/docs/20150710-gg38978_gen699_3_MarikanaReport.pdf.

The verdict in the Timol case resets the clock that has told the time for us in the years since the end of the Truth Commission hearings, a clock that represents the inertia of the transition, ostensibly moving forwards, in reality trapped like the hands of a stopped clock that only ever jitters a second forward and a second back. This is the significance of Imtiaz Cajee's long quest in pursuit of justice for his uncle, his family and for the country as a whole – he has forced us awake. The re-opened case and its findings do not undo the past, but they make possible a new and different course, one that sets out from the premise that justice in the aftermath of apartheid need not always be infinitely deferred. The logics of the promise of the gradual realization of rights guaranteed by the Constitution and the endless deferral and suspension that characterizes the postapartheid condition (waiting for houses, waiting for safety, waiting for equal education, waiting for employment, waiting for a living wage, waiting for justice to be done) has been overturned, the clock switched back. As a result, the path of history opens up to present an as yet uncharted future, one in which it feels slightly less foolish to harbor hope.

Postscript

During the time it took to reopen the Timol inquest, all the Security Police officers directly involved in the matter died. Rodrigues, the final witness, died in September 2021. He never disclosed the truth about how Timol was murdered and never stood trial.

Works cited

Aboueldahab, Noha. "Writing Atrocities: Syrian Civil Society and Transitional Justice." *Brookings Doha Center Analysis Paper* 21 (2018). https://www.brookings.edu/research/writing-atrocities-syrian-civil-society-and-transitional-justice/ (Accessed April 6, 2023).

Arendt, Hannah. *Eichmann in Jerusalem: A Report on the Banality of Evil*. London: Penguin, 2006.

Benjamin, Walter. *Selected Writings Volume Four: 1938–1940*. Ed. Howard Eiland and Michael W. Jennings. Cambridge, MA: Harvard University Press, 2003.

Biko, Steve [Frank Talk]. "I Write What I Like." *SASO Newsletter* (January/February 1972). DISA Archive. https://disa.ukzn.ac.za/sites/default/files/pdf_files/sajan72.pdf (Accessed April 3, 2023).

Biko, Steve. *I Write What I Like: Steve Biko. A Selection of His Writings*. Ed. Aelred Stubbs. Portsmouth: Heinemann, 1987.

Bizos, George. *No One to Blame? In Pursuit of Justice in South Africa*. Cape Town: David Philip Publishers, 1999.

Cajee, Imtiaz. *Timol: A Quest for Justice*. Johannesburg: STE Publishers, 2005.

Cajee, Imtiaz. *The Murder of Ahmed Timol*. Johannesburg: Jacana, 2020.

Fullard, Madeleine. "Dis-Placing Race: The South African Reconciliation Commission (TRC) and Interpretations of Violence." Johannesburg: Centre for the Study of Violence and Reconciliation, 2004. https://www.csvr.org.za/docs/racism/displacingrace.pdf (Accessed April 3, 2023).

Hirsch, Marianne. *The Generation of Postmemory: Writing and Visual Culture after the Holocaust.* New York: Columbia University Press, 2012.

"High Court Halts Auction of Steve Biko's Autopsy Report." *Mail and Guardian* (December 2, 2014) www.mg.co.za/article/2014-12-02-biko-family-files-interdict-to-stop-auction-of-slain-activists-autopsy/ (Accessed April 3, 2023).

Khatib, Sami. "No Future: The Space of Capital and the Time of Dying." *Former West: Art and the Contemporary after 1989.* Cambridge, MA: MIT Press, 2017. 639–652.

Khoza, Amanda. "Timol's Cousin Fought Tears during Funeral, Fearing Arrest." *News24* (August 2, 2017). www.news24.com/SouthAfrica/News/timols-cousin-fought-tears-during-funeral-fearing-arrest-20170802 (Accessed May 5, 2019).

Kisla, Atilla. "Prosecuting Apartheid Atrocities: Why an Indictment for a Single Murder in the Ahmed Timol Case Is Not Enough." *Daily Maverick* (April 9, 2019). www.dailymaverick.co.za/article/2019-04-09-prosecuting-apartheid-atrocities-why-an-indictment-for-a-single-murder-in-the-ahmed-timol-case-is-not-enough/ (Accessed April 21, 2019).

"Laaste Ure Van Timol Besryf." *Die Transvaler* (April 27, 1972b). https://www.ahmedtimol.co.za/down loads/archive/articles/1972NewspaperArticles/19720427DieTransvalerDonderdag.pdf (Accessed April 3, 2023).

Masilela, Brenda. "I Didn't See Any Torture at JV Square." *The Star* (August 1, 2017). https://www.iol. co.za/the-star/i-didnt-see-any-torture-at-jv-square-10575657 (Accessed November 29, 2021).

"Memorandum Submitted by the African National Congress of South Africa to the U.N Decolonisation Committee." *South African History Online* (October 20, 1979 [April 17–21</day>, 1972]). https://www.sahistory.org.za/archive/memorandum-submitted-african-national-congress-south-africa-un-decolonisation-committee (Accessed April 3, 2023).

Pather, Ra'eesa. "NPA Admits to Political Interference in Prosecutorial Decisions." *Mail and Guardian* (February 6, 2019). https://mg.co.za/article/2019-02-06-npa-admits-to-political-interference-in-prosecutorial-decisions (Accessed May 5, 2019).

Pillay, Kamcilla. "'Biko's Son Must Apologise to Us'." *Independent Online* (December 5, 2014). https://www.iol.co.za/news/south-africa/gauteng/bikos-son-must-apologise-to-us-1791642 (Accessed November 21, 2022).

Pillay, Suren. "The Partisan's Violence, Law and Apartheid: The Assassination of Matthew Goniwe and the Cradock Four." PhD dissertation. New York: Columbia University, 2011.

Postone, Moishe. "Anti-Semitism and National Socialism: Notes on the German Reaction to 'Holocaust'." *New German Critique* 19 (1980): 97–115.

Rouhana, Nadim, and Areej Sabbagh-Khoury. "Memory and the Return of History in a Settler-Colonial Context: The Case of the Palestinians in Israel." *Interventions* 21.4 (2019): 527–550.

Sachs, Albie. 1999. "Truth and Reconciliation." *SMU Law Review* 52: 1563–1578. https://scholar.smu. edu/smulr/vol52/iss4/6 (Accessed April 3, 2023).

Sarkin, Jeremy. "Dealing with Enforced Disappearances in South Africa (with a Focus on the Nokuthula Simelane Case) and around the World: The Need to Ensure Progress on the Rights to Truth, Justice and Reparations in Practice." *Speculum Juris* 29.1 (2015): 22–48.

Smith, Tymon. "The Ghost of Room 1026: Inquest to Shine Light into Death of Timol." *Sunday Times* (July 2, 2017). https://www.timeslive.co.za/sunday-times/opinion-and-analysis/2017-07-01-the-ghost-of-room-1026-inquest-to-shine-light-into-death-of-timol/ (Accessed November 29, 2021).

Smith, Tymon. "Timol Murder a Watershed Case." *New Frame* (April 3, 2019). www.newframe.com/timol-murder-watershed-case (Accessed April 21, 2019).

Smith, Tymon. "The Unfinished Business of the TRC." *New Frame* (November 16, 2020). (Accessed June 9, 2021).

Someone to Blame: The Ahmed Timol Inquest – A 46 Year Wait for the Truth. Dir. Enver Samuel, 2018. https://www.youtube.com/watch?v=nKtPpKiAB3w (Accessed April 3, 2023).

Sooka, Yasmin, and Dumisa Ntsebeza. "Call for Apology to Victims & for Appointment of a Commission of Inquiry to Investigate the Suppression of the TRC Cases." *The Institute for Justice and Reconciliation.* www.ijr.org.za/2019/02/08/ijr-endorses-letter-by-former-trc-commissioners/ (Accessed April 21, 2019).

Steve Biko Foundation. "Update: The Steve Biko and Ahmed Timol Autopsy Reports." Press Release. *Steve Biko Foundation* (December 8, 2014). www.sbf.org.za/home/wp-content/uploads/2014/12/PRESS-RELEASE-Update-on-the-Steve-Biko-Autopsy-Report-on-Auction-Legal-Action.pdf (Accessed May 4, 2019).

"This Is Where It Happened." *Rand Daily Mail* (April 27, 1972). https://www.ahmedtimol.co.za/downloads/archive/articles/1972NewspaperArticles/19720427RandDailyMail.pdf (Accessed April 3, 2023).

Thomas, Kylie. "Returning History: Figuring Worlds: Helen Levitt, Jansje Wissema, the Burning Museum Collective and Photographs of Children in the Streets of New York and Cape Town." *Critical Arts* 32.1 (2018): 122–136.

"Timol: Getuienis Oor Geheime Name en Taal." *Die Transvaler* (April 27, 1972a). https://www.ahmedtimol.co.za/downloads/archive/articles/1972NewspaperArticles/19720427%20Die%20Transvaler%20Donderdag.pdf (Accessed April 3, 2023).

Tolsi, Niren. "Timol Inquest: Reliving the Horror." *Mail and Guardian* (June 30, 2017). https://mg.co.za/article/2017-06-30-00-timol-inquest-reliving-the-horror/ (Accessed November 29, 2021).

"Truth and Reconciliation Commission Final Report." Truth and Reconciliation Commission, Volume 5, 1999. www.justice.gov.za/trc/report/finalreport/Volume5.pdf (Accessed April 3, 2023).

Vadi, Zaakirah. "Essop and Abdulhay Jassat: Brothers in Struggle." *Ahmed Kathrada Foundation* (May 8, 2018). www.kathradafoundation.org/download/essop-abdulhay-jassat-booklet/ (Accessed April 3, 2023).

Venter, Zelda. "#AhmedTimol: Joao Rodrigues Wants Permanent Stay of Prosecution." *Independent Online* (March 27, 2019). www.iol.co.za/news/south-africa/gauteng/ahmedtimol-joao-rodrigues-wants-permanent-stay-of-prosecution-20115410 (Accessed May 5, 2019).

wa Bofelo, Mphutlane. "How Many Bullets Will It Take to Kill Us All." *The Journalist* (November 27, 2018). www.thejournalist.org.za/art/how-many-bullets-will-it-take-to-kill-us-all (Accessed April 3, 2023).

Whittles, Govan. "Biko Family to Fight for Ownership of Autopsy Report". *EWN* (December 3, 2014). https://ewn.co.za/2014/12/03/Biko-family-disgusted-at-attempted-autopsy-sale (Accessed November 21, 2022).

Yates, Adam. "Justice Delayed: The TRC Recommendations 20 Years Later." *Daily Maverick* (September 5, 2018). www.dailymaverick.co.za/article/2018-09-05-justice-delayed-the-trc-recommendations-20-years-later/ (Accessed April 28, 2019).

York, Geoffrey. "Apartheid's Victims Bring the Crimes of South Africa's Past into Court At Last." *The Globe and Mail* (April, 6 2019). www.theglobeandmail.com/world/article-apartheids-victims-bring-the-crimes-of-south-africas-past-into-court/ (Accessed April 21, 2019).

Part II: **Reworking Memories of Transitions**

Kostis Kornetis
Memoryscapes of the Southern European Transitions during the Great Recession

Abstract: This chapter illustrates the emergence of a *bras de fer* between past and present and an intergenerational interconnection (obvious or subterranean) between the 1970s and the 2010s in Portugal, Spain, and Greece. It catalogues the ways in which the 1970s compete with efforts to depict the conjuncture of the Great Recession through the aesthetic code of the transitions, examining how a new generation of artists, activists and intellectuals with distant or blurry memories of the transition years makes sense of and appropriates them at present. This aesthetic (and political) re-emergence of codes of the 1970s music and film is re-enacted by contemporary authors and is acclaimed by the public rewatching or re-performing the transitions. This recourse to cultural memory functions as a means of expressing disenchantment with the present-day political situation wherein a certain spectral version of the past in its various manifestations resurfaces; the chapter concludes with the finding that its effect can be both inspirational and debilitating.

Introduction

This chapter focuses on the resurgence of the memory of the transitions to democracy in the cultural/intellectual-artistic domain of Spain, Greece, and Portugal during the Great Recession of 2010. The official discourse of academics and politicians emphasized until recently the positive impact of the institutional legacies of democratization, reading transitions as accomplishments (Kornetis 2019, 509). In Spain and Greece, several intellectuals still hold on to the idea of a 'model' or 'velvet transition.' Spain was put forward as the prototype of a democratic transition, a triumph of political will and negotiation to be replicated (Linz and Stepan 1996). Similarly, scholars traditionally regarded the Greek passage to democracy after seven years of authoritarian rule by the colonels (1967–1974) as both swift and easy (Voulgaris 2001). In Portugal, influential political scientists proposed dropping the 'revolutionary' prefix 'r' when talking about the 1974 revolution on the

Acknowledgments: I am grateful to Ksenia Robbe for her valuable feedback throughout the writing process of this chapter. I would also like to thank the anonymous reviewer and Geli Mademli for their useful suggestions.

https://doi.org/10.1515/9783110707793-007

occasion of its thirtieth anniversary, and to start referring to it as 'evolution' instead, pointing to the country's democratic maturation (Baumgarten 2017).

Even though the revolution in Portugal, the regime collapse in Greece, and the negotiated rupture in Spain of the mid-1970s bore the imprint of political decisions 'from above,' they nevertheless triggered cultural outbreaks, which were inextricably connected to movements 'from below.' After long stretches of repressive time, these grassroots movements were connected to public spaces, such as re-conquered squares, piazzas, and to the public domain in general. The symbolic (and political) edge of these cultural/political battles against authoritarianism, which took place right before and just after the transitions to democracy, silenced for some time, have been appropriated by a variety of memory activists and memory producers in the three countries. This chapter catalogues the ways in which musical or filmic cultural artifacts that were inextricably linked to the transitional periods *re-performed* this political, symbolic and cultural memory during the Great Recession from 2008–2009 onwards, parallel to a critical drive towards the same periods and the articulation of a generational critique regarding the age-group of politicians that navigated the transitional periods (Kornetis 2019). The article uses the notion of memoryscapes, exploring the evocation of selective past scripts, words, and images for different purposes.[1] Affective references to those past moments contributed to the historicization of the crisis, while temporalities collapsed in a Benjaminean way (Tziovas 2021, 81). Building on Ann Rigney's work on the possibility of re-enacting cultures of joy, hope, exaltation and anticipation, rather than just reviving memories of pain, trauma and loss (Rigney 2018), the chapter looks at how the recollection of the transitional moments in Spain, Greece, and Portugal through this revival of transitional cultural politics has contributed in shaping the present political moment and how it is being reflected in contemporary cultural politics.

Cultural artifacts are triggers and mirrors of societal needs with variable potential of promoting certain visions of the past. At the same time, some artifacts take immediate resonance with certain social groups in specific historical junctures, "proposing a certain narrative of the past" (Zamponi 2018, 73–74). Anti-austerity movements in the early 2010s, protesting against the lack of 'real' democracy and bringing back the critique of the limits of democratization, dormant

---

1 This follows Arjun Appadurai's influential work on "scapes" as a means of tracing cultural topographies. Here I follow Phillips and Reyes' conceptualization of memoryscapes as the "complex landscape upon which memories and memory practices move, come into contact, are contested by, and contest other forms of remembrance," Whereas they however look at how older ways of conceptualizing the past are unsettled, in my viewing it is precisely these older frames that structure the new memories and practices of remembrance concerning the transitions. See Phillips and Reyes 2011.

since the 1970s, appropriated to some extent such cultural codes from a different era. From the field of musical production, the paper focuses on the revival of signature songs of three major dissident figures of the late authoritarian periods: Lluís Llach in Spain, Nikos Xylouris in Greece, and José (Zeca) Afonso in Portugal. From the field of cinema, the chapter showcases the emergence of a reflexive filmography since the onset of the crisis, which was tapping into the 1970s, in terms of cinematic models, inspiration, political reference, or direct subject matter for fiction.

My analysis is based on an ethnography that includes interviews with actors of what I call the 'second generation' of the transition (Kornetis 2019), namely young people who have either no recollection of the events or a distant but formative memory bringing them back to their early childhood. These were mostly cultural producers rather than members of the audience, people on the street, or young people energized by the revivals of the cultural life of the transition years. How did they themselves envisage this fine line connecting their early childhood (coinciding with the emergence of the transitions) to their adulthood? In focusing on these artists as 'memory producers,' the article engages with the question of what role this recollection played in their political outlook and how this recollection was connected to specific cultural artifacts that have recently experienced an afterlife (Ross 2002).

The chapter postulates that these recycled performances and revisitations of those past moments attempt to contest the hegemonic memory culture that constructed the transitions as the foundation of the present political order. It further dissects the conditions of possibility of reclaiming the political momentum and aspirations of the transition years.

Cultural icons

In late Francoist Spain, *poète-chansonnier* Lluís Llach (1948–) was a powerful symbol of Catalan politics. Already since the late 1960s Llach had stated clearly that he would not sing in Castilian unless the issues raised through the so-called *Nova Cançó* concerning cultural and linguistic diversity were tackled head-on. Interestingly, in a 1970 interview the 22-year-old Llach reiterated in a manifesto of sorts:

> By singing in Catalan I intend to attract the attention of people in the whole country to the issue of cultural problems. We cannot allow our regions to lose their character. I believe that in a united Europe one has to first secure the culture of every one of the regions that compose the European countries, and second to secure the very countries themselves. (Llach 1970)

The references to a united Europe are striking, perhaps echoing the Spanish petition to join the EEC (1962), at a time, however, in which this was still a distant possibility due to Franco's fiercely negative stance on democracy. The mentioning of 'regions' strikes very close to home in terms of current Catalan appeals to the 'Europe of the regions' in the European Union. Llach's most popular song, *L'estaca* [The stake], became a hymn of the anti-regime youth of the 1970s but also of Catalan cries for autonomy during the transitional years. The final stanza was a clear reference to Francoism and the inevitability of the dictatorship's collapse on the weight of popular resistance:

> If you pull hard from here
> And I pull hard for there
> It is sure that it will fall
> And we can liberate ourselves.

Footage of Lluís Llach's gigantic concert at Barcelona's Palau dels Esports in 1976 shows a stadium vibrating with youthful energy. People are holding Catalan banners, candles, and cigarette lighters, shouting "Llibertat, Amnistía, Estatut de Autonomía," the triptych of demands that characterized the entire Spanish transition – meaning freedom for the country, amnesty for political prisoners, and autonomy for Catalonia and other repressed regions with cultural and linguistic diversity. The next year Llach would write his emblematic "Campanades a morts" on the five workers killed by the police in Vitoria in the Basque country, one of the bloodiest incidents of the Spanish transition.

Similar to Llach, in Greece one of the major cultural figures that sprang out of the post-dictatorship moment was Nikos Xylouris (1936–1980), a performer and lyra-player who turned into a symbol of the Cretan spirit of resistance. As anthropologist Konstantinos Kalantzis notes, "the resonance of lyre-playing and *rizitiko* singing in the context of Greek political demonstrations draws on the 1970s popularization of the genre":

> [*Rizitiko*] achieved great popularity among Greek urbanites, especially during the 1970s anti-junta movement. These urban audiences, like certain folklorists before them, insisted on the lyrics' metaphorical meaning of liberation, using them to speak about political emancipation from the colonels' junta. Xylouris [. . .] became nationally iconic for notions of resistance against the junta . . . (Kalantzis 2019, 171–172)

Xylouris, particularly idolized by anti-dictatorship students between 1967 and 1974, was crucially involved in the staging of the musical theater piece *Our Grand Circus*, dating back to the final year of the Colonels' dictatorship in Athens in mid-1973 (Kornetis 2013, Van Steen 2014). The play, loosely inspired by Arianne Mnouchkine's legendary *1789* (Kiernander 1993), was based on a series of historical vignettes, filled with allusions and references to the Greek people's suffering throughout the centuries from either foreign rule or domestic autocracy. *Our Grand Circus* paralleled authoritarian moments of the past to the rule of the Colonels and to U.-S. neocolonialism and was butchered by censorship. Interestingly the play became a representative artwork of the Greek transition period, featuring a number of remakes, including a sequel. In particular the last song from *Our Grand Circus* (lyrics by Iakovos Kampanellis / music by Stavros Xarchakos) turned into a signature item signifying people's resistance to any kind of oppression:

> People, don't tighten your belts any farther
> Don't pride yourselves on hunger any more
> The battles you have waged will not have merit
> If they do not pay for the blood that has been spilled.
> People, don't tighten your belts any farther
> Hunger as pride belongs to the coward
> To the slave whose future is to be buried.[2]

In Portugal, Zeca Afonso (1929–1987) was the most influential amongst a number of *cantautores* from the 1970s. Afonso's single best-known hit was *Grândola Vila Morena*, a 1972 hymn to people's power:

> Grândola, swarthy town
> Land of fraternity
> It is the people who lead
> Within you, oh city
>
> It is the people who lead
> Land of fraternity
> Grândola, swarthy town
> On every corner, a friend
> In every face, equality
>
> Grândola, swarthy town
> Land of fraternity
> Land of fraternity[3]

Grândola became the tune which gave the secret signal to the rebelling Portuguese armed forces involved in a bloody colonial war in Africa (*Movimento das Forças Armadas*, MFA) to start the April 25 Revolution in 1974. *Grândola* hence became the soundtrack of the entire revolutionary period, succinctly referring to

---

2 I am using the translation of Eva Johanos.
3 I am using the translation of Daniel da Silva.

the country as a 'land of fraternity.' Forty years later, Afonso, just like Llach and Xylouris, became the epicenter of a powerful revival of a cultural and political type, partly connected to the anti-austerity movements forged in 2011, such as the *indignados* or 15M in Spain and Portugal, and their equivalent *aghanaktismenoi* ('exasperated') in Greece. In fact, it might not come as a surprise that all three items include a mythical or not People ("Ourselves"/ "The people"/ "People") leading the way; or rather, there is a direct call or plea to that collective subject to take more agency.

"They started to sing *L'estaca* and I started to cry"

Lluís Llach acquired immediate resonance during the years of the crisis and especially in the Catalanist quest for independence from Spain that reached a peak in 2018. Left-wing political formation Podemos, in government at present, typically wrapped up its rallies singing *El pueblo unido jamas sera vencido* and *A galopar* (a Chilean revolutionary song and one of Spanish *cantautor* Paco Ibañez, based on Rafael Alberti's poetry on the Spanish Civil War, respectively). Podemos invariably added Llach's *L'estaca* to their list of favorite songs, sang collectively at the end of their rallies. The mnemonic project here is clear and so is its transitioning from a cry against Francoism in the 1970s, to a cry against Madrid's centralism and the Spanish state at present. Culture with historical connotations in this respect becomes a strategic toolkit, used by social actors to mobilize emotional resources. As Catherine Boyle notes, "music of resistance, written for specific purposes, can have an artistic, expressive life *beyond* the limits of the context in which it was written" (Boyle 1995, 291). Referring to *L'estaca*, Lluís Llach himself mentions today: "Young people are still seeking freedoms of different types, within their own restraints, prohibitions, and possibilities, but always pulling at the stake to see if it can be toppled and its captives allowed to walk free" (Boyle 1995, 294). This highlights the interesting mixture between past and present militancy, a blending of the conceptual landscape and the poetic popular archive of 1975–1978, or even the one of 1936–1939, with that of 2017.

A noteworthy revival of the song took place during the Catalan referendum for independence on October 1, 2017, which caused a violent backlash on behalf of the Spanish authorities and cries against a 'Francoist come-back' by independentists throughout Catalonia. Journalist Queralt Castillo Cerezuela (born 1985), of Castilian origins, born and raised in Barcelona, offers an interesting episode involving the song's comeback, acquiring entirely different connotations in a hitherto 'alien' setting in the Catalan capital during the tense moments of the referendum:

And at some point, a band arrived, a brass band, and they started to sing *L'estaca* and I started to cry at that moment because it was incredible for me to be singing *L'estaca* in that place where I had grown up, in a totally Castilian environment [of Barcelona]. And the people, my neighbors, singing *L'estaca*. And there, for example, the referendum was experienced as a celebration. As a celebration. And many people went to vote . . . (Castillo Cerezuela 2018, interview)

This is a typical case of 'multidirectional memory'[4] where the collective memory of Franco's dictatorship and the demands for Catalan autonomy dating from the time of the transition double up with present day grievances against Madrid's centralization and cries for independence.

"Resistance, why not?"

Similar to Llach, in Greece long-dead Xylouris experienced a revival of sorts during the crisis years as his signature cortege song *Xasteria* (Clear Skies), a *rizitiko* rendering from Crete, was endlessly reproduced in demonstrations and protests. As mentioned above, while his *rizitiko* songs are supposedly allegorically speaking about the liberation of the island of Crete from its national enemies in the nineteenth century (the Ottoman Turks), according to anthropologist Konstantinos Kalantzis, "for the left, the enemy is identified with the oppressive state (and the police) [. . .]" (Kalantzis 2012, 10). The movement of *aghanaktismenoi* occupying public squares in 2011 claimed the heritage of the Cretan singer as a means of resistance through a number of impromptu uses of his music (Herzfeld 2011). But this revival of Xylouris was not only limited to the movements from below. In summer 2012, the State Theater of Northern Greece, in collaboration with the Akropol Theater, revived *Our Grand Circus* to great critical acclaim, according to Modern Greek specialist Gonda Van Steen. "Director Soteres Chatzakes and his actors touched a raw nerve in the Greek psyche at the height of the country's economic crisis and of resented, foreign-imposed austerity measures," she adds (Van Steen 2014, 190).[5] Contemporary literature specialist Tassos Kaplanis (born 1969) remembers:

---

4 The term coined by Michael Rothberg denotes the memorial connections between different histories and their legacies over time. It "recognizes the dynamic transfers that take place between diverse places and times during remembrance" (Rothberg 2004, 1233–34).
5 An article in the liberal *To Vima* with the telling title "The ghost of a performance" ventured: "We must admit, however, that the modern representation of the work is original, with its historical and stage beginning undoubtedly marking its current reception. As if the then show (in its allotted time) is the (memorial and historical) reserve of today's one (in the current situation) or

Our Grand Circus was the first non-child theater play I saw in my life, I was very little back then, immediately after the transition (in the summer of 1974–1975) in Athens. And still, I remember Xylouris very well, I remember the actor Papagiannopoulos playing [shadow theater character] Karaghiozis and Kazakos (who seemed enormous to me – I was sitting at the front row, but he must have already put on weight), and Karezi.[6]

In Dimitris Tziovas words, "the [financial] crisis has generated a retrospective discourse of cultural trauma, which is a process of reawakening earlier traumatic events ingrained in the collective memory. Past and present also coalesced into a body of knowledge during the dictatorship (1967–1974)." (Tziovas 2021, 62) As in a Chinese box, the very same *Our Grand Circus* performed during the dictatorship, alluding to past sufferings of the Greeks by the Great Powers from 1821 onwards, was now providing the historical context and pedigree of resistance against which the disrupted present was weighed.

An intriguing moment of chronotopical transfer was in 2016, when visual artist Zafos Xagoraris decided to recreate the exact same stage on which Xylouris performed. Xagoraris (born 1964) found a way to revive this 'blurry image' of his childhood back to life and install it in the city center, right where the play was originally staged. Art, in this respect, seems to be exorcizing childhood memories connected to authoritarianism. On the one hand this is connected to 'play' (childhood) and on the other to 'resistance' (Junta) – in fact leading to the concept of 'playful resistances.' Xagoraris remembers:

It is one of those things that are lost in distant memory, like the blurry images I located in a short film that was shot by a television crew. And accordingly, it is lost in my memory because then I had seen something like this, I was nine and a half years old, with my parents who had gone to the show and I vaguely remember what was happening. And I do not remember exactly. What I do remember more precisely is my parents' emotion. There was a festive atmosphere; this was anyway a kind of musical that worked well. With dancing and so on, but these are things that you don't remember if they really happened or not, if they are actual memories, that is, if you have brought them back to your memory. And because my parents are not alive to discuss this, it's quite moving for me. If I remember correctly from descriptions there were essentially two stages and a corridor that connects them in the form of modern catwalks, like a big I or H, and the spectators sat in between. Facing each other. (Xagoraris 2018, interview)

---

vice versa, if the present show functions somewhat as an executor of an unfulfilled legacy". See Pefanis, *To Vima*, October 7, 2012; also see Sykka, 'Ταξίδι στον εθνικό μας εαυτό', *I Kathimerini*, July 22, 2012.

6 Tassos A. Kaplanis, "To megalo mas tsirko," *Facebook*, https://www.facebook.com, March 2016. Accessed 18 December 2021.

Xagoraris' idea, willingly or not, was inscribed in a series of actions bringing the show, and unmistakably Xylouris' own performance, back to life in a time of crisis. According to his curator, Katerina Gregos, far from a facsimile of the original, the re-creation of the marquee featuring the Cretan idol's name acted as a phantasmatic appearance, "a looming, surreal relic of the past" (Xagoraris 2016, 49):

> Encountering a sign – an illuminated ghost from bygone times – that bears the name of people who are now deceased, is in itself a rupture in the present, and an *activation* of memory, an invitation to re-consider the past from the perspective of the present (Gregos 2016, 50).

Gregos notes that the original theater location was meant to become part of a multinational hotel chain, surrendering what was once the locus of creative resistance to the forces of global capital (2016, 50). This brings to mind the analogous case of the notorious political police PIDE's headquarters in Lisbon, which have been turned into luxury apartments. The haunting and spectral element seems to be doubling up with the neoliberal remaking of these cities, with complete disregard to their painful pasts.

On his part, Xagoraris substantiates his need to reconnect with older moments of defiance by means of a simulacrum. He maintains that "as much as historical conditions have changed, that connection remains the main issue today." In an interview on this very connection between past and present, he concluded with a rhetorical question: "Resistance, why not?" (Kakouriotis 2016).

"We never forget, in a sense"

Zeca Afonso's songs from the 1970s experienced a resurgence, too, in crisis-ridden Portugal. In 2012 protesters stormed the Parliament while Prime Minister Passos Coelho was discussing austerity measures, and interrupted his speech singing *Grândola*. Such impromptu performances of this emblematic song during the recent crisis came to be called *grandoladas*. Coelho himself reiterated that "of all the ways of interrupting proceedings, this was in the best taste" (Wise 2013). Ricardo Noronha, activist and historian at present, born in 1979, remembers:

> There was this thing of interrupting discourses by politicians singing "Grândola," and that had a major impact. Cause it was something that was extremely unpopular for the police . . . or anyone to stop them from doing that, but obviously it had a disruptive factor, that was very well conceived. You cannot charge on people while they are singing Grândola, that's like beating up Liberty, you know? (Noronha 2017, interview)

As for Xagoraris and his childhood memories in Greece, Zeca Afonso is profoundly present in the minds of young people who have been involved in political action in Portugal over the last decade. Historian Daniel Melo, born in Brussels in 1970 where his parents were political exiles, similarly remembers the impact of the *cantautores*, such as Afonso and Fausto. In his words one can discern a certain intergenerational transmission of memory, whereby history is described with a capital H:

> We grew up with José Afonso and that music of the *cantautores*. I met some of them. Fausto, in fact, who has produced the most conceptual albums and who wrote mostly about recent history, or rather about History, period. Fausto is very important . . . I was talking to him because he was a friend of my father. Because my father also sang in the albums of Fausto. (Melo 2017, interview)

But even grassroots activist Ana Mateus, born ten years later, in 1980, was quick to respond to my question on what her first primary political memory was. She describes that she had indeed grown up with the music of Zeca Afonso who, alongside the revolutionary troops, left the most long-lasting impression on her:

> The first [memory]? Oh gosh! (laughter) I must have been really young when I had the first one . . . Maybe it was related to the troops, the Portuguese military, and the songs, Zeca Afonso, mainly. I would say these two, these images, that would be on the television, that would be my first memory, I think. (Mateus 2017, interview)

Same with Ricardo Noronha:

> I was lucky that my primary school teacher was quite towards the left, so she had been involved with the radical left, she was personal friends of this famous singer José Afonso, the guy who sang *Grândola Vila Morena*. I remember she was very depressed when he died, I also remember the day he died, like not the date but the year when he died, it was like 1988 or 1987. She didn't come for a week to school, she was really depressed. (Noronha 2017, interview)

He takes this a step further and remembers how this song deterred people from singing the national anthem in protests.

> Because after a while people started singing *Grândola* all the time. Which is better, in my opinion, than singing the Portuguese national anthem. Although there was a suggestion at the time 'Oh no, we should actually struggle to make *Grândola* the national anthem,' which is funny but at the same time a little bit awkward. (Noronha 2017, interview)

The song's stanza *O povo é quem mais ordena* [It is the people who lead] was used as the motto for the largest protest in the crisis years, on September 15, 2013. (Baumgarten 2017, 56) Renato Miguel Do Carmo, a sociologist and politician and cofounder of the small radical party "Livre," describes this reuse of *Grândola* today:

In terms of a symbolic way, or symbolic point of view, these *Grandoladas* were very effective in the way they appeared in the public space and this was very strong. People with the *Grândola*, using the song to protest and explicitly say to these politicians: "Ok, we have this and you have put this in cause." And mobilizing this awe, the ideology, symbology, the heritage. (Do Carmo 2017, interview)

This is part of performing history, or even performing memory, whereby the past illuminates the present, but also becomes *re-performed* in the present. Portuguese memory performer Joana Craveiro (born 1974) dwells on such a performance in her dense piece "Um museu vivo de memórias pequenas e esquecidas" (Living Museum of Little and Forgotten Memories). The piece is a panoramic view of disparate memories from everyday life and repression under the Estado Novo, the colonies and the war, the Revolution and its contested aftermath and ending.[7] In her five-hour performance of the piece in Lisbon, marking the 43rd anniversary of the Revolution's abrupt and mysterious finale, on November 25, 1975, she included old songs from the 1960s and especially the 1970s, inviting the audience to sing along; *Grândola* was again the most powerful mnemonic vehicle.

To my question on whether the idea or the utopia of the Revolution is still present among people born during or after the Revolution, Craveiro hinted at a strong intergenerational transmission keeping that memory alive:

We never forgot in a sense. That's why my friend Rita still cries with "Grândola Vila Morena," which I also tell in my theater performance "How did the revolution end," now I tell it even more. She cries when she listens to that song and she says: "I always cry with this song," and I go like, well you were there, you know? *But you don't need to [have] be[en] there to cry with this song because it is something that has been transmitted to you throughout the years*, so whenever you listen to the song something awakens in you. I am not sure how much longer we will be able to transmit this, this I am not sure. But I think in my generation definitely up to 1978, 1979, at least there is this thing about the dream . . . Maybe now it is latent and not manifest, but when we were growing up, you know, it was so much there. Everything was about demonstrating, fighting for, you know, writing words by Zeca Afonso on the walls, things like that. (Craveiro 2017, interview, my emphasis)

An intergenerational identification is discernible here, which is both emotive and political. I consider such cultural artifacts a repository of cultural memory, entailing historical and political connotations from a different era that travel across generations. Inevitably the semiotics change, but they carry with them the poetics of that era. Both Afonso and Xylouris appeared during the crisis years in gigantic

---

7 The so-called revolutionary process in Portugal (PREC), namely the months that followed the Carnation Revolution, characterized by an overthrow of social, political and economic realities, was ended abruptly on 25 November 1975, when a supposed coup d'état engineered by the Portuguese Communist Party was halted. See Fishman, 2019.

graffiti and murals in Portugal and Greece, respectively, as mementos to their continuing popular resonance (Rendeiro and Lupati 2019).

Chronotopical contrapositions and iconotexts

For memory theorist Alison Landsberg, who brought forward the idea of 'prosthetic memory,' cinema is a medium that helps fill the void of absent experience (Landsberg 2004). Cinema is the most powerful memory vehicle and the art par excellence that creates the illusion of participating in the actual events and emotions of a different era. A series of films produced between 2012 and 2016 also evoked the revolutionary moment/um, weighing its distance from the present. Here, Mikhail Bakhtin's famous analysis of cultural chronotopes can also be quite useful, whereby the sharp boundaries between (past and present) time and (past and present) space seem to collapse.[8] Portuguese cultural historian Luis Trindade was involved in a series of actions researching the impact of cultural artifacts on young people, in the time-sensitive period of the Grand Recession. José Filipe Costa's film *Linhea Vermelha* (2011), a metafilmic elaboration on *Torre Bela*, a 1975 film by Thomas Harlan on an emblematic occupation of 1974 Portugal, was a case in point. Trindade explains:

> José Filipe has this film called "Red Line" on *Torre Bela*, this very emblematic documentary on the occupation of this land state, by a German filmmaker, one of these militant filmmakers of the 1960s and 1970s who was a globetrotter of the revolutions called Thomas Harlan. He was the son of Veit Harlan, a Nazi filmmaker, so he was this 1960s kid coming to terms with the memory of his father and radicalizing on the left. And José Filipe's film is also about ways in which Thomas Harlan triggered some events in the occupation in order to have stuff to film, including an amazing sequence where the occupiers occupy the palace, and it looks live Buñuel's *Viridiana*, opening the drawers and exposing all the objects, and it's an amazing scene . . . (Trindade 2017, interview)

José Filipe Costa's documentary makes a direct contraposition between 1975 and 2012. He finds the actual protagonists of the documentary, people directly involved in the occupation of Torre Bela, in the outskirts of Lisbon in 1974, and asks them how they feel about it now. The main question that Costa (born 1970) posed about the re-enacted scenes was to what extent the presence of the camera affected the way in which people reacted. But the real issue here is the temporal

---

8 According to Bakhtin, "spatial and temporal indicators are fused into one carefully thought-out, concrete whole. Time, as it were, thickens, takes on flesh, becomes visible; likewise, space becomes charged and responsive to the movements of time, plot and history" (1981, 84).

and symbolic distance between 'then' and 'now,' posed by the director directly. Filipe took this a step further, by including a scene in his documentary where he brings the film *Torre Bela* to a local school in which a history teacher asks fifteen- and sixteen-year-old students to discuss the plot. Trindade comments on that particular sequence:

> Most of the kids were in favor of the occupation. You know, one was thinking 'Oh, people should be ashamed of themselves, of occupying other people's houses,' but others 'what if you were hungry, wouldn't you do the same then?' So, it's interesting . . . It didn't seem it was [stemming] from some kind of family memory, it was, you know, political common sense. If you are hungry, are you entitled to occupy? (Trindade 2017, interview)

Just like in Portugal, in Spain too young filmmakers have dealt with the moment of the Transición (either its beginning or its end) with a critical eye. Luis López Carrasco's El futuro (2014), about the celebration of the socialist victory of 1982 and Daniel Castro's *Ilusión* (2013), a comedy about a young filmmaker who tries to produce a musical on the Moncloa Pacts,[9] are typical examples of this trend – that also broke a long cinematographic silence regarding the Transición. In a joint interview they were both dubbed the 'hijos cabreados de la Transición' (angry kids of the transition) – as Carrasco was born in 1981 and Castro in 1972. They provided a ferocious critique of the films produced in the era of the 'Cultura de la Transición' that focused on contemporary understandings of Spanish history as essentially Manichean and simplistic.

Alberto Rodríguez Librero's *La Isla Mínima* (2014), on two cops in 1980 Spain, was openly critical of the way the transition unfolded and represents the most important of such critiques in recent years. The film, on the permanent clash between two police officers, one directly descending from the Franco regime, and a younger, 'progressive' one, is set against the background of a country still permeated by the fear and violence emanating out of four decades of dictatorship. The film represents a very interesting direct dialogue with an iconic sequence of documentaries from the late 1970s and early 1980s under the rubric *Después de . . .* (1981), filmed by siblings Cecilia and Juan José (Pepe) Bartolomé, students of the Chilean cineaste Patricio Guzmán Rodríguez says:

> Two documentaries, 'Atado y bien atado' [Tied up and well tied up] and 'No os puede dejar solos' [They won't leave us alone], by the Bartolomé siblings, gave me the interpretative keys. Made at street level, they study the Transition without the filter of time, because they are set up in 1981. I suddenly found meaning in everything. (Belinchón 2015)

---

9 Luis López Carrasco, Daniel Castro, "Hablan los hijos cabreados de la Transición." *El Confidencial*, 20 January 2014.

These documentaries were indeed a rare, à chaud retelling of the Transition years 'from below,' with an avalanche of ordinary people partaking in the footage, both passively but also actively, expressing their opinions on all possible things. They capture a slice of life on all sides of the spectrum, from early exhumations of dead republicans by their families, to a filming of a fascist pilgrimage in Valle de los Caídos.

Pepe Bartolomé stressed to me the climate of fear and uncertainty that characterized those dark years (1979–1981), which comes in contrast to the subsequently idealized narrative of the Transition, that was "neither miraculous, nor sacrosanct," in his words. He also tried to explain the success of his film during the Great Recession years through a certain type of revival, mentioning the fact that younger generations inevitably discovered the dark sides of the transitions, also pointed out by the documentary itself at the time:

> The consensus was mythologized in the sense that the result of the Transition was the result of Franco dying in bed, as is also mentioned many times in the film. In other words, there was no force capable of taking Franco down when Franco died. With the exceptions of Catalonia and the Basque Country, the attempts to make a general strike, a national mobilization, all failed . . . So people were demanding, they were asking, including a part of the Franco regime, for normalization. But undoubtedly, we did not have the capacity at that time to overthrow the regime, as did the Carnation Revolution, a great movement type. So, the mistake is that at that moment an agreement was reached, or a series of things were agreed or accepted. The bad thing is that that moment was sanctified . . . Forty years have passed and it has remained sanctified. The whole process that ended up there was also mythologized and that's how we have been until now. With which it is normal that younger generations rediscover that it was not so miraculous, nor so holy. (Bartolomé 2016, interview)

Pepe Bartolomé and his sister Cecilia were taken aback by the enthusiastic participation of young people, such as Rodríguez, in the screenings of this film in the years 2013–2018, which from an almost prophetic filmic testimony of the tense climate in the country prior to the failed coup d'etat by Colonel Tejero in 1981 (the film was only screened in 1983) transitioned to becoming a cult of the new critics of the Transition (Alvarado Jódar 2015). This, among others, constitutes a spectacular revival of 'iconotexts' from the 1970s during the Great Recession (Burke 2001, 65).

Similarly, during the crisis years the legendary Catalan film director from the 1970s Pere Portabella reflected on his own film *Informe General*, a key filmic text on the Spanish Transition (1977). Just like Fernando Solanas, the Argentine filmmaker of the legendary *The Hour of the Furnaces* (1968) went back to film-making and generated a series of films on the 2001 crisis in Argentina,[10] Portabella de-

---

10 *Memoria del saqueo* (2004) and *La tierra sublevada* (2009).

cided to make a film-commentary on the current state of affairs in Spain, with direct references to his previous work. While *Informe General* tried to make sense of the democratic transition, *Informe General II* called attention to a new democratic order that has not yet materialized.[11] Journalist Guillem Martínez (born 1965), one of the writers of a seminal collection of texts that tried to dissect the 15M movement titled *CT o Cultura de la transición* hints at the fact that Portabella who now appears critical of the transition was personally involved in Catalan president Josep Taradellas' return from exile to Barcelona in 1977. Martínez catalogues Portabella among the seminal intellectuals who 'deactivated culture' in post-transitional Spain by establishing a new order whereby culture ceased to be a political battlefield and went mainstream (Martínez 2012).

> Portabella is Portabella. He's the one who organized the return of Tarradellas. Actually not the return, the civil governor organized that, but he is the one who organized the protocol when Tarradellas came to Barcelona. And he is one of the deactivators of culture. And surprise, surprise, he made a comeback with 15-M and made a second part of *Informe General.* (Martínez 2018, interview)

In Greece, filmmaker Giorgos Tsemberopoulos, together with Sakis Maniatis, tried to make a revival of their signature film *Megara* (1974) – a documentary glorifying the farmers' movement against a powerful landowner in dictatorial Greece around the time of major social explosions. The film, a cult of sorts, was revisited by the two filmmakers who went back in situ 45 years later, and was shown in an art-house film festival in Athens in 2018 (FLix 2018). Still, it did not manage to acquire a massive 'fresh' audience, like Solanas in Argentina and Portabella in Spain, despite its attempt to tap into the recent malaise of ecological deterioration.

'Sarcastic' nostalgia?

While in Spain and Portugal the revival of the past relies on a solidly political demand regarding the reappraisal of the transitions, in Greece it seems to be a mixture between aesthetics and politics, or at times a more nostalgic pop aesthetic that supersedes the purely political. The most direct filmic reference to the 1970s during the crisis years in Greece was *Mythopathy* (2015) by Tassos Boulmetis (born 1957), which reconstructs the post–1974 condition in Greece through the life and romances of a young leftist student and a would-be cinematographer. The entire microcosm of young radicals in post-Junta Greece is carefully portrayed,

---

11 I owe this remark to Bryan Cameron. Also see Fanés 2008.

wherein the depiction of leftist cultural politics and liberated everyday life habits is appealing but somewhat caricaturist. Beyond the colorful appearance of the protagonists, the various collectivities parading throughout the film, and the obligatory openness in sexual encounters, the viewer is at times left wondering which were the real political issues at stake. While the spectator's identification with the projected images is perhaps predictable, the film perpetuates a highly problematic filmic canon of bittersweet depictions of the dictatorship years and their aftermath, with sexual awakenings and the coming of age as the dominant elements, with regime violence relegated to the backdrop (Kornetis 2014a; Halkou 2019).

Things seemed to be changing during the time of the economic crisis with a shift in the filmic treatment of the 1970s, whereby especially the post-dictatorship transition to democracy was seen as directly linked to the present juncture. Yet *Mythopathy* brought back nostalgia to the fore: representing this era through the lens of adolescents reinforces a de-politicized, de-historicized nostalgia for the period of the transition to democracy. Boulmetis himself believes that young people would recognize parts of the past in the present: "Young spectators today recognize parts of the present in the past. And, of course, there is a connection, inevitably, especially on the political sphere since everything that we are going through today is inextricably linked to all the things said and narrated in the 1970s." (Euronews 2020)

Journalist Myrsini Lionaraki, daughter of the late Nikitas Lionarakis, a dissident student leader during the Junta years, whose young self could have exponentially been one of the movie's main characters, did not like this rendering, rejecting its 'nostalgia' as well as its aesthetics, which she considers too stylized: "It's a bit mignon. It's 'how cool is life.' It's a bit like 'shiny happy people.'" (Lionaraki, interview). Having said that, Lionaraki goes on to wonder whether there was indeed a verisimilitude between the depiction of youngsters in the 1970s and her father's milieu. To my observation that the film might be using caricature characters who are constantly debating, chain-smoking, and voting in assemblies for the most banal matters she uttered: "I'm not sure of this but I'm afraid that it might have been exactly like that. I think that they were such morons." Her observation about a scene in the movie in which two different generations of militants fraternize in a taverna, whereby several real time members of the anti-dictatorship struggle and old friends of Lionarakis senior appear in cameo roles, is also telling of her critical attitude:

> He was always telling me stories when I was little and we laughed a lot about the first years of the *Metapolitefsi* when the main entertainment was to go to the tavernas, tavernas with music, so whenever they played some heroic tune, they would stand up raising their fists like that [she holds her fist high]. In the taverna . . . (Lionaraki, interview)

At any rate, a major difference from filmic examples elsewhere is that *Mythopathy* did not become a generational exponent of any sort as it was a rather commercial/ized product by someone who had experienced the transition first-hand, thus featuring certain autobiographical elements. Moreover, the frequent comical occurrences in the film bring to mind not only the established tropes of Greek comedy, but also the ones of acclaimed Spanish TV-series *Quéntame como paso?* (Tell Me How It Happened, 2001–the present), which aestheticized the Spanish *Transición*, currently copied by Greek Television in the sitcom on the dictatorship years *Our Best Years* (ERT, 2020). Despite its drawbacks, however, nostalgia can arguably play a 'reflective' role, to quote Svetlana Boym's term, by being ironic and humorous (Boym 2001, 41).[12] In this sense *Mythopathy* acted potentially soothingly in the crisis-ridden Greek society of 2015. Moreover, Boulmetis dubbed the sense of nostalgia that emanates from his film as "sarcastic," as he equally longs for and keeps a critical distance from his past.[13]

On the opposite side of *Mythopathy* stands Daphne Hérétakis short documentary *Au Revoir* (2016), a clever, albeit at times banal and wordy cine-tract on Greece right after the 2015 referendum.[14] One of the most striking moments features young women reading poetry from the 1970–1980s, especially the iconic Katerina Gogou, a renegade self-destructive poet-actor of the time, symbolizing the dark underbelly of the Greek 1970s (Demetriou 2015). The film was produced during the crisis, but it employed visible 1970s techniques and features, such as intertitles, music from the Greek long 1960s (Mikis Theodorakis), and poetry such as Gogou's famous "Provocateur," a poem with direct references to the grassroots movements and the underground of the 1970s. In terms of aesthetics, the use of Super-8 and 16mm camera work and film constitutes, according to theorist Geli Mademli, embalming memories of times past with a self-reflexive quality which renders film makers media archeologists of sorts (Mademli 2018a). A certain commercialized 'pastness' and constructed authenticity here is an element that stands out and that characterizes the film, due its affective qualities, which are transmitting a sense of knowing and re-experiencing the past.[15]

---

12 For a general overview of theoretical views on nostalgia, see Mademli 2018b.
13 At about the time of the film's opening, literary critic Thanasis Th. Niarchos (2016) argued in the Greek daily *Ta Nea*, albeit on a different occasion, that nostalgia can never be "sarcastic".
14 An avalanche of young art house filmmakers worked on crisis-related subjects, including Antonis Glaros, Stella Theodoraki, and Maria Kourkouta.
15 Hérétakis' film was selected by the "Europa. Futuro-Anterior" [Europe. Past-Future] Festival at San Sebastian, run by film theorist Pablo La Parra Pérez, as part of a project that precisely spotted artworks bringing out the political past in the disrupted present.

A major difference from filmic examples in Portugal or Spain, however, is that *Mythopathy* or *Au Revoir* did not trigger a generational reflection of any sort as they were a rather commercial/ized product by someone who had experienced the transition first-hand and a film with a specific and limited audience by a member of the younger generation, respectively. In both cases aestheticization went hand-in-hand with a certain anaesthetization to the practical and political dimensions inherent in this past, to paraphrase Georges Didi-Huberman (2016, 18).

Conclusion

This chapter looked at the resurgence of the cultural memory of transitions to democracy in Spain, Greece, and Portugal during the Great Recession. It demonstrated the multiple and intricate ways in which past and present interact in terms of the memory of the transitions and its representations in the artistic field. Iconic figures of the 1970s experienced a revival while iconotexts of that same period also made a comeback. At the same time representations of the 1970s compete with efforts to depict the current conjuncture, using the aesthetic code of the transitions. The chapter, lastly, catalogued the ways in which a new generation of artists, activists and intellectuals with distant or blurry memories of the transition years makes sense of them and appropriates them at present. A certain aesthetical (and political) reemergence of codes of the 1970s music and films is re-enacted by contemporary authors and is acclaimed by the publics re-watching or re-performing them. One mode of reception of these past tropes is nostalgia (sarcastic, restorative, and/or reflective). Beyond recalling the unfulfilled expectations of the 1970s, "cultural" nostalgia, in film theorist Maria Halkou's words, engages "with the lived or mediated memories of the audience and, through an investment in the popular culture and the material legacy of the era" (2019, 195). This recourse to cultural memory often functions as a means for dealing with the disenchantment with the present-day political situation.

All the above relates to the Benjaminean concept of the appropriation of the past as it flushes up by listening to its echoes in the present (Benjamin 2010 [1942]). The question, however, that remains is why do activists (including memory activists and at times the living artists of the 1970s themselves) tend to privilege past scripts over present circumstances or, even more so, national-historical narratives and local frames over international and contemporary ones. What are the limits, if any, to such memory work (Zamponi 2013), and what is the extent to which the past can be manipulated and strategically used for political reasons by present day actors? An issue that arises here is the malleability of historical material such as Llach's past repertoire with all its connotations (Spillman 1998, 445). Podemos' attitude towards the past, for instance, is far from unproblematic as a nostalgic drive towards the contentious past of mobilizations runs parallel to the critical drive towards post-authoritarianism in Spain.

Does the use of the 1970s memoryscape, furthermore, indicate or suggest a certain entrapment in a past aesthetics? Catalan journalist and chronicler of the 15M movement in Spain Guillem Martínez rightly wonders: "Hay un futuro en todo este pasado?" [Is there a future in all this past?] (Martínez 2012; see also Kornetis 2014) This more than simply a revisiting and reappropriation of the past, points towards a confinement in past historical frames, the 1970s and their aesthetic code (Karpozilos 2014; Kornetis 2014b). Already in 2004 Greek 1970s student leader Mimis Androulakis (born 1951), an emblematic figure of the so-called Polytechnic Generation that rebelled against the Colonels' regime in 1973 and former MP, published a book pointing at this phenomenon which he calls 'vampirism,' namely the symbolic imprisonment of future generations in the foundational moments and intrinsic myths of another time and another generation, intrinsically that of the 1970s. His generation, he explains, absorbed younger age groups in its own past rather than allowing them to develop their own genuine breakthroughs (Androulakis 2004).[16]

In conclusion, the above discussion has demonstrated the varying ways in which the memory of the transitions still matters for society and politics today. The legacies of these formative periods of Southern European democracies acted as powerful symbols for social mobilization but also for the understanding of oneself as part of history during the crisis in Spain, Greece, and Portugal. This article lastly illustrated the emergence of a *bras de fer* between past and present and an intergenerational interconnection (obvious or subterranean) between the 1970s and the 2010s. This signified a dialogue between a moment of political exaltation (where everything seemed possible) and a moment of political despair (where all seemed lost), experienced differently by successive generations.

Works cited

Alvarado Jódar, Alejandro, *La postcensura en el cine documental de la transicion española*. Unpublished
    PhD Thesis. Malaga: University of Malaga, 2015.
Androulakis, Mimis. *Βαμπίρ και κανίβαλοι. Το ρίσκο μιας νέας σύγκρουσης* [Vampires and Cannibals.
    The Risk of a New Conflict]. Athens: Kastaniotis, 2004.
Bakhtin, Mikhail. *The Dialogic Imagination: Four Essays*. Austin: University of Texas Press, 1982.

---

16 On a similar critique in France regarding the generation of 1968, see Remy 1990.

Baumgarten, Britta. "The Children of the Carnation Revolution? Connections between Portugal's Anti-Austerity Movement and the Revolutionary Period 1974/1975." *Social Movement Studies* 16.1 (2017): 51–63.

Belinchón, Gregorio. "En las marismas de la Transición. Alberto Rodríguez compite por la Concha de Oro con 'La isla mínima', 'thriller' policial." *El País* (January 15, 2015).

Benjamin, Walter. *Über den Begriff der Geschichte*. Berlin: Suhrkamp Verlag, 2010 [1942].

Boyle, Catherine. "The Politics of Popular Music: On the Dynamics of New Song." *Spanish Cultural Studies. An Introduction*. Ed. Helen Graham and Jo Labanyi. Oxford: Oxford University Press, 1995. 291–294.

Boym, Svetlana. *The Future of Nostalgia*, New York: Basic Books, 2001.

Burke, Peter. *Eyewitnessing. The Uses of Images as Historical Evidence*. Ithaca: Cornell University Press, 2001.

Carrasco, Luis L., and Daniel Castro. "Hablan los hijos cabreados de la Transición." *El Confidencial* (January 20, 2014).

Demetriou, Demetra. "'I Defend Anarchism.' Deconstructing Authority or Mythicizing Terrorism in Greece's Metapolitefsi: The Poetry of Katerina Gogou." *Forum for Modern Language Studies* 51.1 (2015): 68–84.

Didi-Huberman, Georges. "Introduction." *Uprisings*. Paris: Gallimard, 2016.

Fanés, Fèlix, *Pere Portabella. Avantguarda, cinema, política*. Barcelona: Filmoteca de Catalunya, 2008.

Fishman, Robert. *Democratic Practice: Origins of the Iberian Divide in Political Inclusion*. Oxford: Oxford University Press, 2019.

Gregos, Katerina. "The Performance. Between Phantomatic Presence and Suspension of Disbelief." *The Performance*. Ed. Zafos Xagoraris. Athens: Neon, 2016. 48–50.

Halkou, Maria. "Childhood Memories, Family Life, Nostalgia, and Historical Trauma in Contemporary Greek Cinema." *Retelling the Past in Contemporary Greek Literature, Film and Popular Culture*. Ed. Trine S. Willert and Katsan Gerasimus. Lanham: Lexington Books, 2019. 185–199.

Herzfeld, Michael. "Crisis Attack: Impromptu Ethnography in the Greek Maelstrom." *Anthropology Today* 27.5 (2011): 22–26.

Kakouriotis, Spyros. "Ζάφος Ξαγοράρης: Αναζητώντας μια «Παράσταση» και τη μνήμη της" [Zafos Xagoraris: Looking for a 'Performance' and its Memory]. *Monopoli* (December 6, 2016). http://www.monopoli.gr/EDITORS/item/151398-Zafos-Xagorarhs-Anazhtwntas-mia%C2%ABParastash%C2%BB-kai-th-mnhmh-ths (Accessed October 16, 2020).

Kalantzis, Kostis, "Crete as Warriorhood. Visual Exploration of Social Imaginaries in 'Crisis'." *Anthropology Today* 28.3 (2012): 7–11.

Kalantzis, Kostis. *Tradition in the Frame: Photography, Power, and Imagination in Sfakia, Crete*. Bloomington: Indiana University Press, 2019.

Karpozilos, Kostis. "Παγιδευμένοι στην ιστορία. Η ριζοσπαστική σκέψη του 21ου αιώνα σε αδιέξοδο" [Trapped in History. 21st Century Radical Thought in Impasse]. *Levga* 13 (February 17, 2014) (Accessed October 16, 2020).

Kiernander, Adrian. *Arian Mnouchkine and the Théâtre du Soleil*. Cambridge: Cambridge University Press, 1993.

Kornetis, Kostis. "From Politics to Nostalgia – and Back to Politics: Tracing the Shifts in the Filmic Depiction of the Greek 'Long 1960s' over Time." *Historein* 14 (2014a): 89–102.

Kornetis, Kostis. "Is There a Future in this Past? Analyzing 15M's Intricate Relation to the *Transición*." *Journal of Spanish Cultural Studies* 15.1–2 (2014b): 83–98.

Kornetis, Kostis. "Projections onto the Past: Memories of Democratization in Spain, Greece, and Portugal during the Great Recession." *Mobilization: An International Quarterly* 24.4 (2019): 511–524.

Kornetis, Kostis. "The Memory of Southern European Military Dictatorship in Popular TV Shows." *Contemporary European History* (2023): 46–51.

Landsberg, Alison. *Prosthetic Memory. The Transformation of American Remembrance in the Age of Mass Culture.* New York: Columbia University Press, 2004.

Linz, Juan J., and Alfred Stepan. *Problems of Democratic Transition and Consolidation.* Baltimore, MD: Johns Hopkins University Press, 1996.

Llach, Luis. "Me gustaría cantar en castellano. Pero cuando se resuelvan los problemas que motivaron el nacimiento de la 'cançó'." *Diario Madrid* (March 20, 1970).

Mademli, Geli. "Diaries in Flux: The Aesthetics of Obsolescence in New Greek Essay Documentaries." Paper presented at the conference Contemporary Film Cultures III: Strategies for the Documentary, Vienna, Department of Byzantine & Modern Greek Studies, University of Vienna, May 16–18, 2018.

Mademli, Geli. "Genre as Laboratory: Pastiche in Contemporary Greek Cinema." Unpublished article.

Martínez, Guillem, ed. *CT o la Cultura de la Transición.* Madrid: Debolsillo, 2012.

Niarchos, Thanasis Th. "Το χαστούκι που τρως αντηχεί σ' όλη τη γειτονιά" [The Slap You Took Echoes in the Whole Neighborhood]. *Ta Nea* (August 25, 2016).

Phillips Kendall R., and G. Mitchell Reyes, "Introduction. Surveying Global Memoryscapes: The Shifting Terrain of Public Memory Studies." *Global Memoryscapes.* Ed. Kendall R. Phillips and G. Mitchell Reyes. Tuscaloosa: The University of Alabama Press, 2011. 13–14.

Remy, Jacqueline. *Nous sommes irréstistibles. (Auto)critique d'une generation abusive.* Paris: Le Seuil, 1990.

Rendeiro, Margarida. "Streets of Revolution. Analyzing Representations of the Carnation Revolution in Street Art." *Challenging Memories and Rebuilding Identities: Literary and Artistic Voices.* Ed. Magarida Rendeiro and Federica Lupati. Abingdon: Routledge, 2019. 98–120.

Rigney, Ann. "Remembering Hope: Transnational Activism Beyond the Traumatic." *Memory Studies* 11.3 (2018): 368–380.

Ross, Kristin. *May 68 and its Afterlives.* Chicago: Chicago University Press, 2002.

Rothberg, Michael. "The Work of Testimony in the Age of Decolonization: 'Chronicle of a Summer', Cinema Verité, and the Emergence of the Holocaust Survivor." *PMLA* 119.5 (October 2004).

Signoret, Simone. *La Nostalgie n'est plus ce qu'elle était.* Paris: Seuil, 1976.

Spillman, Lyn. "When Do Collective Memories Last?" *Social Science History* 22.4 (Winter 1998): 445–477.

Tziovas, Dimitris. *Greece from Junta to Crisis. Modernization, Transition and Diversity.* London: Bloomsbury, 2021.

Van Steen, Gonda. *Stage of Emergency. Theater and Public Performance under the Greek Military Dictatorship of 1967–1974.* Oxford: Oxford University Press, 2014.

Voulgaris, Yannis. *Η Ελλάδα της Μεταπολίτευσης: σταθερή δημοκρατία σημαδεμένη από τη μεταπολεμική ιστορία* [Greece of the Metapolitefsi: Stable Democracy, Stigmatized by Postwar History]. Athens: Themelio, 2001.

Wise, Peter. "Lisbon Anti-Austerity Groups Get Creative." *Financial Times* (February 22, 2013). https://www.ft.com/content/3f9e0c50-7cf6-11e2-afb6-00144feabdc0 (Accessed October 16, 2020).

Xagoraris, Zafos, ed. *The Performance.* Athens: Neon, 2016.

Zamponi, Lorenzo. "Collective Memory and Social Movements." *The Wiley-Blackwell Encyclopedia of Social and Political Movements.* Ed. David A. Snow, Donatella della Porta, Bert Klandermans, and Doug McAdam. London: Blackwell, 2013. 225–229.

Zamponi, Lorenzo. *Social Movements, Memory and Media Narrative in Action in the Italian and Spanish Student Movements*. London: Palgrave Macmillan, 2018.

"Τα «Μέγαρα» των Σάκη Μανιάτη και Γιώργου Τσεμπερόπουλου 45 χρόνια μετά" ['Megara' by Sakis Maniatis and Giorgos Tsemberopoulos, 45 Years Later], *FLix* (April 27, 2018).

"«Νοτιάς»: Ο Τάσος Μπουλμέτης και οι ηθοποιοί του μιλούν στο Euronews" ['Mythopathy': Tassos Boulmetis and His Actors Talk to Euronews]. *Euronews* (January14, 2020).

Films

Mythopathy. Dir. Tassos Boulmetis, 2015.

Linhea Vermelha. Dir. José Filipe Costa, 2011.

Au Revoir. Dir. Daphne Hérétakis, 2016.

Megara. Dir. Giorgos Tsemberopoulos and Sakis Maniatis, 1974.

Despues de . . . Dir. Cecilia and José Juán Bartolomé, 1983.

Informe General. Dir. Pere Portabella, 1976.

Informe General II. El nuevo rapto de Europa. Dir. Pere Portabella, 2015.

Torre Bela. Dir. Thomas Harlan, 1975.

La Isla Mínima. Dir. Alberto Rodríguez Librero, 2014.

El future. Dir. Luis López Carrasco, 2013.

Ilusión. Dir. Daniel Castro, 2013.

Interviews

Bartolomé Pepe, interview, Madrid, December 2016.

Castillo Cerezuela Queralt, interview, Porto, July 2017.

Craveiro Joana, interview, Barcelona, April 2018.

Do Carmo Isabel, interview, Lisbon, November 2017.

Lionaraki Myrsini, interview, Athens, January, 2018.

Martínez Guillem, interview, Barcelona, April 2018.

Mateus Ana, interview, Coimbra, November 2017.

Melo Daniel, interview, Lisbon, November 2017.

Noronha Ricardo, interview, Lisbon, November 2017.

Trindade Luis, interview, Lisbon, November 2017.

Xagoraris Zafos, interview, Athens, September 2018.

Andrei Zavadski

Remembering the 1990s in Russia as a Form of Political Protest: Mnemonic Counterpublics

Abstract: This chapter analyzes the projects dedicated to remembering the 1990s in Russia and launched by the independent online magazine *Colta.ru* (now blocked within the country) in 2014–2015: *The Museum of the 90s, The School of the 90s*, and *The Island of the 90s*. These remembrance efforts are viewed as a form of dissent in which the platform and its partners engage in order to resist the simplified official narrative about the first post-Soviet decade. The analysis employs the author's concept of 'mnemonic counterpublics,' theorized as groups whose members feel excluded with regard to particular memories and, in their resolve to overcome that exclusion, challenge not only the collective remembrance framework, but also the power structure of society and its political status quo. The chapter delineates the official narrative about the 1990s within Russia's memory politics and, against this background, dissects the mnemonic counterpublic emerging around *Colta.ru*'s projects. The author shows that the projects resist the official narrative by actualizing/constructing countermemories of the numerous freedoms that the decade brought about, which, in the context of the overarching memory politics imposed by the authorities, implies resistance to the regime as such. The chapter examines nostalgia as a tool that the projects' creators use to reach wider publics (a prerequisite for the emergence of counterpublics), arguing that its purpose is to attract passive onlookers and draw them into the process of active counter-remembrance. The chapter concludes with a discussion of reasons for the mnemonic counterpublic's ultimate failure.

Introduction

In 2011 and 2012, Russia witnessed large-scale demonstrations against the regime of Vladimir Putin and the ruling party, United Russia [*Yedinaya Rossiya*]. Provoked by massive fraud during the December 2011 parliamentary elections, pro-

Acknowledgments: I am deeply thankful to Florian Toepfl, Anna Litvinenko, Ksenia Robbe, and the anonymous reviewers for their helpful comments and suggestions. This research was funded by an Emmy Noether grant sponsored by the German Research Foundation (DFG) and was partially supported by Sharon Macdonald's Alexander von Humboldt Professorship.

https://doi.org/10.1515/9783110707793-008

tests took place in cities across the country. The state responded with criminal cases against the protests' active participants, a tightening of public assembly regulations, a strengthening of control over the internet, and a number of other measures (Koposov 2018, 277–278; Volkov 2012). These actions, combined with a gradual decline in citizens' interest in coming out into the streets and a failure of the specially elected Russian Opposition Coordination Council to overcome the fractured nature of the opposition (Toepfl 2018), led to a successful suppression of offline protest activity. The oppositional sentiment, or what remained of it, was confined to social media and, during the next four years, hardly left their ghetto.[1]

Around that time, a less explicit form of dissent against the political regime in Russia came to the fore. It manifested itself in the actualization of memories of the 1990s that, in one way or another, resisted the official narrative about the decade and thus challenged the authorities' memory politics and the political status quo more broadly. Significantly, the remembrance efforts that followed the 2011–2012 protests were not limited to recurrent invocations of the 1990s by independent media (Fredheim 2016), but amounted to a series of entire media projects actualizing *countermemories* (Wegner 2020) of the decade. In light of the failure of state-focused political activism, these projects can be viewed as a "culturally driven discursive politics," to use the term of Catherine Helen Palczewski (2001, 161). In the distinction of Palczewski (2001), state-focused activism is directed at political change, and culturally driven discursive politics at social change. However, the actualization and mediation of memories that are (seen as) excluded from the official discourse lead to articulations of marginalized identities. Since "identity formation is not external to politics and public discourse" (Downey and Fenton 2003, 193), remembrance practices that resist the official memory politics amount to a specific form of dissent against the political present. Potentially, it can provide larger emancipatory opportunities, and not only social, but political as well.

I conceptualize this form of dissent as *mnemonic counterpublics*, understood as groups whose members feel excluded with regard to particular memories and, in their resolve to overcome that exclusion, challenge not only the collective remembrance framework, but also the power structure of society and its political status quo. Drawing on the ideas of Michael Rothberg (2006, 2009) and other memory scholars (Ryan 2011; Wegner 2020), and building on the developments in counterpublic theory (Asen 2000; Fraser 1990; Toepfl 2020; Toepfl and Piwoni

---

1 The status quo changed in March 2017, with the eruption of protests provoked by the oppositional politician and activist Alexei Navalny's film *He Is Not Dimon to You* [*On vam nie Dimon*], about the alleged corrupt doings of Prime Minister Dmitry Medvedev. These anti-corruption rallies, as well as the subsequent demonstrations against the government's raising of the retirement age, gradually subsided. In 2019, a new wave of protest activity erupted in the country.

2015; Warner 2005), I argue that shared memories of the past that oppose the official memory politics of a non-democratic regime can give rise to counterpublics.

This chapter looks at a mnemonic counterpublic that emerged around the independent online contemporary culture magazine *Colta.ru*. In 2014–2015, the magazine launched, in cooperation with different partners, three projects dedicated to remembering the 1990s in ways that differ from – and oppose – the authorities' official memory politics. They are *The Museum of the 90s* [*Muzei 90-kh*], *The School of the 90s* [*Shkola 90-kh*], and *The Island of the 90s* [*Ostrov 90-kh*].[2] I argue that these projects focus primarily on the decade's flourishing culture and present freedom as its key phenomenon. The project's speakers – mostly representatives of the cultural intelligentsia – voice feelings of exclusion with regard to this aspect of the 1990s, largely absent from the official narrative. Thus, they resist the latter's "absolute truth claims" (Wegner 2020, 1221) by actualizing memories of the decade that are omitted by the Russian authorities' memory politics. By so doing, and reaching wider publics in the process, they give rise to a mnemonic counterpublic.

The chapter is structured as follows. First, it theorizes mnemonic counterpublics and examines their differences from *communities of memory* (Irwin-Zarecka 1994; Zerubavel 1999). Then, it delineates the official narrative about the 1990s within Russia's official memory politics, and analyzes the mnemonic counterpublic emerging around *Colta.ru*'s projects. The chapter goes on to discuss nostalgia as a tool that the projects' speakers use in order to reach wider publics, and concludes with a consideration of the counterpublic's dissent potential as well as reasons for its ultimate failure.

Counterpublics and memory

At the center of counterpublic theory is the phenomenon of social inequality that manifests itself in the exclusion of people from dominant (wider) publics based on their gender, ethnicity, and/or other characteristics (Asen 2000; Fraser 1990). Members of thus excluded social groups tend to form their own, alternative publics that Nancy Fraser (1990) famously called *subaltern counterpublics*, defined as "parallel discursive arenas where members of subordinated social groups invent

---

2 *Muzei 90-kh*: https://www.colta.ru/90s; *Shkola 90-kh*: https://www.colta.ru/school90; and *Ostrov 90-kh*: https://www.colta.ru/ostrov90. In the analysis that follows, all translations into English are my own.

and circulate counterdiscourses, which in turn permit them to formulate oppositional interpretations of their identities, interests, and needs" (67). In turn, Robert Asen's (2000) conceptualization emphasizes the importance of how individual members of counterpublics perceive themselves. He argues that, in order to form a counterpublic, individuals need to *feel excluded* and *recognize* their own exclusion: ". . . counterpublic signifies the collectives that emerge in the recognition of various exclusions from wider publics of potential participants, discourse topics, and speaking styles and the resolve that builds to overcome these exclusions" (Asen 2000, 438). For him, identifying a counterpublic requires "seeking the counter" in it, which implies understanding the grounds on which its participants feel left out as well as the measures they take in order to reach wider publics and thus resist the status imposed on them (Asen 2000).

Reaching wider publics is crucial here: to become a counterpublic, a social group has to not only share something that makes them oppositional in relation to other groups (for example, an identity), but also strive to communicate this 'something' across the group's boundaries (Fraser 1990, 68). With regard to the latter, Michael Warner (2005) writes about *circulation*, seeing it as a defining feature of (counter)publics. For him, circulation is not the same as *conversation*: the circulation of a text implies its going beyond the "sender/receiver or author/ reader models" (Warner 2005, 90) inherent in private discourse. It demands an audience for which the text was not intended – "onlookers, strangers, and passive interlocutors," in the words of Michael Rothberg (2006, 172).

The question of whether publics and counterpublics can emerge in nondemocratic contexts requires a separate discussion, which remains beyond the current chapter's scope. However, since the (multiple) public sphere was predominantly theorized in relation to democracies, with "a favorable organization of civil society" (Calhoun 1993, 276; Downey and Fenton 2003) deemed necessary for its existence, it is worth saying that a series of studies published in recent years have argued in favor of the existence of multiple publics in countries beyond the democratic world (Denisova and Herasimenka 2019; Litvinenko and Zavadski 2020; Rauchfleisch and Schäfer 2015; Shklovski and Valtysson 2012; Toepfl 2020). Against this background, this chapter discusses mnemonic counterpublics in the context of contemporary Russia.

Memories, as well as people's engagement with the past more broadly, are closely connected to individual and collective identities and hence, to the issues of power and resistance (Ryan 2011; Wegner 2020). Lorraine Ryan (2011) argues that shared memories are instrumental to any social group's endurance. According to her, "memory conflates identity and power as the memory narrative restricts the communal identity to one that serves the legitimization strategies of the dominant" (Ryan 2011, 158). Along similar lines, Michael Rothberg (2006, 2009) argues that memories help constitute the multiple public spheres and its subjects; as a result, the articulation of memory "becomes a site of political engagement" (2006, 161–162).

Rothberg (2006; 2009) discusses how the French writer Charlotte Delbo's 1961 book *Les belles lettres* contributed to the emergence of public Holocaust memory and, crucially, the genre of *counterpublic testimony*. Drawing on Michael Warner's (2005) theory of publics and counterpublics, he analyzes Delbo's mobilization of Holocaust memory for the purpose of resisting the violence of decolonization. For *Les belles lettres*, Delbo selected letters published in French periodicals in 1959–1961 and highlighting controversies of the French-Algerian War, and supplied them with her own commentary, including references to Auschwitz. By drawing a parallel between decolonization and the Holocaust, the book sought to construct a new (counter)public sphere and thus challenge the dominant system of meaning regarding colonialism and decolonization (Rothberg 2006). While acknowledging that the book failed to radically change "the conditions of national publicity" in France, Rothberg argues that such efforts are nevertheless able to put "the past into circulation, opening up possibilities for unexpected acts of solidarity" (2006, 180). Building on Rothberg (2006), I argue that memories recognized by social groups as excluded from dominant publics and stimulating efforts to overcome said exclusion can give rise to mnemonic counterpublics.

Non-democratic contexts demonstrate some inherent specificity in this regard. In contexts like Russia, where memories about a particular fragment of the past are often defined by an overarching memory politics aimed at uniting people around the political leader and legitimizing the regime (Koposov 2018; Wijermars 2018), questioning a particular memory narrative imposed by the authorities involves questioning the political status quo more broadly. Attempts at overcoming exclusions of particular ways to remember a fragment of the past by definition challenge not only the narrative promoted by the authorities or even the official remembrance as a whole, but also the political regime as such. Thus, mnemonic counterpublics in Russia present a form of memory-driven dissent, or "culturally driven discursive politics" (Palczewski 2001, 161). For such counterpublics, overcoming their own exclusion from wider publics signifies the goal of a transformation not only of the way a particular past is remembered, but of the political present more broadly.

In the resolution to overcome exclusion and thus challenge the political present, I argue, lies the crucial difference between the concept of mnemonic counterpublic, on the one hand, and the established concept of the community of memory (Irwin-Zarecka 1994) or mnemonic community (Zerubavel 1999), on the other. A mnemonic community is one that is created by people who bond on the basis of a shared past experience and a consensus on what that experience means (Irwin-

Zarecka 1994, 47–49; Zerubavel 1999, 96). Of course, mnemonic communities can pursue "outspoken activity" and acquire "public resonance" (Irwin-Zarecka 1994, 51). Moreover, they can engage in internal and external mnemonic battles over particular ways to remember the past (Zerubavel 1999, 98). However, members of a mnemonic community do not necessarily feel excluded. Iwona Irwin-Zarecka (1994), writing about exclusion, talks about *groups* rather than *communities*. The next theoretical step would be to differentiate between two kinds of groups. The first kind, a mnemonic community, forms on the basis of shared memories about a particular past. Such groups can – but not necessarily do – pursue outspoken activity in their efforts to secure a representation of those memories in the collective remembrance framework. By way of example: parliamentary parties, who represent particular groups of the population, can fight over memory narratives; however, proper representation denotes the absence of exclusion, which means that no counterpublic is involved. The second kind, a mnemonic counterpublic, is a group whose members feel excluded with regard to particular memories. In their resolve to overcome that exclusion (by reaching wider publics), such groups challenge not only the collective remembrance framework, but also the power structure of society and its political status quo. Building on the previous example, one could refer here to oppositional groups without political representation, who are excluded from dominant publics, recognize that exclusion, and strive to overcome it. Thus, while in the focus of mnemonic communities are memories as such, mnemonic counterpublics regard memories as a key factor able to determine the political present more broadly. For the latter, overcoming their own exclusion from dominant (wider) publics signifies a possible transformation of the political reality.

The questions that this research asks are as follows: What memories of the 1990s are actualized by *Colta.ru*'s projects and what kind of mnemonic counterpublic do they constitute? How does this mnemonic counterpublic emerge? And what tools does this counterpublic use in attempts to overcome its own exclusion? The case is examined through an analysis of one of the three components that make up any counterpublic: *discourse topics* (*discursive practices*) (Asen 2000; Toepfl 2020; Toepfl and Piwoni 2015). The other two components – *participants* (as *speakers* and *listeners*) and *environments* (*places*) – are, due to space constraints, largely left out of the current analysis and only referred to when necessary (as in the case with reaching wider publics). I review how feelings of exclusion with regard to particular memories manifest themselves and how these memories are then conveyed to wider audiences, thus leading to the emergence of a counterpublic.

"Chaos, downfall, mayhem": The official narrative about the 1990s

The 1990s was not an easy time in Russian history, but neither was it black-and-white. Russian citizens experienced it very differently, and their attitudes to it were ambivalent. Sociological surveys conducted in the 1990s and early 2000s "suggest that, among the general public, the idea that this decade was 'terribly hard' took shape retrospectively" (Malinova 2021, 429; see also Levinson 2007). By the mid-2000s, the ambivalence in attitudes to the 1990s had given way to increasing negativity. For instance, a 2006 Levada-Center survey showed that a 61% majority of Russian citizens saw the decade negatively and only 22% positively (Levinson 2007). By that time, Alexey Levinson (2007) argues, the 1990s had undergone the process of not only homogenization, but also significant revision. The period had become a key staple of the official memory politics, aimed at emphasizing the stability under Vladimir Putin. Olga Malinova (2021) even sees the decade as "the second [alongside the 'Great Patriotic War'] 'crucial pillar' of Putin's regime legitimation strategy" (431). Analyzing representations of the decade in Putin's speeches between 2000 and 2008, and in Dmitry Medvedev's rhetoric between 2008 and 2012, she demonstrates that the two Russian presidents significantly contributed to constructing a one-dimensional view of the 1990s (Malinova 2018, 2021). The term *turbulent 1990s* [*likhie devyanostye*], however, first made its way into the official discourse rather late: during the 2007 State Duma election campaign (Malinova 2021; Slobodchikova 2015). Around that time, the Russian authorities took to using the adjective *likhie* when describing the 1990s, with the aim to emphasize the contrasting stability of the 2000s. Since then, in a process that entailed "a routinization of the developments of the previous twenty years" (Gudkov 2009), the first post-Soviet decade has come to be presented almost exclusively as a time of instability, chaos, and rowdiness or, to quote the *Komsomol'skaya pravda* columnist Ul'yana Skobeida, of "chaos, downfall, mayhem" [*razrukha, razval, bespredel*] (Skobeida and Sazonov 2016).

It is worth noting that since 2000, the (early) 1990s have been a point of reference not only for the authorities, but also for opposition members. According to Rolf Fredheim, the "Russian opposition found in the end of communism an especially instructive lens through which to analyze the Medvedev–Putin handover" (2016, 210). Similarly, during the protests of 2011–2012, independent media in Russia actively invoked the collapse of the USSR and specifically the 1991 August Putsch. Fredheim, who analyzed half a million Russian newspaper articles published between January 2003 and May 2013, as well as the email correspondence between members of the Russian political elite leaked in early 2012, concludes:

Certain oppositional voices in independent media consistently draw on the image of Soviet collapse to foreshadow the demise of Putin's Russia. At the same time, in the winter of 2011–12 when the regime was faced with unprecedented opposition, figures aligned with the Kremlin were increasingly reluctant to use historical allegories at all, even when attacking the opposition through references to 'the 90s.' The inevitable conclusion to be drawn in this regard is that the past was of peripheral relevance to efforts aimed at guaranteeing Putin's return to office, while it was central to attempts to mount a challenge to his rule. (2016, 222)

After the protests had been suppressed, this trend seems to have acquired a new vigor, transforming into a form of dissent in its own right. Media projects, festivals, flash-mobs, smartphone applications, documentaries, and television series sought to look at the 1990s in ways that differed from the simplified official narrative, highlighting the decade's positive aspects. Here, I focus on the three media projects launched by *Colta.ru*, viewing them as an environment that gives rise to a mnemonic counterpublic.

Colta.ru's projects on the 1990s

In May 2014, *Colta.ru* and the Yegor Gaidar Foundation [*Fond Egora Gaidara*], a non-profit institution promoting, according to its website, "dialog and knowledge in the areas of economics, modern history and humanities," launched *The Museum of the 90s*. This online journalistic project is based on the idea that the 1990s, which saw the demise of the USSR and the formation of a new post-Soviet Russian state, laid the foundation for contemporary Russia, but "today we are still far from a full understanding of this period." The project consists of four 'museum halls': *Freedom of Speech*, *Freedom of Choice*, *Freedom of Action* [*Svoboda dela*], and *Freedom of Everyday Life*. The founders call it "an invitation to discussion" by sharing "memories, interpretations, and artifacts." The project culminated in 2016 with the release of a book entitled *The Museum of the 1990s: Freedom Territory* [*Muzei 90-kh: territoriya svodoby*] (Belenkina et al. 2016).

In February and in September 2015 respectively, *Colta.ru* launched two more projects on the 1990s: *The School of the 90s* and *The Island of the 90s*. The former was created in cooperation with the educational portal *Your History* [*Tvoya istoriya*] and the foundation *Lessons of the 90s* [*Uroki 90-kh*], and it sought to look at the decade from within the context of Russian history. For this reason, key participants of the project were school teachers of history and literature.

The latter, *The Island of the 90s*, was launched by *Colta.ru* in cooperation with the Boris Yeltsin Presidential Center [*El'tsin Tsentr*] and the portal *Your History*, and with the support of the Zimin Foundation [*Fond Dmitriya Zimina 'Dinastiya'*]. At the very start, the project's offline and online components were to complement each other, with the online part (a collection of journalistic texts) aimed at promoting an offline festival of the same name. However, it effectively grew into a transmedia project comprising, in addition to the texts and festival, a flash-mob on social media that had several waves. The first festival was held in Moscow's Muzeon Park of Arts on 20 September 2015. It enjoyed so much success (around twenty thousand people – against the expected two-three thousand – attended) that it was followed by three more editions: two in Yekaterinburg (24 April 2016 and 25 November 2017) and another one in Moscow (20 August 2016).

"Seeking the counter" in the projects' discursive practices

The discursivity of *The Museum of the 90s* manifests itself already in its structure. The five 'museum halls' constituting the project highlight the lens through which its speakers offer to look at the 1990s. Inferring that the authors want to focus solely on the decade's positive aspects, however, would be misleading. The introductory text, for instance, announces that the project seeks to determine and analyze distinct features of the 1990s as "a contradictory epoch" that brought about political and social transformation (Fond Yegora Gaidara 2014). Descriptions of the five 'halls' refer to informational and oligarchic wars as one such feature. This suggests that freedom is viewed as a basic value, a kind of 'ontological necessity' that can contain many, and not only positive, things. At the same time, the project's authors argue that "myths of 'the turbulent 90s' will sooner or later disappear, and artifacts, documents, and witness accounts of [that] epoch of unprecedented openness and freedom will be in demand" (Fond Yegora Gaidara 2014). This invites a contrary interpretation: that the narrative of the turbulent 1990s is reduced to myths. Combined with the foci dominating in the descriptions of the 'museum halls' (access to uncensored information; freedoms of self-expression and thought; freedom of professional, personal, political, and electoral choice; the revival of business and personal initiative; and so on), it becomes clear that freedom and the positive transformations it conduced are of primary importance to the project.

The book *The Museum of the 90s* (Belenkina et al. 2016) is based on the online project, with a few additional texts. The overall framework has also remained intact. While emphasizing that "the 90s did not leave behind any consensus; an intelligible conversation [about the decade] has been substituted with myths; the struggle for the legalization [of these myths] is continuing to this day" (Belenkina et al. 2016, 9), the book's introduction presents *freedom* as the central concept for describing the epoch: "Understood and named in different ways – as 'opportunities,' 'changes,' 'breakdown,' 'chaos' – it appears in almost all of the book's texts" (Belenkina et al. 2016, 10). The key to how the authors understand freedom, however, is also clearly pronounced: it is first and foremost freedom from the state: "the 90s was one of the decades, rare in Russian history, when the state weakened, rather than strengthened, its influence" (Belenkina et al. 2016, 10).

Katerina Belenkina does not deny that her personal beliefs had an impact on the project: "My personal position consists in [thinking] that freedom is above all things in the world. It can have the scariest, the most unpleasant consequences, but it is still above all else" (Belenkina and Nemzer 2018, interview). Another author, Anna Nemzer, is less straightforward. The authorities, she argues, labeled the 1990s as "turbulent" in the course of the regime legitimization process. It had been unclear for them how to talk about the decade because "for better or worse, it was a period of absolute freedom, in all its positive and negative manifestations," which is why they decided to turn the 1990s into a cemented cliché (Belenkina and Nemzer 2018, interview). But breaking that cement was not difficult, "simply because of people's willingness to speak":

> We as authors understood very clearly with what take on the 1990s we would not agree: with these 'bloody 90s,' where nothing beyond blood existed. [. . .] So, on the one hand, [our project] was an attempt to deal with this myth, and, on the other hand, we did not want to create an alternative, cheerful myth. We wanted, as much as it was possible, to paint a multidimensional picture, but without betraying our own stances. (Belenkina and Nemzer 2018, interview)

While the book does present more diverse memories of the 1990s than the online project (including more recollections of poverty and life breakdown), its overall focus on freedom can scarcely be ignored. Notably, Belenkina and Nemzer point out that they consciously, due to methodological considerations, did not ask their interlocutors about freedom. However, it inevitably came up in almost each conversation they conducted. In the words of Belenkina, "it could be cursed freedom or blessed freedom," but it "crept out from everywhere" (Belenkina and Nemzer 2018, interview).

The School of the 90s also places freedom at its center, but constantly compares the 1990s to the Russia of today. The project starts with an introductory essay by Alfred Kokh ("The School of Growing Up"), a writer and economist who briefly served as deputy prime minister under President Boris Yeltsin. He reflects on how the way towards freedom turned out to be much more difficult than expected. One of the mistakes that, according to him, were made was the period's economic determinism: too much attention given to life's economic dimension and too little to the social one. Acknowledging that in the 1990s, there "was a lot of shooting and blood," he nevertheless argues against the official interpretation of the period:

> It was a time of freedom. But this freedom did not create any image that would generate optimism. Gaidar's tragicness – that's the image of the 90s. We ourselves have given our freedom up. Some of us have traded it in for money. Others for the possibility to moralize endlessly. [. . .] So, why weren't we happy about this freedom? Why have we agreed so easily that the 90s were 'turbulent'? That it was a time of decline, decay, degradation ... You know it is not true! Yet, mass consciousness has already agreed to that. (Kokh 2015)

The core of the project consists in the monologues of several school teachers. They discuss the 1990s primarily in relation to their work, comparing it to the late Soviet times and to the 2000–2010s. One of the things that comes up repeatedly is the enormous bureaucratization of their current day-to-day activities. But central to the teachers' monologues is the discussion of the changes that the 1990s brought about. Tamara Eidelman, an honored (history) teacher of Russia, unequivocally refutes the official narrative ("If All Teachers Are Fired, Who Will Teach?"):

> 'The turbulent 90s' is a preposterous term that was consciously conjured up and introduced in order to discredit this beautiful period of freedom. [This term] overshadows all those wonderful beginnings, initiatives, and generally all of the good things that were achieved at the time. (Eidelman 2015)

Marietta Chudakova ("Turning 90s"), an author and historian of literature, does not speak of freedom per se. However, relating to the political process of the 1990s and her own participation in it, she defines the decade as follows: "I have no doubt as to the epithet for the 90s: 'the turning 90s'" (Chudakova 2015). She goes on to defend both Yegor Gaidar and Boris Yeltsin, arguing how important their work was for the creation of a new Russia.

Another common feature that unites this project's speakers is the comparison of the 1990s to the current status quo. Leonid Katsva (2015), for instance, dissects the approach to the 1990s within the "so called historical cultural standard," a document that defines how all history textbooks are to be written and history is to be taught in Russia ("Ostensibly True, but False Really!"). Katsva (2015) shows that this document's text about the 1990s, which is to form the basis of any textbook or class, "creates an absolutely negative feeling" about the decade. Some of the cause-effect relations, he argues, are misinterpreted, with the tone of the document changing dramatically when it goes on to describe the time after Putin's rise to power. In turn, Eidelman (2015) argues that, when she looks at Russia in 2015 (the year when the interview was conducted), it becomes clear that "our country has failed the freedom and responsibility exam. But it can always take it again." The Russian literature teacher Elena Vigdorova's (2015) ("We Blew Our 1990s") conclusion is similar, if somewhat less optimistic: "The freedom test ...

what can I say. We have not passed it." Finally, Chudakova (2015) provides a more hopeful outlook. She claims that it was Yeltsin who had laid the foundation of Russia's democracy, and that it was because of that foundation that current attempts to destroy that democracy to the core were failing: "I have no doubt that we will not let [them] destroy it."

The Island of the 90s uses similar metaphors, descriptions, and rationales for introducing the project to the public. The 1990s, the project's (unnamed) editors write in the introduction ("An Invitation for a Trip"), was

> a time of Russia's youth, a time when everything turned upside down, all winds started to blow at once, and one had to learn to breathe this unusual and crisp air of freedom anew. A hard time – living in an epoch of change is never easy. We do not wish to idealize the 1990s. But we do not wish to put up with how [the decade] is persistently being cast in a dark light either. ("Priglashenie k puteshestviyu" 2015)

Explaining their decision to turn to the topic for the third time, the editors argue that it is inexhaustible; "besides, each new turn of our current life makes it timely in a fresh way" ("Priglashenie k puteshestviyu" 2015). This inconspicuous reference to Russia's present as well as the hint at the official narrative of the turbulent 1990s signify a continuity of *The Island of the 90s* with *The Museum* and *The School*. Also significant is the explanation behind calling the project an 'island':

> We suggest discovering [the 1990s] anew. Seeing [this period] as multidimensional and colorful, rather than flat. Realizing how much the end of the decade differs from its beginning [. . .] Learning about the feelings and moods of that time first-hand. [. . .] Understanding what that period of unparalleled opportunities, intensive searches, experiments, and discoveries meant for literature, music, media, fine arts, cinema, theater. ("Priglashenie k puteshestviyu" 2015)

As in *The Museum* and *The School*, freedom occupies a prominent place in *The Island* as well. Most of the project's participants touch upon it in one way or another. Thus, while the complexity of the decade – its poverty, the traumatizing changes, the loss of the sense of security – is present in their recollections more prominently than in the other two projects, at *The Island*'s center are invariably freedom, opportunity, and the creation of the new: a new language, a new art market, and so on. The writer Vladimir Voinovich ("Even If Literature Plays a Lesser Role, Let There Be Freedom"), if perhaps prompted by his interviewer, notably compares the first post-Soviet decade with the current situation in Russia. Asked if he would find an alternative to the epithet 'turbulent' with regard to the 1990s, he replies:

> I would say 'the years of hope.' One could also say 'the years of failed hopes.' But not entirely, not entirely. I'd say (I have a more optimistic view of the future) that the first step towards

democracy has been taken, and it cannot be reversed. Now, of course, we are experiencing reactionary politics, long-running reactionary politics, but a second step will be taken, I think. And this second step will probably be a more decisive one. (Vasilevskaya 2015)

The writer Boris Minaev ("A Different Truth about Yeltsin Needs to Be Told"), the author of a 2010 biography of Boris Yeltsin, has an even clearer stance. Minaev's decision to take on the task of writing about the first Russian president was, according to him, "emotional" (Boyarinov 2015). As he watched how the 1990s were increasingly presented as a solely negative, "turbulent" decade, he wanted to tell "a different truth" about Yeltsin, "at least tell the facts in the correct order" (Boyarinov 2015). For him, understanding the 1990s in all their complexity is not simply about the past: "[E]mploying mythologems and schemes, using simplistic and superficial answers to complex questions, we take away our own future. We live as if we had plastic bags on our heads" (Boyarinov 2015).

One of the more complex and multidimensional statements about the 1990s is voiced by the writer Vladimir Sharov ("The 1990s, I Think, Have Not Ended"), for whom it was "the brightest time," "a time of our avalanching acquaintance with all things new" (Drobiazko-Parshchikova 2015). Still, Sharov sees it not only as a period of "an ocean of hopes," but also – and "even more" so – of "disappointments and puzzlements" (Drobiazko-Parshchikova 2015). The latter includes the belief of most people in Russia that the direction of development taken in the 1990s "turned out to be the wrong one," and the frustrations related to it. But crucially, he argues that both those who accepted and supported the changes, and those who "outright rejected" them "had it equally hard" (Drobiazko-Parshchikova 2015). He concludes by pointing out that, in order to understand the 1990s fully, more distance is required, but goes on to acknowledge that there were a lot of "personal tragedies of people who did not manage to cope with all that [change]. But in this very place, in this very pot, there were quite a lot of the brightest (perhaps, for the first time in many centuries) hopes. All of this got woven into a very peculiar ball" (Drobiazko-Parshchikova 2015).

A key aspect of *The Island* is the successful transition of the digital memories (Hoskins 2018) actualized by the online media project into the offline realm (the festivals) – and vice versa. Having launched the project on *Colta.ru*, the festival's organizers started to post their own photographs from the 1990s on Facebook and Instagram. This spontaneously grew into a flash-mob: people shared *Colta.ru*'s texts about the 1990s and/or photographs of themselves from the decade. The posts were accompanied by captions filled with memories and interpretations of the period. *Colta.ru*'s deputy editor Gleb Morev (2019, interview) claims that the partners did not plan the flash-mob, did not invest any money in it, and were surprised by the scale of what was happening as much as anybody else. However, once they saw that the flash-mob was working, they contributed to fuelling it. Be it as it may, this activity proved to be very effective: about twenty thousand people showed up at the first festival, including those who were not *Colta.ru*'s readers.

Some of the lectures and discussions held at the first festival were not only published online in the form of videos, but transcribed and presented on *Colta.ru* as articles. One such lecture, given by the publisher Irina Prokhorova ("How a New Language Was Born"), deals with attempts at describing the new reality of the 1990s and the resulting birth of a new language. However, a significant place in Prokhorova's talk is occupied by discussing the 1990s as an epoch. Here, all of the key themes of *The Island* and of *Colta.ru*'s recollection of the decade in general come to the fore: freedoms, the official narrative about the 1990s, and the importance of debating and thinking about that time in connection to the current state of affairs in Russia. For Prokhorova,

> [t]hat freedom, with all its disappointments and hardships, is a most valuable experience that is impossible to drive out of a whole generation's consciousness; it makes us see the world absolutely differently, [it makes us] act. (Prokhorova 2015a)

She concludes by calling for a shrewd look at the 1990s and an analysis of the decade's mistakes, hoping that it will allow for the creation of a better strategy for further development: "I do not think that the 1990s can be canceled, even if we silence [those years] down. The foundation already exists. So, let's try erecting a new building on top of this foundation" (Prokhorova 2015a).

The most complex discussion of the decade took place in the form of a roundtable that brought together Aleksandr Baunov, Dmitry Butrin, Linor Goralik, Aleksandr Drakhler, Anna Narinskaya, Kirill Rogov, and Marietta Chudakova ("Do You Realize That It Was Given to You in the 90s?"). Most of these people participated in the other *Colta.ru* projects on the 1990s. However, it is their dialogue at the first offline festival, which was then transcribed and published by *Colta.ru*, that produced the most diverse memories and opinions about the decade. Goralik, who moderates the conversation, starts with observing that the festival has created a space for discussion which, by the end of the day, "became emotional, not to say conflictual, and it is wonderful because it means that the elephant we are touching is alive" (Baunov et al. 2015). Referring to the emotionality of debates around the 1990s at the festival is important, as it not only illustrates that memories, especially living memories, are inherently affective, but also stresses that different memories and opinions were voiced and juxtaposed at the festival. This is also supported by my personal observations, which speaks in favor of the festival's reaching across publics.

Chudakova, Narinskaya, and other speakers invoke the cliché of the turbulent 1990s. Chudakova denounces it, arguing that "fabulous things" happened during the decade (Baunov et al. 2015). Yet, according to her, liberal elites should have done more to explain why the dismantling of the USSR was important, and to contradict the rise of the official narrative about the 1990s; instead, they indulged in personal ambitions. Narinskaya takes a different stance, pointing out that Chudakova's explanation is further complicated by two factors. First, by the official historical politics, "when television shows 'rowdy' series and films about criminals killing everybody, and so on" (Baunov et al. 2015). And second, it involves explaining to people the time through which they lived themselves. Baunov also speaks about "a gigantic trauma" that Russian people experienced as a result of the collapse of the USSR. He, too, sees the main difficulty of discussing the 1990s in the necessity to maneuver between the myths created by the authorities and people's living memories:

> That's why you are torn between the task of ultimate honesty and the task of resisting the lies you encounter. Which is why this festival solves the second task: it is not so much about whitewashing the 90s, not about their idealization, but about an objective conversation of sorts. (Baunov et al. 2015)

This observation is central to understanding what kind of memories are actualized/constructed by *The Island* and, generally, *Colta.ru*'s three projects on the decade. If one were to identify a 'meta-memory' of the 1990s conveyed by *Colta.ru*, it could be the theater director Henrietta Yanovskaya's ("We Attempted to Be a Free Country") phrase "these hard, wonderful 90s" (Vasilevskaya and Golubeva 2015). The emphasis in this phrase – despite some of the participants' genuine eagerness to acknowledge the hardships of many Russian citizens in the 1990s – is on the word 'wonderful.' The projects are about "the blossoming of intellectual media and intellectual life that, perhaps, were in contrast with the economic misery," as Morev (2019, interview) puts it. They focus on the freedoms of speech, movement, consciousness, choice, and so on, and the transformations of culture they brought about; on remembering the new, the particular, 'the wonderful.' What is 'counter' about this way of remembering the 1990s?

In her radio program *Culture of the Everyday* [*Kultura povsednevnosti*], Prokhorova (2015b) interviewed, among others, Denis Boyarinov, an organizer of the festival *The Island of the 90s*. Asking Boyarinov about *Colta.ru*'s projects, she remarks: "Somehow the decade got engraved with the cliché of 'rowdiness,' and for a long time, discussing it in any positive way seemed inappropriate" (Prokhorova 2015b). This comment could serve as a gist of the feelings of exclusion in relation to the 1990s experienced by the projects' participants. As formulated by Baunov, in a passage cited above, "you are torn between the task of ultimate honesty and the task of resisting the lies you encounter" (Baunov et al. 2015). "Ultimate honesty" is hard to achieve when one sets out to oppose an overarching official memory politics, for this would require partial agreement with and, hence, a certain validation of the official narrative. Hence, despite the promise of *The Island* to look at the period as "multidimensional and colorful," the project – as well as *Colta.ru*'s recollection of the decade in general – tends to add color to the grim turbulent 90s narrative and thus *add* to the dominant memories of the 1990s. Thus, *Colta.ru*'s projects resist the official narrative by, in a way, *complementing* it with countermemories of freedoms. Countermemories are always *oppositional* – they contradict or even resist "official acts of remembrance," and at the same time *relational* – they are necessarily defined against, and thus connected to, "official" or "authoritative" memories (Wegner 2020, 3–6). In this light, the 'counter' of the memories actualized/constructed by *Colta.ru* consists in their relationship to the official narrative. Focusing primarily on culture and viewing freedom as the decade's key phenomenon, the projects oppose and challenge that narrative's "absolute truth claims" (Wegner 2020, 4) by actualizing positive memories of the 1990s omitted by it.

Nostalgia as a tool of reaching wider publics

Why and how does this actualization of countermemories lead to the emergence of a mnemonic counterpublic? In the case studied, I argue, it is achieved through a certain instrumentalization of nostalgia used as a way of reaching across publics, vital for the emergence of a counterpublic (Warner 2005). Nostalgia, Svetlana Boym writes, "is a yearning for a different time – the time of our childhood, the slower rhythms of our dreams" (2001, xv). This kind of longing for one's childhood/youth has been instrumentalized by the projects' participants to attract audiences, creating the possibility of *Colta.ru*'s communicating across publics, for even passive onlookers and strangers were tempted to join the conversation.

In the press release following the first *The Island of 90s* festival ("The Island of the 90s: Find Yourself"), the organizers confess to having been afraid that the vintage fashion flea market and music concerts, which constituted the festival's important part, would attract more attention than the discussions. Yet, people "firmly and massively occupied our lectures, discussions, exhibition, and film platforms. All of them without exception" (Golubeva 2015). My field research confirms this: when asked why they came to a lecture or a discussion held at the festival, many people would say they had been attracted by the opportunity to hear their favorite musician or attend the 1990s-themed flea market. Popular musicians and bands from the 1990s (*Auktyon*, *Vezhlivyi otkaz*, Vyacheslav Butusov, and others) served as key attractions for wider publics. In fact, my observations confirmed that even passers-by were stopped by the sounds of music coming from the Muzeon Park and prompted to enter the venue (the fact that the festival was free of charge also played a role). Some respondents would also say that they had seen information about the festival on Facebook or would even mention the flash-mob. Notably, the news program *Vesti* (2015), reviewing the festival for a federal audience, also invokes that flash-mob, charging *Colta.ru* with starting it. The reporter Anastasia Efimova accuses the festival's organizers of nostalgically idealizing the 1990s and thus whitewashing the decade's grim history. If anything, this kind of attention from a federal TV channel (the program is produced by *Rossiya-1*), a key actor in the official memory politics (Wijermars 2018), points to the festival attracting much broader publics that initially expected by the authorities.

The quiz format was also used to attract wider audiences. The three most viewed pieces of *The Island* are quizzes (for example, "The TV Series of the 90s"). *The School*'s and *The Museum*'s materials that enjoyed the biggest number of views share the same format: for instance, "Yupi, Barbie, Tamagotchi: What Do You Know about the Things of the 90s?" and "The Discotheque of the 1990s." They have similarities in content, as well as form: most of these tests present a nostalgic take on the decade. Anna Nemzer admits to consciously using "memory triggers" in *The Museum*:

> Memory works in a very particular way. So, of course, there were quite a few triggers [used in the project]. They are triggers of recognition: "Try to remember," "Let's remember the sound of a loading [computer]", "Let's remember the sound of Tetris," "Let's remember that sound." Of course, it works with those who can actually remember. In this sense, moving on from Tetris to Gaidar's first speech and [other] serious events was convenient. That's why we shook [readers] up, stirred [them] up a bit – and moved on to something else. [. . .] At the same time, we did not feel that we thus lost the younger audience completely. We understood, of course, that they wouldn't remember Tetris and we would partially lose them. For them, there were other triggers. [. . .] The task was to talk to those who remember first [. . .] and then through them, and with the help of human stories, involve others." (Belenkina and Nemzer 2018, interview)

In addition to the book (Belenkina et al. 2016), which allowed the project to leave the confines of the digital, these nostalgic 'triggers' contributed to the project reaching wider publics. But what specific role does nostalgia play in this – and *Colta.ru*'s efforts in general?

Otto Boele, analyzing *The Museum of the 90s*, the festival *The Island of the 90s*, and the related Facebook flash-mob, writes that they instrumentalize "nostalgia as weapon" (2019, 204). He understands this type of nostalgia as a kind of oppositional memory that "allows marginalized groups in society to resist 'official historical knowledge' and construct their own vision of the recent past" (Boele 2019, 204). The projects' participants, he writes,

> questioned and openly challenged the 'official' view of the decade by drawing on personal memories and offering an alternative picture of the way things had 'really' been. By [. . .] so doing they helped to define and simultaneously break a new taboo: to disregard the national trauma of the 1990s by remembering the decade with a mixture of fondness and regret, that is by remembering it nostalgically. (Boele 2019, 219)

Nostalgia can undeniably be a form of oppositional remembrance, but Boele's (2019) reading of the projects nevertheless seems reductionist. While rightly identifying the act of breaking the taboo of speaking about the decade fondly, it does not allow for any other active stance with regard to the current political reality. This, as I demonstrated above, is not the case with *Colta.ru*'s projects. Nostalgia is indeed used by their participants as an affective tool, but it should be seen as a bait, rather than a weapon. Its purpose is not limited to countering the official narrative about the 1990s. This tool is also used to attract, consciously or inadvertently, passive onlookers and draw them into the process of active counter-remembrance, which, in turn, involves challenging the official narrative about the 1990s and questioning the political status quo.

Interestingly, the projects' nostalgia – or, more broadly, the romanticization of the 1990s – was also criticized from outside dominant publics (Narinskaya 2015). Alexandra Polivanova, a human rights activist, educator, and International Memorial member, who essentially does not belong to Russia's dominant publics (more often than not participating in various counterpublics instead), also criticized *Colta.ru*'s projects, especially *The Island* and the related flash-mob. According to her, the mechanism that makes people feel nostalgic about the 1990s is the same one that makes many Russian citizens experience, "not very responsibly," nostalgia for the late Soviet times (Polivanova 2015). This criticism is not irrelevant, for it stresses that people's emotional responses to the 1990s could be, and indeed *were*, used for essentially political purposes. But nostalgia's role here was different. If one sees nostalgia per se as a kind of passive protest, then *Colta.ru*'s projects instrumentalized it to attract broader audiences – reach across publics – and engage them in more active memory work. This led to the emergence of a mnemonic counterpublic.

Colta.ru's counterpublic and its effects

Memory has power. It can act as a tool of resistance against the exclusion of individuals and groups from the multiple public sphere and a motor of struggles for equality. But how successful can memory-driven dissent be? Feeling exclusion, articulating that exclusion, and seeking to overcome it, participants of *Colta.ru*'s projects resisted the simplified official narrative about the 1990s. Actualizing memories of the decade that differ from that narrative and reaching wider publics in the process, they gave rise to a mnemonic counterpublic. But in order to consider what effects and potentials this form of dissent had (and has), one has to examine the counterpublic's sustainability. Unlike communities, counterpublics are temporary: public attention has a fleeting nature, and, depending on the circulation of discourse, counterpublics come together and inevitably dissolve (Warner 2005). This is one reason for *Colta.ru*'s mnemonic counterpublic failing to offer a significant challenge to the political regime in Russia. However, the circulation of discourse is subtle and takes place in forms that go far beyond two-person conversations (Warner 2005). Had *Colta.ru* (as well as Facebook and other social networks) not been blocked by the authorities following the beginning of Russia's full-scale invasion of Ukraine, re-emergence of the mnemonic counterpublic around *Colta.ru*'s projects would theoretically be possible due to what I call 'circumstantial circulation' – incidental liking and sharing on social networks, for example (as demonstrated by a second wave of the Facebook flash-mob in September 2018). This could reignite discourse circulation and lead to the counterpublic's re-actualization.

Another reason behind the mnemonic counterpublic's ultimate failure is likely to have been its elite (albeit not elitist, as illustrated, among other things, by the free entrance to the offline festivals) nature: in its attempts to actualize/construct countermemories of the 1990s, *Colta.ru*'s projects appealed first and foremost to those whose memories went against the official narrative in the first place. Such memories are primarily shared by people who enjoyed certain privileges – education, travel opportunities, and similar – already in the 1990s. Constituting the core of *Colta.ru*'s (potential) readership, these people successfully partook in the actualization of their memories together with the projects' masterminds. As for others, whose memories of the 1990s lay less in the realm of freedom and more in the struggle for survival, they must have got a glimpse of 'the other side' of the period's remembrance – and remained unconvinced. The chance to convince them, considering counterpublics' transitory nature, did not come to pass. Thus, despite reaching wider publics, *Colta.ru*'s mnemonic counterpublic did not expand enough to make a difference.

Works cited

Asen, Robert. "Seeking the 'Counter' in Counterpublics." *Communication Theory* 10.4 (2000): 424–446.
Baunov, Aleksandr, Dmitry Butrin, Linor Goralik, Aleksandr Drakhler, Anna Narinskaya, Kirill Rogov, and Marietta Chudakova. "Ty osoznayosh', chto eto tebe podarili v 90-e?" [Do You Realize That

It Was Given to You in the 90s?]. *Colta.ru* (October 22, 2015). https://www.colta.ru/articles/os
trov90/8957-ty-osoznaesh-chto-eto-tebe-podarili-v-90-e (Accessed April 10, 2023).

Belenkina, Katerina, Ilya Venyavkin, Anna Nemzer, and Tatiana Trofimova, eds. *Muzei 90-kh: territoriya
svobody* [Museum of the 1990s: Freedom Territory]. Moscow: Novoe literaturnoe obozrenie, 2016.

Boele, Otto. "'Perestroika and the 1990s – Those Were the Best Years of My Life!' Nostalgia for the
Post-Soviet Limbo." *Post-Soviet Nostalgia: Confronting the Empire's Legacies*. Ed. Otto Boele, Boris
Noordenbos, and Ksenia Robbe. New York: Routledge, 2019. 203–223.

Boyarinov, Denis. "Boris Minaev: 'Nuzhno skazat' o Yeltsine druguyu pravdu'" [Boris Minaev: "A
Different Truth about Yeltsin Needs to Be Told"]. *Colta.ru* (November 23, 2015). https://www.
colta.ru/articles/ostrov90/9336-boris-minaev-nuzhno-skazat-o-eltsine-druguyu-pravdu
(Accessed April 10, 2023).

Boym, Svetlana. *The Future of Nostalgia*. New York: Basic Books, 2001.

Calhoun, Craig. "Civil Society and the Public Sphere." *Public Culture* 5.2 (1993): 267–280.

Chudakova, Marietta. "Povorotnyye 90-e" [Turning 90s]. *Colta.ru* (April 3, 2015). https://www.colta.ru/
articles/school90/6866-povorotnye-90-e (Accessed April 10, 2023).

Denisova, Anastasia, and Aliaksandr Herasimenka. "How Russian Rap on YouTube Advances
Alternative Political Deliberation: Hegemony, Counter-Hegemony, and Emerging Resistant
Publics." *Social Media + Society* 5.2 (April–June 2019): 1–11.

Downey, John, and Natalie Fenton. "New Media, Counter Publicity and the Public Sphere." *New Media
& Society* 5.2 (2003): 185–202.

Drobiazko-Parshchikova, Ekaterina. "Vladimir Sharov: 'Ya dumayu, chto 90-e nie kon'chilis.'" [Vladimir
Sharov: "The 1990s, I Think, Have Not Ended"]. *Colta.ru* (December 4, 2015). https://www.colta.ru/
articles/ostrov90/9459-vladimir-sharov-ya-dumayu-chto-90-e-ne-konchilis (Accessed April 10, 2023).

Eidelman, Tamara (recorded by Denis Boyarinov). "Yesli vsekh uchiteley vygonyat', to kto uchit'
budet?" [If All Teachers Are Fired, Who Will Teach?]. *Colta.ru* (February 12, 2015). https://www.
colta.ru/articles/school90/6289-esli-vseh-uchiteley-vygonyat-to-kto-uchit-budet (Accessed
April 10, 2023).

Fond Yegora Gaidara. "O 'Muzeye 90-kh'" [About "The Museum of the 90s"]. *Colta.ru* (May 15, 2014).
https://www.colta.ru/90s/about (Accessed April 10, 2023).

Fraser, Nancy. "Rethinking the Public Sphere: A Contribution to the Critique of Actually Existing
Democracy." *Social Text* 25/26 (1990): 56–80.

Fredheim, Rolf. "August 1991 and the Memory of Communism in Russia." *Memory in a Mediated
World: Remembrance and Reconstruction*. Ed. Andrea Hajek, Christine Lohmeier, and Christian
Pentzold. Basingstoke: Palgrave Macmillan, 2016. 210–228.

Golubeva, Anna. "'Ostrov 90-kh': naydite sebya" ["The Island of the 90s": Find Yourself]. *Colta.ru*
(September 22, 2015). https://www.colta.ru/articles/ostrov90/8611-ostrov-90-h-naydite-
sebya#ad-image-0 (Accessed April 10, 2023).

Gudkov, Lev. "Zachem vlastyam nuzhna reabilitatsiya obraza Stalina" [Why the Authorities Pursue
the Rehabilitation of Stalin]. *Vedomosti* (September 30, 2009). https://www.vedomosti.ru/opin
ion/articles/2009/09/30/zachem-vlastyam-nuzhna-reabilitaciya-obraza-stalina (Accessed
November 24, 2021).

Hoskins, Andrew, ed. *Digital Memory Studies: Media Pasts in Transition*. New York: Routledge, 2018.

Irwin-Zarecka, Iwona. *Frames of Remembrance: The Dynamics of Collective Memory*. New Brunswick, NJ:
Transaction, 1994.

Katsva, Leonid (recorded by Denis Boyarinov). "Vrodie vsyo pravda, no ved' nepravda zhe!"
[Ostensibly True, but False Really!]. *Colta.ru* (February 17, 2015). https://www.colta.ru/articles/
school90/6357-vrode-vse-pravda-no-ved-nepravda-zhe (Accessed April 10, 2023).

Kokh, Alfred. "Shkola vzrosleniya" [The School of Growing Up]. *Colta.ru* (February 9, 2015). https://www.colta.ru/articles/school90/6252-shkola-vzrosleniya (Accessed April 10, 2023).

Koposov, Nikolay. *Memory Laws, Memory Wars: The Politics of the Past in Europe and Russia*. Cambridge: Cambridge University Press, 2018.

Levinson, Alexey. "1990-e i 1990-yi: sotsiologicheskiye modeli" [The 1990s and the Year 1990: Sociological Models]. *Novoe literaturnoe obozrenie* 2 (2007): 489–503.

Litvinenko, Anna, and Andrei Zavadski. "Memories on Demand: Narratives about 1917 in Russia's Online Publics." *Europe-Asia Studies* 72.10 (2020): 1657–1677.

Malinova, Olga. "Obosnovanie politiki 2000-kh godov v diskurse V.V. Putina i formirovanie mifa o 'likhikh devyanostykh'" [Justifying the Political Course of the 2000s and Constructing the Myth about 'The Hard Nineties' in Vladimir Putin's Discourse]. *Politicheskaya nauka* 3 (2018): 45–69.

Malinova, Olga. "Framing the Collective Memory of the 1990s as a Legitimation Tool for Putin's Regime." *Problems of Post-Communism* 68.5 (2021): 429–441.

Narinskaya, Anna. "Ves' kuryatnik vspoloshilsya. Anna Narinskaya ob udivitel'nom fleshmobe pro 1990-e gody" [The Buzzard-Roost Astonished. Anna Narinskaya Explains the Surprising Flash-Mob on the 1990s]. *Meduza* (September 23, 2015). https://meduza.io/feature/2015/09/23/ves-kuryatnik-vspoloshilsya (Accessed November 24, 2021).

Palczewski, Catherine H. "Cyber-Movements, New Social Movements, and Counterpublics." *Counterpublics and the State*. Ed. Robert Asen and Daniel C. Brouwer. Albany: SUNY Press, 2001. 161–186.

Polivanova, Alexandra. *Facebook* (September 20, 2015). https://www.facebook.com/search/posts/?q=%23%D0%BE%D1%81%D1%82%D1%80%D0%BE%D0%B290%D1%85&epa=SERP_TAB (Accessed November 24, 2021).

"Priglashenie k puteshestviyu" [An Invitation for a Trip]. *Colta.ru* (September 2, 2015). https://www.colta.ru/articles/ostrov90/8394-priglashenie-k-puteshestviyu (Accessed April 10. 2023).

Rauchfleisch, Adrian, and Mike S. Schäfer. "Multiple Public Spheres of Weibo: A Typology of Forms and Potentials of Online Public Spheres in China." *Information, Communication & Society* 18.2 (2015): 139–155.

Prokhorova, Irina. "Kak rozhdalsya novyi yazyk" [How a New Language Was Born]. *Colta.ru* (October 13, 2015a). https://www.colta.ru/articles/ostrov90/8847-kak-rozhdalsya-novyy-yazyk (Accessed April 10, 2023).

Prokhorova, Irina. "Kultura povsyednevnosti. 1990-e: opyt svobody" [Culture of the Everyday. The 1990s: Experience of Freedom]. *Snob.ru* (October 6, 2015b). https://snob.ru/selected/entry/98811/ (Accessed November 24, 2021).

Rothberg, Michael. "Between Auschwitz and Algeria: Multidirectional Memory and the Counterpublic Witness." *Critical Inquiry* 33.1 (2006): 158–184.

Rothberg, Michael. "The Counterpublic Witness: Charlotte Delbo's *Les belles lettres*." *Multidirectional Memory. Remembering the Holocaust in the Age of Decolonization*. Stanford: Stanford University Press, 2009. 199–224.

Ryan, Lorraine. "Memory, Power and Resistance: The Anatomy of a Tripartite Relationship." *Memory Studies* 4.2 (2011): 154–169.

Shklovski, Irina, and Bjarki Valtysson. "Secretly Political: Civic Engagement in Online Publics in Kazakhstan." *Journal of Broadcasting & Electronic Media* 56.3 (2012): 417–433.

Skobeida, Ul'yana, and Evgeny Sazonov. "Napishem pravdivuyu istoriyu 90-kh!" [Let's Write the True History of the 90s!]. *Komsomol'skaya pravda* (August 24, 2016). https://www.kp.ru/daily/26435.7/3306369/ (Accessed September 30, 2019).

Slobodchikova, Olga. "'Likhie' ili 'raznye': pochemu v Rossii snova sporyat o 90-kh?" ["Turbulent" or "Miscellaneous": Why the 1990s Are Debated Again in Russia?]. *BBC Russian Service*

(September 24, 2015). https://www.bbc.com/russian/society/2015/09/150924_90s_argument_rus
sia (Accessed November 25, 2021).

Toepfl, Florian. "From Connective to Collective Action: Internet Elections as a Digital Tool to Centralize
and Formalize Protest in Russia." *Information, Communication & Society* 21.4 (2018): 531–547.

Toepfl, Florian. "Comparing Authoritarian Publics: The Benefits and Risks of Three Types of Publics
for Autocrats." *Communication Theory* 30.2 (2020): 105–125.

Toepfl, Florian, and Eunike Piwoni. "Public Spheres in Interaction: Comment Sections of News
Websites as Counterpublic Spaces." *Journal of Communication* 65.3 (2015): 465–488.

Vesti (September 21 2015). "Idealizatsiya 90-kh: chego dobivayutsya organizatory vystavki v
Muzeone?" [Idealization of the 90s: What Do the Organizers of the Exhibition in the Muzeon
Strive to Achieve?]. https://www.vesti.ru/videos/show/vid/657269/cid/7/# (Accessed
November 25, 2021).

Vigdorova, Elena (recorded by Elena Rybakova). "My prosvisteli svoi 90-e" [We Blew Our 1990s].
Colta.ru (March 3, 2015). https://www.colta.ru/articles/school90/6473-elena-vigdorova-my-
prosvisteli-svoi-1990-e (Accessed April 10, 2023).

Vasilevskaya, Nadezhda. "Pust' literatura igraet men'shuyu rol', no pust' budet svoboda" [Even If
Literature Plays a Lesser Role, Let There Be Freedom]. *Colta.ru* (September 10, 2015).
https://www.colta.ru/articles/ostrov90/8485-pust-literatura-igraet-menshuyu-rol-no-pust-budet-
svoboda (Accessed April 10, 2023).

Vasilevskaya, Nadezhda, and Anna Golubeva. "My pytalis' stat' svobodnoy stranoy" [We Attempted to
Be a Free Country]. *Colta.ru* (September 2, 2015). https://www.colta.ru/articles/ostrov90/8393-
my-pytalis-stat-svobodnoy-stranoy (Accessed April 10, 2023).

Volkov, Denis. *Protestnoe dvizhenie v Rossii v kontekste 2011–2012 gg.: istoki, dinamika, rezul'taty* [Protest
Movement in Russia in the Context of 2011–2012: Origins, Dynamics, Results]. Moscow: Levada-
Center, 2012.

Warner, Michael. *Publics and Counterpublics*. New York: Zone Books, 2005.

Wegner, Jarula M. I. "Rethinking Countermemory: Black-Jewish Negotiations in Rap Music." *Memory
Studies* 13.6 (2020): 1219–1234.

Wijermars, Mariëlle. *Memory Politics in Contemporary Russia: Television, Cinema and the State*. London:
Routledge, 2018.

Zerubavel, Eviatar. *Social Mindscapes: An Invitation to Cognitive Sociology*. Cambridge, MA: Harvard UP,
1999.

Zintsov, Oleg. "Festival 'Ostrov-91' sdelal iz vremeni mesto" [Festival 'Island-91' Makes a Place out of a
Time]. *Vedomosti* (August 21, 2016). https://www.vedomosti.ru/lifestyle/articles/2016/08/22/
653872-festival-ostrov-91-sdelal-iz-vremeni-mesto (Accessed November 24, 2021).

Interviews

Belenkina, Katerina and Anna Nemzer, interview, Moscow, October 3, 2018.
Morev, Gleb, interview, Berlin, April 16, 2019.

Mykola Makhortykh

We Were Hungry, but We Were Also Free: Narratives of Russia's First Post-Soviet Decade on Instagram

Abstract: The first post-Soviet decade occupies an important place in the Russian collective memory. Associated with the transition to democracy, but also economic hardships and violence, it constitutes a complex amalgamation of traumatic and nostalgic recollections. The ambiguous role of the 1990s memories is further complicated by their intense instrumentalization by the Kremlin for consolidating the public support as well as their counter-instrumentalization by the civil society for criticizing the revival of authoritarian tendencies in Russia. Under these circumstances, it is important to understand how the remediation of narratives about the first post-Soviet decade is influenced by social media platforms capable of both countering and reinforcing hegemonic discourses about the past.

With this aim, the chapter examines how trauma and nostalgia associated with the 1990s are remediated via Instagram. Using a sample of Instagram data, it examines whether memory remediation on the platform reflects the above-mentioned intense politicization of nostalgia and trauma associated with this period and how this remediation is affected by the consumption-oriented nature of Instagram. The chapter's findings demonstrate that Instagram is primarily used for showcasing cultural products associated with the 1990s and expressing a yearning towards childhood and teenage years that coincided with the post-Soviet transition. Despite the absence of explicit political statements, however, nostalgic content on Instagram can still be seen as a form of challenging the hegemonic narrative of the 1990s as a time of misery and hardships.

Introduction

The first post-Soviet decade – or 'the 1990s' – occupies a special place in the Russian collective memory. The abolishment of the planned economy and the opening of the Russian market to the Western material and cultural products were the integral part of Russia's transition to democracy and normalization of relationship with the West. However, the downside of these transformations was the rise of poverty and crime amplified by the dismantlement of the Soviet social security system and a series of armed conflicts in the former Soviet republics. This combination of economic and creative opportunities, but also disillusionments and hardships, explains why this period is collectively known as *likhie devianostye* ('the rowdy 1990s' in Russian; Boele 2019).

Until now, memories of the first post-Soviet decade maintain a substantial presence in the Russian public sphere. During the third presidential term of Vladimir Putin, references to *likhie devianostye* and the hardships brought by them became a recurring element of the Kremlin's rhetoric (Malinova 2018). Employed for consolidating public support by contrasting current economic stability with the chaos of the post–1991 transformations, the 1990s are referred to as "the tragic years" (Putin 2019), when Russia was "on the edge of losing its sovereignty and being dismantled" (Putin 2019a). Yet, the very same contrast also inspires more nostalgic feelings, with the post-Soviet transition being praised as a period of unprecedented economic and political freedom which contrasts with the revival of authoritarian tendencies in the 2000s (Medvedev 2019).

An important factor in the interactions between different narratives of the 1990s is the digital turn in individual and collective remembrance in the post-Soviet countries (Rutten, Fedor and Zvereva 2013). By enabling new possibilities for cultural and political self-expression (Kukulin 2013), digital platforms facilitate the construction of mnemonic counter-narratives which have the potential for exposing and revitalizing suppressed memories. At the same time, the digital turn can also be used to reinforce hegemonic historical narratives via new digital formats (Makhortykh and Sydorova 2019) and subjugate alternative views by abusing platform affordances.

To achieve a better understanding of how the digital memory turn impacts memories of the post-Soviet transition, the chapter examines how trauma and nostalgia associated with the transition are remediated via Instagram. Instagram is a Western digital platform that is used for storing, sharing, and discussing photos and videos. Before its ban in Russia in 2022 as part of the reinforcement of the Kremlin's control over the domestic information sphere following the Russian large-scale invasion of Ukraine, Instagram was highly popular in Russia (more than 47 million users; Statista 2020), in particular among female and younger (25–34 years) audiences with average (39.2% of users) and above average (32% of users) income (data for 2020; Gaitbaeva 2020).

Instagram features prominently in digital memory research[1] with its affordances enabling different forms of sharing and engaging with individual and collective past. Simultaneously, the platform's frequent use for business purposes makes it rather consumption-oriented, which makes Instagram an important component in the process of "memory commercialization" (Björkdahl and Kappler 2019). Furthermore, Instagram is less subjected to Russian state censorship,

---

1 For some examples see Hochman and Manovich 2013, Avedissian 2015, Commane and Potton 2019.

which facilitates its use for online (counter)memory campaigns, including the ones focused on memories of the 1990s (IRK 2018, Merzliakova 2020).

Based on a sample of Instagram data dealing with the first post-Soviet decade, the chapter examines how the platform is used to produce and communicate memories of the post-1991 transition, to what degree these processes reflect the intense politicization of nostalgia and trauma associated with this period, and how these processes are affected by the consumption-oriented nature of the platform. By doing so, the paper addresses the following questions: How are post-1991 socioeconomic transformations in Russia presented and interpreted via Instagram? What are the recurring visual tropes employed by Instagram users to communicate nostalgia and trauma related to this transition period? And to what degree does Instagram serve as a platform for countering official narratives of the 1990s and promoting alternative interpretations of the period?

Post-post-soviet digital trauma and nostalgia in Russia: Theoretical background

Trauma and nostalgia in digital environments

The unprecedented saturation of contemporary societies with digital technologies has a significant impact on how the past is engaged with on the individual and collective levels (Hoskins 2017). The growing connectivity between individuals enabled by platforms and mobile devices accelerates the formation and contestation of memories in digital environments (Hoskins 2009). Together with the extensive possibilities for capturing and storing memorabilia, these factors shift the balance between remembrance and forgetting with the former becoming a default condition in human relationship with the past (Mayer-Schonberger 2011).

This digital turn also has profound implications for the ways in which feelings of trauma and nostalgia are formed and processed. While often conceived as opposite states, both trauma and nostalgia characterize a condition under which the past intrudes on the present (Arnold-de Simine 2013). This intrusion is accompanied by a sense of rupture and radical discontinuity caused by the "irretrievable loss" (Horowitz 2010, 49). Yet, in the case of nostalgia the intrusion of the past is centered around the positive attachment, whereas in the case of trauma "the negative inability" (Legg 2004, 103) to deal with the past prevails.

Besides both being located on the same "threshold between remembering and forgetting" (Arnold-de Simine 2013, 62), nostalgia and trauma are often causally related to each other. Nostalgia is frequently viewed as a consequence of trauma, both on individual (Talu 2009) and collective level (Kalinin 2011), with nostalgic feelings being a reaction to post-traumatic shock (Mazur 2015). However, trauma not only causes nostalgia by creating a yearning for the time preceding the loss as, for instance, in the case of post-Soviet nostalgia caused by the dissolution of the Soviet Union (Mazur 2015), but also can be an object of longing itself. Arnold-de Simine (2013) discusses how the sinking of the Titanic or the German bombing of Britain stimulate nostalgic feelings for the time of greatness and the communal spirit despite being highly traumatic events. Similar logic can explain the nostalgic longing for the Stalinist period in post-Soviet countries, where it is associated with strong leadership despite it also being related to many unresolved traumas of mass atrocities (Gugushvili and Kabachnik 2019).

The process of digitization creates new venues for expressing and interacting with nostalgia and trauma. The platform-based connectivity facilitates establishment of mnemonic communities, where nostalgic and traumatic recollections can be shared (Kalinina and Menke 2016), thus countering silence which is particularly prominent in the case of trauma (Menyhert and Makhortykh 2017). By offering a venue through which trauma can be shared, platforms can help to cope with the past and prevent secondary traumatization related to a society's unwillingness to listen to the victims (McKinney 2007). At the same time, memory digitization also increases possibilities for accidental encounters with the content that triggers nostalgic or traumatic experience. This can lead to re-traumatization of individuals who experienced trauma (Majeed, Sudak and Beresin 2019) as well as their successors in the case of historical traumas (Carlson et al. 2017).

The digital turn also influences the societal uses of nostalgia and trauma. Because of their strong affective potential, both of them serve as powerful factors of mobilization and are often instrumentalized for political aims, e.g., collective identity-building (Kalinina and Menke 2016). While such instrumentalization can empower grassroots initiatives and counter memory hegemonies, there is also the growing recognition that the exclusive focus on the democratizing potential of digitally mediated trauma and nostalgia can be misleading (Makhortykh and Aguilar 2020). The nostalgic yearning for a 'golden age' (Elgenius and Rydgren 2019) is increasingly utilized by populist politicians around the world to secure their political gains (Kenny 2017, Buzalka 2018). Similarly, traumatic recollections of past injustices such as 'one hundred years of humiliation' in China (Wang 2008) or the October revolution in Russia (Chatterje-Doody and Tolz 2020) often serve as important elements of neo-authoritarian 'identitarian' (Kneuer 2017) narratives.

At the same time, the affectivity of trauma and nostalgia also encourages their use in other domains, such as commerce. Nostalgia in particular has long served as an important element of the advertisement industry, where sentimental yearning for an idealized past was used to drive consumption (Volčič 2007). The growing visibility and frequency of interactions with the past online facilitates commodification of nostalgia as a commercial device in the structure of global capitalism (Jeziński and Wojtkowski 2016). The examples of platform affordances which further stimulate commercial uses of nostalgia are low costs of retrieval and actualization of mnemonic content (Lizardi 2014) as well as affect circulation in online communities (Keightley and Niemeyer 2020).

Digitization of trauma and nostalgia in Russia

Digitization of trauma and nostalgia is a particularly important topic in relation to the post-Soviet states due to the multiple unresolved traumas caused by political repressions and armed conflicts. These historical conditions result in a complex amalgamation of traumatic and nostalgic feelings towards the past, and specific features of public interactions with memory in the local context. Many of these countries, including Russia, demonstrate what Michael Bernhard and Jan Kubik called 'fractured memory regimes,' in which political actors try to control public memory practices and use them to legitimize their own status (2014, 17). Consequently, ordinary citizens have limited possibilities to influence how the past is publicly remembered with the state using multiple means to sustain its mnemonic hegemonies. These means vary from legal repercussions for promoting alternative narratives as in the case of Russian memory laws (Koposov 2017) to hijacking grassroots memory movements such as the Immortal Regiment (Fedor 2017).

Under these circumstances, digital platforms offer Russian citizens a space where the past can be discussed and engaged with.[2] While the process of reactivating memories often involves discursive clashes about what is true and what is not (also known as 'web wars'; Rutten, Fedor and Zvereva 2013), it still allows individuals to reflect on their affective attachment to the past and, potentially, process it constructively (Trubina 2010). However, the combination of the profound disagreements about what shared (mnemonic) symbols of the Russian collective identity should be (Morenkova 2012) and of unresolved traumas related to the past make such constructive processing a challenging task and result in frequent contestation of online engagements with memory.

Another challenge of digitization of nostalgia and trauma in Russia is the growing use of platforms by pro-Kremlin forces for targeting their opponents and

---

2 The chapter has been written before the 2022 Russian invasion in Ukraine and the subsequent changes in Russian digital media landscape. While after 2022 digital platforms still provide some space for counter-state reflection and self-expression, the intense suppression of the dissent by the Russian state limits their use for critical engagement both with the historical and the recent past.

mobilizing popular support. Such instrumental uses often involve appropriation of trauma for constructing negative identities of political opponents to undermine their reputation or even dehumanize them. Recent examples of such abuses of affective attachment to the past come from Russia's war against Ukraine, where references to Second World War memories were employed to stigmatize the Ukrainian side and draw parallels between the new pro-Western Ukrainian government and Nazi Germany (Gaufman 2017, Makhortykh 2018).

Besides the new possibilities for political uses of trauma and nostalgia in Russia, the digital turn also enables new ways of using nostalgia in commercial contexts. Despite the slower shift towards online marketing by local businesses, Russia currently is one of the major digital markets – the situation that leads to the intense use of platforms for product advertisement. The large pool of digital memorabilia available for the use in commercial purposes (Kalinina 2014), together with the ability to deliver them in a more individualized manner (e.g., via Facebook news feed), facilitates evocation of nostalgic feelings, which are used by by Russian companies for increasing profits.

Post-post-Soviet nostalgia and trauma

In contrast to the numerous studies devoted to the nostalgia and trauma associated with the Soviet period,[3] there is relatively little research on affective attachments to the post-Soviet era and how these attachments are influenced by digitization. One reason for this discrepancy is that the first post-Soviet generation has just recently reached maturity. In addition, the discontinuity between the Soviet and the post-Soviet periods can be argued to be more pronounced than in the case of the transition from the 1990s to the 2000s, albeit the rise of authoritarian tendencies in Russia in the 2000s results in a strong discontinuity between the 1990s and the 2010s.

These two factors can explain why the feeling of rupture and loss associated with the 1990s has only recently become mediatized on a larger scale and, thus, attracted more scholarly attention. So far, however, the research on post-post-Soviet nostalgia tends to focus on the analogue media. Boele (2019), for instance, examines TV series dealing with the first post-Soviet decade and points out the complex composition of the period's perceptions, varying from the appreciation of the freedom and the prowess required to survive its excesses. Mazur (2015)

---

3 See, for instance, Boym 2001, Todorova and Gille 2010, Kalinina 2014 and Boele, Noordenbos and Robbe 2019. For the research on digital forms of post-Soviet nostalgia, see Kalinina and Menke 2016, Duijn 2019, Semolina 2013.

identifies a similar mix of feelings, varying from the nostalgic recollection of the end of Soviet-era deficits and the possibility to travel abroad to the less sentimental recollections of the consequences of the diminishing social security net.

The larger volume of research on post-post-Soviet trauma similarly tends to discuss it in the analogue context. Shevchenko (2009) examines the perception of the 1990s in Moscow and shows how the post-Soviet transition was interpreted as a perpetual crisis with a few isles of stability such as family. Similar observations come from Gorkshkov (2016), who shows how the period of transition is remembered as the time of anguish and insecurity, in particular as a result of the financial crises. Hashamova (2007) shows how these traumatic feelings are also reflected in popular culture with wounded national pride and anxiety about the unclear future having a substantive impact on post-Soviet Russian cinema.

The relatively limited scope of scholarship on nostalgia and trauma of the 1990s is contrasted by their intense instrumentalization. The traumatic aspects of *likhie devianostye*, in particular the loss of the superpower status and economic decline, are intensively used in the rhetoric of the Kremlin (Malinova 2018) and other political actors, e.g., the Communist Party (Malinova 2020), to mobilize public support. Simultaneously, nostalgia about "the most free, the most remarkable" (Medvedev 2019) period of the Russian history is used to oppose the authorities' attempts to strengthen control over the public sphere. Such opposition involves the use of platforms to organize mnemonic flash mobs, such as "#my90s" (Merzliakova 2020), where Russian citizens share their personal experiences that often contradict the narrative of the 1990s as a time of misery and geopolitical weakness.

The intense exploitation of the feeling of rupture associated with the first post-Soviet decade is also observed in the context of Russian commerce. Similar to the Soviet nostalgia, which was used to promote multiple commercial brands (Kusimova and Schmidt 2016), the 1990s increasingly become an influential factor in promoting different kinds of services/goods, in particular the ones related to post-Soviet popular culture that intensively developed in the 1990s (Merzliakova 2020). The effects of this commodification of the 1990s nostalgia, however, remain rather unclear as well as the way commodification interacts with narratives of the first post-Soviet decade thriving on online platforms.

Capturing (counter-)narratives of the 1990s

For implementing the study, I looked at Instagram posts with the #90ые ('the 1990s') hashtag. The choice of the hashtag was made based on the examination of the search queries corresponding to different terms associated with the post-

Soviet transition (e.g., #девяностые, #лихие90е, #90е, #ностальгия). The choice of the #90ые is attributed to three reasons. First, this hashtag was less emotionally predefined than some other popular options (e.g., 'the rowdy 1990s'). Second, compared to other queries, it provided a more diverse composition of results addressing various aspects of the post-Soviet transition. Finally, the corpus size for #90ые (less than 20 thousand Instagram posts) made it easier to retrieve, in particular considering data retrieval limitations enforced by Instagram.

The posts with the chosen hashtag were crawled using Phantombuster's automated programming interface (API) for Instagram. Phantombuster is a commercial company specializing in cloud-based marketing APIs which can be used for retrieving data from different platforms. The resulting dataset included 10, 221 Instagram posts published between 2012 and 2019. From this dataset, a random sample of 222 posts with the equal number of posts sampled for each year[4] was selected. Then, the sampled posts were manually examined and classified using the inductive coding approach (Thomas 2006).

The classification included three coding schemas and was conducted by a single coder. The first schema – affective attachment to the past – included three options: 1) *nostalgic*: posts that expressed nostalgic feelings in relation to the past; 2) *traumatic*: posts that referred to individual/collective trauma associated with the past; 3) *non-affective*: posts that did not express any clear emotional attachment to the past.

The second coding schema – the mnemonic function – included five memory-related functions performed by the Instagram posts: 1) *abstract nostalgia*: posts expressing nostalgic feeling in general terms and without a clear attachment to the 1990s; 2) *specific nostalgia*: posts expressing nostalgic feelings in relation to the specific aspects of the period; 3) *commercialized nostalgia*: posts utilizing nostalgic feelings for promoting specific products and commercial goals; 4) *showcasing*: posts showcasing aspects of the period without expressing an emotional attachment to them; and 5) *cultural referencing*: posts appropriating aspects of the 1990s as a form of cultural reference for today, but without a clear emotional attachment to the past. For trauma-related posts, no differentiation between specific functions was introduced because of the small number of such posts.

The final coding schema – objects of memory – classified aspects of the 1990s which were referenced on Instagram. In those cases when a post could be attributed to several different categories, the choice was made according to the image's focus as well as verbal cues (e.g., the image description). The following options were used: 1) *economics*: posts referring to the economic situation in the 1990s; 2)

---

4 For each year from 2013 to 2019 a random sample of 30 posts was generated. For 2012, all 12 posts retrieved for this year were used.

food: posts discussing different food products; 3) *games*: posts referring to specific games or toys; 4) *lifestyle*: posts referencing specific features of 1990s life or distinct subcultures; 5) *location*: posts describing specific locations; 6) *mass media*: posts discussing mass media (e.g., TV channels); 7) *people*: posts referring certain people (e.g., family members); 8) *popular culture*: posts referring to specific cultural products (e.g., popular songs); 9) *politics*: posts referring to political matters; 10) *technology*: posts referring to specific gadgets and vehicles (e.g., cars).

Between nostalgia, trauma, and showcasing: The mnemonic functions of the '90ые'

Nostalgic timelines: The rise of the '90ые' on Instagram

I started the analysis by examining the use of #90ые on Instagram. Figure 1 shows that the hashtag became intensively used in 2014 and since then shows a growing trend. Despite several "memory marathons" dealing with the 1990s in 2015 and 2018 (Merzliakova 2020, Maksimova 2016), there are no peaks of hashtag use during these two years. The absence of such peaks might suggest that either the marathons did not make a substantial difference for the overall dynamics of engaging with the 1990s on Instagram or they did not involve the hashtags used for data collection.

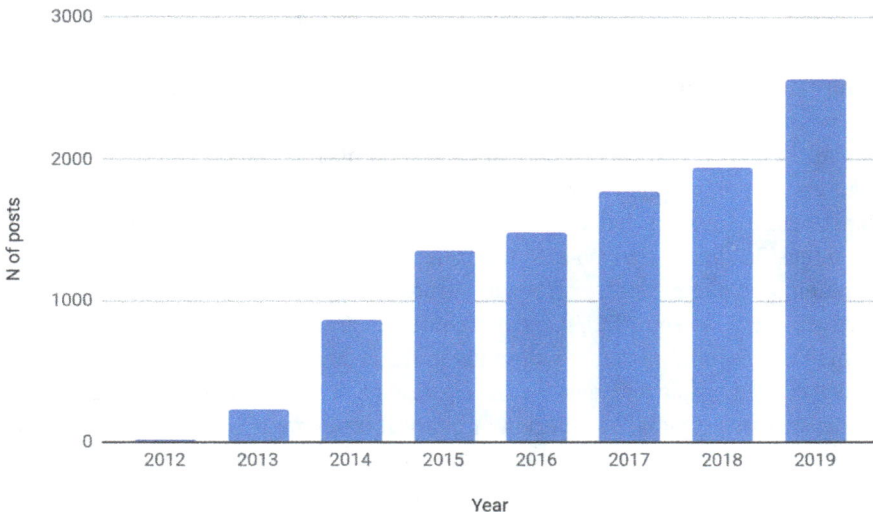

Figure 1: The use of 90ые hashtag on Instagram.

However, it is important to take into consideration that older Instagram posts are more likely to get deleted, which can influence the distribution shown.

It is also important to emphasize once more that Figure 1 shows the distribution of only the posts with 90ые hashtag and not all the posts dealing with the 1990s on Instagram. Some of the 1990s–related posts did not necessarily include the hashtag, in particular as it takes time for the hashtag to become adopted. Furthermore, the examination of the use of #90ые should also take into consideration the overall dynamics of Instagram use in the region. According to Brand Analytics data, in the winter of 2014–2015, the number of active Instagram users in Russia was 2.6 millions (Brand Analytics 2015), whereas in the winter of 2015–2016 the number increased to 10.6 millions (Brand Analytics 2016), followed by 23.7 millions in autumn 2018 (Brand Analytics 2018). At the same time, the trend of growth is not necessarily linear as shown by data for the summer of 2017, when the number of active users dropped to 7.1 million (Brand Analytics 2017) compared to 10.6 million in 2016. Under these circumstances (and considering the often fragmentary reporting on the number of Instagram users in Russia), it is difficult to normalize the growth in the use of #90ые by the overall increase in the number of Instagram users in the region, in particular considering that the hashtag might not necessarily be used only by users from Russia.

One particular observation concerning the timeline of the use of #90ые is that it started to be intensively used from 2014. Such timing can be attributed to the growing online presence of the first post-Soviet generation for which the 1990s are associated with childhood memories that can stimulate yearning for "a return to an ideal childhood" (Kalinina 2016, 7). From this point of view, the growing interest towards the 1990s on Instagram can be viewed as a form of reflective nostalgia, defined by Boym (2001) as a more individualized and fragmentary form of nostalgia that differentiates it from restorative nostalgia which deals with collective recollections of the past and desires to revive it.

At the same time, the particular timing can also be related to the changes in the Russian public sphere following the beginning of Russia's war against Ukraine (Mazur 2015). Under the conditions of the growing confrontation with the West and the intensification of the neo-authoritarian tendencies, including the increased use of mnemonic narratives for strategic purposes (Gaufman 2017, Makhortykh, Lyebyedyev and Kravtsov 2021), invocation of the 1990s memories can be viewed as a form of protest aiming to draw attention to the changes in the political sphere. The choice of the post-Soviet transition as a reference of such protest can be explained by the fact that it signifies a period of political freedom; it can also be a counter-reaction to the instrumentalization of the 1990s by the Kremlin for the sake of mobilizing public support towards its aggressive political course.

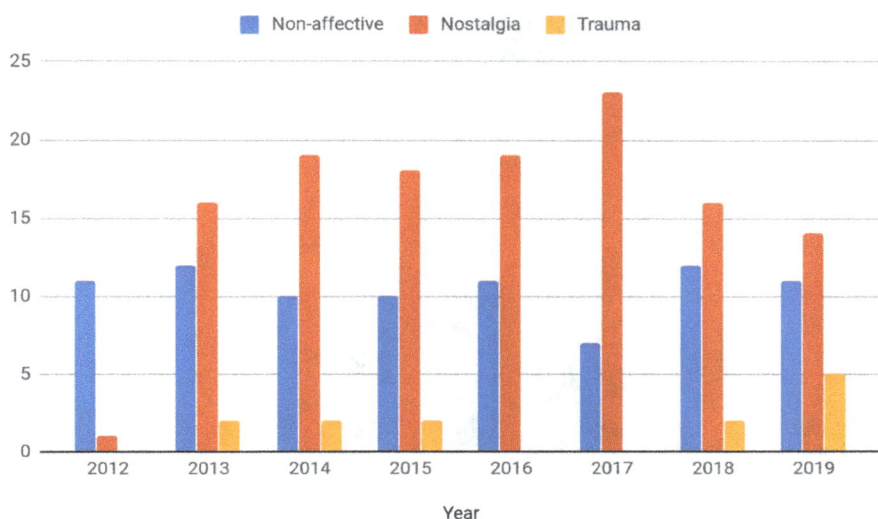

Figure 2: The dynamics of posts with emotional attachment to the past (sample).

Following the examination of the dynamics of the use of #90ые, I examined specific memory functions of the content with the hashtag. Figure 2 shows that the majority of examined Instagram posts deal with nostalgic and non-affective references to the past with the former being prevalent during the whole period with a single exception of 2012. By contrast, references to trauma occur rather sporadically and appear just in a few posts during the period of observation. A small increase of trauma-related content in 2019 is attributed to the A.U.E[5] Instagram campaign that used references to the 1990s to promote the movement.

Finally, I looked at the distribution of posts with specific mnemonic functions. Despite the rather small sample size, Figure 3 still provides interesting insights into the changing function of nostalgic and non-affective posts.[6] For instance, the figure points out the prevalence of the showcasing function in the first few years of the use of #90ые on the platform. This gradual rediscovery of the 1990s on Instagram is then followed by the growing use of memories about the period for cultural reference. The intensification of using 1990s for creative re-interpretation of the present from 2016 is also accompanied by the rise of commercialized nostalgia and the adoption of 1990s for advertising events and products.

---

5 A.U.E. is an acronym for Arestantskii Ustav Edin (Convict's Codex is Universal), an informal organization of Russian criminals, mainly consisting of children and teenage members.
6 The figure does not include trauma-related posts due to the small number of these posts, which does not allow for differentiating between their various functions.

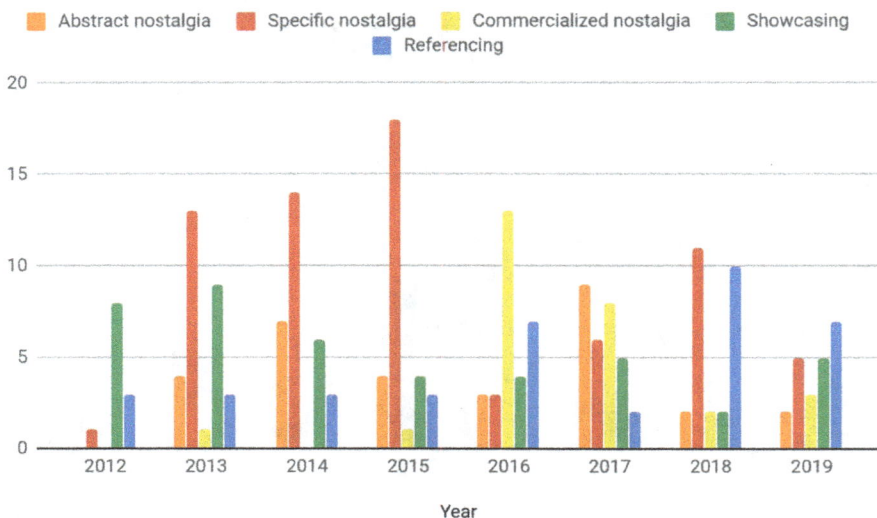

Figure 3: The dynamics of posts with specific mnemonic functions (sample).

Abstract, specific, and commercialized: Nostalgia for the 1990s

The above-mentioned focus on the positive and neutral attachment to the 1990s can be viewed as a form of resistance to the hegemonic narrative of 'likhie devianostye' sponsored by the Russian state (Malinova 2018). However, the examination of nostalgic posts suggests that very few of them focus on political aspects of the 1990s, such as the higher level of personal and societal freedom (Medvedev 2019). Similar to "memory marathons" on Facebook (Maksimova 2016), most nostalgic content on Instagram did not include direct political messages and did not compare the 1990s to the current political situation.

The absence of such explicit comparisons can be attributed to the usual focus of nostalgic content on more intimate and biographical aspects of the past. However, in the post-Soviet context, where references to the past are often used for interpreting and commenting on the present (e.g. Rutten et al., 2013), such absence is surprising. It is particularly astonishing in the case of references to the 1990s for which, as shown by Zavadski (in this volume), the the process of challenging hegemonic narratives of the post-Soviet transition often goes hand in hand with the challenging of the political status quo.

Instead, a large number of posts express a yearning for childhood and teenage years. These abstract nostalgic feelings that are also prevalent in the case of

Facebook (Maksimova 2016) do not seem to be explicitly related to the economic and cultural realities of the post-Soviet transition, but refer to the time when the Instagram users were younger than they are now. This specific form of nostalgia that looks back to the earlier days of one's life can be related both to the concepts of reflective nostalgia (Boym 2001) and of personal nostalgia (Holak, Matveev, and Havlena 2007). In this context, the use of #90ые will not differ much from #80ые ("the 1980s") or #70ые ("the 1970s") or any other hashtag denoting a specific time period, which a certain part of the platform's population recalls as the time of being innocent and careless.

Figure 4: Instagram content and abstract nostalgia.Here and for the subsequent figures the faces and account names are blurred on purpose as an additional safeguard for users' privacy.

Two examples of the use of Instagram as a means of expressing personal nostalgia are shown on Figure 4. The image on the left shows a typical family photo featuring a father and a daughter. The daughter, now an Instagram blogger, posted the photo together with several hashtags "#childhood, #childhoodwhereareyourunning, #iaminchildhood, #iamsmall, #photoarchive, #photoalbum, #oldphoto, #itwaslongtimeago, #90ые, #withdad, #daddy, #children, #kids." The image on the right is also a family photo showing two brothers standing in tall grass. The signature says "It does not matter that you are poor, but you have a soul and you have a brother: 90ые."

These images highlight one particular difference between nostalgic posts on Instagram and the ones produced during the Facebook mnemonic marathons. Unlike Facebook, where women predominantly presented themselves as "sexually appealing objects" (Maksimova 2016, 409) and men posted content of themselves working and studying, Instagram users publish content about their early childhood. This distinction can be related to Instagram's audience in Russia being younger than on Facebook (Pokrop 2019) and supports the earlier suggestion that the use of 1990s content can be related to Instagram users reaching maturity and starting feeling nostalgic about their earlier years, but not necessarily connecting their nostalgia to specific political features of the post-Soviet transition.

In terms of sex distribution on Instagram., men were substantially more present compared to women. Such an unequal distribution is observed only for abstract nostalgia- and trauma-related content with other 1990s–related posts being distributed more equally between sexes. While a similar observation is reported by Maximova (2016) for Facebook, it is hard to explain considering the prevalence of female users on Russian Instagram (Pokrop 2019). At the same time, recent studies in cognitive psychology (Kim and Yim 2018) suggest that while sex has little effect on the nostalgic feelings among younger individuals, there is a substantial difference between older males and females with the former being more eager to engage with content stimulating nostalgic feelings.

Compared to abstract nostalgia, Instagram content with nostalgic references to specific aspects of the 1990s occurs more frequently. Usually, these references concern cultural products associated with the period, in particular pop music (e.g., Laskovyi Mai and Ruki Vverh groups). Again, the political realities of the period are not referenced at all with a single exception of a post describing clashes between punks and police during the concert of Grazhdanskaya Oborona and noting that it was a glorious time. The absence of political or commercial references behind this category of content aligns it with the notion of aesthetic nostalgia, namely a reverenced attitude towards the culture from the past that focuses on its preservation for the sake of its aesthetic value (Volčič 2007).

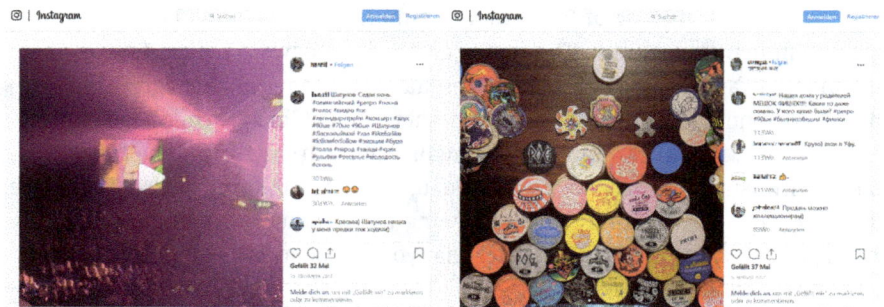

Figure 5: Instagram content and specific nostalgia.

Figure 5 shows two examples of specific nostalgia. The first shows a post referring to a performance of Yuri Shatunov, a front man of Laskovyi Mai pop group. The video showing the performance is signed as 'Shatunov – Sedaia Noch.' #Olimpiiskii #retro #song #voice #video #sk #legendsofretrofm #sound #80s #70s #90ые #Shatunov #LaskovyiMai #hall #liketolike #followtofollow #emotions #storm #crowd #people #dance #shout #smiles #joy #youth #fire". Another image refers to a popular game from the 1990s. The signature says "I found A SACK OF TOKENS at the parent's house!!!! I even remember some of them. Which one did you have? #retro #90ые #iwasundefeatable #tokens."

A related category of content also focuses on specific objects associated with the 1990s, but instead of expressing appreciation, it uses nostalgic feelings for commercial purposes. A number of examined Instagram posts evoke nostalgia to promote certain events (e.g., musical performances) or to sell specific products. Such instrumental use of sentimental feelings is not a new phenomenon and can be viewed as a form of escapist or utopian nostalgia (Volčič 2007) that focuses on commodified narratives of the past and employs them to attract the attention of prospective customers.

Similar to Yugonostalgia (Volčič 2007), such utopian references to the past are often involved in the marketing of popular culture (e.g., 1990s music bands). In some cases, the sellers explicitly appeal to the generation of the 1990s, inviting its members to dive into the memories and dance to your favorite hits or asking if oldies are ready to play the legendary games. In other cases (e.g., the advertisement campaign of the Nora shop specializing in second-hand clothes), the emphasis was made on the vintage nature of items from the 1990s without any additional means of nostalgia activation.

Figure 6: Instagram content and commercialized nostalgia.

Figure 6 offers two examples of commercialized nostalgia. One is an image advertising "a nostalgic evening from the Hightower Band" taking place in a restaurant in Saint-Petersburg. The image of a retro phone and a cassette player is accompanied with a description that draws upon the knowledge of the 1990s popular culture:

"Take me fast, take me beyond one hundred seas, and kiss me everywhere, I am already eighteen." If you did not just read the line above, but sing it and your soul is filled with a pleasant nostalgia, then get your jeans and leggings out of your wardrobes, the 90s come back to Floor 41. Our residents, the Hightower Band, have already made the chart of the best hits of those times and are ready to perform for you on June 28 on the stage of our restaurant!

The second advertisement shows a similarly intense reliance on memories of the 1990s. Published by a Kazakh enterprise known as "a shop of unusual presents," it promotes an iconic chewing gum, Turbo, which was popular in post-Soviet countries. The description of the image states:

Turbo chewing gum – how many of your memories are related to it? Did you know that small marks on the gum itself imitate the traces of car wheels? Today Turbo is not just a chewing gum, but a cultural phenomenon, an iconic product from the 90s. One plate of Turbo is enough to transport you to the world of childhood and the inserted image will bring you great mood! There are 100 chewing plates in one block.

Altogether, these observations highlight two points concerning interactions with nostalgia on Instagram. First, there are few references to politics in the narrow sense of the term (e.g., contrasting political freedoms of the 1990s with the current situation in Russia). Yet, the promotion of narratives that are different from the hegemonic narrative of the post-Soviet transition as a grim warning for the miserable consequences of the regime change can by itself be viewed as political. By constructing a different story of the 1990s that revolves around childhood memories, Instagram users oppose the state-sponsored narrative of the period, albeit in a different way than the usual interpretations of the notion of countermemory presume.[7]

The intense use of nostalgia for the 1990s for commercial purposes adds to this complexity. By relying on the references to the first post-Soviet decade for generating feelings of utopian nostalgia (Volčič 2007) to promote certain products, Instagram focuses on the positive aspects of the first post-Soviet decade and presents it as a time period with its own merit. By doing so, Russian companies relying on the use of nostalgia as part of their marketing strategies also to a certain degree challenge the negativist narrative of the 1990s by presenting the period as the one that is worth yearning for.

---

7 Often, countermemory is associated with narratives that provide a comprehensive alternative to the dominant narrative. See, for instance, Foucault 2003.

Black-and-white past: Trauma of the 1990s

The posts referring to the post-Soviet trauma are distinguished both by their scarcity and explicit references to the socioeconomic realities of the 1990s. Unlike the nostalgic references, which can often be applied to other periods, posts dealing with trauma are more specific and highlight particular traumatic aspects of the time. In particular, they refer to the poverty and the high level of crime which characterized the first post-Soviet decade. An interesting visual aspect of such posts is their tendency to use black-and-white images as contrasted to the almost exclusively colorful images used for nostalgic and non-affective posts.

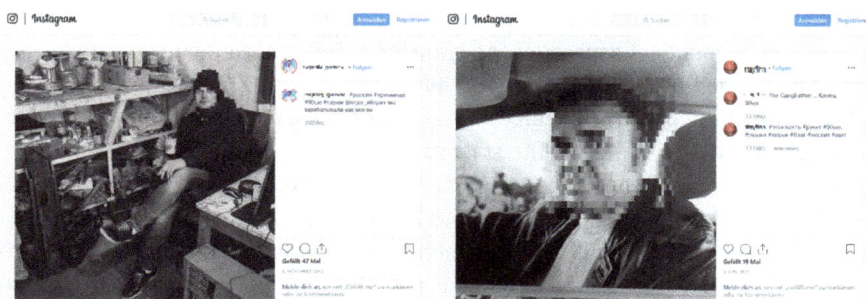

Figure 7: Instagram content and trauma.

Figure 7 shows two examples of trauma-focused posts. The first one shows an image of a trading post signed as "#russia, #criminal, #90ые, #garage – we earned money in all the ways we could." The second one is an image of a driver (potentially, a reference to the 'bombilas,' the illegal cab drivers from the 1990s) signed as "The Gang Father . . . late 90s #danger, #raket, #90ые, #guns, #knives, #blat, #nesvit, #shield." Judging by the text descriptions, both images are of autobiographical kind and belong to the users who posted them.

The above-mentioned posts can be read in different ways. One potential reading is that these posts reiterate popular stereotypes of tough experiences during the 1990s for the purpose of self-aggrandizement. However, they can also be treated as a socially acceptable form of communicating trauma, in particular considering the "remasculinization" (Riabov and Riabova 2014) of Russia during Putin's presidential terms. Earlier research (e.g., Erwin 2022) demonstrated that hegemonic masculinity has substantial implications for conveying traumatic experiences, especially by males, and some of these implications might include inability to speak about trauma directly and the tendency to hide traumatic experiences behind the use of memories for bragging.

Besides the black-and-white stylistics and references to economic hardships, both images show men, which is another common feature of trauma-related posts. This observation aligns with the findings by Maksimova (2016), who compared content produced by male and female users on Facebook and found that male users focus more often on the traumatic aspects of the post-Soviet transition. One possible explanation of such discrepancy is related to the different perceptions of nostalgia: women seem to be focusing on their individual perceptions of the past (i.e., reflective nostalgia) while men concentrate on the collective views on the period (i.e., restorative nostalgia).

Another feature of the trauma-related content is its alignment with the hegemonic narrative of the 1990s as a time of misery. Such an alignment is not necessarily explicit: none of the posts expresses support for the Russian authorities or focuses on geopolitical aspects of the transition that are the key elements of the above-mentioned hegemonic interpretation (Malinina 2020). Yet, by presenting the 1990s through the prism of genuine experiences of economic hardships and crime, these posts can also reinforce the state-sponsored story of the *likhie devianostye*. Even in the case of rather anti-state posts (e.g., the ones associated with the A.U.E self-promotion campaign referring to the 1990s as the time when state apparatus was less capable of controlling organized crime), the depressing image of the decade can lend credibility to the hegemonic narrative instrumentalized by the Kremlin, in particular considering the above-mentioned narrative being deliberately broad and Instagram posts often being too concise to provide a more nuanced interpretation of the period. This observation highlights that hegemonic memory narratives do not necessarily have to be reinforced via organized top-down campaigns, but can also be strengthened by the pluralization of the mnemonic sphere.

Showcasing and referencing: Non-affective references to the 1990s

The final type of the 1990s-related content on Instagram did not have a strong affective attachment to the past unlike the posts mediating nostalgia and trauma. These more neutral cultural expressions usually perform one of the two mnemonic functions: showcasing the past or appropriating certain elements of it as a form of cultural reference.

The showcasing posts are usually devoted to a specific material or cultural product coming from the post-Soviet transition period. These products vary from cars used during the 1990s to iconic drinks to popular music groups and movies. A few exceptions also include showcasing a specific episode from the past such as a New Year celebration with the family. In all these cases, however, the presentation is devoid of emotional cues which would allow identifying any affective attachment to the showcased object.

Figure 8: Instagram content and showcasing.

Figure 8 offers two examples of Instagram posts performing a showcasing function. The one on the left shows the images of two iconic juices – Zuka and Yupi – which became available to Russian citizens in the 1990s. The image is accompanied only with the 90ые hashtag that does not allow to identify any affective attachment. Similar lack of distinct sentiment towards the portrayed subject is observed for another post which shows portable console videogames. The image is accompanied with a signature "Portable consoles 'Elektronika' in EndlesSstory videogames museum by John Isaev #games #museum #consoles #endlessstory #electronics #90ые."

Except for the lack of emotional attachment, showcasing posts share multiple similarities with specific nostalgia which in its turn aligns with the notion of aesthetic nostalgia (Volčič 2007). Like aesthetic nostalgia, showcasing presents artifacts of the 1990s for the sake of preserving their authenticity; however, in the absence of statements elaborating on how users feel about the items, it is hardly possible to judge whether these artifacts are cherished or despised. Another, albeit significantly less common, function of the non-affective posts relates to the appropriation of recognizable elements from the 1990s as a form of cultural reference to the post-Soviet transition. The majority of appropriated elements reference the lifestyle of the transition period using particular types of clothes associated with it.

Figure 9 shows two examples of such cultural references. The first features a selfie made by a young man dressed in a crimson suit with the signature "Hello, bandits." The selfie refers to a stereotypical image of the New Russians, a post-Soviet business elite who acquired their wealth using illegal market operations and who were identifiable by rather tasteless wardrobe choices (including, among others,

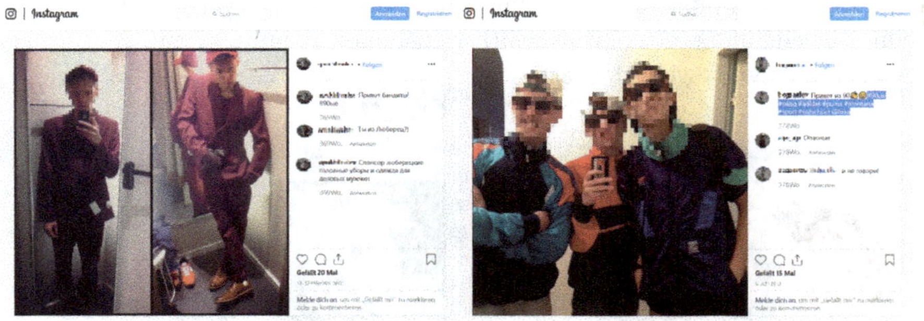

Figure 9: Instagram content and cultural referencing.

iconic crimson suits). A similar way of appropriating the past is shown on the second image with three teenagers in sport suits and a signature "Hello from the 90s #90ые #swag #adidas #puma #montana #sport #oldschool." Similar to the previous post,, the image refers to the stereotypes associated with young males involved in petty crime during the 1990s (also known as the *gopniki*).

One distinct feature of using 1990s as a cultural reference is it being similarly appealing for male and female users on Instagram (as contrasted by the higher presence of males for other categories of 1990s–related content). At the same time, the type of references used by sexes varies substantially. For men, the common source of reference are criminals, whose high visibility is viewed as one of the features of the 1990s. In the case of women, there is no distinct attachment to a specific group used as a reference; instead, women just reused the style of clothing popular at the time, in particular for partying.

Games, lifestyle, and economics: The 1990s memorabilia

In the last part of the analysis, I examined how memory of the 1990s is represented via specific objects. Figure 10 shows that posts referring to the lifestyle of the first post-Soviet decade are particularly frequent on Instagram. Most of these references concern the distinct style of clothing common to the period, in particular the growing adoption of the new Western elements. Some posts also refer to the low standards of life and the rise of crime, which also became part of the lifestyle during this time. Such references, however, remain rare, so the distinct cultural (life)style which formed after the dissolution of the Soviet Union remains a major visual association for the post-Soviet transition on Instagram.

The reasons for such popularity of lifestyle content can be explained by its close relationship with the teenage years, a period which together with childhood

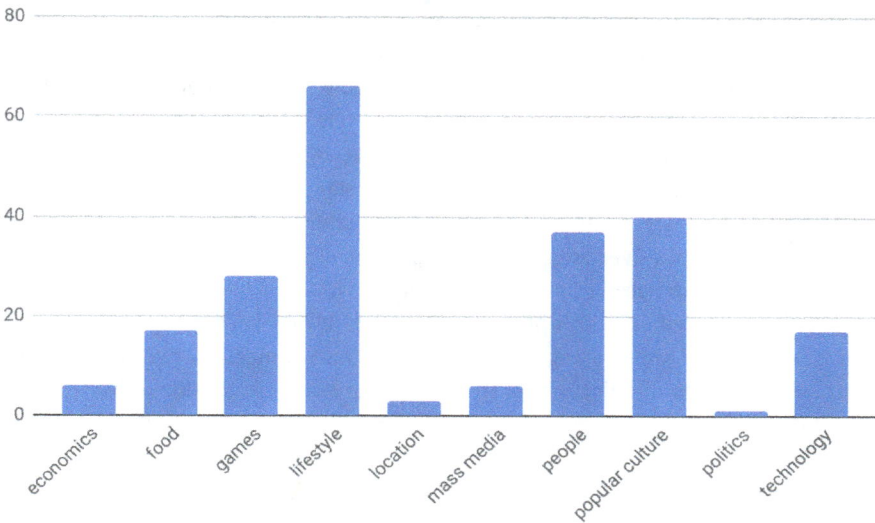

Figure 10: Distribution of memory objects (sample).

is essential for nostalgic feelings. Similar to the toys, which are another common object of post-post-Soviet nostalgia (Duijn 2019), images of the parties and creative use of clothing trigger memories of youth that coincided with the first post-Soviet decade and reflect an idealized perception of the time. Unlike toys, however, lifestyle perceptions are more focused on the feelings of freedom and independence associated both with the youth and the post-Soviet transition.

Two other types of memory objects commonly found on Instagram are images of people (e.g., relatives and friends) from the 1990s and references towards popular culture (e.g., music and movies). In the latter case, references to the musical groups such as Laskovyi Mai and Ruki Vverh are particularly frequent. Other common objects include material products of the post-Soviet time, in particular toys and technological gadgets. In the case of gadgets, the majority of references are focused on cars and sound recording devices, whereas toys vary from computer games (e.g., *Tiberium Sun*) to analogue games involving tokens and chewing gum inserts.

The least frequently referenced objects are the ones related to politics and economics. Only one post included an object directly related to politics, namely a video interview of Boris Netmstov from the time of him serving as a governor of the Nizhny Novgorod oblast. A few objects related to economics include price tags from the 1990s and images from trade markets.

Following the examination of the general distribution of memory objects, I looked at their distribution among the posts with specific mnemonic functions. Figure 11 shows that some functions relied on a few categories of objects, such as people (in the case of abstract nostalgia) and lifestyle (in the case of trauma focusing on the poverty and crime-related lifestyle). A slightly broader selection of objects is found in the case of commercialized nostalgia and cultural referencing content. While lifestyle-related objects are prevalent in these two cases, being used as a means of advertisement or commentary, popular culture objects and games are also referenced relatively frequently.

The most varied selection of memory objects is observed in the case of specific nostalgia and showcasing. Popular culture and games are two particularly common categories of objects referenced in these two cases. Unlike other categories, references to lifestyle and people are quite rare for these two functions which focus on material traces of the past. For the same reason, references to food and gadgets occurred here more frequently.

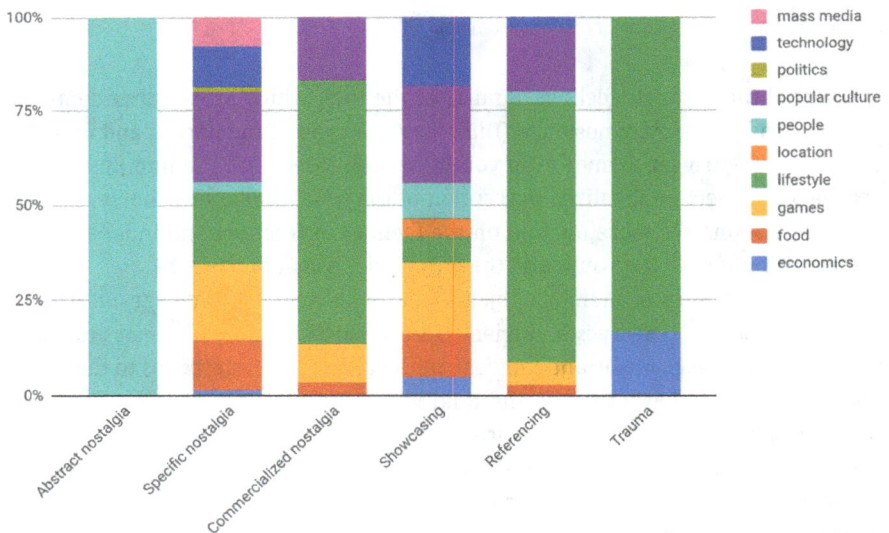

Figure 11: Distribution of memory objects per function (sample).

Finally, I examined how the distribution of posts referencing specific memory objects changed over time. Figure 12 shows that in many cases the presence of objects varied significantly, but references to some categories were more consistent. The objects which were referred to quite consistently include games, elements of popular culture, and people. This consistency can suggest that these categories cause

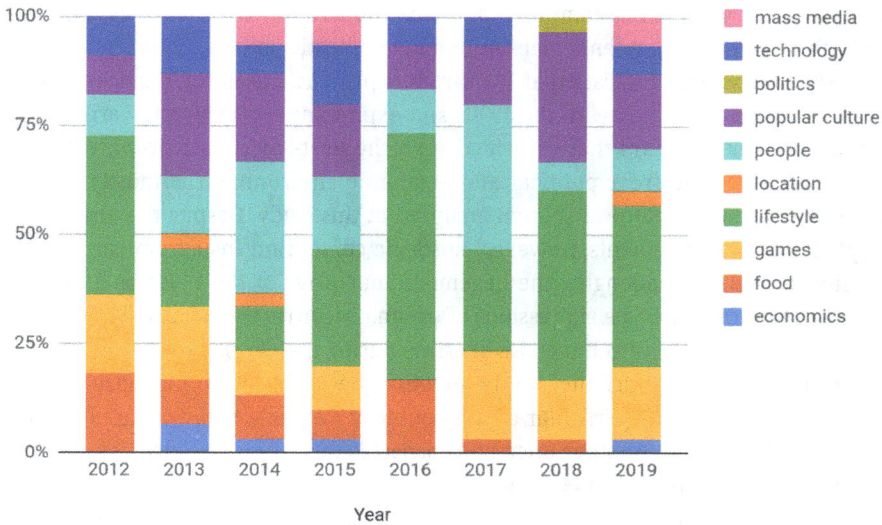

Figure 12: Distribution of memory objects per year (sample).

particularly strong attachments to the past which is also supported by observations on the relationship between specific objects and nostalgia as well as trauma (Shevchenko 2009, Duijn 2019).

More variation was observed in the case of references to technology-related objects, food, and lifestyle items. References to the former two categories occurred more frequently from 2012 till 2016 (the period when the showcasing function prevailed), whereas posts referring to lifestyle became more prominent from 2016, when the objects from the 1990s became increasingly used as a cultural reference. Unlike the more consistently used objects, these three categories seem to be referred to in a more situational way.

Conclusions

The analysis of Instagram content points to the increasing number of references to the first post-Soviet decade on the platform since 2012. Such an increase can have multiple reasons, varying from the first post-Soviet generation reaching maturity to the profound changes in the Russian public sphere following the growing hostilities with the West since the annexation of Crimea and beginning of Russia's war against Ukraine. The latter events in particular signify a dramatic rupture with Russia's post–1991 attempts to advance cooperation with the West and the growth of authoritarian tendencies in Russian domestic politics.

My observations indicate that Instagram is primarily used for showcasing cultural products associated with the 1990s and expressing a yearning towards childhood and teenage years that coincided with the post-Soviet transition, whereas nostalgia about the freer political and economic environment is mostly absent from the sample of platform content analyzed in this study. Despite the absence of explicit political statements, however, nostalgic content on Instagram can still be seen as a form of challenging the hegemonic narrative of the 1990s as a time of misery and hardships. The expressions of trauma occur rarely and usually focus on the economic insecurity and the rise of crime during the period. Such a low visibility of trauma can be attributed to the unwillingness of users to publicize painful episodes of the past, in particular as only publicly available data was used for implementing the study. Another interesting aspect is that trauma-related content features primarily men and is mainly published by male users.

Another aspect of mediating memories of the 1990s is their intense commercialization. While commodification of affective attachment to the past is a well-known phenomenon (Volčič 2007), my analysis suggests that digitization of memory can accelerate this process by facilitating the use of nostalgia as a form of promotion by both individual vendors and larger companies. The commercial uses of nostalgia further complicate interactions between state-sponsored and alternative narratives of the 1990s by highlighting how profit-driven presentation of the decade as a desired past can turn into a political message. These observations align with Boele's (2019) call for a more nuanced view of nostalgia's role in contemporary Russia and stress the importance of a broader understanding of the political uses of memory.

The analysis also points out a number of possible directions for further study. The use of memories of the 1990s as a cultural reference and the different ways in which specific user groups (e.g., males and females) engage with various types of mnemonic content is one question which deserves more attention. Another interesting direction for future research is the use of 1990s memories for commercial purposes and self-promotion and its relationship with hegemonic memory narratives such as the one of the *likhie devianostye*.

Finally, some limitations of the current analysis should also be mentioned. Despite its popularity in Russia before the 2022 invasion in Ukraine, Instagram is just one of many online platforms which are used for remediating and reinterpreting memories of the 1990s. It is also the platform with a rather distinct audience, at least in the case of Russia – i.e., predominantly female, young people with relatively high income (Gaitbaeva 2020) – which has implications for how it is used to engage with the past. Further research can benefit not only from a comparison between Instagram and other platforms used for engaging with memories of the 1990s (e.g., TikTok; Makhortykh 2021), but also a more in-depth discussion of the role of a medium in this process. Similarly, only a single hashtag was used to collect the data, whereas the pre-data collection examination of the platform's content pointed to the presence of multiple hashtags that can be related to the period of the post-Soviet transition.

Works cited

Arnold de-Simine, Silke. *Mediating Memory in the Museum: Trauma, Empathy, Nostalgia*. Bern: Springer, 2013.

Avedissian, Karena. "Clerics, Weightlifters, and Politicians: Ramzan Kadyrov's Instagram as an Official Project of Chechen Memory and Identity Production." *Caucasus Survey* 4.1 (2016): 20–43.

Bernhard, Michael, and Jan Kubik. "A Theory of the Politics of Memory." *Twenty Years After Communism: The Politics of Memory and Commemoration*. Ed. Michael Bernhard and Jan Kubik. Oxford: Oxford University Press, 2014. 7–37.

Björkdahl, Annika, and Stefanie Kappler. "The Creation of Transnational Memory Spaces: Professionalization and Commercialization." *International Journal of Politics, Culture, and Society* 32.4 (2019): 383–401.

Boele, Otto. "'Perestroika and the 1990s – Those Were the Best Years of My Life!' Nostalgia for the Post-Soviet Limbo." *Post-Soviet Nostalgia: Confronting the Empire's Legacies*. Ed. Otto Boele, Boris Noordenbos, and Ksenia Robbe. London: Routledge, 2019. 203–224.

Boele, Otto, Boris Noordenbos, and Ksenia Robbe, eds. *Post-Soviet Nostalgia: Confronting the Empire's Legacies*. London: Routledge, 2019.

Boym, Svetlana. *The Future of Nostalgia*. New York: Basic Books, 2001.

Brand Analytics. Sotsialnye seti v Rossii, zima 2014–2015. Tsifry, trendy, prognozy. 2015. https://br-analytics.ru/blog/socialnye-seti-v-rossii-zima-2014-2015-cifry/ (Accessed December 5, 2022).

Brand Analytics. Sotsialnye seti v Rossii, zima 2015–2016. 2016. Tsifry, trendy, prognozy. https://br-analytics.ru/blog/socialnye-seti-v-rossii-zima-2015-2016-cifry-trendy-prognozy/ (Accessed December 5, 2022).

Brand Analytics. Sotsialnye seti v Rossii, leto 2017: tsifry i trendy. 2017. https://br-analytics.ru/blog/sotsialnye-seti-v-rossii-leto-2017-tsifry-i-trendy/ (Accessed December 5, 2022).

Brand Analytics. Sotsialnye seti v Rossii: Tsifry i trendy, osen' 2018. 2018. https://br-analytics.ru/blog/socseti-v-rossii-osen-2018/ (Accessed December 5, 2022).

Buzalka, Juraj. "Post-Peasant Memories: Populist or Communist Nostalgia." *East European Politics and Societies* 32.4 (2018): 988–1006.

Chatterje-Doody, Precious, and Vera Tolz. "Regime Legitimation, Not Nation-Building: Media Commemoration of the 1917 Revolutions in Russia's Neo-Authoritarian State." *European Journal of Cultural Studies* 23.3 (2020): 335–353.

Commane, Gemma, and Rebekah Potton. "Instagram and Auschwitz: A Critical Assessment of the Impact Social Media Has on Holocaust Representation." *Holocaust Studies* 25.1–2 (2019): 158–181.

Duijn, Mandy. "Journeying to the Golden Spaces of Childhood: Nostalgic Longing in the Online Community the USSR Our Motherland through the Visual Image of the Soviet Toy." *Post-Soviet Nostalgia: Confronting the Empire's Legacies*. Ed. Otto Boele, Boris Noordenbos, and Ksenia Robbe. London: Routledge, 2019. 21–38.

Erwin, C. "Bearing Witnessing with What We Cannot Speak: The Use of the Abject and Figurative Language in Pat Barker's Regeneration and Union Street." *Narrative*, 30.3 (2022), 344–363.

Fedor, Julie. "Memory, Kinship, and the Mobilization of the Dead: The Russian State and the 'Immortal Regiment' Movement." *War and Memory in Russia, Ukraine and Belarus*. Ed. Julie Fedor, Markku Kangaspuro, Jussi Lassila, and Tatiana Zhurzhenko. Cham: Palgrave Macmillan, 2017. 307–345.

"Fleshmob 90-e: marafon vospominanii." *IRK* (2018). https://www.irk.ru/news/articles/20180927/nineties/ (Accessed September 10, 2019).

Foucault, Michel. *Society Must be Defended*. New York: Picador, 2003.

Gaitbaeva, Sofiia. "Auditoriia shesti krupneishih sotsetei v Rossii v 2020 godu: izuchaem insaity." *PPC World* (August 31, 2020). https://ppc.world/articles/auditoriya-shesti-krupneyshih-socsetey-v-rossii-v-2020-godu-izuchaem-insayty/ (Accessed December 5, 2022).

Gaufman, Elizaveta. *Security Threats and Public Perception: Digital Russia and the Ukraine Crisis*. Cham: Palgrave Macmillan, 2017.

Gorshkov, Mikhail. "Twenty Years that Shook Russia: Public Opinion on the Reforms." *The Social History of Post-Communist Russia*. Ed. Piotr Dutkiewicz, Sakwa Richard, and Kulikov Vladimir. London: Routledge, 2016. 113–147.

Gugushvili, Alexi, and Peter Kabachnik. "Stalin on Their Minds: A Comparative Analysis of Public Perceptions of the Soviet Dictator in Russia and Georgia." *International Journal of Sociology* 49.5–6 (2019): 317–341.

Hashamova, Yana. "Aleksei Balabanov's Russian Hero: Fantasies of Wounded National Pride." *The Slavic and East European Journal* 51.2 (2007): 295–311.

Hochman, Nadav, and Lev Manovich. "Zooming into an Instagram City: Reading the Local through Social Media." *First Monday* (2013). https://firstmonday.org/ojs/index.php/fm/article/view/4711/3698 (Accessed April 7, 2023).

Holak, Susan, Alexei Matveev, and William Havlena. "Nostalgia in Post-Socialist Russia: Exploring Applications to Advertising Strategy." *Journal of Business Research* 60.6 (2007): 649–655.

Horowitz, Sara. "Nostalgia and the Holocaust." *After Representation? The Holocaust, Literature, and Culture*. Ed. Clifton Spargo and Robert Ehrenreich. New Brunswick: Rutgers University Press, 2010. 41–58.

Hoskins, Andrew. "The Mediatisation of Memory." *Save as . . . Digital Memories*. Ed. Joanne Garde-Hansen, Andrew Hoskins, and Anna Reading. London: Palgrave Macmillan, 2009. 27–43.

Hoskins, Andrew. *Digital Memory Studies: Media Pasts in Transition*. New York: Routledge, 2018.

"Instagram by the Numbers: Stats, Demographics & Fun Facts." *Omnicore* (2020). https://www.omnicoreagency.com/instagram-statistics/ (Accessed July 21, 2020).

"Instagram Users in Russia from September 2018 to April 2020." *Statista* (2020) https://www.statista.com/statistics/1024741/instagram-users-russia/ (Accessed July 21, 2020).

Jeziński, Marek, and Łukasz Wojtkowski. "Nostalgia Commodified." *M&Z* 4 (2016): 96–104.

Kalinin, Ilya. "Nostalgic Modernization: The Soviet Past as 'Historical Horizon'." *Slavonica* 17.2 (2011): 156–166.

Kalinina, Ekaterina. *Mediated Post-Soviet Nostalgia*. Södertörn: Södertörn University, 2014.

Kalinina, Ekaterina, and Manuel Menke. "Negotiating the Past in Hyperconnected Memory Cultures: Post-Soviet Nostalgia and National Identity in Russian Online Communities." *International Journal of Media & Cultural Politics* 12.1 (2016): 59–74.

Kenny, Michael. "Back to the Populist Future?: Understanding Nostalgia in Contemporary Ideological Discourse." *Journal of Political Ideologies* 22.3 (2017): 256–273.

Keightley, Emily, and Katharina Niemeyer. "The Commodification of Time and Memory: Online Communities and the Dynamics of Commercially Produced Nostalgia." *New Media & Society* 22.9 (2020): 1639–1662.

Kim, Young Kyu, and Mark Yi-Cheon Yim. "When Nostalgia Marketing Backfires: Gender Differences in the Impact of Nostalgia on Youthfulness for Older Consumers." *Applied Cognitive Psychology* 32.6 (2018): 815–822.

Koposov, Nikolay. *Memory Laws, Memory Wars: The Politics of the Past in Europe and Russia*. Cambridge: Cambridge University Press, 2017.

Kukulin, Ilya. "Memory and Self-Legitimization in the Russian Blogosphere: Argumentative Practices in Historical and Political Discussions in Russian-Language Blogs of the 2000s." *Memory, Conflict and New Media: Web Wars in Post-Socialist States*. Ed. Ellen Rutten, Julie Fedor, and Vera Zvereva. London: Routledge, 2013. 112–129.

Kusimova, Tamara, and Maia Schmidt. "Nostal'gicheskoe potreblenie: sotsiologicheskii analiz." *Journal of Institutional Studies* 8.2 (2016): 121–132.

Legg, Stephen. "Memory and Nostalgia." *Cultural Geographies* 11.1 (2004): 99–107.

Lizardi, Ryan. *Mediated Nostalgia: Individual Memory and Contemporary Mass Media*. Lanham: Lexington Books, 2014.

Makhortykh, Mykola. "#NoKievNazi: Social Media, Historical Memory and Securitization in the Ukraine Crisis." *Memory and Securitization in Contemporary Europe*. Ed. Vlad Strukov and Viktor Apryshenko. London: Palgrave Macmillan, 2018. 219–247.

Makhortykh, Mykola. "#givemebackmy90s: Memories of the First Post-Soviet Decade in Russia on Instagram and TikTok." *Cultures of History Forum* (2021). https://www.cultures-of-history.uni-jena.de/exhibitions/givemebackmy90s-memories-of-the-first-post-soviet-decade (Accessed April 3, 2023).

Makhortykh, Mykola, and Juan Manuel González Aguilar. "Memory, Politics and Emotions: Internet Memes and Protests in Venezuela and Ukraine." *Continuum* 34.3 (2020): 342–362.

Makhortykh, Mykola, Lyebyedyev Yehor, and Daniel Kravtsov. "Past Is Another Resource: Remembering the 70th Anniversary of the Victory Day on LiveJournal." *Nationalities Papers* 49.2 (2021): 375–388.

Makhortykh, Mykola, and Maryna Sydorova. "Animating the Subjugated Past: Digital Greeting Cards as a Form of Counter-memory." *Visual Communication* 21.1(2019): 28–52.

Maksimova, Olga. "Konstruirovanie gendernoi identichnosti v virtualnoi politicheskoi kommunikatsii: diskursivnye strategii i praktiki samorepresentatsii v sotsialnykh setiakh." *Vestnik Rossiiskogo universiteta druzhby narodov. Seriia Sotsiologiia* 2 (2016): 403–416.

Malinova, Olga. "Obosnovanie politiki 2000-h godov v diskurse VV Putina i formirovanie mifa o 'likhih devianostyh'." *Politicheskaia Nauka* 3.3 (2018): 45–69.

Malinova, Olga. "Tema likhih devianostykh v diskursah rossiiskikh kommunistov i natsional-patriotov. " *Bulletin of Perm University. Political Science* 14.2 (2020): 53–63.

Mayer-Schönberger, Viktor. *Delete: The Virtue of Forgetting in the Digital Age*. Princeton: Princeton University Press, 2011.

Mazur, Liudmila. "Golden Age Mythology and the Nostalgia of Catastrophes in Post-Soviet Russia." *Canadian Slavonic Papers* 57.3–4 (2015): 213–238.

Medvedev, Sergei. "Likhie devianostye' kak opyt svobody." *Radio Svoboda* (September 16, 2015). https://www.svoboda.org/a/27252441.html (Accessed September 10, 2019).

Menyhért, Anna, and Mykola Makhortykh. "From Individual Trauma to Frozen Currents: Conceptualising Digital Trauma Studies." *Studies in Russian, Eurasian and Central European New Media* 18 (2017): 1–8.

Merzliakova, Valentina. "Mediatizatsiia kollektivnoi pamiati o 1990-h gg. v Runete." *Vestnik RGGU. Seriia Literaturovedenie. Iazykoznanie. Kul'torologiia* 8.2 (2020): 289–302.

Morenkova, Elena. "(Re)creating the Soviet Past in Russian Digital Communities. Between Memory and Mythmaking." *Studies in Russian, Eurasian and Central European New Media* 7 (2012): 39–66.

Pokrop, Jan. "Facebook & Instagram users in Russia 2019." *NapoleonCat*. https://napoleoncat.com/blog/social-media-users-in-russia/ (Accessed September 10, 2019).

Putin, Vladimir. "Priamaia liniia s Vladimirom Putinym." *President of Russia*. http://kremlin.ru/events/president/news/60795 (Accessed September 10, 2019).

Putin, Vladimir. "Beseda s rabotnikami Kazanskogo aviatsionnogo zavoda imeni S.P.Gorbunova." *President of Russia*. http://kremlin.ru/events/president/news/60506 (Accessed September 10, 2019).

Rutten, Ellen, Julie Fedor, and Vera Zvereva, eds. *Memory, Conflict and New Media: Web Wars in Post-Socialist States*. London: Routledge, 2013.

Shevchenko, Olga. *Crisis and the Everyday in Postsocialist Moscow*. Bloomington: Indiana University Press, 2009.

Smolina, N. "'Sovetskoe' v postsovetskov prostranstve: Analis nostal'gicheskih soobshestv." *Vestnik Cheliabinskogo gosudarstvennogo universiteta* 17.346 (2014): 133–136.

Talu, Niluefer. "Home as Nostalgic Myth and Lost Object of Memory: Transcendental Homelessness and Pathological Home Desire in Modern Culture." *Memory & Nostalgia*. Ed. Atilla Silkue, Murat Erdem, and Patrick Folk. Izmir: Ege University Press, 2009. 251–281.

Thomas, David. "A General Inductive Approach for Analyzing Qualitative Evaluation Data." *American Journal of Evaluation* 27.2 (2006): 237–246.

Todorova, Maria, and Zsuzsa Gille. *Post-Communist Nostalgia*. New York: Berghahn Books, 2010.

Trubina, Elena. "Past Wars in the Russian Blogosphere: On the Emergence of Cosmopolitan Memory." *Studies in Russian, Eurasian and Central European New Media* 4 (2010): 63–85.

Volčič, Zala. "Yugo-nostalgia: Cultural Memory and Media in the Former Yugoslavia." *Critical Studies in Media Communication* 24.1 (2007): 21–38.

Wang, Zheng. "National Humiliation, History Education, and the Politics of Historical Memory: Patriotic Education Campaign in China." *International Studies Quarterly* 52.4 (2008): 783–806.

Ioana Luca

Romanian Transition and Transnational Crossings: A Well-Traveled Communist Biddy

Abstract: My chapter argues for transnationalism as lens and method for examining cultural memories of the transition in Romania so as to capture the multiscalar, complex articulations informing them. I focus on *I am an Old Commie!* by Dan Lungu (*Sînt o babă comunistă!* 2007), its national remediations, and regional travels, and analyze its transnational relationalities, both at the diegetic and extra diegetic level. A transnational approach to the novel, to Stere Gulea's 2013 film, and to Antonella Cornici's 2019 play highlights, I claim, how multifaceted global/local interactions and the multidirectional forces of globalization post–1989 shape both representations of the *longue durée* transition in Romania and forms of remembering the communist past. The coda provides a brief view of the reception of the novel in the former socialist bloc and surveys the 'minor transnationalisms' (Lionnet and Shih 2005) it has enabled. I show how Lungu's much remediated and well-traveled novel fleshes out overlooked global entanglements of the Romanian transition and unexpected post–1989 transregional variabilities, which re-orient us toward complex circuits, relations, juxtapositions, and encounters. Such configurations, I hold, unmoor national frames of reference that have been a given in the understanding of the postcommunist transition and its literary representations in Romania, and point to the relevance of comparative approaches when examining the evolving heterogeneity of cultural memories within the former socialist bloc.

Introduction

Academic calls "to recognize how painful the postcommunist transition was – and, for many, continues to be" (Ghodsee and Orrenstein 2019) or hyperbolic comparisons of the transition to a struggle and catastrophe of "biblical" proportions (Ghodsee and Orrenstein 2021, 22; 192) have been echoed in opinion pieces, editorials, or new political platforms throughout the region. Generational change, com-

Acknowledgments: This chapter is the result of a research project supported by a Taiwan Ministry of Science and Technology grant (109–2410-H-003 −010 -MY3). I am grateful to Ksenia Robbe, Oana Popescu-Sandu and the external reader for insightful comments.

https://doi.org/10.1515/9783110707793-010

bined with the alarming rise of instability, populism and strong nationalism throughout the former Eastern Europe since 2015, is behind such ongoing reevaluation of the immediate aftermath of 1989/1991. Scholarly endeavors of "taking stock of the shock" (Ghodsee and Orenstein 2021) and positioning the post–1989 changes both within a *longue durée* and a global perspective (Mark et al. 2019) have, however, long been predated by artistic projects. These have brought to light narratives unacknowledged by the mainstream discourses of the time and also alternative ways of recording and remembering the post-communist transition. The highly acclaimed Romanian novel *I am an Old Commie!* by Dan Lungu (*Sînt o babă comunistă!* 2007)[1] is one such instance in which a retired woman worker, an emblematic, but overlooked character of the post–1989 changes, and a figure "pushed to the margins of contemporary European culture," more broadly (Scribner 2001, 5), is given a voice.

My chapter focuses on Lungu's novel, its national remediations, and regional travels, and proposes a transnational lens for examining the Romanian transition and its memories. I examine how diegetic transnational connections frame the protagonist's reminiscences, affect her life in the present, and turn her memories and life story into commodity and spectacle. At the extra-diegetic level, I briefly discuss the regional travels of the novel in translation. I reveal the "interlocking scales" of memories which involve several "intersections" and "articulations" (De Cesari and Rigney 2014, 5) and position remembering communism and experiencing the transition within the broader frames of references that have informed these processes. My investigation thus switches the focus of current scholarship on Lungu's novel away from communism and toward the post–1989 transition, and also to a transnational rather than national context.[2]

Let me begin with the old biddy's memories. "Lord, how good we had it under communism" (63); "I had everything my heart desired" (64): these are just two of the many similar statements made by Emilia Apostoae, the protagonist of the novel. As a first-person narrative confession, the novel is centered on her joyful reminiscences about life under communism during the early years of the Roma-

---

1 The literal translation of the title is "I am an Old Communist Biddy." I draw on the English version of the book which opts for "commie" in the title but keeps the gendered noun throughout the text. The film title has been rendered as *I am an Old Communist Hag* but the noun "hag" does not do justice to its protagonist.

2 Scholarship on Lungu's novel highlighted the end of an "ethical paradigm" in remembering *communism* (Simuţ 2015, 136–138), showed its relevance as a means of "cultural memory" of *communist* times (Mironescu 2013, my emphasis), examined forms of nostalgia the character evidences, and provided insightful comparisons of the novel and its film adaptation (Turcuş 2013, Komporaly 2014).

nian transition, which she also documents. A detailed, often humorous remembering of everyday life with its many challenges and also joys, Apostoae's narrative offers no idealized version of the communist regime, but rather a series of vivid recollections imbued with a strong affective attachment to times past while describing the present. The stances valiantly adopted by the retired factory worker in Lungu's novel came counter to the mnemonic practices flourishing in postcommunist Romania and the mainstream depictions of the Romanian transition. Romania's mnemonic practices have been instrumentalized and entwined with the political, from the official "forget-and-forgive" of the 1990s (Stan 2013) to the presidentially-sanctioned incrimination of the communist regime in 2006 (Tismăneanu 2007). All along, the official discourse has been paralleled by strong public anticommunism, combined with a confident teleological view of the transition, supported by the cultural and intellectual elites and reinforced by a large number of publications about the past – prison memoirs, various life stories of sacrifice and heroism – authored by famous victims, exiles, and dissidents. While, more recently, ironic artistic engagements with the past (Dobre 2017) as well as memories of childhood or teenage years under communism are broadening this narrow spectrum, historians correctly mention that the "persistence of a collective representation of the past [. . .] is hardly able to absorb the multifarious memories of Romanian communism" (Petrescu and Petrescu 2014, 68). Overall, there is still a dearth of narratives capable of doing justice to the manifold nature of memories about communism (Georgescu 2016, Pohrib 2019). Moreover, the transition period is only now beginning to be systematically addressed by both artists and scholars. Discussions of its artistic representations are scarce and its transnational dynamics are completely missing.[3] Against this background, Lungu's 2007 old commie was particularly unexpected and, unsurprisingly, triggered mixed reactions in the country's cultural press: while most critics highlighted the novelist's talent, the novel's very topic and main protagonist attracted significant criticism.

Sixteen years later, however, Lungu's novel is enjoying a lasting legacy. Nationally, it has come out in six editions with a major publisher. It has been turned into a successful movie, a dance show, and several plays staged throughout the country. The catchy title has entered common parlance, and references to the protagonist are frequent. Moreover, seen retrospectively, the old biddy's perspectives seem uncannily prescient of survey polls showing a retroactive positive assessment of the communist regime by the older generation in Romania (Dragomir 2011) and also indicating large-scale dissatisfaction with the post–1989 political

---

3 Stan (2021) offers an excellent analysis of the 2000s literary landscape and points to the tensions of "millennial realism" and Iovănel's (2021) literary history is a case in point.

scene.[4] On the other hand, Lungu's focus on microhistory and everyday life, as well as the humorous view he adopts, foreshadowed the recent boom in Romanian letters of light-hearted everyday memories and alternative mnemonic practices about the communist regime flourishing in online venues (Petrescu 2017, Pohrib 2019). It also etched vivid glimpses of post-communist times from the perspective of the older generation in a humorous memorable way.[5] Internationally, Lungu's novel has been translated into thirteen languages, has won awards in France and Poland, and theater adaptations have been staged in the Netherlands and Hungary, to great acclaim.[6] It is fair to say that the communist biddy has become nothing short of a phenomenon, and together with her, memories of communist and postcommunist times have traveled widely and accrued a large range of affective reactions and social constellations.

My chapter argues for a transnational approach that "hollow[s] out [national] pressing and peremptory claims to legitimacy" (Giles 2010, 45) and highlights the multidirectional forces of globalization post–1989, and the multifaceted interactions across time and space informing the transition and its cultural memories. As my analysis shows, teasing out the relevance of transnational relationalities, both at the diegetic and extra diegetic level, of Lungu's well-traveled biddy fleshes out often overlooked global entanglements and transregional variabilities of transition, which re-orient us toward complex circuits, relations, juxtapositions and encounters. Such new configurations, I argue, direct us to alternative memory cultures in the postsocialist period and memories of crisis during the transition. They also unmoor national frames of reference that have been a given in understanding post-communist transition and its literature in Romania. Last but not least, such transnational configurations point to the evolving heterogeneity of cultural memories within the former socialist bloc. More specifically, by examining Lungu's novel and two of its remediations, i.e., Stere Gulea's 2013 film and Antonella Cornici's 2019 play, I reveal how the intertwining of local and global contexts informs cultural representations of the Romanian transition and memories about communist times. I highlight how these artistic representations depict the

---

4 The staggering 9% votes in 2020 for a newly established populist party, Alliance for the Union of Romanians is one such example.

5 The landscape of the transition is present in the 'ego fiction' of the 2000s through the biographical perspective of the younger generation, the existential angst of its members and their explorations of ontological precarity; such views however did not gain the national attention and appeal Lungu's book and its filmic adaptation triggered.

6 As of January 2020, the play staged at József Katona theater in Budapest had 125 representations and excellent reviews in major Hungarian publications. See Komporaly 2014, for a discussion of this stage adaptation.

transition while also engaging self-reflexively with the processes of remembering everyday communism. The analysis of the many travels (Erll 2011) and remediations (Erll 2008, Rigney 2008, 2015) of the "old biddy's" memories foregrounds the still unsettled and unsettling memories about communism during the *longue durée* Romanian transition. The coda provides a brief view of the reception of the novel in the former socialist bloc and examines the "minor transnationalisms" (Lionnet and Shih 2005) it has enabled. By foregrounding the interconnections of the Romanian "old commie's" life and memories with the global and the regional, I probe into the paradoxes, apparent contradictions, and ambivalences of encounter informing Romanian transition and the literature about it.

Dan Lungu's *I am and Old Commie*: Trans/national itineraries of personal and collective pasts

Dan Lungu, a writer by calling and a sociologist by training, has produced academic studies in parallel with his literary pieces. *Povestirile vieții: teorie și documente* (*Life Stories: Theory and Documents* 2003) is one such innovative scholarly work. In it, Lungu takes the focus away from the heroic resistance or forced compliance with the communist regime and puts it on people whose life-style matched the images churned out by communist propaganda under Nicolae Ceaușescu – namely, the upwardly mobile, happy workers. The story of a metal worker woman, Florentina Ichim, came counter to all interviews Lungu was conducting, triggered his interest in blue collar workers' memories of communism and was the starting point for the fictional Emilia Apostoae.

I am an Old Commie! presents the childhood and young years of Emilia, who toiled daily in a very poor village. The experience of turning cow manure into fuel makes her desperately dream of becoming a "townie," and exuberant flashbacks show how she does become a city-dwelling, working-class woman who does well in life: she takes evening classes, marries, gets an apartment, a propane tank and a TV set –everything with support from her factory. She works hard to produce metalwork for export and relishes the comradery of her fellow workers, who enjoy themselves whenever the opportunity arises. The novel opens in the present, in post-communist times, when the factory has closed down and Emilia finds herself overlooked by the processes of transition. Her only daughter, Alice, emigrates to Canada right after the revolution, and briefly comes back to introduce her Canadian fiancé, Alain. Her daughter's trajectory is emblematic for the youth migration and brain drain which has defined Romania since 1989. When back in Canada, Alice phones her mother in order to make sure she does not vote for the ex-communists. Actually, it is her daughter's short visit and the transatlantic phone conversations that trigger Emilia's intense reminiscing about her life in the village (chronologically the first temporal layer), and, mostly, her golden years as a self-fulfilled factory worker (the second temporal frame of the novel).

Emilia's recollections are relational and processual mnemonic acts prompted by her daughter and future son-in-law, and the transnational connections the two bring in. Alain "stared in amazement" at Emilia's honest answer that she was "worse off now" than before the Revolution, thus displaying a Cold War mentality – i.e., there is no bigger evil than communism. Emilia's inner comments speak about the difficulty of truly sharing your past, just as they point to the impossibility of explaining one's postcommunist predicament to foreigners: "a foreigner [. . .] is not interested in our beggarly pensions, and they've got no idea how things are over there [. . .] How could I explain it to him?" (25). A similar disconnect is present in the subsequent transatlantic phone calls with her own daughter who, on behalf of a Romanian overseas association, is "trying to persuade" Emilia to vote for "democracy" and not for the "ex-communists" (44–45). The mother points to the many challenges the present poses, and holds her ground. To her daughter's indicting statement "you are more of a communist than I thought" she calmly retorts "Well . . . I am an old commie, if you really want to know. That's what I am" (46). The connotations of the word "communist" are derogative in post–1989 Romania, asserting a strong disregard for elderly people and highlighting their inability to adapt to the new, allegedly better, times. Moreover, the unavoidably gendered version of the original – "communist biddy" – makes the whole phrase further deprecating. While the mother respects and comprehends her daughter's decision to emigrate – she herself left the poor village – the reverse does not happen. Everything that matters to Emilia is discarded by her daughter, who literally and symbolically "marries" into the neo-liberal paradigm.[7] The phone conversations point to the daughter's total lack of interest or even empathy, and also to the dignified existence of the mother, who does not give in. Their brief encounters – emblematic for the early years of the postcommunist transition – are to be seen in terms of a generational clash, but with class distinctions sometimes marked. Alice stands for the youngsters of the post–1989 period, who have no understanding for the older generation and readily assign (insulting) labels ("commie"). Read more broadly, Alice and Alain can also stand symbolically for global forces that claim lofty intentions (IMF, World Bank, etc.) but are incapable of, or uninterested in, really understanding the local context.

---

7 For a discussion of "marrying west," see Sadowski-Smith (2018) on post-Soviet migrant women's smooth integration into the neoliberal systems.

The crossings with the global embodied by Alice and Alain prompt Emilia's intense reminiscing, opening for readers the two interrelated past temporal layers that reveal the heroine's life. Her dream of being a "townie" illustrates the communist progressive ethos of modernization; at the same time, the material benefits and the upscale mobility, rather than any communist credos, are what counts for her and make her happy. The communist times are figured as moments of intense labor but also fun. The factory workshop is a tight community, where people work and rejoice together. Ideological motivations for Emilia's life decision are absent, and even becoming a party member is a pragmatical choice.

Unlike Alain, the reader does get a glimpse into Emilia's inner life, her thoughts, and her psychological mechanisms, as the first-person narrative abounds in long inner monologues which constantly juxtapose the past and the present. A gifted storyteller, Lungu makes Emilia a highly enjoyable biddy, who views herself from a distance, often with detached self-irony and humor. This gives the text much liveliness. At the same time, Lungu the inquisitive sociologist also surfaces in several instances. The nostalgia Emilia experiences is constantly analyzed and dissected by the protagonist herself, who is on a quest for self-understanding and self-discovery: "To us, it wasn't the Party members who were communists, but the political instructors and the fanatics . . . Now, the communists were the ones who lied, who confiscated, who threw people into jail and tortured them, and did all kinds of other things. I was neither the one, nor the other. What kind of communist was I?" (48). While she distances herself from the communist ideology, the much longed for propane tank, the apartment and the TV set were all inextricably linked to the factory, the very product of the communist system, and she herself stands for "lives lived," lives made, "not lost" under communism (Iacob 2016, 30).[8] At the same time, when seen against the complex "polysemy" of post-communist nostalgia (Nadkarni and Shevchenko 2004) one encounters in the Romanian popular culture (Popescu-Sandu 2010, Georgescu 2010), Emilia's nostalgic sensibilities look rather straightforward: as with people elsewhere in the former socialist bloc, there is a strong attachment to a life she lost (Todorova 2010) as well as a form of contestation of the present (Berdahl 2010). The way the past and the present are brought together offers a clear indictment of the transition, and Emilia's dissatisfaction echoes millions of other people's harsh lives in Romania after 1989. However, the past is in no way just a springboard for the critique of the transition. Emilia's memories about her life under the communist regime are joyful even when *not* contrasted with the

---

8 The daughter's trajectory to the West is underpinned by the same search for a "better life" and her democratic activism, never examined in the book, seems more an effect of her relocation rather than its very cause.

present; Emilia's life story complements the mainstream discourse about Romanian communism which by late 2000s had not included multilayered narratives.

The atmosphere in the workshop and the numerous communist jokes the factory workers shared are extensively depicted. Entire chapters function as an amusing interlude both for the conflicting present Emilia inhabits and for the reader familiar with communism. The references to local brands and imported products turn the text from a vehicle of memory for the protagonist to a prompt for remembering for the in-the-know reader, as the cascading effect of these names generates a stream of memories for a readership sharing the same cultural background. As such, the chapters dedicated to jokes and storytelling can be seen as a means of turning "communicative memory" into "cultural memory" (Assmann 2008), with such a process short-circuited in the case of younger or (most) foreign audiences (the context and the gags are hard to grasp). The brands that get mentioned also mean little without the associations they entailed during communism, and the puns remain difficult to convey no matter how masterful the translation.[9] Even so, the extensive mélange of jokes – the shared subversive knowledge of the times – frame the individual story within a shared collective past that readers who experienced communism easily relate to and which can still remain somewhat meaningful – via footnoting – for the non-initiated reader.

Emilia's disillusionment with the transition is echoed by her neighbor, Mrs. Stroescu, an aspiring artist from a relatively well-off family that the communist regime destroyed. The two women had strikingly different life trajectories under communism ("lives lost" vs. "life made"), but their encounter entails mutual respect. Symbolically, this encounter stands for alternative versions of transition in Romania, as respectful dialogue and meaningful listening between people at opposite ends of the ideological spectrum has almost never happened. While the two women's memories of communism could not have been more different, they both voice clear indictments of the transition, while also harboring quixotic dreams about the future. The reader does not learn what happens with Mrs. Stroescu's plans of recovering the nationalized small tailor workshop of her family. We do find out, however, that Emilia's utopic visions – restarting the factory workshop, bringing the team together again, and creating jobs so that people making a livelihood abroad can come back (another clear reference to migration, this time the large-scale labor exodus) – are shattered by her former workmates whom she brings together one afternoon. Neither Emilia's sister, who had once

---

9 The English translation opted for footnotes and explanations for several puns and rhyming nicknames; a reviewer found the rendition of these chapters difficult for a non-native speaker (Szilagy 2018).

begged Emilia to help her out of the village, nor her best friend in the workshop, now a busy small shop owner – a representative embodiment of the successful transition type – would even consider ever going back and working in the factory. Moreover, neither shares, to Emilia's surprise, her own strong affective memories about the workshop.

Other unexpected and divergent life trajectories during the transition become apparent during Emilia's chat with her former workmates. She learns that the former factory party secretary, the one who used to be in charge with the ideological indoctrination of the cadres, has become a pious monk. The beloved foreman of her memory, who cheered them up recounting political jokes, turns out to have been a secret police informer, who is currently running in the elections on behalf of a far-right party; on top of that, it transpires he was also a lecher, constantly hitting on the younger women around him. Surprised by how differently she and her friends remember the past and relate to the present, Emilia no longer brings up her idea of restarting the workshop. She also questions her perspectives, but in no way is she repentant about how she views her past. She does not, however, vote in the elections and the ending of the book is open-ended. The novel captures well the multifaceted life trajectories during transition, pointing to always in flux personal itineraries and multilayered experiences.

As stated above, the initial critical reception of the novel was mixed. The author was praised for a well-written book, his humor and knack as a storyteller, and also for bringing the novel closer to the readers (Axinte 2007, Burţa-Cernat 2007, Ursă 2007 respectively). On the other hand, the "verisimilitude" of the protagonist was challenged (Gorzo 2013, among many others). Emilia was found to be shallow, unconvincing, flat, or taken to task for experiencing no remorse about her feelings and for her general attitude about the past (Creţu 2007, Axinte 2007). The nostalgia Emilia experiences was commonly regarded as not genuine, but rather expressing a fad, a bandwagon the novelist jumps on in order to make the book marketable abroad (Luca 2008, Cristea-Enache 2008).[10] To put it simply, a character joyfully reminiscing about the communist times and criticizing the present was not seen as a genuine and plausible one. At the other end of the ideological spectrum, left-leaning critics (an exception in the late 2000s) blamed Lungu for following a disguised anticommunist agenda through his naïve working-class woman, who only *apparently* regrets the past and actually functions as an "ideological puppet" revealing the strengths of the communist regime only by comparison to the bankruptcy of the present transition (Iovănel 2007). Even

---

10 For a strikingly different view about this aspect see Rogozanu (2007), the first to laudatory mention the possible "translatability" of the novel for its *intrinsic* strengths.

when Lungu's focus on individual destiny and his keen eye for microhistory were positively noted, his work was viewed against the haunting absence of the "grand *communist* novel" literary critics long expected and which he himself also failed to deliver (Conkan 2009, my emphasis). All in all, the immediate critical reception of the novel, just as that of the film at a later date, became the springboard for various engagements with the past and the politics of memory in Romania rather than an acknowledgment of the multiplicity of memories, life trajectories during the communist times, and the complex dynamics of the transition period, which, at that time, was still viewed as the teleological narrative of political and material progress.

What Lungu achieves through Emilia's memories is that he gives voice to an emblematic and overlooked character of transition, and offers a new perspective on the communist past and the transition. She stands for the unadjusted type, who has often been blamed for the failures of transition and even scapegoated for the fiascos of the (former) elites in power. As a social category, this little understood type – but with significant voting power and strong social traction[11] – has often been looked down upon, sometimes blatantly disregarded and, at times, downright manipulated by a large number of Romanian politicians. Culturally or artistically, the Emilia Apostoae type had not been given a voice before Lungu's novel, although it has been a strong presence in the Romanian transition. Furthermore, the transatlantic conversations and the encounter with the future son-in-law make clear the "interlocking scales," involving several "intersections" and "articulations" of memories (De Cesari and Rigney 2014, 5) which position remembering communism and experiencing the transition within broader frames of references. By not judging her, and by allowing her to speak and analyze herself and the others – with much wit, humor, and irony – Lungu builds Emilia into a vivid, funny, and very likeable biddy who keeps travelling across spaces and media.[12]

---

11 Women have constituted a significant electoral base for the ex-communists or their revamped versions of "social democrats."

12 Interestingly enough, a review of Lungu's academic monograph featuring the interview with Florentina Ichim brings up not only the very prevalence of many such people in post-communist Romania but the reviewer's very encounter with such a group, and his dismay at hearing their stories on a long train ride (see Mihăilescu 2003).

"Archive of feelings" or why does the biddy travel?

Florentina Ichim's fond personal memories of everyday communism traveled to the fictional Emilia Apostoae, who thus gave voice to a whole generation of over-looked and misunderstood people of the transition. To put it otherwise, one can argue that the novel and its remediations can all be seen as forms of remediated nostalgia, i.e., sophisticated actualizations of the original metal worker's memories about the past offered to readers/viewers with complex artistic tastes. As scholars note, "memory fundamentally means movement, traffic between individual and collective levels of remembering, circulation among social, medial, and semantic dimensions"; also, "cultural memory must travel, be kept in motion, in order to stay alive, to have an impact both on individual minds and social formations" (Erll 2011, 15). The old biddy's memories have kept travelling and remediations have thrived after Lungu's novel came out. Before discussing the 2013 film and the 2019 stage adaptation, one question is in order: What makes the old communist biddy such a well-traveled, popular and compelling character? A focus on audiences and their changing knowledge and interpretative frames about the past provides one possible answer for the old biddy's many travels across media and spaces.[13] At the same time, Emilia's extensive memories of everyday life under communism, her self-ironic and self-questioning nature, her struggles after 1989 as well as her stoic resilience all play a key role in the character's wide-ranging appeal. Moreover, there is a continuous overt or implied request for empathy, from other characters and also from us, an invitation, as she tells her daughter, to "be in her shoes"; it is this affective power of the protagonist, its ability to draw people into her universe, that the reactions of a wide range of directors, script writers and actors highlight.

The director of the 2016 stage adaptation at the Sibiu National Theater perceived the novel as a "testimony" and "sensed an almost umbilical connection with the text" (Mihu-Plier qtd. in *Teatrul* 2016), as it felt like a book about her own mother. Consequently, she "envisioned a show full of love and humor" (Mihu-Plier qtd. in Micu 2016). Stere Gulea, the director who authored the film version, relived his own experience of leaving his home village (Costanda 2013), even though he himself hails from the other end of the ideological spectrum. The more senior cast of the movie either found themselves autobiographically connected with the story or emotionally involved in the self-ironic but resilient way of going

---

13 It is *not* the left-leaning artists who further remediated Lungu's biddy, and the protagonist's appeal is very broad, thus the ideological stake of artists/viewers is negligible for now.

through difficult situations – the way of making lemonade when life gives you lemons, as Emilia illustrates. Younger actors also described the story as "comprising bits of everybody's life" (Costanda 2013). A New Zealander chorographer relocated to Romania, Aleisha Gardner, who initiated the 2015 dance show in Sibiu, also resonated with the protagonist and, after intensive research, offered the public a show in which they "[could] find parts of their past" (*Sînt o babă*, Gardner 2015). In an interesting twist, the old biddy of the 2019 play staged in Timişoara (and streamed online during the Covid-19 pandemic) is no longer old, as the stage director found her way of thinking emblematic not only for Emilia's generation but also for numerous young people who were not even born during communism but "think like" a communist old woman (Cornici qtd. in Leonte 2019).

Such views are replicated by more recent readers' reviews in the Romanian blogosphere and invite one to see the text as "an archive of feelings" (Cvetkovich 2003, 7) about everyday life under communism and postcommunism, which is of interest for people coming not only from different generations and social layers but also from different ideological positions. Ann Cvetkovich's term refers to "cultural texts as repositories of feelings and emotions, which are encoded not only in the content of the texts themselves but in *the practices that surround their production and reception*" (2003, 7 my emphasis); in our case, it is these very practices of production and reception that multiply and generate the range of feelings and affects about the communist past and post-communist transition in both national and regional contexts. Lungu's novel came counter to both main narratives of communism and the transition, this together with the strong affective power, the empathy the character benefits from a wide range of readers, and the strong representativeness of the character, have enabled the many travels and remediations of Emilia so far. In view of the scholars' insight that numerous travels and remediations play a decisive role in "stabilizing" memories (Erll 2008, 393–395), one would expect that Emilia's recollections of everyday life under communism and the complex transition that followed would have sedimented and crystalized themselves in Romanian culture by now, but such a process of stabilization is far from having been achieved, as my next sections show.

Stere Gulea's cinematic biddy: Between local transition and the global crisis

The transnational connections embodied by the daughter and her fiancé which frame Emilia's reminiscences in the book drive the plot in Gulea's film *I am an Old Communist Hag*, which centers on the visit of the young couple in Romania. Moreover, the movie is set almost twenty years after the fall of communism, namely right after the global financial crisis of 2007–2008, which made its long-lasting effects painfully felt throughout Eastern Europe. Unlike the book, the movie is a soberer affair, even though humor, wit and (self-)irony are never missing. The joy Emilia and her husband feel when finding out that their daughter and her fiancé, coming from the US this time, are going to briefly visit them is clouded by the financial difficulties this visit entails for the old couple (Figure 1). The parents need to borrow money in order to welcome the young couple, but they are not the only ones experiencing many difficulties. Numerous other protagonists are struggling, and there is an all-pervading sense of stasis that captures quite well the precariousness of a large segment of the population in the early 2010s.

Figure 1: Financial difficulties this visit involves for the old couple.

The visual depiction of the small town further encapsulates the Romanian transition: huge fancy billboards with glamorous models share the same space with poorly dressed people and a motley array of stores. The flamboyant retired worker from Lungu's novel looks lost and awkward when faced with the weight of transition in Gulea's film. The attempt to find her old-time hairdresser takes her to a privately-owned salon where the young "hairstylist" suggests her a look "à la Lady Gaga." There is dark humor and much empathy for Emilia, who, as we shall see, is *not* portrayed as a helpless victim but rather as a strong, resourceful, and resilient woman. The joyful memories of Emilia's communist years are rendered here through black-and-white flashbacks, just like her early years of toil in the native village. These strikingly different periods of her life come together and are both, visually, faded and old. The flashbacks – which also include archival footage – present Emilia as a spectator to her own life, and thus the communist times are nothing but a thing from bygone days that has relevance for the protagonist only. The challenging present, the *longue durée* transition which Emilia navigates with difficulty but much dignity, takes center stage in Gulea's movie.

The multiple crossings between the local and the global keep the story evolving. Alice's successful immigration story gradually unravels, and we find out that the young couple are currently unemployed –their company's branch had closed because of the crisis – and she is three months pregnant. Her fiancé, always optimistic but mostly naïve, has countless business ideas that always fail. Moreover, their unpaid mortgage amounts to 15.000 USD, and the bank threatens foreclosure. Emilia, upon realizing her daughter's difficulties, tries all along to help, and the old couple end up mortgaging their apartment, in extremely disadvantageous conditions, to a Chinese money lender for exactly 15.000 USD. The yuppie-styled Alice, when leaving the small provincial town, accepts the envelope with the money. The ending of the movie shows the old couple on a country road in an old Romanian car loaded with their belongings and moving to the countryside.

The Chinese money lender points both to new transnational routes and local forms of ruthless capitalism. He embodies the present while also representing a vision of the future – the Chinese immigrant, i.e., allegedly a former communist, is now the ruthless capitalist (the exorbitant commission means that the couple actually give up on their apartment) who is the only one enabling them to help the family out. Read in a symbolic key, the former communist becomes a successful capitalist in the Wild East of never-ending transitioning, exemplifying the trajectory numerous communist elites actually followed after 1989 in Romania, and becoming emblematic for how postcommunist countries have turned into "poster children of neoliberalism" (Chelcea and Druță 2016, 538). Following the local/global imbrications the movie reveals, the future of Alice (and her child) in the US seems predicated on her parents' sacrifice. Romanian reviewers derided the ending (Pleşu 2013), but read symbolically it shows how global capitalism, and global crisis, do entail the exploitation of former communist countries. The transnational connections the book foregrounds show Emilia's memories as generated by the "multidirectional flows of people, ideas" (Fishkin 2005, 22), and the film portrays her political stance further strengthened by her daughter's challenges in the US. The movie illustrates how the former communist space is transnationally constituted, "embedded and influenced" (Levitt and Khagram 2008, 5) by larger arenas (the 2008 crisis, the Chinese entrepreneur), and also how utopic visions about the US are challenged. Emilia's already difficult existence during the postcommunist transition is further affected by the global crisis her daughter experiences, and she goes back to the country-side she struggled to leave in her youth (Figure 3). Her return to the village completely erases even the shallow progress achieved by the communist system. Paradoxically, the globalizing processes sends her back full-circle.

The destiny of another character, a homeless old woman (Maricica) who finds shelter in a dilapidated Trabant, is symptomatic for the hopelessness of transition (Figure 2). Maricica represents the precarious conditions of those too old or simply unable to make it after 1989, and the Trabant– a symbol of socialist affordability and sturdiness – is the only roof the homeless woman has, thus further pointing to the failures of the postcommunist transition. The implied death of Maricica at the end of the movie parallels but also contrasts Emilia's return to the village, as the old biddy has both the strength and the humor to start over again. Regardless, in Gulea's movie the Romanian transition, with its multiple transnational entanglements, has devastating effects on the individuals.

Figure 2: Trabant, the only shelter for Maricica.

Figure 3: Emilia going back full-circle to the countryside.

The evolving frameworks of memory about the communist past are a constant thread in Lungu's novel and its remediations, all of which engage self-reflexively with recording or remembering it. For instance, in the novel a journalist interviews Emilia about her communist life and sympathies (just as Lungu did with the real metal worker), while in the film Emilia and Ţucu (her husband) become film extras in a documentary about the communist times at her factory. While the film crew – young people with not much knowledge of communism – are well-intended, they have no interest in considering Emilia's suggestions as far as accuracy is concerned. Moreover, she is just one of the many background cast of the film and this further emphasizes her insignificance. The film within a film is not only a nod to Gulea's on-going endeavor (a film about an old communist biddy) and thus a filmic recasting of Lungu's own implicit self-reference to the young journalist interviewing Emilia, but also functions as a signpost that the challenges of the present relegate communism to the past, which, when depicted, follows clear established templates (re-enactment according to generic archival footage).

Gulea's movie was unequivocally praised for its extraordinary cast, with both well-known actors and newcomers making remarkable roles. On the other hand, scholars viewed it as a "commentary" on the book (Komporaly 2014) or an "unfaithful adaptation" (Turcuş 2013). Still, just like the book, Gulea's film became the springboard for ideological conflicts and debates. One of the few reviews that lauded the film beyond its excellent cast and showed how it deals with anti-communism tropes (Burţa-Cernat 2013) became a major bone of contention, with leading intellectuals reacting to it (Tismăneanu 2013, Manolescu 2013). New debates about (out of place) nostalgia for the communist past also ensued, as the movie brought the novel back into the public attention. It also bolstered its popularity, and a new, limited edition of the novel was released with a new cover: the main protagonist of the movie is shown wearing a red head scarf and an "I love PCR" T-shirt (the famous "I love NY" logo now refashioned with the initials standing for the Romanian Communist Party), showing how communism and consumerism come together. This was very much of a common phenomenon in the late 2000s Romania. It was also a fascinating recasting of the globalizing tendencies within the national context, which occupies an important part in the play staged in Timişoara in 2019, to which I now turn.

Antonella Cornici's biddy on stage: The "communist girl" on reality show

The most recent stage adaptation of the novel makes another leap in time and brings us to the present and to a reality show where Emilia, the well-known "old communist biddy" made famous by Lungu's novel, is invited to share her life under communism on TV with a live audience, and also talk about the effect Lungu's novel has had on her life. If the movie foregrounds the local/global imbrications during the world economic crisis and the added difficulties these brought to those transitioning through postcommunism, the play concentrates on how the globalizing forces are morphed and appropriated in local social milieus. Specifically, it accurately portrays the mass media in the transition while also dramatizing the reception of memories about communism. The play had its premiere in November 2019 in Timişoara, a major city with a strong symbolic connection to the fall of communism: the Revolution of 1989 started in Timişoara and the strongest anticommunist declaration demanding lustration was read in the same city in March 1990. During the Covid-19 lockdown the recorded premiere night was streamlined online and enjoyed a warm welcome from a national audience.

Antonella Cornici, the director, found Lungu's Emilia to be emblematic for a current phenomenon – what scholars call "second-hand nostalgia" (Oushakine 2019), with reference to the increasing number of people who did not experience communism but regret its demise.[14] Accordingly, the old biddy is now a good-looking and well-dressed middle-aged woman who talks about her youth under communism, while also praising "Dănuț" (the "Danny boy" she has long known) who is now Lungu, the writer, and who accurately captured her memories and life story for the wider public. She objects the title though, which implies an old person and is thus inappropriate for her – she could have been referred to as "comrade" or just a "communist girl." Such remarks justify the play's script and also self-reflexively draw attention to how artistic representations successfully remediate genuine memories and give them a long-lasting life.

The TV show format is particularly inspired, as it enables an engagement with the *longue durée* of the transition (the time frame nods both to the present and to the 2000s, when such reality shows enjoyed significant popularity), proposes a debate about the role of memories about communism and highlights their value as precious commodity and spectacle to be capitalized on.[15] Clearly modeled on an imported long-lasting and particularly popular show in Romania,[16] *Cineva, Cândva* (*Somebody, Sometime*) reveals the precariousness behind the glamorous TV setting. Both the host and the show director encourage Emilia to allow her emotions overcome her, and cry or at least let some tears off: "Tears bring in advertising, advertising brings in money and thus salaries come on time. Do cry so that I can get my paycheck on the 23rd!" candidly tells her the show director. The current episode is to be followed by one devoted to a "capitalist biddy." Thus, memories and life stories about communism have become just a part of a commercial media package meant to produce ratings and money. To put it simply, in the play communist times encounter capitalist realities live on TV: the global practices of the early 1990s with communist memorabilia from the East acquiring currency in Western marketplaces are recast within the national context.

---

14 From this perspective, the protagonist's nostalgia as understood by the scriptwriter and director emphasizes the mutability of the phenomenon, or what Velikonja calls the "ahistoricity, extemporality, ex-territoriality, sensuality, complementarity, conflicted story lines, unpredictability, polysemism and episodic nature" of nostalgic narratives (2008, 28).

15 The debate exists on the extradiegetic level as well, as the premiere was followed by an onstage discussion hosted by the theater director and having Dan Lungu as part of it.

16 *Suprize, Suprize* (*Guess Who, Guess What!*) a reality show created by Valeriu Lazarov, a Romanian-born television producer and director who defected to Spain in 1968, ran weekly from 1999 to 2007 on the national network; the show invited ordinary people to talk about their life challenges, while it also enabled them to meet (unexpectedly) lost lovers or people from whom they have been separated. A large number of similar such shows captured national audiences along the transition years.

Figure 4: Biddy on TV, the *Cineva, Cândva* show.

Well-looking and dressed up in an elegant, black-dotted white deux-pièces suit,[17] Emilia appears out of place in these unfamiliar surroundings and finds it hard to stomach the glitzy atmosphere (Figure 4), even though she does come to life when she gets to share her life story. As expected in such a show, a whole gallery of family members or acquaintances gradually show up – Țucu, the daughter with her husband flown in from Canada, the former party representative (now a pastor), and Emilia's neighbor, Rozalia Stroescu. The diva host embodies the shallow TV glamour – she is always exuberant when the cameras are on and has ready-made show-biz questions and reactions irrespective of what happens in the studio.

Images of communist memorabilia Emilia treasures – her party membership card, her national savings' certificates, various products from the communist times – are projected on large screens, helping her bring dear memories back while expressing her strong affective attachment to the communist past. For the audience, the projection of memorabilia looks like the musealization of communist everyday life, but the different unfolding discourses about it point to the unsettled and unsettling nature of the past. Emilia's husband provides here constant counterpoints to her story – there is almost no remark she makes without Țucu punctuating her enthusiasm about the past. Such clashes between the low-key husband, who stands here for the voice of an 'unadulterated' memory of the past,

---

17 The colors of the entire setting are highly symbolic, in this case Emilia's white and black *deux-pièces* suit points to her overall 'innocence,' but also to her mistakes.

and the enlivened Emilia, who comes to life only when bringing the communist past back, are often dramatic and offer moments of good humor for the audience, while also articulating very distinct narratives.

The climax of the play is represented by a cameraman's outburst during a commercial break, when he shames the guest and everybody around: "Shame on you! Your nostalgia legitimizes the communist regime, its cruelty and injustice! How dare you not remember the endless humiliations, the queues, the winter cold, the lack of liberty?" The show resumes with the neighbor's story who highlights Emilia's genuine care about her, "an enemy of people," during the communist regime, to then switch to the final guest of the show, Dan Lungu himself. An excerpt from a televized interview is projected on wide screens and Lungu, as a professor of sociology, explains the 'roots' of the protagonist's nostalgia – these are indeed in the past but they are also connected to the future, which such people cannot foresee because of feeling marginalized and overlooked.

The show ends with a short monologue in which Emilia seems to make the difference between her youth, her life, and the communist regime. Though not exactly convincing and definitely not apologetic, the brief monologue seems very much in the spirit of show-biz, a means to bring closure and reconcile the heated spirits, to then enable the entire cast to dance happily in the TV studio. The ending of the play follows – the stage lights dim and the merry soundtrack of the show turns into a well-known, forward-looking pioneer song, with lyrics about a hopeful (communist) future with children becoming themselves (communist) heroes in the year 2000 (a simplistic recasting of Emilia's view about the past). Romania's coat of arms in socialist times is projected on the center screen, while the two side screens show white text rolling on: "Over 2 million people were imprisoned, tried or tortured for political crimes." Next, a list of famous cultural and political figures precedes the reference to "the thousands and thousands of pages of autobiographical literature which document the means of torture the secret police used" (a reference to the mainstream narrative about Romanian communism). All along, the socialist coat of arms has been gradually vanishing, until the line about the "genocide and atrocities committed by the communist regime against the Romanian nation" takes center stage, just as the young pioneers continue singing about future communist glory. The ending posits clear contrasts and reflects a "competitive memory" approach (Rothberg 2009) which denies the existence of multiple versions about the past.

The play ironically engages with the politics of the spectacle during transition. Emilia's memories are commodified and all things about the communist past become a spectacle. The genuine affective attachment of the protagonist to her past is constantly spectacularized and turned into a source of entertainment, melodrama, and anything that can bring in ratings and timely salaries. The extensive mélange of jokes from the novel are now entertaining musical or dramatic interludes, where performers who bring to mind protagonists in *The Matrix*, *Men in Black*, and contemporary rap and fashion shows models declaim in utter seriousness the jokes of the times against contemporary sounds of techno music and the like. Unlike in the novel and in Gulea's film, transnational crossings neither frame Emilia's memories, nor drive the plot. Instead, in Cornici's play world-wide practices of spectacularizing communism or its musealization are localized and define the national context in the indeterminate time frame of the transition the play alludes to. At the same time, the engagement with the past is unpredictable and still unsettled, as the outburst of the middle-aged cameraman makes clear.

As already stated, the play emphasizes a clear and constant clash between Emilia's and others' discourses about the past. Emilia is a kind-hearted person and well-intended human being, but her stance about the past remains an issue that needs to be addressed. All the other perspectives the play presents (Țucu's, her daughter's, Mrs. Stroescu's) offer correctives to Emilia's version; the very ending, which aims to symbolically counteract Emilia's naïveté, i.e., the pioneer song and text emphasizing the crimes of the communist regime, is didactic and does not leave room for alternative views. Aligning itself with the mainstream discourse about the memory of communism, the play definitely opts away from the open-endedness of the novel and the non-judgmental approach of its character. The on-stage discussion following the premiere, which was hosted by the theater director and had Dan Lungu, together with the entire artistic team as participants, also highlighted the need to "contextualize" Emilia's memories and remember the regime in view of "accurate historical knowledge." This is how the theater director put it when inviting the audience to read published memoirs and the literature on the topic. The show's extradiegetic layer points to clear anticommunist mnemonic regimes that have to be internalized and followed, and in which dissenting voices should be put in context.[18]

Irrespective of this rather didactic and institutionalized view (explainable perhaps by the play's staging in Timişoara, the city of the Romanian revolution), this remediation captures well how processes of exoticizing and spectacularizing of communism or its commodification have been naturalized in the local context. It also points to the unsettled and still fluid nature of the cultural memory of communism. Moreover, it highlights once again how wide-ranging and representative

---

18 Lungu was part of the on-stage discussion that followed the premiere. His 2019 status of senator for a liberal progressive party (as of 2016) apparently toned down his inquisitive and critical sociological stand of the early 2000s.

the protagonist actually is. The play, just like the 2013 movie, does provide a viable Emilia in a realistic context. Thus, she can be representative for some of the disillusioned younger generation, who appropriate nostalgia for communist times and render it into a completely empty signifier. She can equally sacrifice herself and start her life again in the countryside, but she can also be made aware of her naïve, one-sided view of the communist regime, without however repenting about her past. The protean nature of the character owes much to the times she straddles, whose complexity and multilayered nature have been neither acknowledged nor accommodated in mainstream representations.

Lungu's novel functioned as a "relay station" for the real metal worker's memories – it was "built on" these memories, and "recycled" them (Rigney 2008, 350). Lungu brought a new angle to both the communist past and the postcommunist transition, revealing memories about everyday communism that have resisted "the politics of memory produced by authorities and institutions" and which are "reductive by definition" (Todorova 2014, 7). The remediations of the novel have dramatized the intertwining between the past and present, the local and the global (the film), and the naturalizing of global processes within the national context as far as the communist past is concerned, its musealization, commodification, and spectacularizing (the play). The novel definitely presaged a wide range of light-hearted mnemonic engagements with the communist past,[19] but, as my analysis has shown, its remediations have not led to solidifying the cultural memory (Erll 2008, 393) of communism that Emilia's narrative embodies or of the transition she faces with much difficulty. On the contrary, the biddy's remediations point to dynamic, unsettled, and still unsettling processes of remembering the communist past and portraying the transition, all of which are predicated on complex transnational developments past and present.

Coda: The communist biddy's travels within the former socialist bloc

Transnational crossings (at the diegetic level) trigger Emilia's fond reminiscences about communist times, shape her life during the transition, and position the precarity of postcommunist times within a larger global orbit. What happens at the extra-diegetic level when the biddy travels, in translation, within the former socialist countries? The reception of the book within the former Eastern Europe

---

19 See for instance the omnibus film *Tales from the Golden Age* (Mungiu et al. 2009).

points to forms of "minor transnationalism," namely a space of exchange, a possibility, where cultures interact without necessary mediation by a center (Lionnet and Shih 2005, 5). Lionnet and Shih's concept denotes transversal movements of culture that include "minor to minor networks" and "circumvent the major altogether" (Lionnet and Shih 2005, 8). In regard to *I am an Old Commie!*, its reception within former socialist countries points to such alternative circuits of knowledge about transitions, through minor-to-minor transnational relationalities that are otherwise overlooked. It also further emphasizes the diversity of transitions and the very different understandings of the communist past in the region.

The countries in the former socialist bloc are viewed by scholars as having a family resemblance, and the almost half a century of communism they all shared (with a wide range of differences) has been seen as the major factor giving them a common regional identity since 1945 (Todorova 2014, 8). Scholars in memory studies have highlighted the commonalities of memory across the region, proposing "regional frameworks" of memory which are due to "specific sets of discursive practices related to particular events that happened in this part of Europe" (Pakier and Wawrzyniak 2015, 15–16). Consequently, one could expect that the memories of the old commie would have a similar resonance throughout the region. A quick search on the reception of the book's translation in Hungary, Bulgaria, Ukraine, and Poland proves otherwise. While numerous mentions do exist, and the translation of the book is reviewed and recommended on different culture-related websites and blogs, the reactions the novel has produced varies widely, with the warmest welcome coming from Poland.

Different from the early reception in Romania (and Bulgaria) where the focus was on how the *communist past* is portrayed, the focus of most Polish book reviews and presentations highlights the depiction of the transition which in Poland, just like Romania, did not provide any "magical solution," with politicians never delivering the expected changes. Moreover, if in Hungary the book is seen as casting light on Romania, and thus on one particular context (Csilla 2008), the Polish media emphasize the *familiarity* with the Emilia type ("we all have heard such an uncle or grandparent") and with the problems the book raises about both the past and the present ("change a name or two and this could easily be a book about Poland under communism" (Wysocki 2009)). Such Polish pieces also bring up connections the novel invites in relation to *Polish* recent history ("Recenzja" 2018). In other words, if both the verisimilitude and the plot of the novel were a bone of contention for Romanian critics in the late 2000s, in Poland the book was widely embraced for its very authenticity. Lungu's book captivated Polish readers through its humor, irony, and keen sense of rendering the absurd characterizing both the communist and postcommunist times. Titles such as "Romanians and Poles are Kin" ("Polak" 2012) point to relationalities between two former communist countries that may be less apparent otherwise and which the reception of the novel clearly reveals.

A move to Bulgaria, shows how Lungu's biddy goes against familiar types of post–1989 Bulgarian culture. The Bulgarian book presentation highlights how Emilia is "neither a victim of communism nor a perpetrator," but a "*curious* character when viewed against the literary narrative of the Bulgarian transition" ("Chervena," my emphasis). Thus, the presentation suggests similarities between (restrictive) mnemonic canons in Romania and its southern neighbor. In Ukraine, Emilia is the Soviet "affected" type (Daphnia 2019) who would never vote for change and who would have supported Viktor Yanukovych, the pro-Russian former president (Vieru qtd. in Lukyashko 2018). Emilia is thus a familiar phenomenon to the Ukrainians as well, and one to be blamed because of the political implications of her vote. Another Ukrainian book presentation states with much relief that the "modern versions of women in the Warsaw Pact countries" are not only the Soviet ones, but their former socialist neighbors ("Literaturnyj" 2018). That is, not only women's Soviet mentality affects the present, and is an impediment for changes, but the socialist one just as much. In other words, any possible ideological split between the USSR and the Eastern Bloc is bridged by our character, and possible communist leanings are to be blamed for the failures of the present.

Why would such relationalities and transregional dis/connections matter, and what do they tell us about remembering transition and the local and (trans) regional crossings in culture and media? The reception of Lungu's novel in the former socialist countries signals the unpredictable, reciprocal (though often asymmetrical) associations between different minor networks and makes room for "the minor's inherent complexity and multiplicity" (Lionnet and Shih 2005, 8). Specifically, it draws attention to relationalities and solidarities but also to the evolving heterogeneity of postsocialist mnemonic contexts across the region. Moreover, it points to the need for a broader comparative scale, and the relevance of postsocialist comparative memory cultures, which would better map the variegated itineraries of postcommunist transitions as well as the subjectivities and agencies at work.

As my analysis has shown, in Romania the reception and several remediations of Lungu's novel are themselves emblematic for the processes of the transition and the complexities of remembering the communist past. They also illustrate the transition that contemporary literature has undergone, as the novel and its author have been gradually canonized in Romanian culture. In light of the focus of the current volume, one can confidently assert that the artistic embodiments of the communist biddy and her memories open up alternative ways of representing the painful *longue durée* transition in Romania. Just as importantly, by drawing attention to the multifaceted interfaces between the local, global, and the regional informing or deriving from such representations, my chapter argues for transnationalism as lens and method of engagement with post–1989 transitions and mnemonic framing of post/communism, as a means of capturing the multiscalar, complex articulations informing both the past and the present.

Works cited

Assmann, Jan. "Communicative and Cultural Memory." *Cultural Memory Studies: An International and Interdisciplinary Handbook.* Ed. Astrid Erll and Ansgar Nünning. Berlin: De Gruyter, 2008. 109–188.

Axinte, Serban. "Drama Emiliei Apostoae, dincolo de ficţiune." *Tribuna* 117 (July 6–13, 2007): 4–5.

Berdahl, Daphne. "*Good Bye, Lenin!* Aufwiedersehen GDR: On the Social Life of Socialism." *Post-Communist Nostalgia.* Ed. Maria Todorova and Zsuzsa Gille. New York: Berghahn, 2010. 177–189.

Burţă Cernat, Bianca. "Anticomunismul nostru postfactum." *Observator Cultural* 691 (September 18, 2013). www.observatorcultural.ro/articol/anticomunismul-romanesc-post-factum-i-2/ (Accessed June 10, 2020).

Burţă Cernat, Bianca. "Să scrii bine despre universurile derizorii." *Observatorul Cultural* 363 (March 15, 2007). www.observatorcultural.ro/articol/sa-scrii-bine-despre-universurile-derizorii-2/ (Accessed April 15, 2020).

Chelcea, Liviu, and Oana Druţă. "Zombie Socialism and the Rise of Neoliberalism in Post-Socialist Central and Eastern Europe." *Eurasian Geography and Economics* 57.4–5 (2016): 521–544.

Creţu, Bogdan. "Ascensiunea si declinul omului nou." *Observator Cultural* 363 (March 15, 2007). https://www.observatorcultural.ro/articol/ascensiunea-si-declinul-omului-nou-2/ (Accessed April 15, 2020).

Conkan, Marius. "*Sînt o babă comunistă* sau 'romanul cu poantă'." *Revista Echinox* 5–12 (2009).

Costanda Alexandra. "VIDEO: Stere Gulea, regizorul filmului "Sunt o babă comunistă!": "Degeaba ai idei bune dacă nu-i convingi pe spectatori de aici şi acum." *adevărul.ro.* https://adevarul.ro/showbiz/film/video-stere-gulea-regizorul-filmului-sunt-o-baba-1466808.html (Accessed April 15, 2020).

Cristea-Enache, Daniel. "Răpirea din Serai – *Sunt o babă comunistă!* de Dan Lungu." *Liternet* (March 17, 2008). https://atelier.liternet.ro/articol/5596/Daniel-Cristea-Enache/Rapirea-din-Serai-Sunt-o-baba-comunista-de-Dan-Lungu.html (Accessed April 15, 2020).

Csilla, Zólya A. "Komcsi-e a nyanya?" *ujszo.com* (October 24, 2008). https://ujszo.com/kultura/komcsi-e-a-nyanya (Accessed June 1, 2020).

Cvetkovich, Ann. *Archive of Feelings.* Durham: Duke University Press, 2003.

Daphnia. "Review." *Live.ru* (October 23, 2019). https://www.livelib.ru/review/1210258-ya-sche-ta-komunistichna-baba-dan-lungu (Accessed May 15, 2020).

De Cesari, Chiara, and Ann Rigney. "Introduction." *Transnational Memory: Circulation, Articulation, Scales.* Ed. Chiara De Cesari and Ann Rigney. Berlin: De Gruyter, 2014. 1–29.

Dobre, Claudia-Florentina. "Memorial Regimes and Memory Updates in Post-Communist Romania." *Sensus Historiae* 27.2 (2017): 115–130.

Dragomir, Elena. "In Romania, Opinion Polls Show Nostalgia for Communism." *Balkanalysis.com* (December 27, 2011). www.romaniannewswatch.com (Accessed June 10, 2019).

Erll, Astrid. "Literature, Film, and the Mediality of Cultural Memory." *A Companion to Cultural Memory Studies*. Ed. Astrid Erll and Ansgar Nünning. Berlin: De Gruyter, 2008. 389–398.

Erll, Astrid. "Travelling Memory." *Parallax*. 17.4 (2011): 4–18.

Fishkin, Shelley F. "Crossroads of Cultures: The Transnational Turn in American Studies: Presidential Address to the American Studies Association, November 12, 2004." *American Quarterly* 57.1 (2005): 17–57.

Georgescu, Diana. "Between Trauma and Nostalgia: The Intellectual Ethos and Generational Dynamics of Memory in Postsocialist Romania." *Südosteuropa* 64.3 (2016): 284–306.

Georgescu, Diana. "'Ceauşescu Hasn't Died': Irony as Countermemory in Post-Socialist Romania." *Post-Communist Nostalgia*. Ed. Maria Todorova and Zsuzsa Gille. New York: Berghahn Books, 2010. 155–176.

Giles, Paul. *Transnationalism in Practice: Essays on American Studies, Literature and Religion*. Edinburgh: Edinburgh University Press, 2010.

"Chervena babichka s'm. Dan Lungu." [I'm a Red Granny. Dan Lungu] *Faber-bg*. https://www.faber-bg.com/%D1%87%D0%B5%D1%80%D0%B2%D0%B5%D0%BD%D0%B0-%D0%B1%D0%B0%D0%B1%D0%B8%D1%87%D0%BA%D0%B0-%D1%81%D1%8A%D0%BC (Accessed May 20, 2020).

Ghodsee, Kristen, and Mitchell Orenstein. "Revolutions for Whom?" *Project Syndicate* (November 1, 2019). https://www.project-syndicate.org/commentary/most-postcommunist-citizens-worse-off-by-kristen-r-ghodsee-and-mitchell-a-orenstein-2019-11?barrier=accesspaylog (Accessed July 15, 2021).

Ghodsee, Kristen, and Mitchell Orenstein. *Taking Stock of Shock: Social Consequences of the 1989 Revolutions*. Oxford: Oxford University Press, 2021.

Gorzo, Andrei. "Noul şi vechiul." *Dilema veche* 498 (August 2013). https://agenda.liternet.ro/articol/17007/Andrei-Gorzo/Vechiul-si-noul-Sint-o-baba-comunista.html (Accessed April 15, 2020).

Iacob, Bogdan C. "History's Debris. The Many Pasts in the Post-1989 Present." *Südosteuropa* 64.2 (2016): 119–141.

Iovănel, Mihai. "Scufiţa Roşie în lumina luptei de clasă." *Cultura* 60 (2007).

Iovănel, Mihai. *Istoria literaturii române contemporane, 1990–2020*. Bucharest: Editura Polirom, 2021.

I'm an Old Communist Hag. Dir. Stere Gulea. MediaPro Pictures, 2013.

Khagram, Sanjeev, and Peggy Levitt. "An Introduction." *The Transnational Studies Reader: Intersections and Innovations*. Ed. Sanjeev Khagram and Peggy Levitt. London: Routledge, 2008. 23–35.

Komporaly, Jozefina. "'Don't You Dare to Vote with the Communists!': Timeliness, Nostalgia, and the Authenticity of Experience in *I'm a Communist Biddy!*" *Adaptation* 7.2 (2014): 169–179.

Leonte, Florin. "*Baba comunistă* a lui Dan Lungu jucată la Naţionalul timişorean." *7Iasi.ro* (November 7 2019). https://www.7iasi.ro/baba-comunista-a-lui-dan-lungu-jucata-la-nationalul-timisorean/ (Accessed August 10, 2020).

Lionnet, Françoise, and Shu-mei Shih. "Introduction: Thinking through the Minor, Transnationally." *Minor Transnationalism*. Ed. Françoise Lionnet and Shumei Shih. Durham: Duke University Press, 2005. 1–26.

"Literaturnyj dajdzhest. Yakby ne bulo komunistychnyx bab, to nixto b ne diznavsya pro isnuvannya Yanukovycha." [Literary Digest. If there were No Communist Women, No One would Know about Yanukovych's Existence] *Bukvoid.com.ua* (March 16, 2018). http://bukvoid.com.ua/digest/2018/03/16/091039.html (Accessed August 14, 2020).

Luca, Maria. "O tranziţie fragilă." *Observator Cultural* 412 (February 28, 2008).https://www.observatorcultural.ro/articol/o-tranzitie-fragila-2/ (Accessed April 15, 2020).

Lukyashko, Kateryna. "За комуністів було краще. Це – шокуюча правда" [It Was Better under the Communists. This is the Shocking Truth]. *Gazeta.ua* (20 March 2018). https://gazeta.ua/articles/culture-newspaper/_za-komunistiv-bulo-krasche-ce-shokuyucha-pravda/826835 (Accessed May 10, 2020).

Lungu, Dan. *I Am an Old Commie!* Trans. Alistair I. Blyth. London: Dalkey Press, 2017.

Lungu, Dan. *Sînt o babă comunistă!* Iaşi: Polirom, 2013 [2007].

Mark, James, Bogdan C. Iacob, Tobias Rupprecht, and Ljubica Spaskovska. *1989: A Global History of Eastern Europe*. Cambridge: Cambridge University Press, 2019.

Manolescu, Nicolae. "Anticomunismul, terorism intelectual?" *Adevărul* (October 4, 2013). https://adevarul.ro/cultura/carti/anticomunismul-terorism-intelectual-1_524ee41ec7b855ff56fcb8a1/index.html (Accessed June 1, 2020).

Micu, Mădălina. "Luna noiembrie la Teatrul Naţional 'Radu Stanca'. Premiere şi evenimente speciale." *Turnul Sfatului* (November 5, 2016). www.turnulsfatului.ro/2016/11/05/luna-noiembrie-la-teatrul-national-bdquo-radu-stanca-rdquo-premiere-si-evenimente-speciale-70829 (Accessed April 10, 2020).

Mihăilescu, Dan C. "La chermeza proletară." *Ziarul Financiar* (December 17, 2003). www.zf.ro/ziarul-de-duminica/la-chermeza-proletara-2967307 (Accessed May 5, 2020).

Mironescu, Andreea M. *Textul literar şi construcţia memoriei culturale. Forme ale rememorării în literatura română din postcomunism*. Bucharest: Editura Muzeul Literaturii Române, 2013.

Nadkarni, Maya, and Olga Shevchenko. "The Politics of Nostalgia: A Case for Comparative Analysis of Post-Socialist Practices." *Ab imperio* 2004.2 (2004): 487–519.

Oushakine, Serguei A. "Second-Hand Nostalgia: On Charms and Spells of the Soviet Trukhliashechka." *Post-Soviet Nostalgia*. Ed. Otto Boele, Boris Noordenbos, and Ksenia Robbe. London: Routledge, 2019. 38–69.

Pakier, Małgorzata, and Joanna Wawrzyniak. "Introduction: Memory and Change in Eastern Europe: How Special?" *Memory and Change in Europe: Eastern Perspectives*. Ed. Małgorzata Pakier and Joanna Wawrzyniak. Oxford: Berghahn Books, 2015. 1–20.

Petrescu, Cristina. "Nostalgia, Identity and Self-Irony in Remembering Communism." *Justice, Memory and Redress in Romania: New Insights*. Ed. Lavinia Stan and Lucian Turcescu. Newcastle upon Tyne: Cambridge Scholars Publishing, 2017. 192–213.

Petrescu, Cristina, and Dragoş Petrescu. "The Canon of Remembering Romanian Communism: From Autobiographical Recollections to Collective Representations." *Remembering Communism. Private and Public Recollections of Lived Experience in Southeast Europe*. Ed. Maria Todorova. Budapest: Central European University Press, 2014. 43–70.

Pleşu, Andrei. "Nostalgia cu 'chip uman.'" *Adevărul* (August 26, 2013). https://adevarul.ro/entertainment/film/nostalgia-cu-chip-uman-1_521af264c7b855ff5613676f/index.html (Accessed June 1, 2020).

Pohrib, Codruţa A. "The Romanian 'Latchkey Generation' Writes Back: Memory Genres of Post-Communism on Facebook." *Memory Studies* 12.2 (2019): 164–183.

"Polak, Rumun dwa bratanki." *Miasteczko Krajeńskie* (November 2012). www.miasteczkokrajenskie.pl/asp/polak-rumun-dwa-bratanki,29,artykul,2,470 (Accessed June 1, 2020).

Popescu-Sandu, Oana. "'Let's All Freeze up until 2100 or so': Nostalgic Directions in Post-Communist Romania." *Post-Communist Nostalgia*. Ed. Maria Todorova and Zsuzsa Gille. New York: Berghahn Books, 2010. 113–128.

"Recenzja 'Jestem komunistyczną babą!' Dan Lungu." *Melancholia Codzienności* (April 2018). http://melancholiacodziennosci.blogspot.com/2018/04/recenzja-jestem-komunistyczna-baba-dan.html (Accessed June 1, 2020).

Rigney, Ann. "Cultural Memory Studies: Mediation, Narrative, and the Aesthetic." *Routledge International Handbook of Memory Studies*. London: Routledge, 2015. 87–98.

Rigney, Ann. "The Dynamics of Remembrance: Texts between Monumentality and Morphing." *Cultural Memory Studies: An International and Interdisciplinary Handbook*. Ed. Astrid Erll and Ansgar Nünning. Berlin: De Gruyter, 2008. 345–353.

Rogozanu, Costi. "Cum explici că nu e comunismul bun?" *Suplimentul de Cultură* 118 (March 10–16, 2007). http://suplimentuldecultura.ro/1259/cum-sa-explici-ca-nu-e-bun-comunismul/ (Accessed June 1, 2020).

Rothberg, Michael. *Multidirectional Memory: Remembering the Holocaust in the Age of Decolonization*. Stanford: Stanford University Press, 2009.

Sadowski-Smith, Claudia. *The New Immigrant Whiteness: Race, Neoliberalism, and Post-Soviet Migration to the United States*. New York: NYU Press, 2018.

Scribner, Charity. *Requiem for Communism*. Cambridge, MA: MIT Press, 2003.

Simuţ, Andrei. *Romanul românesc postcomunist între trauma totalitară şi criza prezentului. Tipologii, periodizări, contextualizări*. Bucharest: Editura Muzeul Literaturii Române, 2015.

Sînt o babă comunistă! by Dan Lungu, directed by Antonella Cornici, Teatru Naţional din Timişoara (November 3, 2019) [recording].

Sînt o babă comunistă! by Dan Lungu, choreographed by Aleisha Gardner, Teatrul de Balet Sibiu, April 28, 2015 [recording https://www.youtube.com/watch?v=s3QWSBWAEag] (Accessed May 10, 2020).

Stan, Adriana. "Post-Socialist Realism. Authenticity and Political Conscience in the Romanian Literature of the 2000s." *Critique: Studies in Contemporary Fiction* (2021): 1–12.

Stan, Lavinia. *Transitional Justice in Post-communist Romania: The Politics of Memory*. Cambridge: Cambridge University Press, 2013.

Szilagyi, Anikó. "Dan Lungu: *I'm an Old Commie!* translated by Alistair Ian Blyth; Ignacy Karpowicz: *Gestures*, translated by Maya Zakrzewska-Pim." *Translation and Literature* (2018): 379–383.

Teatrul Naţional Radu Stanca. *Sunt o babă comunistă!* November 10, 2016. https://www.tnrs.ro/ro/events/sunt-o-baba-comunista-9. (Accessed August 20, 2020).

Tismăneanu, Vladimir. "Comunism, Anticomunism si Terorism Intelectual." *Romclub* (October 18, 2013). https://romclub.wordpress.com/2013/10/18/comunism-anticomunism-si-terorism-intelectual-de-vladimir-tismaneanu/ (Accessed April 3, 2023).

Tismăneanu, Vladimir, Dorin Dobrincu, and Cristian Vasile, eds. *Raport final*. Bucharest: Humanitas, 2007.

Todorova, Maria. "From Utopia and Propaganda and Back." *Post-Communist Nostalgia*. Ed. Maria Todorova and Zsuzsa Gille. New York: Berghahn Books, 2010. 1–13.

Todorova, Maria. "Introduction: Similar Trajectories, Different Memories." *Remembering Communism: Private and Public Recollections of Lived Experience in Southeast Europe*. Ed. Maria Todorova, Augusta Dimou, and Stefan Troebst. Budapest: CEU Press, 2014. 1–26.

Turcuş, Florin-Claudiu. "Recycling and Confronting Ostalgie under the Romanian Transition. *I'm an Old Communist Hag* – An Unfaithful Adaptation." *Ekphrasis. Images, Cinema, Theory, Media* 10.2 (2013): 63–76.

Ursă, Mihaela. "Baba comunistă c'est moi!" *Apostrof* 6 (2007). http://www.revista-apostrof.ro/ (Accessed April 10, 2020).

Velikonja, Mitja. *Titostalgia: A Study of Nostalgia for Josip Broz*. Ljubliana: MediaWatch, Peace Institute, 2008.

Wysocki, Grzegorz. "Dan Lungu 'Jesterm komunistyczną babą?'" *Dwutygodnik.com* (November 2009) https://www.dwutygodnik.com/artykul/624-dan-lungu-jestem-komunistyczna-baba.html (Accessed May 20, 2020).

Cara Levey

Writing Exile(s) from the Periphery: *Hijos del exilio* and Transnational Memory of the Southern Cone Democratic Transitions

Abstract: Exile and migration to, from, and between the Southern Cone countries have been commonplace throughout the history of the region. However, from the 1960s onwards forced displacement would become a 'ubiquitous phenomenon' (Roniger et al. 2018, 32), with Europe a natural destination for an unprecedented exodus of individuals, as well as families, fleeing dictatorships from across the region, including Argentina (1976–1983) and Uruguay (1973–1985) (Graham-Yooll 1987). As this chapter elucidates, for the *hijos del exilio* – those who were born and/or brought up in exile – there is no neat division between country of origin and country of exile; their lives reveal ebbs and flows, multiple journeys and 'returns' during the democratic transitions of the 1980s, some permanent, others fleeting. Whilst there has been notable academic interest in the first generation of exiles – those who were adults when they left South America – there is a general absence of the *hijos del exilio* from the dictatorship and transitional memory landscape, which obfuscates the microhistories and diverse hidden voices of transition. This chapter challenges the exclusion of second-generational exile voices from dictatorship and transitional memory landscapes, by comparing the work of two child-exile writers: *De exilios, maremotos y lechuzas* (1990) by Dutch Uruguayan author Carolina Trujillo and *El azul de las abejas* (2013) by Franco-Argentine writer Laura Alcoba. These semi-autobiographical works challenge widely held assertions and myths about exile that circulated during the dictatorship and, in particular, the transitional periods, and allow for a deeper and more nuanced approach that destabilizes the notion of transition as a top-down or national process.

Introduction

> Hundreds of us children are burdened with this gaping wound, a legacy of the dictatorship: (we are) broken, placeless, orphaned and in search of identity.[1] (Carolina Meloni, Argentine brought up in exile in Spain, quoted in Conde 2019)

---

1 "Cientos de niños argentinos cargamos con esta brecha imborrable, herencia que nos ha dejado la dictadura: fisurados, desterritorializados, huérfanos y en busca de identidad." All quotes in Spanish have been translated by the author.

https://doi.org/10.1515/9783110707793-011

Exile and migration to, from, and between the Southern Cone countries have been commonplace throughout the history of the region; however, from the 1960s onwards forced displacement would become a 'ubiquitous phenomenon' (Roniger et al. 2018, 32), with Europe a natural destination for an unprecedented exodus of individuals as well as families fleeing dictatorships from across the region, including Argentina (1976–1983) and Uruguay (1973–1985) (Graham-Yooll 1987). The words of Carolina Meloni, a child when her family went into exile in Spain, where she still lives, offers us a stark reminder about the profound intergenerational reverberations of exile and the legacy of violence beyond the geographical boundaries of the Southern Cone. As this chapter elucidates, for the *hijos del exilio* – those who were born and/or brought up in exile – there is no neat division between country of origin and country of exile; their lives reveal ebbs and flows, multiple journeys and 'returns,' – often during the democratic transitions of the 1980s – some permanent, others fleeting. Whilst there has been significant academic interest in the first generation of exiles – those who were adults when they left South America – Meloni alludes to what I assert is an absence of the *hijos del exilio* from the dictatorship and transitional memory landscape, which obfuscates the microhistories and myriad 'hidden' voices of transition. Further, she raises the more pronounced marginalization of those *hijos* who never returned to the Southern Cone, a transnational group that Mariana Norandi has called the *no retornados* [non-returnees] (2016).

Challenging this lacuna, this chapter offers a nuanced depiction of the Argentine and Uruguayan dictatorships and transitions as experienced by children and adolescents, by foregrounding analysis of the child-exile in work that is also *by* two *hijas del exilio*: French-Argentine Laura Alcoba and Dutch-Uruguayan Carolina Trujillo, two writers whose biographies abound comparisons.[2] Alcoba was born in Cuba in 1968, before returning to La Plata with her activist parents a few months later. Amidst the escalation of violence and with her father imprisoned from 1975, she and her mother were forced into hiding in the so-called *casa de los conejos* – the rabbit farm that served as a front for the opposition printing press *Evita Montonera* – the events surrounding which are fictionalized and inspired the 2008 eponymous novel (originally published in French in 2007). While Alcoba's mother fled to France in 1976, the young Alcoba would remain with her grandparents in La Plata, visiting her father in prison on a fortnightly basis before joining her mother in Paris at the age of ten in 1979. Born in 1970, Carolina Trujillo's biography reveals a similar trajectory to Alcoba and many other Uru-

---

2 I use these terms to acknowledge the dual or hybrid identities adopted by the authors themselves.

guayan exiles, first fleeing with her mother and sister to Argentina in 1974 while her father remained in prison in Uruguay, before leaving for the Netherlands in 1976, when the Argentine military took control of government. Both authors therefore could be considered *exiliadas hijas* themselves as well as *hijas del exilio*.[3] Although this suggests slippage between the first and second generations, there is, as we shall see, a clear ontological difference between those who were adults when they went into exile and the *hijos* – undergoing "an exile that comprises the country of childhood" (Arfuch 2018, 688) – coming of age *after* dictatorships ended in the early-mid 1980s and their home countries grappled with nascent democratic transitions. Furthermore, while Alcoba would remain in France permanently, Trujillo and her family went back (including her father who had been released) in 1985. She eventually returned to the Netherlands in the early 1990s, before finally settling there in 2005. Both writers can thus be viewed as belonging to the category of *no retornados*.

Meanwhile, exile and state violence are recurrent themes in the authors' work, inspired by real events, from Alcoba's parents' journey to Cuba in *Los pasajeros del Ana C.* (2012) to Perón's exile in Spain. In terms of overlap with Alcoba's own lived experience, *La casa de los conejos* can be viewed as part of a trilogy, along with *El azul de las abejas* (2015, published in French in 2013) and *La danza de la araña* (2014), that explicitly engage with the child's life during dictatorship, or in the case of *la danza*, a teenager. Whilst *la casa* explores a seven-year-old girl's experience of internal exile in Argentina, *El azul* is based on Alcoba's weekly correspondence with her father while in exile in Paris, deploying the child-narrator to shed light on the departure for and arrival to Parisian exile for the post-dictatorship generation. It is thus a fitting text to be read alongside Trujillo's 1990 young adult novel *De exilios, maremotos y lechuzas* [*Of Exiles, Tsunamis and Barn Owls*], written from the perspective, for the most part, of a child narrator and depicting the before, during and *after* of Dutch exile from Uruguay. Covering a slightly longer timespan than *El azul*, the work was conceived and drafted as the then-teenaged Trujillo was grappling with the problematic 'return' to a country dealing with the reestablishment of democracy. Preoccupation with state violence and exile appear in two of Trujillo's other novels: her 2002 *De Bastaard van Mal Abrigo* [The Bastard of Mal Abrigo], is set in an undisclosed Latin American country and, more recently, *De Terugkeer van Lupe García* [The Return of

---

3 Alberione favors the term *exiliados hijos* over the 'second-generation' and other possible terms, placing the verb before the noun for emphasis of the effects of the dictatorship for these children. Here, I use the term *hijos del exilio* as a term that allows for the slippage between first and second-generation exiles, acknowledging that many of those who were born in exile were in fact exiles themselves, as is the case with both the authors explored here.

Lupe Garcia], 2009, which, as the title suggests, deals with the return of the children of exile. However, *Exilios* is the only of these to be written and published in Spanish.

By bringing these two second-generation exilic narratives into dialogue with one another, the chapter's contribution is two-fold. First, I advocate a move away from postmemory (Hirsch 2008), the lens through which much second-generation memory work in the Southern Cone has been viewed. (Blejmar 2016, Levey 2015, Ros 2012, Serpente 2011) By now it is well-established that memory may be transmitted to those who did not live through or remember a particular event or period. However, there has been limited discussion on memory work situated at the interface of generational and geographical displacement. Second, the chapter views these voices as a challenge to the widely held assertions about exiles (and their children) that circulated during the dictatorship and the transitional periods: first, the 'Golden Exile' myth, prevalent during the Southern Cone democratic transitions, which depicts exile as an overwhelmingly positive experience occluding the hardship and challenges, and second, the idea that the second-generation of *no-retornados* are fully integrated in host or receiving societies. By exposing exile and being the child of exiles as a more complex and multilayered experience, such ostensibly transnational iterations of memory place the transitions in a different light, advocating new ways of thinking about the lasting and deep impact of the dictatorship on the children of exile. In doing so, the chapter offers an alternative and nuanced perspective on democratic transitions, which, for the most part, have focused on the process as experienced by the nation and concerning elites and judicial and political institutions, rather than the individual voices impacted in and by transition. Thus, we can challenge the gap between what happens at national level and the microhistories obfuscated by transitional 'macronarratives.'

The chapter begins with a discussion of the absence of the *hijos del exilio* (including the *no retornados)* from transitional and, contemporary memory landscapes, in order to frame the authors' respective bodies of work, advocating for an approach to transition that encompasses hidden or marginal voices The second, more substantive, section compares the novels in detail. Split into three parts, the first, "Rupture and Adapting to Exile," looks at the use of the child's gaze, and the blurring of fiction and autobiography, as a way of depicting the integration and daily lives of the *hijos del exilio*. The second, "Writing Home," considers the narrators' epistolary relationships with their incarcerated fathers, which serve as a reminder of the ongoing violence in their home countries. The third part, "After Exile," deals with depictions of the transitions that followed the dictatorship periods and the (potential) return of the, by now teenage, protagonists. There is here a mirroring of the nation going through transition and the transitional turbulence of adolescence in the young protagonists' lives. The chapter closes by revisiting Fanny Söderback's (2012) concept of 'temporal revolt' in order to position the texts as a destabilizing force from the periphery in response to transitional memory narratives that are often (quasi)hegemonic and might otherwise have gone unchallenged.

Absent voices: Hegemonic memory narratives of transition

Post-dictatorship memory narratives concerned with truth, justice, and redress for the victims of state terrorism in the Southern Cone have tended to exclude or marginalize the exile experience, adopting an historical approach to exile, focusing on the period during which human rights violations were taking place (Franco 2008, Markarian 2006). More recently, the introduction to Roniger et al.'s (2018) volume centers on the contribution of returning exiles to the culture and politics of the Southern Cone, yet little is said about those who did not return during or since the democratic transitions. Responding to this lacuna, Miorelli and Piersanti (2021) have conducted in-depth interviews with Southern Cone exiles, many of them *no retornados,* in London from the first generation (those who were adults when they were exiled). Indeed, the Roniger et al volume explicitly identified the need for more work on the consequences of exile on the second generation. Here, we may interpret this as both during the dictatorship but also the legacy during transition, when many returned, whilst others remained in Europe. Yet a decade later, this literature remains scant. This is in spite of the increasing public presence of the second-generation in the Southern Cone since the mid-1990s, which accounts for an upsurge in scholarly interest on post-dictatorship cultural production (Blejmar 2016; Ros 2012) and identity and activism (Fried 2016; Jara 2016). Together these important works have offered insight into how the second-generation experience of dictatorship differs from the experience of those who were adults during the dictatorship and transitions, pointing to a constellation of different perspectives. However, much of this work has focused on the children of the *desaparecidos* and murdered. In excluding the *hijos del exilio*, this body of work does not offer a nuanced picture of post-dictatorship generational change and the ongoing engagement with dictatorial rule and the democratic transitions that followed. This is particularly surprising when one considers the questions about exiles that the end of dictatorships brought into sharp focus – in particular whether their return to the Southern Cone would be feasible and how this would be facilitated.

Notwithstanding, when surveying the scholarly landscape on the *hijos del exilio*, several notable exceptions emerge. In Dutrénit's 2006 collection on Uruguayan exile, Porta's chapter specifically turns to the Uruguayan second-generation to shed light on the impact of exile, yet the focus is generally on those who returned to Uruguay (2006). In a similar vein, Serpente (2011) has explored the children of Argentine and Chilean migrants in London, not only those displaced by state violence, but those who migrated for other reasons. Whilst scholars like Norandi and Serpente, themselves members of second-generation diasporic communities, make invaluable contributions to diversifying the impact of dictatorship and exile beyond the Southern Cone, the emphasis on individual cases tends to prevent a comparative approach between different originating countries, something this chapter builds on by turning to literary narratives of exile.

The peripheral position of *hijos del exilio* in general, and the *no-retornados* more specifically, can be attributed to their young age during dictatorship and them only coming of age in the democratic transitions (from the mid-1980s onwards)[4] translating into a lack of public presence and political protagonism until the mid-1990s. However, it is also closely connected to the narratives surrounding exile that emerged during dictatorships and persisted well into the democratic transitions, which excluded exiles from the category of victims. A reason for this is the historical and cultural formulation of the exile figure in terms of victimhood, the result being that the exile experience was "sidelined by other forms of exclusion" (Roniger 2007, 32), particularly by forced disappearance in the case of Argentina. This arguably inhibited collective claims of victimhood and discussion of exile within a human rights frame throughout the transitions, and even beyond. Furthermore, this gulf between victimhood and exile continued through region-wide transitions to democracy in the 1980s and early 1990s, during which narratives of suffering and the claims for legal redress tended to focus on the emblematic victims (the disappeared in Argentina, and the long-term political prisoners in Uruguay) as activists and relatives took to the streets to demand justice. After the dictatorship, turning to the transition, returning exiles were treated

---

4 Defining the parameters of the democratic transitions is not an exact science. The end of Southern Cone dictatorships involved negotiation through elections and the eventual transfer of power, which ranged from a relatively short year in Argentina to several years in Uruguay, as in Chile. For the most part, the 1980s were dominated by discussions over how to address human rights violations. By the start of the 1990s, both Argentina and Uruguay had undergone two democratic presidential terms, without violent transfer of power, marking the end of the transitional phase of democratic handover. Having said this, many of the issues at the fore in the 1980s remained persistent throughout the 1990s, and questions emerged about the quality of these (re) emerging democracies.

with suspicion, partly because of widely held assumptions about their time in exile. As Jensen (2010) has found in the case of Argentina, those who left were commonly viewed as fortunate to have survived, leading to their erasure as victims from national consciousness, but also obfuscating more nuanced formulation of exile. In Argentina, this was likely exacerbated by the lack of official expulsion by the regime, but it is apparent that the myth of, or at least some version of, *exilio dorado* [golden exile], through which exile is construed as a more positive experience, permeates most of the Southern Cone country studies.[5] It was also exacerbated, as Jensen explains, by the narrative of the regimes themselves, that the exiles had left voluntarily and abandoned the struggle, a viewpoint that was also shared by members of the revolutionary left. This is problematic given that many of those who left for exile had disappeared family members or had been imprisoned and tortured themselves or that families were separated for prolonged periods. There is, therefore, no neat distinction between the exile as 'fortunate' survivor and the exile as victim or having suffered upheaval, displacement, and issues of integration in the host countries. In the case of Argentina, Roniger et al. highlight an even more hostile depiction of exiled citizens, citing the dictatorship's demonization of exiles as a strategy that led to their isolation from the political scene (2012, 100–101). This may have been more prevalent in Argentina, because, unlike Uruguay, there was no state policy to facilitate the return and reintegration of exiles after the dictatorship.[6] However, it is clear that hierarchical formulations of victimhood have resulted in the marginalization of exile from broader post-dictatorship memory culture, including the literature on first and second generations. These features have obfuscated the child-exile by tending to view the latter's experience as an extension of that of their parents (Norandi 2016). The result is a tendency to downplay the long-term psychological and societal effects of exile, and their legacy for future generations, something that for much of the transitional periods went unchallenged.

Attention to these other experiences, through the work of Trujillo and Alcoba, refocuses our gaze on other aspects or layers of democratic transition. As noted above, in the case of Latin America, scholarly attention on transitions tend to focus

---

5 For discussion of this phenomenon in Argentina, see Franco 2008, Jensen 2010; for Uruguay, see Porta 2006.

6 In Uruguay, the reintegration of the country's large number of exiles was a key strand of the Sanguinetti administration's policy to address the past. In 1985 the government created the *Comisión Nacional de Repatriación* [National Repatriation Commission], the explicit goal of which was to support returning exiles. Chile experienced a similar trend of assistance from 1990 onwards. In contrast, in Argentina, in the absence of official support for the return of exiles, this task was mainly left to the voluntary sector, for example the *Oficina de Solidaridad para Exiliados Argentinos* [Office of Solidarity for Exiled Argentines].

on elites, institution building, markets and truth and justice processes (cf. Barahona de Brito et al. 2001, Remmer 1992, Hagopian and Mainwaring 2012). In this way, transitions in general are often portrayed as a national process, a period of flux that a country must pass through in order to achieve some form of democratic consolidation. Instead, I propose that it helps to think of the transition in plural, as a multilayered set of interconnected, yet distinct, processes in which memory is shaped and shapes. As well as helping us to understand the lack of visibility or nebulous approach to distinct groups during transition, the focus on truth and justice processes at national level also tends to occlude certain categories of voices, in this case the diverse community of exiles who spent the dictatorships and beyond outside the Southern Cone. Furthermore, the view of the transitions as experienced by and in a particular territory can occlude transnational voices from beyond the region. A nuanced approach to transition as an evolving and multilayered process permits closer scrutiny of the stakeholders and voices that emerge during transitional periods.

Indeed, a combination of generational displacement and the dispersal or scattering of second-generation exiles across contrasting linguistic, cultural, and historical contexts, has made in-depth comparative analysis of the *hijos del exilio*, and in particular, the *no-retornados*, more complicated. That both authors write in the languages of the host country is, of course, the direct result of their exilic childhoods, and in the case of Trujillo (whose writing is mainly in Dutch), can explain why much of her writing has remained outside the post-dictatorship memory canon. Similarly, Ferrari has described Alcoba as part of "a minority, given that Spanish is their mother tongue and they have adopted French as their second language . . . because of exile," functioning as a type of "double displacement"[7] (Ferreri 2017), simultaneously spatial and linguistic.[8] However, it is also because they have re-

---

7 "un grupo minoritario dado que han pasado por el español como lengua maternal y han adoptado como lengua extranjera el francés . . . a causa del exilio."
8 Although there is, as noted, a dearth of scholarly work to date on *hijos del exilio/no-retornados*, it is worth briefly inserting a caveat vis-à-vis Alcoba's work. Indeed, her trilogy of novels dealing with her own experience of dictatorship (*La casa de los conejos, El azul* and *La danza de la araña*) have not only circulated widely in translation in Argentina, but have been published and framed by the Argentine publishing house Edhasa as Argentine/national literature. In particular, *La casa de los conejos* has been incorporated into analysis of the child's experience of dictatorship in Argentina (Blejmar 2016; Bonatto 2018; Ros 2012), finishing where *El azul* picks up. However, there has been less written about *El azul*, the novel discussed here. Arfuch (2018) has compared *El azul* with similar autobiographical works. Her work is a notable contribution, but I propose comparative work that goes *beyond* the preoccupation with biography and genre, to elucidate the ways in which the texts unsettle dictatorship and transitional narratives vis-à-vis the *hijas del exilio*, by shedding light on neglected voices affected by transi-

mained in the countries of exile as adults. Writing during the transition, Andrew Graham-Yooll (1987), editor of the *Buenos Aires Herald,* predicted that the children of exile who did not return to their countries of origin would fully integrate into the European host societies. These cases problematize the notion of 'full' integration by showing that in spite of writing in Dutch and French, they remain deeply affected by state violence and engage with the dictatorship period and its aftermath in different ways. Although this chapter is more explicitly concerned with the textual portrayal of the *hijos del exilio* during and after dictatorship, rather than assessing the veracity of Graham-Yooll's claim, the synergies between Trujillo and Alcoba's biographies and work imply that the *hijos del exilio,* and particularly the *no-retornados* inhabit a unique transnational space that differentiates them from their exiled parents and generational contemporaries in the Southern Cone, but situates them as transitional voices that merit further attention. Moreover, a comparative reading poses a challenge to the peripheral status within the regional and national canons of these authors' works in which they engage with recent transitions.

Tales of/from two writers: Child-exile in *El azul* and *Exilios*

Rupture and adapting to exile: The child's gaze

Both texts are narrated in first person by young female protagonists, and begin in dictatorship-era Argentina and Uruguay, amidst escalating violence and threats to the lives of the parents of the child narrators (six-year-old Laura in *Exilios,* and the unnamed eight-year-old in *El azul).* They take the reader through the various stages of exile: the before, during, and after: preparation, the departure, the journey (in the case of *Exilios),* and their integration and settling in to these new surroundings (through language, play, and letter-writing). Although the texts were written by the now-adult authors, the narrative voice in both texts is, predominantly a young child. In *El azul* the reader is never informed of the name of the child-narrator, but in the first pages of the novel she tells us, through conversational French lessons with her teacher, that she is eight and then eleven towards the end of the book

---

tion, yet obfuscated by the reductionist focus on transitions as an essentially national, elite or institution-building process Furthermore, bringing Trujillo's lesser-known work into dialogue with Alcoba's narrative challenges the peripheral position or 'placelessness' of the *hijos del exilio,* including the *no retornados.*

after the several years in exile spanned by the novel, roughly corresponding to the age, dates, and location of Alcoba's own exile. *Exilios* reveals a similar pattern of coincidence with Trujillo's own experience in the Netherlands, although the characters are given different names (her younger sister "América" becomes Cristina). There is a clear blurring between the adult author (as well as the occasional adult narrator in *Exilios*) and the child narrator, between autobiography and fiction, as well as approximation with the past viewed through the lens of the present. As Arfuch has said in the case of Alcoba, this work sits at "thresholds of the autobiographical, a story that recognizes a self-fictional trace" (2018, 88). Similarly, the preamble to Trujillo's novel describes the work as an example of "autobiografía enmascarada" ["concealed autobiography"], one in which, like Alcoba's work, the various characters correspond to real-life people (Alcoba 2014, 15). Interestingly, the subtle changes between the autobiographies of the author and child-narrator draw our attention to the fictional element. In this way, the child-exile's voice is deployed to go beyond the singularity of one person's biography. Indeed, as Alcoba asserts, "I'm not working with my own story, although it is related, but it is one that is connected to the history of many others"[9] (quoted in Menestrina 2020).

The fictionalization of the lived experiences of the authors, particularly the use of a fictional narrator, points to the wider experience of the *hijos del exilio,* often neglected, as noted, from work on the post-dictatorship and obscured by their parents' exiles. For Trujillo and Alcoba, who were both able to remember aspects of the before and aftermath of exile, these semi-fictional accounts is a way of making visible the child-exile and explore the unique, but not uncommon, positioning of the *hijos del exilio.* As Alcoba has argued, the child's perspective also permits a certain amount of critical distancing vis-a-vis the past, to broach subjects that the adult narrator may not be able to without accusations of politicizing the text. The texts may be written from a child's perspective, but, as Blejmar has astutely distinguished vis-à-vis *La Casa de los Conejos*, without "infantilizing the child" (2016, 99). The adult's perspective on the childhood exile is ever present, through reminders that the adult author is recounting and revisiting the past from the present, with phrases such as "I don't remember" etc. In *Exilios* the adult-narrated chapters, as we see in more detail, reveal a marked difference in the way that adults and children experience displacement, but also hint at the profound impact of exile on the entire family.

The narrators' young age, and the difficult experience of leaving their homelands is highlighted in different ways throughout the texts. In *Exilios* each section

---

9 "no estoy trabajando sobre mi historia personal sino con una historia que tiene que ver, en parte, pero que se conecta a partir de la historia de otros".

is split into short vignettes, often entitled with a list of randomly asserted nouns, like the novel's title. The effect for the reader is a more immature way of thinking and seeing the world. This is also evident in the lack of overly elaborated scene setting. Instead, the reader is given a number of clues or allusions to the wider dictatorship contexts. For example, Alcoba's narrator mentions early on her regular prison visits to her father (Alcoba 2014, 11), then later "the disappearances, the murders and the fear"[10] (20) although the dictatorship is never explicitly named. In *Exilios* the scene is set by the dialogues between mother and daughter, with the young child's persistent questioning about the reasons why her father is in prison. But it is actually the adult voice, Laura and Cristina's mother, Sara, who narrates the first two chapters, before handing over to her daughter, before resuming this role., Finally, as they journey into exile, Laura becomes the eyes through which the reader views exile. Sara's adult voice conveys the fear and panic, but also the worry over what to tell the children about the father's imprisonment: "I don't know how to tell Laura the truth, mum says not to tell her, to lie about it"[11] (Trujillo 1990, 21). The narrative then switches to Laura, and the shift in narrative voice is quite clear: "I understood everything mummy had told me about daddy, that he was in prison because he thought differently to the *milicos* and the *milicos* wanted everyone to think like them and how . . . and also that daddy did not want children to go hungry and . . ." (Trujillo 1990, 25).[12]

The sense here is of the child repeating what they have been told almost parrot fashion (adopting "milicos," the derogatory term for members of the armed forces), but the stream of lengthy sentences gives away their young age and that they do not quite understand the implications. The child-like naivety surrounding exile in *Exilios* is emphasized again: "I later discovered that the world is round and is full of countries all over the place and you can never fall off a country because right next to it is another one and another and another and another."[13] (Trujillo 1990, 25) Again it also highlights the difference between children and adults vis-a-vis the exile experience. Articulating the child's voice on difficult pasts also means trying to find subtle ways of establishing the wider historical context for the reader and the ways in which even very young children can pick up things that are said or not said, the stories told by adults, overheard conversa-

---

10 "las desapariciones, los asesinatos y el miedo."
11 "no sé cómo decirle a Laura la verdad, dice mamá que no se lo diga, que le mienta . . .".
12 "yo había entendido todo lo que mamá me había explicado de papá, eso de que estaba preso porque pensaba diferente que los milicos y que los milicos quieren que todos piensen igual que ellos y como . . . y además papá no quería que los niños tuvieran hambre . . .".
13 "Después me enteré de que el mundo es redondo y está lleno de países por todos lados así que nunca te podés caer de un país porque enseguidita pegadito al lado hay otro y otro y otro y otro."

tions, what Fried (2016) has called the intersubjective spaces. *Exilios* hints at this through play in the scene where Sara finds her daughters playing 'mummies and daddies.' Yet in this scene, the children are using a window to separate them, acting out the prison visit experience (Trujillo 1990, 26). This ludic example is a way of exploring a serious issue – how children are affected by events they may not understand – but also asserting the difference between the way children and adults perceived this period.

Meanwhile, the child's perspective also says something about the different positions of children and adults and highlights the former's lack of agency. Laura says: "Mummy says we are going to Argentina, I don't know what that is"[14] (Trujillo 1990, 25). Similarly, Alcoba's narrator states this when she learns French in preparation for joining her mother in exile: "I only know that an adult told me that I had to start some time before."[15] The occasional adult voice, usually a grandparent, updates the narrator on her impending departure. The implication here is that for the child-exiles more generally, the decision was out of their hands. Norandi (2016), who fled with her family from Uruguay to Spain at the age of eight, describes the exile experience as one of confusion for children as they were unable to fully understand a decision that affected them so deeply yet was simultaneously beyond their control. Whilst there are references to the issues the parents face, the financial hardship, struggle to secure a home, or the sense of fear and worry from other exiles which is picked up by the child-narrator on the journey to the Netherlands (Trujillo 1990, 27), many of the episodes recounted are to do with the challenges and obstacles that specifically affect them: settling in at school (46), friendships, whether to disclose the whereabouts of the absent fathers, and stigma surrounding exile (77). Or in *El azul*, the shock and disillusionment that exile in France is not in the Paris that she had imagined, in the role play conversations she had enjoyed with her teacher back in La Plata, but a small town some distance away. This chapter, entitled "casi verdadero" (almost true) is about her negotiation of truth when writing to her friend back in Argentina, "because you couldn't really say that Blanc-Mesnil was very close to Paris, in fact it was really almost quite far"[16] (Alcoba 2014, 16) but it is ostensibly a nod to the reader about Alcoba's own fictional embellishment of this exile.

Language is also a clear part of the adaptation process for the child-narrators. This is particularly the case for those *hijos* who were exiled to non-Spanish speaking countries, like Trujillo and Alcoba, as well as the child-narrators. At the same

---

14 "Mamá dice que vamos a la Argentina, no sé qué es eso".
15 "solo sé que un adulto me dijo que tenía que empezar cuanto antes."
16 "porque no puede decirse que el Blanc-Mesnil quede muy cerca de Paris, en realidad casi cada un poco lejos . . .".

time, for the *hijos*, linguistic immersion is a more prominent feature of exile life, particularly because their schooling and many of their social interactions were in the language of the host country, but also because the possibilities of going beyond proficiency and attaining fluency are much higher for pre-adolescents or very young children. For those who remained in the exile countries permanently, what was a foreign language became their own. Alcoba herself has described exile as "the departure from silence and arrival to a new language"[17] (interview with Menestrini 2020), not only a journey from dictatorship to democracy, but to a new linguistic space. In *El azul* the pursuit of linguistic proficiency is established from the outset, with the opening lines forging the link between exile and language: "my journey started, in some way, behind my nose" (9).[18] Later we learn that this is connected to the narrator's almost obsessive attempts to learn French and pronounce the vowels like a native speaker. However, once in exile, language is also connected to fitting in and muting difference: "I would like to erase it, make it disappear, rid myself of this Argentine accent" (Alcoba 2014, 34) and later "in spite of my efforts, I still speak with an Argentine accent, an accent I despise more than ever" (72).[19] As well as attempting to master the language, the narrator questions what it must be like to be a native speaker of French, drawing the distinction between those who 'inherit' the language from birth, "passed down from parents to child over generations,"[20] compared to those who learn as older children (Alcoba 2014, 56). Yet, by the end of the novel, three years later, she achieves this much desired fluency: "Until finally one day I thought in French. Without realizing and without meaning to. I thought and spoke in French at the same time . . . my mother expressed her shock in Spanish: 'You spoke in French,' she repeated. And it was actually very strange." (119)[21]

This is a milestone moment in which French, the language she is using outside the home, infiltrates the domestic Spanish-speaking space. This is the moment when she acquiesces to her father's repeated requests for a photograph of her and her mother for his cell. In this sense, the transformation from her self-consciousness when speaking in French to speaking without thinking is a crucial

---

17 "la salida del silencia y la entrada de otro idioma."
18 "mi viaje comenzó en alguna parte detrás de mi nariz".
19 "Quisiera borrarlo, hacerlo desaparecer, arrancarlo de mi a este acento argentino". . . "a pesar de los esfuerzos que hago . . . .todavía hablo con acento argentino . . . un acento que detesto más que nunca . . . ya siento vergüenza."
20 "viene transmitiéndose de padre a hijos desde hace generaciones."
21 "Hasta que un día por fin pensé en francés. Sin darme cuenta y sin quererlos. Pensé y hablé en francés al mismo tiempo . . . . mi madre se había asombrado en castellano. "Hablaste en francés" repitió. Y de verdad era raro'.

part of her adaptation to exile, suggesting that she finally feels comfortable enough to be photographed in the exilic space.

Language is similarly highlighted in *Exilios*, although less explicitly, becoming a point of tension and difference between the various generations. On a family trip for the holidays the two sisters sing Christmas songs in Dutch, and their grandmother expresses annoyance at not being able to understand the lyrics, so teaches them a song in Spanish that is not even vaguely festive (Trujillo 1990, 51). As the novel progresses, the narrator's mother corrects her Spanish (Trujillo 1990, 73) and the letters to the father in prison reveal a number of spelling errors and phonetic spellings of basic Spanish verbs (74). Furthermore, language is also invoked to make a wider comment on exile, through games played with the other exiled children at the refuge, a halfway house where the girls and their mother spend the first four years. The game involves one of the children taking on the role of 'vendepatrias' or 'traitor' (8). Later in the novel, the target of the game is repeated. With a more sarcastic tone, the narrator notes the divide between the 'perfect' or 'model' exiles who have their suitcases packed, ready to return, who never learn the language with those who do: "little by little the traitors started to really understand Dutch" (38).[22] Here the adult voice is more keenly felt, pointing to the underlying tension within the exile community as well as alluding to the accusations levelled at them from those who stayed in their home countries. Trujillo addresses the problematic exile figure but also positions herself, her mother, and sister on the side of the 'traitor exiles' as her mother gets a job and a more permanent residence. Indeed, their ties to the wider exile community shift with the passing of time: in the early period of exile their mother has a Chilean boyfriend, also an exile; by the time the father is released from prison, she has a Dutch partner. Cristina has become "Cris" (Trujillo 1990, 66) adopting a less Spanish-sounding moniker, a subtle erasure of cultural difference in order to blend in, which also points to fluid and mobile identities around naming repertoires reported in other exilic and migratory contexts (Lulle 2021). These changes and the increasing integration and immersion, both linguistic and cultural, is hinted at through both novels with the passing of time (the narrator in *El azul* reaching puberty, examples of teenage activities – a point I return to below). Language is connected to geographical distance, conceived as cutting or loosening ties with the homeland, generational difference (experienced differently by the second generation), and adaptation to life in exile.

---

22 "de a poco los vendepatria empezaron a entender bien el holandés."

Writing home: Exilic epistles to absent fathers

If the last section was concerned with the adaptation to and impact of exile for the child-narrator, this section turns to these child-narrators' engagement with their home countries through the act of writing home. Here I take as a starting point something that both narratives have in common: the epistolary communication with absent political prisoner fathers. As other scholars have noted, the epistle is a recurring trope in diasporic cultural production, in cinema (Naficy 2001, 5) and exile narratives more specifically (Arfuch, 693). In the texts under consideration, the letters are just one example of the various fragments and strands by which the memory of a childhood in exile is constructed, alongside anecdotes, diary entries (in *Exilios*), recounted conversations, anecdotes, photographs, songs, etc (Alberione 2016, 7). In the case of *El azul*, as explained in the Epilogue, the novel is based on Alcoba's encounter, many years later, with the letters her father wrote to her over a period of two years. As the letters were lost, this re-reading was only based on the letters her father wrote to her, a somewhat one-sided conversation. This piecing together of the past is a reminder that childhood exile is viewed and filtered through the present by the now adult writer.

In both texts, the letters to and from exile replace the routine prison visits to their fathers that precede the girls' departures for Europe. These trips give brief insight to the strict controls, the culture of fear, and the inhumane treatment of prisoners. Before departing for Europe, both child-narrators make a final prison trip, which marks the beginning of the epistolary relationship with the absent father. In *Exilios* this unfolds in the chapter entitled "El Ultimo Padre" ("The Last Father"), foreshadowing the family separation and breakup of the family. Here, the narrative voice switches backwards and forwards between Laura and the girls' father: "I know that they are leaving, I don't know where to, but it will be far enough away that I won't be their father anymore, it already astonishes me to see them so big . . . now these are the last visits, the last daughters, the last identifiable pieces of me. I'm broken . . ." (Trujillo 1990, 28)[23]

Here the father's fears are voiced as he laments what he sees as the end of the paternal relationship in its current form, while alluding to the uncertainty and open-endedness of that exile journey. The shift in narrative voice gives different perspectives on the same set of events, the child's voice not fully grasping the severity of the situation, with the father's words portraying panic. Similarly, in

---

23 "Sé también que se van a ir, no sé a dónde, pero será lo suficientemente lejos como para que yo deje de ser padre, ya me asombra verlas tan grandes . . . ya son las últimas visitas, las últimas hijas, y los últimos trozos de mí mismo que veo, yo quedé roto."

the opening pages of *El azul*, the narrator is heading off to a fortnightly visit to her incarcerated father, her habitual absence from school shrouded in silence (Alcoba 2014, 12). In the visit, the narrator's father urges her to write to him each week, so that they can keep up "some sort of conversation" (12) in spite of the distance. Indeed, although the letters are rarely reproduced in the text (they are mainly recounted by the child-narrators), they become part of a ritual of exile for both protagonists. In *Exilios* we are rarely aware of the father's voice (it is Laura's letters that are included very occasionally), only the daughter's perspective on what becomes "casi un ritual" ("almost a ritual") (Trujillo 1990, 46). The author explores this in the section entitled "familias de papel" ("paper families"). Here the physical presence of their father, the suspension of which was hinted at by "el último padre", is replaced with letters. In *El azul*, this is not only through writing to each other, but reading together (the father in Spanish, prohibited from reading any foreign language books and the narrator in French). For most of the text, this is the challenging text, *le Vie des abeilles* [The Life of the Bee] written by Belgian apiarist Maurice Maeterlinck. The narrator recounts these epistolary communications at various points and her encounters with Maeterlinck's book, interwoven with her accounts of increasing linguistic and cultural integration in France. Writing and reading become a way of negotiating the distance between them, but also keeping the family together symbolically. Indeed, Naficy (2001, 5) has argued that the epistle can make presence felt, in other words collapsing the distance that marks family separation.

The male characters are conspicuous in their absence. Their letters, mediated by the young female narrators, are a reminder of the ongoing dictatorships back in the Southern Cone and the treatment of political prisoners. We learn for example, that the father in *El azul* is only allowed five photos in his cell (Alcoba 2014, 43) and that there are very strict controls about letters or texts written in foreign languages. The long-term absent father, a trope that has appeared in the cultural production of *hijos del exilio* and Latin American cinema more broadly (Levey 2021), is a frequent reminder of family separation, but it also subverts the portrayal of exiles as 'fortunate survivors,' showing that many left in fear for their lives were themselves imprisoned or threatened with incarceration. The relationship between exile and victimhood is thus considerably more blurred. Indeed, the wider backdrop of dictatorship is implied through interactions with other exiles (from Latin America and from elsewhere in Europe) in both novels, as a frequent reminder of the context of the narrators' exiles, that they are not the only ones to be displaced. The visit from Fernando and Raquel, friends of the narrator's mother who are in exile in Sweden, in *El azul* is a case in point. The child-narrator listens to them go through the sad inventory of the fates of their *compañeros*, as they are confirmed as disappeared, imprisoned or in exile, or in other cases unknown (Alcoba 2014, 87). In this way, exiles are incorporated into the widening circle of those affected directly by dictatorship, as the reader is reminded what may have happened to the narrator's mother, had she not left Argentina.

Whilst the father in *El azul* remains out of reach, only contactable by letters, Laura and Cristina's father, released during the final months of the dictatorship, joins them in exile during the second half of *Exilios*. His much-heralded depature from prison soon gives way to the stark reality: the clear psychological damage he has sustained and his trouble reintegrating, not only into Dutch society, but into the family unit after a decade of incarceration. Again, the discussion of his breakdown and intrusion into the exile space is posed as very problematic; in a way the child's gaze opens up a way of talking about these aftereffects. In documenting the father's release from prison and the family's possibility of return, we are given insight into a more complex constellation of victimhood, in which Laura and Cristina can be understood as the children of exiles, exiles themselves and children of a political prisoners. This poses a critique of the prevailing tendency to view exile as outside other forms of victimhood, something that has only changed very recently in the region. Indeed, from the late 1990s, the *Comisión de Exiliados Retornados* [the Returning Exiles Commission] led a campaign in Argentina to demand state reparation for foreign exile. Debate also centered on whether the children who left for exile would be eligible, highlighting their positioning as 'almost' victims and 'not quite' exiles. In response to this, in recent years second-generation groups of returned *hijos del exilio* have emerged in the Southern Cone: for example, *Hijas e Hijos del Exilio* in Argentina (since 2006) and *Hijas e Hijos del Exilio Chile,* formed in 2018, to contest the notion of exile as a space of refuge (a challenge to Golden Exile), and frame exile as a serious human rights violation that has affected, and continues to affect, multiple generations.

After exile: Transitional returns and (non)returns

If the previous two sections were about living and writing exile, here we turn to the aftermath. The onset of democratic transitions from the early 1980s and the end of dictatorship in 1983 in Argentina and 1985 in Uruguay, brought with them the possibility for forcibly displaced Argentines and Uruguayans to return to their homelands. As mentioned in the first section, the return to Argentina and Uruguay was difficult for the first generation of exiles, as they sought to reintegrate but also dealt with the ongoing stigma of being exiles. As Jensen reminds us, for many, "instead of ending the obvious decentralization that has shaped the positioning between the displaced with others and deemed them to be 'inside' or 'outside', the return actually reinforces and deepens this" (2011).[24] Thus, the collapse of geographical boundaries did not mean the end of exiles being seen as outsiders or treated with suspicion, but the transitional possibilities brought their futures into stark relief. Furthermore, the upheaval of 'return' was not only an issue for the first generation of exiles but also for their offspring, many of whom were now teenagers or young adults, who "suffered the return to a country that was not the one they left, a far cry from the 'imagined Paradise,' that they yearned for from afar, or chose the option of 'no return,' to stay in the host country" (Alberione 2016, 4).[25] The upheaval and difficulties of exile and the return are explored in Trujillo's 2009 *De Terugkeer van Lupe García* (*The Return of Lupe García*), which look at the childhoods of a number of returning *hijos del exilio*, one of whom is now an alcoholic, another involved in petty crime, to explain "why we are all so messed up."[26] Not only does she highlight tricky reintegration in a country where the *hijos* may only briefly have lived or not even ever visited, but she indicates the different transitional trajectories that are explored or alluded to in the texts under consideration, shedding light on the transitional periods as experienced by the *hijos*.

Indeed, it is the treatment of the transition where the novels diverge considerably. When the narrator of *El azul* leaves Argentina in the late 1970s, she states: "Until one day I left, and for good."[27] (Alcoba 2014, 15) It is evident that, like Alcoba, when she left, she had no way of knowing she would never return to live in Argentina, instead here the adult voice is strongly asserted. Whilst *El azul* ends some time before the Argentine transition, in *Exilios*, the potential, and then eventual, return to Uruguay after the father is released and joins his family in the Netherlands, dominates the final three sections of the novel. By this point, Laura and her sister are teenagers, a reminder that most of those who were babies or small children in exile were adolescents or nearing adulthood by the end of dictatorial rule. The physical and emotional changes in the *hijos del exilio*'s lives were thus closely linked and paralleled with the rupture implicated by return, and more broadly, the fledgling democratic processes in their countries of birth. Here, there is a clear mirroring of adolescence as a transitional phase and the transition from authoritarianism to democracy. The transition away from childhood is

---

24 "el regreso, lejos de anular el descentramiento vital que condiciona la relación y los desplazados con el mundo y los lleva a definir 'adentras' y 'afueras' se reedita y/o profundiza."
25 "les tocó luego sufrir el retorno a un país que ya no era el que dejaron, que distaba mucho de ese 'Paraíso imaginado' que anhelaban a la distancia, u optaron por el 'no retorno', por la permanencia en el país de acogida."
26 "Por qué estamos todos hechos mierda".
27 "hasta que un día partí, y para siempre."

strongly hinted at in both novels, with the narrator of *El azul* telling the reader she is now eleven, and noting her body's changes, as she becomes a '*señorita*' (young woman). The events of *Exilios* span a longer period of exile, and after nearly a decade, Cristina and Laura are in their mid-teens, at secondary school and engaging in small acts of teenage rebellion like smoking. Laura's thoughts on her everyday life are also voiced in her teenage diary entries. The dialogue between the sisters in which the return is first discussed marks a shift from the earlier child-like prose employed when they went *into* exile:

– Cris, do you really want to go back to Uruguay?
– I dunno, the thing is that I'm kind of bored here, I don't like it anymore.
– Totally, I want to leave here, I don't care if it's Uruguay or Africa.
– The only thing that I'm upset about is leaving my friends, I'll really miss them. (Trujillo 1990, 87)[28]

Here, the direct and persistent questioning of their mother, is replaced by hushed conversations in the teenagers' bedroom, in an exchange that demonstrates their growing age. Rather than repeating what they have been told is happening by an adult, the sisters have their own opinions on the return and its implications, conflicted between wanting adventure and leaving friendships behind. However, because they were not yet adults, the option of staying or returning, as for many of the *hijos del exilio*, was out of their hands.

Exilios also points to a considerable difference for those who were children or babies when they went into exile, encapsulated in the lexical precision of the return. For Cristina and Laura, they are undecided on whether to use 'volver' (return) or 'ir' (to go) whereas for their mother this is a definite 'volver' (Trujillo 1990, 93) suggesting a point of tension between the generations. This is not to say that all adult exiles wanted to return or did, but the notion of 'volver' for those with very limited memory of their homelands suggests a different type of exile and a different type of transitional return. This is elucidated in the final section before the return, when the narrator offers the reader two different endings of the classic fairytale, one which is more of a summary of the facts; the second posits a more uncomfortable account of the father's release and intrusion into their lives, as their mother starts selling their furniture and the house becomes empty (Trujillo 1990, 93). This subversion of the fairy-tale is told bitterly by the teenaged

---

28 – Cris, en serio que querés volver para el Uruguay?
  – No sé, es que acá estoy media aburrida, no me gusta ya . . .
  – Claro, yo quiero irme de acá, no me importa si es a Uruguay o a África.
  – Lo único que me da pena es los amigos, los voy a extrañar mucho.

narrator, who no longer believes in, or can be consoled by, fictitious happy endings.

The final two sections of the novel give us a glimpse into life after return, and the issues that the second-generation face. The teenaged Laura's innermost thoughts and perspective on the return is made present through the series of diary entries that track impending departure from the Netherlands, and their arrival and (re)adaptation in Uruguay. For those who spent exile in non-Spanish-speaking countries, the reintegration is not only cultural, but also linguistic. Indeed, one diary entry says: "Yesterday, at school, I understood a total of sixty-three words. I am sure I'm going to fail. Laura (sad)."[29] (Trujillo 1990, 104) These worries, and also the various examples of reintegrating in school and society at large draw a parallel with the challenges depicted in both books during the early days of exile, especially the *El azul* narrator's obsession with thinking in French. As Laura states, "Cris and I tried to be as Uruguayan as possible"[30] (Trujillo 1990, 106). Rather than slot in back to their old lives, they have to relearn being Uruguayan and integrate, although this time they are much older and more self-aware. A few pages later, their metamorphosis (as it is referred to) is complete: "we have learnt to be Uruguayan"[31] (107). Their transformation in the Uruguayan transitional space, bringing into comparison the girls' complex emotional state and that of a society emerging from authoritarianism, can be contrasted with Alcoba's character's own linguistic and cultural metamorphosis in the exile space, while the (re)learning and inhabiting a language (even your mother tongue) complicates the notion of language and identity as 'inherited'. What is interesting is that they ultimately adopt a hybrid, transnational identity. Although they have relearned being Uruguayan, Laura says: "I can still feel the Dutch language, but it is more muted, more deaf and more blind [. . .] always a little bit further away, a little closer, always, always, it is there".[32] (Trujillo 1990, 112) This suggests an embodied and sensory relationship to the exile space that is in constant flux. The real metamorphosis is, I would argue, the transnational positionality of the *hijos del exilio* in which the two spaces are constantly interacting, often below the surface, jostling and moving against one another, like tectonic plates. Here, as an extension of this, the transitions themselves are re-

---

29 "Ayer, en el liceo, en total entendí ciento sesenta y tres palabras. Estoy segura que voy a repetir. Laura (triste)."
30 "Cris y yo tratábamos de ser lo más uruguayo posibles."
31 "hemos aprendido a ser uruguayas."
32 "todavía me siento el holandés aunque más mudo, más sordo, más ciego" . . . . "siempre está un poco más lejos, un poco más cerca, siempre, siempre, está."

visited and restaged as multilayered and complex, not only political and collective, but individual, societally, *and* transnationally entangled.

This dialectical relationship is also obvious when looking at the authors themselves. Trujillo, somewhat disillusioned with fledgling Uruguayan democracy and transitional impunity for the perpetrators of human rights violations, returned to the Netherlands for good. At the same time, she is described as "at ease with her dual identity,"[33] self-translating and moving freely within and between two identities. Even in the case of Alcoba, a clear case of *no retorno*, she says that since the end of the dictatorship, "my links with Argentina, where I regularly return, have intensified. There they see me as an Argentine writer. I see myself as a French and Argentine writer" (quoted in Chaplain Riou 2014).[34] Her experience of non-return, rather than slackening ties with Argentina, suggests that the situation for *no retornados* is rather more nuanced than Andrew Graham-Yooll might have predicted in 1987. The literary works of the two authors foreground the *hijos del exilio* (as children), destabilizing some of the assertions about them during the dictatorships and transitions; as now adult *no-retornados*, the writers alert us to multiple spatial and temporal identities that are not easily disentangled from one another. In this sense, placelessness does not, as might first be suggested, denote belonging 'nowhere', but is suggestive of a form of transnational positionality, not of the relocation of one identity or temporality to a new context, but a complex process of exchange in which temporalities and geographies are negotiated and transformed, resulting in the creation of a new or alternative transitional memory (de Chesari and Rigney 2014). The *hijos del exilio* have a different way of seeing the world, and *being* in it (Dutrénit 2006, 16).

Towards a conclusion: Exilic writing and the child's gaze as temporal revolt

At the heart of both authors' works is the creation of an exilic or even transnational literary space that subverts temporal and/or geographical distance from dictatorship to revisit the recent past. Read together, they expose and elucidate the child's inhabitance of exile and the aftermath of this exile during transition; in doing so they carve out a space for their voices, one that critiques the narra-

---

33 "a gusto con su identidad dual."
34 "mis vínculos con Argentina, adonde regreso regularmente, se intensificaron. Allá me consideran como una escritora argentina. Yo me veo como una autora argentina y francesa."

tives around exile that were forged in dictatorships and that permeated the transitions. They offer a more complex and bottom-up depiction of transition, one in which voices often excluded from high politics and memory narratives surrounding victimhood come to the fore.

To close, I draw briefly on Fanny Söderbäck's seminal work on revolutionary time. Although her discussion of the displacement of linear time emerged in relation to feminism, it is, I propose, applicable to the ways in which the texts here engage with the *hijos del exilio* and with transition (2012, 316). Revolutionary time is forward-looking in transgressing and surpassing the linear/cyclical dichotomy, moving in multiple simultaneous directions, adopting both distance and approximation to the past, reminiscent of postmemory in some respects. This is important because, as Söderbäck has argued, "the linear-progressive time paradigm is problematic as it runs the risk of forgetfulness and of *repetition*" (2012, 303). In other words, writing from the post-dictatorship, created by former child-exiles who are now adults, adopts and inhabits a child's perspective, piecing together letters, memories, dialogues, songs, and photos, in order to create an alternate, and highly mediated, vision of the past. To stay with Söderback, repeating the past means we will not learn, thus hindering our ability to move forward. Indeed, the examples discussed in this chapter mobilize the recent past and create a space for the *hijos del exilio*, reminding us of what was, but with a certain amount of critical distance, generational, geographical, and, as we saw, linguistic. As such, they encapsulate what Söderbäck describes as "a model of time that allows us to redeem the past and the present without instrumentalizing them in the name of a future always already defined in advance" (2012, 304). Rather than return to a specific period (Southern Cone dictatorships) and place (a country of origin, the exile country, or that of a parent) they bring to light in the present what state power has attempted to erase or control, and the broader societal narratives that stem from dictatorship and transition, shaped by distinct local factors in a new transnational context. As Söderbäck continues, we can view this practice as a form of revolt in that it constitutes "continuous displacement" (2012, 311) in which the borders or boundaries of time and place are not easily disentangled. This is, I assert, particularly resonant for the *no-retornados*. As this chapter has shown, they revolt against the restoration of a 'normal' national being and sense of belonging, insomuch as 'transitions' imply a linear or chronological movement towards a predetermined goal, one that will be duly concluded at a future point in time. These novels not only challenge the myths surrounding such temporalities, but they also expose the limitations of these transitions (the overwhelming focus on specific victims, certain geographies and a particular generation or generational unit). These narratives are attentive to an expanded transitional and transnational memory field, placing the transitions in a new light and incorporating a wider set of implicated and affected voices.

Works cited

Alberione, Eva. "Narrativas contemporáneas de los *exiliados hijos*: Esa particular manera de contarse." *Exilios: un campo de estudio en expansión*. Ed. Soledad Lastra. Buenos Aires: CLACSO, 2018. 197–210.

Alcoba, Laura. *El azul de las abejas*. Buenos Aires: Edhasa, 2014.

Arfuch, Leonor. "Childhood Exile: Memories and Returns." *Auto/Biography Studies* 33.3 (2018): 687–704.

Barahona de Brito et al. *The Politics of Memory and Democratization*. Oxford: Oxford University Press, 2001.

Blejmar, Jordana. *Playful Memories: The Autofictional Turn in Post-Dictatorship Argentina*. New York: Palgrave, 2016.

Bonatto, Virginia. "Memoria infantil, género y dictadura: Maria Laura Fernández Berro, Laura Alcoba y Leopoldo Brizuela." *Acta literaria* 57 (2018). https://www.scielo.cl/scielo.php?script=sci_arttext&pid=S0717-68482018000200071 (Accessed June 16, 2021).

Chaplain Rieu, Myriam. "Laura Alcoba, contar de otra forma la dictadura." *Gaceta* (March 21, 2014). https://www.gacetamercantil.com/notas/48819 (Accessed June 16, 2021).

Conde, Paula, "La última dictadura: Cómo vivieron el exilio quienes fueron niñas en los 70." *Clarín*, 27 June 2019. https://www.clarin.com/cultura/vivieron-exilio-ninas-70_0_FOFuvGXab.html. (16 June 2021).

Cordeu, Mora. "Las huellas de la represión en la escritura de Carolina Trujillo". *Telam*. 6 March 2013. https://www.telam.com.ar (Accessed June 16, 2021).

de Cesari, Chiara, and Ann Rigney, eds. *Transnational Memory: Circulation, Articulation, Scales*. Berlin: De Gruyter, 2014.

Dutrénit Bieloust, Silvia, ed. *El Uruguay del exilio: Gente, circunstancias, escenarios*. Montevideo: Trilce, 2006.

Ferreri, Natalia. "Memorias y olvidos en la conformación de las literaturas Francesca, francófona y extraterritoriales." III Coloquio Internacional "Francia y Latinoamérica en el imaginario de escritores, cronistas y cineastas," Lima (July 19–21, 2016).

Franco, Marina. *El Exilio: Argentinos en Francia durante la dictadura*. Buenos Aires: Siglo XXI, 2008.

Fried, Gabriela. *State Terrorism and the Politics of Memory: Transmissions across the Generations of Post-Dictatorship Uruguay*. New York: Cambria, 2016.

Graham-Yooll, Andrew. "The Wild Oats They Sowed: Latin American Exiles in Europe." *Third World Quarterly* 7.3 (1987): 246–253.

Hagopian, Frances, and Scott Mainwaring. *The Third Wave of Democratization in Latin America: Advances and Setbacks*. Cambridge: Cambridge University Press, 2001.

Hirsch, Marianne. "The Generation of Postmemory." *Poetics Today* 29.1 (2007): 103–128.

Jara, Daniele. *Children and the Afterlife of State Violence: Memories of Dictatorship*. London: Palgrave, 2016.

Jensen, Silvina. *Los Exiliados: La lucha por los derechos humanos durante la dictadura*. Buenos Aires: Sudamericana, 2010.

Jensen, Silvina. "Exilio e Historia Reciente: Avances y perspectivas de un campo en construcción." *Aletheia* 1.2 (2011). https://www.memoria.fahce.unlp.edu.ar/art_revistas/pr.4806/pr.4806.pdf (Accessed April 7, 2023).

Levey, Cara. "Of HIJOS and Ninos: Revisiting Postmemory in Post-Dictatorship Uruguay." *History and Memory* 26.2 (2015): 5–39.

Levey, Cara. "Documenting Diaspora, Diasporizing Memory: Mediation and Memory among Chilean and Uruguayan *no-retornados*" *Bulletin of Latin American: Research* 42.2 (2023): 189–203, first published online (early view) December 2021

Lulle, Aije. "'Repertoires of 'Migrant Names': An Inquiry into Mundane Identity Production." *Social and Cultural Geography* 23.9 (2021): 1294–1312.

Markarian, Vania. "From a Revolutionary Logic to Humanitarian Reasons: Uruguayan Leftists in the Exile and Human Rights Transnational Networks." *Cuadernos Del CLAEH* 1 (2006) 85–108.

Menestrina, Enzo M., "'La experiencia del exilio determina y deja una huella para siempre' Entrevista a la escritora Laura Alcoba." *Anaclajes* 24.2 (2020). https://cerac.unlpam.edu.ar/index.php/an clajes/article/view/4318 (Accessed June 16, 2021).

Mierelli, Romina, and Valentina Piersanti. "Staying Alive: 1970s Southern Cone Exiles in the UK." *Bulletin of Latin American Research* 40.2 (2021): 220–234.

Naficy, Hamid. *An Accented Cinema: Exilic and Diasporic Filmmaking.* Princeton: Princeton University Press, 2001.

Norandi, Mariana. "Hijos del Viento." *Brecha* (June 2, 2016). https://brecha.com.uy/hijos-del-viento/ (Accessed July 7, 2020).

Porta, Cristina. "La segunda generación: los hijos del exilio." *El Uruguay del exilio: gente, circunstancias, escenarios.* Ed. Silvia Dutrénit Bieloust. Montevideo: Trilce, 2006. 488–505.

Remmer, Karen. "The Process of Democratization in Latin America." *Studies in Comparative International Development* 27 (1992): 3–24.

Roniger, Luis. 2007. "Citizen-Victims and Masters of Their Own Destiny: Political Exiles and Their National and Transnational Impact." *MARLAS* 1.1: 30–52.

Roniger, Luis, James N. Green, and Pablo Yankelevich, eds. *Exile and the Politics of Exclusion in the Americas.* Sussex: Sussex Academic Press, 2012.

Roniger, Luis, Leonardo Senkman, Saúl Sosnowski, and Mario Sznajder, eds. *Exile, Diaspora, and Return: Changing Cultural Landscapes in Argentina, Chile, Paraguay, and Uruguay.* Oxford: Oxford University Press, 2018.

Rowe, William, and Teresa Whitfield. "Thresholds of Identity: Literature and Exile in Latin America." *Third World Quarterly* 9.1 (1987): 229–245.

Ros, Ana. *The Post-Dictatorship Generation in Argentina, Chile, and Uruguay: Collective Memory and Cultural Production.* New York: Palgrave, 2012.

Serpente, Alejandra. "The Traces of 'Postmemory' in Second-Generation Chilean and Argentinean Identities." *The Memory of State Terrorism in the Southern Cone: Argentina, Chile, and Uruguay.* Ed. Francesca Lessa and Vincent Druliolle. New York: Palgrave, 2011. 133–156.

Söderback, Fanny. "Revolutionary Time: Revolt as Temporal Return." *Signs: Journal of Women in Culture and Society* 37.2 (2012) 301–324.

Trujillo Piriz, Carolina. *De exilios, maremotos y lechuzas.* Buenos Aires: Colihue, 1990.

Ksenia Robbe

Remembering Transition in Contemporary South African and Russian Literatures: Between Melancholia and Repair

Abstract: This chapter outlines and conceptualizes intersections between the structures of post-transitional time and its transformations between the 1990s and the present in South Africa and Russia. It suggests that a transregional consideration of the ways in which the 1980–1990s transitions are recalled in contemporary cultures reveals the emergence of *other times* that interrupt the disenchanted present and differ from memories of colonial/imperial oppression or nostalgic longing. These temporalities elucidate the *longue durée* of current crises and invoke past hopes for emancipation while refusing teleological temporalities. By turning to works of Russophone and South African literature of the 2010s I explore the mnemonic modes through which they engage with the 'structures of feeling' that reflect the conditions of the post-Cold war neoliberal present, *after* socialist and *after* anticolonial visions of history as emancipatory processes mobilized in struggles for social equality. My reading juxtaposes four novels – first, Alexei Ivanov's *Nenastye* (Nasty Weather) and Nthikeng Mohlele's *Small Things*, and second, Nadia Davids' *An Imperfect Blessing* and Daria Dimke's *Zimniaia i letniaia forma nadezhdy* (Winter and Summer Forms of Hope) – and outlines two modes of memory that each pair exemplifies: melancholia and repair. Despite the difference of temporalities and affect, these texts share a structure of ambiguity in their remembering transitions as times of crisis, loss, or even trauma, but simultaneously of hope, of aspiration, and the shock of new possibilities. Thus, the chapter begins theorizing *memories of transition* as a possible nexus between postsocialist and postcolonial perspectives on transformation.

Other times

> For many South Africans, the present state of the nation is not the future imagined during the anti-apartheid struggle: *that* time is no time like *this* present. (Van der Vlies 2017, 1)

Acknowledgments: I am grateful to the Polish Institute of Advanced Studies (PIASt), during the stay at which in 2019 I wrote the first draft of this chapter. This stay and research was supported by the EURIAS Fellowship Program of the Europeam Commission (Marie-Sklodowska Curie Actions – CO-FUND Program –FP7).

https://doi.org/10.1515/9783110707793-012

In the contemporary Russian discourse on the 1990s, this period is regularly characterised in terms of 'timelessness' (*bezvremenie*), a veritable black hole in between the crisis of the Soviet order and the reassertion of the Russian 'liberal bureaucratic' state under President Putin. [. . .]. The 1990s are indeed a time like no other. (Prozorov 2007, 4–5)

These two quotations, placed alongside one another, juxtapose the peculiar senses of time generated by frustrated experiences of transitions in South Africa and Russia. In his book *Present Imperfect*, reflecting on South African literature's preoccupation with the sense of aborted futures in the aftermath of revolutionary struggle and transition to democracy, Andrew van der Vlies diagnoses this predominant temporality as "no time," drawing on the metaphor of Nadine Gordimer's novel *No Time Like the Present* (2012). The protagonists, who are former fighters in the liberation struggle, meet the transition with high hopes for the 'new' South Africa in which a cross-racial relationship like theirs will be a norm, and the new government will establish structures for achieving freedom and equality. However, a decade and a half later, they find themselves disillusioned by everyday racism, violent bursts of xenophobia, staggering inequality, and the corruption of the ruling party. "[I]f the revolution has run out of time, has been suspended, then characters in *No Time Like the Present* find themselves in a present also somehow outside of time [. . .] a present that did not feature in the past's privileged narrative of time's future unfolding" (Van der Vlies 2017, 5–6). In Van der Vlies' reading, this sense of a post-revolutionary suspension which he traces in a range of contemporary South African literary texts, is, however, more than a dead-end, the end of historical time; it is also a Benjaminian "now time" which suggests a non-progressivist historicity and 'weak messianic' hope (Van der Vlies 2017, 6–9).

Reflecting on the imaginaries of post-Soviet transformation in his 'historical ontology' of Russian postcommunism in the mid-2000s (i.e., also two decades after the 'transitional' time was initiated during the perestroika), Sergei Prozorov (2007) identifies the temporal and affective structures that involve perhaps unexpected similarities to the postapartheid sensorium. During the late 1980s and early 1990s, socioeconomic and political transformation was a vague perspective for most Russians. But, despite the fears of the loss of stability, during the early 1990s democratic transformations were welcomed by the majority, even if very diverse and sometimes radically different expectations were projected onto these changes (Levinson 2007). While the 'transition' decade was experienced by many as the time of chaos, uncertainty, and conflict, people were adapting and responding to these experiences by producing new socialities, identities, and genres of communication (Oushakine 2009, Ries 1997, Shevchenko 2009). In Prozorov's interpretation, this was "a time of trials, of trying out every possible pathway of future development at the same time, without a final commitment to any single of them," which meant radical suspension of any certainty, any teleological time (2007, 7). He calls this the "timelessness" of the 1990s, which like the postapartheid "no time" is different from and opposite to the teleological 'end of history' (Prozorov 2007, 11); read in Benjamin's and Agamben's terms, this timelessness "was an effect of *messianic suspension* of teleological temporality" (Prozorov 2007, 18).

I begin with these resonances between theorizations of (post-)transition temporalities generated in postapartheid and post-Soviet contexts in order to initiate a broader consideration of intersections and differences between perceptions of time and practices of memory since the end of the Cold War, particularly in the current times of global uncertainty about the directions taken by the late twentieth-century 'transitions.' Can these transitions still serve as ideals for resisting injustice and imagining transformations? Or are these imaginaries, once widely circulating and still enjoying considerable authority, nothing more than mythologizations of far more contradictory historical events? Should we differentiate between the emancipatory visions of transformation and the *realpolitik* that betrayed these ideals? Each of these positions, and the many variations within and across them, involve different ways of interrelating past and present, and of actualizing the past in contemporary political circumstances. Looking at the expressions of disappointment and frustrated hope (however differently such emotions are 'managed' by the states and populist politicians in the two countries), we may discern shared 'structures of feeling' which reflect the conditions of the post-Cold war neoliberal present, *after* socialist and *after* anticolonial visions of history as emancipatory process mobilized in struggles for social equality.

The transitions' "no(w) time" and "time like no other" both involve feelings of melancholia and messianic hope, and both look back at the transitions as a time of suspended potentialities and disavowed loss.[1] While the 'no(w) time' conveys an experience of dreaming and the 'time like no other' focalizes practices of living, both of these ontological perspectives are retrospective, mnemonic constructions. It is significant that both authors motivate their reflections on the time of transformation by referring to the collectively shared perception that this time has ended and that we find ourselves in a new temporal regime which reduces the possibility of past hopes. In Russia, the paradigm shift had to do with the politics of 'stabilization' during the presidency of Vladimir Putin, who built his image upon the contrasting of his 'strong' leadership to the 'disorder' and 'weakness' of the state during the 1990s. According to Prozorov, this post-2000 official discourse

---

1 See Agamben 1999. Also see Sami Khatib's (2013) discussion of time in Benjamin's materialist messianism and in later iterations of the non-religious messianic, in particular by Agamben and Derrida.

was a "perpetuation of the 'timelessness' of the 1990s," although it introduced a crucial difference as it involved the "suspension of the messianic" (2007, 18). Thus, the new time regime displaced the radical openness of the 1990s, framing it as the time of national trauma (Malinova 2021, Oushakine 2009, Sharafutdinova 2020). It is only during the mid-2010s that Russian state begins elaborating new messianic discourses – the process that intensifies towards the early 2020s, justifying the war in the East of Ukraine and preparing the full-scale invasion of 2022. This messianic imperialism focused on resurrecting a mythical past of 'unity' of the peoples is, however, significantly different from the unruly messianism of the 1990s, which did not have an ideological direction. In South Africa, a symbolic closure of the transitional period was introduced by the massacre of striking mine workers by the police at Marikana in 2012 – an unprecedented case of state violence after the end of apartheid. For many South Africans, this meant the end of hope that the current dispensation would break up with the system of racial exploitation instituted during apartheid. As many commentators observed, this event struck the final blow to the transition narratives of the 'rainbow nation' and made apparent the cruel cynicism of politicians and the continuing workings of racial biopolitics after the formal end of apartheid.

Thus, while the hopes of transitions were foreclosed in different ways, in both contexts we could speak of the late 1980s–1990s period as having been pushed back into a past that is discontinuous from the 'now.' Certainly, 'transition' still serves as a reference point in political or everyday discourse, but it functions rather as an overused sign denoting a symbolic turn or gap, a myth, not a living memory. Using Aleida Assmann's term, lived experiences of transitions have largely become the stuff of 'storage memory' which "contains what is unusable, obsolete, or dated; it has no vital ties to the present and no bearing on identity formation" (2011, 127). Such shifting of past imaginations and enactments of change into a 'storage,' however, also produces a counter-reaction since this memory "holds in store a repertoire of missed opportunities, alternative options, and unused material" (Assmann 2011, 127). Hence, as retrospective constructions, transitions may become 'now times' or 'times like no other,' or simply *other* times, alternative to the oppressive past and the disenchanted present. They might elucidate the origins of (or sometimes interrupt) the "states of affective dysphoria and temporal disjuncture" (Van der Vlies 2017, 7) often mediated by contemporary South African literature; they may also convey a radical "refusal of any idea of 'transition'" as a teleological project (Prozorov 2007, 11).

This chapter reflects on such re-imaginings of transitional past in contemporary Russian and South African literature, within the broader cultural-historical contexts which I outline below. My focus is on the acts of remembering societal change during the late 1980s–early 1990s which depict transitions in their ambiguities, i.e., neither in an entirely negative nor fully positive light. This is not to ignore the more affirmative or humoristic projects of remembering the decade, or, on the other hand, the role of dystopian fictions. However, such ambivalent memories that represent both the hopes and failures, the losses and new beginnings of the transitions are particularly intriguing mediations that are likely to resonate with larger audiences and reflect the complexity of vernacular, living memories of those times. This reading begins by defining and conceptualizing the modes that these acts of ambiguous recall take in contemporary literary productions, drawing on examples from a postsocialist and a postcolonial context.

The four novels which I read comparatively – Alexei Ivanov's *Nenastye* (Nasty Weather), Nthikeng Mohlele's *Small Things*, Nadia Davids' *An Imperfect Blessing*, and Daria Dimke's *Zimniaia i letniaia forma nadezhdy* (Winter and Summer Forms of Hope) – all involve the above-mentioned ambiguity: they recall the transitions as times of crisis, loss or even trauma, but simultaneously of hope (against all odds), aspiration, the shock, of new possibilities, and similar affects. I begin by laying the ground for this comparison – first, by discussing the ways in which transitions have been engaged with in postapartheid and postsocialist critique and how studies of memory can be the next step in theorizing these entangled conditions; second, by outlining the modes of 'melancholia' and 'repair' against the background of earlier narratives of transitions in South African and Russian literature. The last two sections provide brief comparative readings of the novels that trace these developing modes of memory.

Transitions as foundations of the present: From turning points to returning pasts

The idea of unidirectional development of societies undergoing transitions as part of the so-called "third wave of democratization" (Huntington 1991), propelled by the "end of history" prognoses (Fukuyama 1992) and resulting in the whole field of 'transitology,' has been largely discredited or seen as mistaken even by its proponents (Fukuyama 2018). My reading, as the initial theoretical approaches sketched above indicate, is not underpinned by any such idea of (failed) teleological development. It seeks to elaborate approaches to a *different* type of interconnectedness and parallelism between post-Soviet and postapartheid temporalities, which can be regarded as instances for considering elective affinities between postsocialist and postcolonial senses of time on a larger scale. Several prominent studies in the past twenty years have observed the necessity of scrutinizing the interconnected structures of feeling in societies that emerged on the ruins of socialist and anticolonial utopianism. This is an entwinement that involves power asymmetries and diverging historical time frames (Tlostanova 2017); it also necessitates consideration of material and economic factors of (post)colonialism and (post)socialism (Mezzadra 2020).

Despite "possible mismatches," Monica Popescu suggests, "the reward [of comparing] lies in the wealth of similarities, mirrorings, and reverse-mirrorings" between these diverging yet entangled contexts (2003, 421). Writing a few years later, Sharad Chari and Katherine Verdery argued about the productivity of comparing postcolonial and postsocialist aftermaths with the aim of "restor[ing] research connections [between the former Second and Third Worlds] that should have never been separated" (2009, 12). Like Popescu, the authors underscore *the centrality of transitions* in the efforts of both 'posts' to define themselves. "Think[ing] [. . .] about colonial relationships together with market and democratic transitions" (2009, 12), they propose, can facilitate reflection on the retaining of revolutionary, emancipatory visions within the more sober perspectives of postcolonial and postsocialist studies. This thinking can liberate postsocialist and postcolonial theory from the narrow spatial and temporal categories and interlink them within the critical visions of "post-Cold War" (2009, 29). Approaching the above argument from a decolonial perspective, Madina Tlostanova proposed that the intersections between postcolonial and postsocialist practices should be viewed not as necessarily having similar sources or trajectories; nevertheless, we can observe "similar results and even possible coalitions [. . .], because ultimately they [postsocialism and postcolonialism] manifest [. . .] different reactions to the coloniality of power" (2017, 13).

More recently, a number of studies have provided close historical examinations and conceptualizations of the ways in which socialist and anticolonial perspectives interacted and influenced each other, particularly in art, literature, and other cultural practices, during the Cold War (Djagalov 2020, Lee 2014, Popescu 2020). In parallel, theorizations of *post*socialism drawing on post- and decolonial critique have developed approaches for comprehending Cold War aftermaths beyond Eurocentric or Occidentalist frameworks (Atanasoski and Vora 2018, Karkov and Valiavicharska 2018, Kurtović and Sargisyan 2019). My reading draws on both of these strands that examine historical pasts and contemporary 'posts,' but zeroes in on another nexus of (post)socialism and (post)colonialism: the current remembering of transitions. I am interested in the *difference* of these re-imaginations from transitional temporalities developed in national and transnational public cultures during the 1990s and 2000s. While earlier critical reflections on postsocialist and postcolonial intersections regarded transitions as points of mainly symbolic significance and focused on either 'before' or 'after,' my examination inquires into the practices of *memory* – of re-actualizing the times of transitions from various positions and agendas of the present.

As research into cultural practices of rethinking transitions asserts, the beginnings of 'the contemporary' remain a salient point of reference (and, I would add, of imaginative return) in postapartheid and post-Soviet contexts. "The entire field of South African writing since 1990," Rita Barnard observes, "pivots around the idea of transition" (2019, 11). "And to say that 'transition' is pivotal," she continues, "is to say that postapartheid literature is fundamentally animated by temporal concerns and questions" with the problem of how to represent the relationship between past (pre–1994), present, and future occupying center stage (2019, 11). Timothy Wright (2019) stresses, more specifically, the shift in such temporal constructions during the 2010s: "If the South Africa of 1994 to 2012 was haunted by the spectre of apartheid, most visibly in its obsession with the Truth and Reconciliation Commission (TRC), South Africa post-2012 can broadly be said to be haunted by a new ghost: the ghost of 1994 itself" (200). Indeed, when it seemed that South African social imagination has moved beyond the 'post-transitional' (Frenkel and McKenzie 2010), notable works of literature, film, and art along with broader public discourses started returning to the time of transition or the practices of the Left during the 1980s (Robbe 2018, Wright 2019). In Russia, similarly, the late 2000s suggested a shift beyond the dominant 'post-Soviet' temporality (as in assessing everything in the present via comparison to the Soviet) towards a multiplicity of co-existing times (Platt 2009). However, as Kevin Platt observes a decade later, this multiplicity has resulted in a temporal "cacophony" – a regime in which "a powerful state [. . .] has actively fostered an uncontrolled and disordered multiplicity of temporalities – one that has yielded particular advantage for the maintenance of power" (2020, 401). The framing of the early 1990s, the most active stage of transition, as the exemplary "'pro and contra' period, event or figure, on which no consensus can be reached" (Platt 2020, 401) plays a key role in the construction of this time regime.

Thus, in both contexts the present is haunted by 'transitions.' This ghostly presence troubles established interpretations and unsettles possibilities of a consistent narrative, such as the case with the instrumentalization of this ghostliness in Russian official memory discourse. Whether such unsettling produces or closes off potentially transformative engagements with the past, as long as this haunting persists, it begs to be addressed. The increasingly *mnemonic* forms of approaching these pasts – particularly as new generations try to create ways of 'owning' them – require close examination. My reading engages with literary narratives of transitions, focusing on the role of memory as a vehicle for rearranging time, shaping new temporalities and subjectivities, making sense of haunting pasts, or providing itineraries for social connectivity. I focus on literature as the medium for this exploration due to its ability to provide texture to the past by recollecting ambiguities and (re)shaping modes of narrating and remembering while attending to practices and senses of the everyday. Comparing literary representations can help us discover how memories of transition in specific national and local contexts are entangled globally, in particular across the postsocialist and postcolonial contexts.

Temporalities of transition: The death and latency of utopianism

In order to outline modes of remembering the 1980–1990s in contemporary literature, we need to understand the background against which they unfold and which they reimagine, i.e., the dominant temporalities of (post-)transition as developed in cultural representations during the 1990s. Despite the welcoming of political transformations by the majority in both societies, and certainly the majority of writers and other cultural producers, the spirit of anticipation in Russian and South African literatures of the late 1980s and early 1990s was often apocalyptic. This tendency augmented during the later 1990s and the 2000s, giving shape to dystopian genres. We can recall Elleke Boehmer's (1998) observation that South African writing of the 1980s struggled to imagine 'new beginnings' in its catastrophic expectations of a revolution;[2] or her registering of "hiatus, abrupt halt, suspended action, especially but not only at the end of narratives" (2012, 35) as dominant temporal forms of postapartheid fiction during the 1990–2000s.[3] Michael Titlestad, furthermore, has written about the effect of "South African apocalyptic anticipation" (2014, 55) in 'white writing' since mid-twentieth century. This affect, grounded in fears of mass mobilizations of racial and class 'others,' intensified during the transition and persisted during the 2000s. Today, it finds expression in dystopian representations of 'white' anxieties that rehearse old phantasms, often with the use of satire (Titlestad 2014).

---

2 Drawing on a wide range of fiction in English, including the novels of J.M. Coetzee, Nadine Gordimer, Miriam Tlali, Lewis Nkosi, and Mongane Serote, Boehmer asserts that South African literature of the 1980s failed to develop any vision of a definite end and, thus, of a possible future after apartheid: "Up to the present [. . .] the bulk of South African writing seems to have willed an ending to the present state of things, but could do no more – the end was left hanging. Politicians on the right and the left projected apocalyptic visions of the future. As if the initiative had thereby been wrested away, fiction, already hesitant about form-giving, could not or chose not to give the future shape." (1998, 51).

3 In her reading of Zakes Mda's *Ways of Dying* as an early post text, Rita Barnard (2004, 279) observes its hesitation to imagine a liberatory future, due to the postapartheid consciousness of the "future *im*perfect" (Kruger 1999, 177) of decolonization in other African countries.

In Russian literature of the same period, we can trace somewhat similar dynamics of apocalyptic temporality. As Ilya Kukulin (2007) observes, catastrophic forebodings are characteristic of literature (and other discourses) during the periods of perceived crisis. However, such 'structures of feeling,' which he finds in the writing of the 1980s and the mid-2000s, differ significantly between the time of the decaying Soviet system in the first case and the eve of presidential elections foreshadowing authoritarianism in the second. If late Soviet writing validates the characters' choice that points towards a different future despite the approaching or already occurring catastrophe, the post-Soviet "fictions of warning" testify to radical disappointment with ideas of activism and possibility of social change. These novels[4] convey what Kukulin (2007) calls "the closure of a temporal horizon" – a refusal of future-oriented projects. In his reading of a similar corpus of texts, Alexander Chantsev (2007) remarks on the "feelings of being lost in the current political situation" and the apparent readers' demand for "phantasmatic catastrophism," which testifies to the widespread "alienation from history."[5]

These tendencies in South African and Russian literatures are, certainly, part of the global proliferation of apocalyptic fictions during the last few decades. This process is related to the disintegration of twentieth-century emancipatory political projects, with the collapse of state socialisms and strong socialist movements, as well as the adoption of neoliberalism, characterized by the lack of future-orientedness (Traverso 2017). As Susan Buck-Morss noted a while back, the 1980s–1990s saw the "dissipation" of an "industrial dreamworld" based on "a utopia of production" in "the East" and "a utopia of consumption" in "the West" (1995, 3). This also holds for many Global South contexts where the erosion of modernization utopias has been aggravated by the "slow violence" of neoliberal capitalism (Nixon 2013). In general, apocalyptic anticipation is a social feeling that underpins neoliberal economies: its focus is the 'homo economicus' (Brown 2015) whose survival-oriented imagination does not extend beyond their selves or their families. While many contemporary dystopias critique the neoliberal condition, more often than not these narratives involve depoliticized representations of catastrophic present/future and fail to provide visions of solidarity (Kunkel 2008). A dialectics of utopia/dystopia, with dystopianism dominating the post-transitional present, is also what interconnects post–1990s Russian and South African cultures (Robbe and Stuit 2021).

---

4 Among the discussed texts are Olga Slavnikova's *2017*, Dmitry Bykov's *Evacuator* and *ZhD*, Vladimir Sorokin's *Day of the Oprichnik*, Alexander Garros and Alexei Evdokimov's *Chukhche*, and Valery Shemiakin's *Eniki-Beniki*.

5 As Kukulin observes, some of these texts involve the use of satire, which creates another parallel to the tendencies traced by Titlestad in South African 'apocalyptic' writing, as outlined above.

An important difference between the post-Soviet and postapartheid social perceptions of time is that the loss of teleological and utopian visions in postsocialism was a result of their gradual erosion and transformation during the late socialist period (Klumbytė and Sharafutdinova 2013, Yurchak 2006), while in South Africa, anticolonial utopianism informed anti-apartheid movements and, to an extent, the transition, but these visions dissipated with the introduction of neoliberal governmentality since the 1990s (Mark and Slobodian 2018, Roberts 2020). However, the early 'transition' in Russia/the Soviet Union saw a brief activation of utopian energies: according to Artemy Magun, "the utopian enthusiasm of the perestroika [. . .] shifted almost overnight into the lamentation of the 1990s" (2013, 41). He sees the catastrophism, typical of the post-transitional decade, as a symptom of post-revolutionary melancholia which structurally succeeds a utopian momentum (as in the 'classical' example of the French revolution). Magun's philosophy of the Eastern European 'transitions' is helpful for placing them in dialogue with decolonization and postcolonial processes in the Global South. Unlike the more common dismissal of the revolutionary character of mobilizations in Eastern Europe, Magun argues that the fact that these transformations were neoliberal or "intercepted by neoliberalism early on" does not "undermine their revolutionary character, the degree of the dethroning of authority that they accomplished, and the sense of novelty that they created" (2013, 29). He defines the type of revolutions that opened itself up to neoliberalism as 'unconscious':

> The revolution did happen, but it happened latently, unconsciously for the actors who were mostly relying on the 'normal' standards of imaginary Western democracy, or on naturalism or neotraditionalism. This unconscious revolution could not, of course, create any lasting democratic institutions and gave birth to an anarchic and anomic society. However, the unconscious character of perestroika created the condition of its return, and we see now, under very different circumstances, a new wave of mobilization that meets a much more serious resistance than 20 years ago, and thus has all chances, in the future, to come to an adequate political self-understanding. (2013, 30)

Orientation towards the imagined 'normality' of the West was, certainly, the driving power behind the anticommunist revolutions in Eastern Europe. Similar aspirations were at work in South Africa during the 1990s, advocated and promoted by postapartheid elites. 'Normalization' became the new keyword in politics and culture (O'Brian 2001, Shapiro 1999), reflecting and further encouraging South African exceptionalism (Magaziner and Jacobs 2012, Mamdani 1996). Behind the teleological visions of the 'new' South Africa were the (colonial) fears of becoming an 'ordinary' African country. As part of this imaginary, South African politics was dominated by attempts at drawing a definitive line between past and present, pushing discursively all experiences and social structures of the apartheid period into a distant past (Grunebaum 2011).

Rather than becoming 'normal' and leaving Soviet or apartheid pasts 'behind,' both societies have witnessed (Russia to a greater extent) what is commonly perceived as the return or repetition of oppressive pasts including growing authoritarianism and state-supported police violence, accompanied in the present by social atomization and generally nihilistic attitudes (although social movements and Left-oriented politics retain their strength in South Africa). According to Magun, this negativity reflected in the social states of melancholia is a typical result of "a revolution in general, and the anticommunist revolution par excellance" (2013, 36); and, we can add, the anti-apartheid revolution which turned out to be also anticommunist, in the sense of giving up socialist aspects of transformation program during the 1990s (Mark and Slobodian 2015). By referring to the 1980s and 1990s revolutions as 'negative' Magun suggests that their negation was, in fact, "incomplete": post-transitional societies retained "libidinal attachment" to Soviet-type authority (2013, 35). In a similar vein, the continuing politics of racial and class violence in South Africa, as has been argued, have to do with the incompleteness of postapartheid transformations and the insufficient reckoning with apartheid, particularly within the everyday (Gready 2011, Grunebaum 2011), finding expression in the psychosocial conditions of 'stuckness' and melancholia (Hook 2013, Thomas in this volume, Van der Vlies 2017).

Melancholia and repair

Melancholia is, certainly, one of the leading structures of feeling in post-Cold War neoliberal societies, and it involves multiple variations and 'uses' in cultural productions as well as everyday performances of subjectivity. Here I reflect on melancholia as a prominent modality of remembering the 1980–1990s transitions that is distinct from the dystopianism or apocalyptic anticipation which I referred to above. It is closer to Benjamin's 'left-wing melancholia' further conceptualized by Enzo Traverso as involving, among other things, the possibility of "channeling" feelings of disappointment "toward a fruitful work of reconstruction" (2017, 21; see also Crimp 1989, Cvetkovich 2003). Drawing on Magun (2013), the 'unconscious' and 'incomplete' character of transformation (which came to be dominated by the neoliberal ethos) are possible reasons not only for post-transitional anomie but also for imaginative returns to the time of transition. Some of these returns suggest positive appreciation of certain aspects of the transition, particularly in the context of the official memory in Russia (see Andrei Zavadski's chapter in this volume). However, such mnemonic returns in literature and film, as my preliminary research shows, almost always involve various aspects of negativity. Some of these productions further elaborate the negativity of transitions (as conveyed in early (post)transitional representations and in vernacular memories), attempting a fuller, more fundamental negation or reflecting on the reasons for the 'negative' turns the transformations took.

In this chapter, I do not discuss the aspect of traumatic repetition in melancholic memories which is present in contemporary recollections of transition as well. Instead, I focus on the modality of 'weak messianism' which Walter Benjamin (1999, 462–463) theorized as dialectical evocation of unrealized hopes from the past. This historical materialist approach has been productively employed in readings of twentieth- and early twenty first-century South African writing evoking the 'afterlives' of revolutionary moments including nineteenth-century anticolonial millenarianism (Wentzel 2009) as well as anti-apartheid struggle and transition (Van der Vlies 2017, 7, 106; Wright 2019). In studies of contemporary Russian culture, messianism has been explored only in its 'negative,' cynic modalities[6] (Kukulin 2018); identifying and theorizing the 'weak messianic,' in turn, can allow for conceptualizing critical possibilities also in the representations that invoke revolutionary "unfailure"[7] to point at the emancipatory desires and potentialities behind and beyond the transition processes.

The second modality, which I illustrate through readings in the last section, is what could be called 'memories of repair.' I borrow the term from Marianne Hirsch's theorization of postmemories' "desire to repair," which she relates to "the child's confusion and responsibility" and "the consciousness that the child's own existence may well be a form of compensation for unspeakable loss" (2008, 112). In a more recent text, she extends this notion beyond postmemory specifically to a range of feminist practices that "demand justice but do not aim at restitution. If they rebuild, they take up temporary, often virtual, spaces. They acknowledge the haunting imprecisions of memory, they perform its wounds but, at the same time, they enable us to imagine alternative histories and queer potentials that can reconfigure painful pasts" (2019, 16).

---

6 Kukulin's theorization of 'messianic cynicism' in the discourses of the Russian state and 'oppositional' artistic expressions come very close to Achille Mbembe's critique of 'negative messianism' which centers on "the will to kill, as opposed to the will to care; a will to sever all relationships with the unwanted, as opposed to the will to engage in the exacting labour of repairing the ties that have been broken" (2017, n.p.).
7 Wentzel's concept of 'unfailure' denotes "not merely a matter of patience (wait long enough, and the prophecy will be fulfilled) but rather a radical patience that keeps past dreams alive as dynamic inspiration for future movements" (Wentzel 2009, 153).

The novels which I examine in this chapter represent transitions through the childhood memories of autobiographical female narrators; they are combined with the narrators' accounts of their older relatives' trauma. The witnessing of these traumas during the transitions is accompanied by memories of intergenerational dialogue which introduce a 'reparative' perspective. This mode of memory, developed by women writers and narrators and foregrounding childhood perspectives, is distinct from the memories of middle-aged male characters in the novels written by men which I discuss under the 'melancholia' rubric. It would be too facile to claim that the 'melancholic' and 'reparative' modes are strictly gendered (in fact, elements of both might be present in a single text). However, the presence of the second mode in works by women writers correlates with feminist theorizations of 'repair'. Along with Hirsch's concept, I draw on Eve Kosofsky- Sedgewick's (2002) outline of 'reparative reading' as an antidote to the tendency of 'paranoid' search for 'true' causes, which often translates into conspiratorial thought. In contrast to the anticipatory qualities of paranoia – a variant of the apocalyptical anticipation that I discussed above – a reparative perspective "entertain[s] such profoundly painful, profoundly relieving, ethically crucial possibilities that the past [. . .] could have happened differently from the way it actually did" (Kosofsky- Sedgwick 2002, 146), thus opening the present up to different futures. Ethically and politically, this perspective is very different from memories developed in alternate histories, which most often normalize the present order.

Recollection of transition periods in a hopeful and affirmative mode, as my reading will show, employs vernacular and local perspectives. It can also be understood as gesturing towards the modes of writing and social imagination developed during the 1980s and 1990s. Despite their hesitance to imagine the future, fiction of that period, compared to that of the 2000s and 2010s, both in Russia and South Africa, has been assessed as casting cautiously hopeful perspectives. Edith Clowes characterized much of the 1980s Russian fiction as "meta-utopian," i.e., subverting the absolute Utopia but "asserting some notions of social vitality" or "utopias in the plural" (1993, 198). Similarly, in several perestroika-time novels, Ilya Kukulin (2007) observes motifs that point to possibilities of futures that are different from the depicted catastrophic present. With regard to South African literature, Rita Barnard's (2004) reading of Zakes Mda's *Ways of Dying*, as a key text from and about transition, considers its development of "a new prosaics" which combines, in grotesque ways, laughter and mourning. The texts I discuss here can be regarded as 're-creating' these practices of tentatively (re)opening horizons in (post)catastrophic circumstances. If the melancholic mode involves, as I noted above, 'weak messianism,' narratives of repair entail a 'weak utopianism'[8] as a strategy of re-engaging hope.

The promise of transition and melancholic attachment

Nthikeng Mohlele's *Small Things* (2013) and Alexei Ivanov's *Nenastye* [Nasty Weather] (2014)[9] are representative of a larger corpus of South African and Russian literary texts that elaborate post-Soviet and postapartheid melancholia and involve a recall of the transition period.[10] Within this broader representational modality, these two novels stand out as validating, in varied ways, the protagonists' desire for a time of emancipatory futurity associated with the experiences or aspirations of the transitions. In both cases, this is a desire for what had (almost) never been and what is recalled as a fleeting moment, a possibility, or an experience of expectation. There is also an important difference between the texts' representations of the transitions. While in Ivanov's novel, the late 1980s and the 1990s are recalled in much detail, from the narrative present of 2008, in Mohlele's text, the protagonist's experience of the late apartheid and early postapartheid period is hardly represented (the narration of the first part of the novel, 'Life', stops in 1976,[11] when Che is imprisoned, and it resumes in the second part titled 'Nausea' in 1994, when he is released; however the 1994–2000 period is not recalled in any detail, and events in the rest of the novel take place, most probably, between 2001 and 2003). This void, however, is structurally significant: against the backdrop of the depressing and tragic present and the nostal-

---

8 O'Connell (2012) theorizes 'weak utopianism' as a version of Derridean 'messianity without messianism' in his re-reading of Ayi Kwei Armah's *The Beautyful Ones Are Not Yet Born*. Contrary to the more conventional approaches to this text as a novel of failed postcolonial nationalism, this reading highlights the presence of promise amid the experience of collapse. Compared to this notion, which comes close to Benjaminian 'weak messianism' as discussed above, I conceptualize the modality of weak utopianism here as involving a stronger emphasis on exploration and emergence, and the absence of melancholia or outright perceptions of catastrophic loss.

9 For a more detailed reading of *Nenastye* see Robbe 2023 (forthcoming).

10 For book-length reflections on post-Soviet and postapartheid melancholia see Etkind 2013, Hook 2013 and Demir 2019. Among the literary texts that relate melancholia in the narrative present to memories of the 1990s transitions are Nadine Gordimer's *No Time Like the Present*, Ivan Vladislavic's *Double Negative*, Sergei Lebedev's *Liudi Avgusta* [People of August], and Alla Gorbunova's *Konets sveta, moia liubov'* [The End of the World, My Love].

11 The year of the Soweto uprising is considered a symbolic turning point for collective resistance against apartheid.

gically recollected youth in Sophiatown,[12] remembering the 1980s and 1990s (the most active phase of anti-apartheid resistance, the transition, and the first post-transition years) as an 'absence' frames this period as waiting or the time when positive expectation was possible, against all odds.[13] This period, spent in prison and on the streets of Johannesburg, is recalled as a time of both traumatic displacement and 'small' hope (the time in prison, he observes, had "slowed down [his] existence" (Mohlele 2013, 43) and minimized his expectations), the time *before* the rapid deterioration of his life and probable death during the 2000s. The novel's narrative present – of consolidated postapartheid socioeconomic order – is experienced by the old, now "hesitant" revolutionary (Mohlele 2013, 85) as the ultimate betrayal of the promise of equality. He observes the emergence of "two Johannesburgs – one for vagabonds and the other for senior executives speaking animatedly into smart phones while cruising in Mercedes Benzes as big as boats. In this other Johannesburg, the one of plush, air-conditioned cars, the revolution is without the slightest meaning" (Mohlele 2013, 126). This loss of meaning, of the promise that would justify the sacrifice, is at the center of the novel's conflict.

Che's ambiguous perspective on the transition is similar to the memories of Ivanov's protagonist German Nevolin. The 1990s in a small, working-class Russian town is depicted as the time of socioeconomic and moral dispossession, of gang wars and corrupt state authorities; this condition is represented as an intensification of the erosion of shared meanings within late Soviet society.[14] At the same time, for the community portrayed in the novel – veterans of the Soviet-Afghan war (1979–1989), German among them – the early transition period (1991–1993) becomes the moment of collective agency when economic collapse and the lack of

---

12 Sophiatown was a suburb of Johannesburg and one of the oldest areas of the city where Black and 'colored' South Africans would settle during the early to mid-twentieth century. During the 1940–50s it was the home of some most prominent developments in Black South African music, literature, and anti-apartheid politics. After the forced removals and complete destruction of the area in the late 1950s, Sophiatown gained a legendary status.

13 Che recollects his time in prison as what conditioned him for "an uncertain life, a life of futile aspirations" (Mohlele 91). While from his viewpoint of the present, these aspirations are seen as "stillborn in a Pretoria penitentiary" (Mohlele 91), this memory nevertheless highlights the aspect of desire and promise.

14 This period (the late 1980s) is recalled through German and his friends' memories of participation in the Soviet-Afghan war. Their remembering generally aligns with the collective memory of this war as meaningless from the perspective of representing state or ideological interests (the war has often been referred to as 'the Soviet Union's Vietnam'). The meaning they generate during the war, as a survival strategy, is the idea of an 'Afghan brotherhood', which creates a support network for this community in the context of the economic and sociopolitical upheaval of the 1990s.

social protection are remedied through the setting up of communitarian structures. These structures are supported by the group's control over semi-legal businesses; the adopted economic model involves social support for all members instead of enrichment of the few under the conditions of emerging 'wild' capitalism. However, with the displacement of the group's initial leader, it deteriorates into a gang and eventually comes under the control of a former KGB officer who 'restores order' by turning the group's economic structure into a private business. In 2008, German finds himself working as a driver for this new company. Witnessing the degradation of his family and friends' lives, and the lack of any possibility of change, he observes that since 1991, everything has remained "just the same. So much newness, it seems, but nothing has changed. By and large. Someone is waging a war in the mountains again. And he, German Nevolin, is still a nobody. Like at that war when he was a soldier." (Ivanov 2014, 192) This loss of meaning and of perspectives for socioeconomic justice is traced back to the failure of the 'Afghan brotherhood' idea which functioned during the early 1990s as an 'ideology' that placed individuals within a (non-national) collective and created bonds of trust.[15] In light of this, German's crime, with which the narrative begins – the heist of a cash-in-transit van carrying the new company's revenues – stands as an act of defiance against the unjust, violent, and future-less neoliberal regime.

Thus, what connects these two novels is their evocation of the transition period, whether fleshed out as a memory or not, as a 'promise' that is irretrievably lost in the present. Both protagonists are, to borrow David Scott's phrase,[16] "conscripts" of anticolonial modernity and its very different yet entangled forms – anti-apartheid liberation struggle and Soviet internationalism (which was the official framing for intervention in the military conflict in Afghanistan). Both recollect struggles for what they perceived as a just cause and find themselves regretting the loss of emancipatory ideals. Their melancholic attachment to the futures that

---

15 The ideas of an 'Afghan brotherhood' and the communities of veterans that were encouraged to start their own businesses (as a result of the corporate tax breaks granted to war veterans) is a recognizable phenomenon of the early 1990s. See Oushakine (2009, 150–190) for an ethnographic study of discourses of the Afghan and the later Chechen war veterans. However, compared to Oushakine's finding that the veterans' "appeals to moral right had no content apart from patriotic experience" (2009, 184–185), the depiction of a post-war community in Ivanov's novel provides a revisionist perspective by stressing socioeconomic rather than nationalist motifs at the core of the veterans' identity. (Robbe 2023, forthcoming).

16 In his book *Conscripts of Modernity*, David Scott (2004, 9) posits that while non-Europeans' "were coercively obliged to render themselves its objects and its agents," the ambiguities and dialectics of their relationship to (Western) modernity – "the complex character of the varied powers that secured those conditions and their effects" – require close scrutiny.

guided their actions in the past is represented as being rooted in this loss. Ironically, though perhaps typically for the states of melancholia, both fail to fully reflect on and acknowledge what exactly was lost: Che refuses "to say for which belief, which idea, he endured such suffering" (Mohlele 2018, 117); German justifies his crime by the wish to 'save' his wife Tania (i.e., provide her with an opportunity to live a good life abroad), but the readers learn about his dreams and longing for the past indirectly, from his memories rather than direct reflections.

In both novels, post-transitional melancholia (displayed by other characters too, but to a greater extent by the protagonists) is represented as an obsession, an almost fatal force beyond control. In *Small Things*, 'being obsessed' is related to revolutionary politics (the policeman mentions this word twice during Che's interrogation), to music (playing trumpet becomes Che's true commitment at the end), and love (his relentless youth-time love for Desirée who always teases him but never reciprocates). Even during his romance with Mercedes, a daughter of a Cuban revolutionary, he remains devoted to his old love; as a result, he chooses to stay in South Africa when Mercedes and her father return to Cuba, asking himself: "How is love of Mercedes greater than love of home?" (Mohlele 2013, 86). As Timothy Wright argues in his reading of the novel, "in the context of the reification of national history, Che's pathological obsession with Desirée becomes a mode, if not of keeping alive the promises of the past, at least of resisting accommodation with the present" (2019, 208). Read as an allegory, Desirée stands for the nation's revolutionary 'future past,' an object of desire that cannot be relinquished. Adopting an allegorical lens to *Nenastye*, Tania's inability to have children (as a result of an abortion) which she perceives as a curse is evocative of the nation's failed transition. German's reckless attempt to 'repair' this trauma, risking his life, is also portrayed as an obsessive devotion to a desire rooted in the past. His inability to leave the past behind is paralleled by his mystical attachment to the old country house where he hides and which he is reluctant to leave until the dramatic ending.

German's crime (justified within the narrative's logic) is a more active attempt at resisting present-day order compared to Che's, although it is also melancholic: from the very start, German gives up on his own life, expecting that he will be arrested. At the same time, Che also makes deliberate (though negative) choices – not using his 'struggle' credentials to get a well-paid job, not leaving South Africa, not stopping to see Desirée, and not committing suicide. Regarding the latter, he mentions that what keeps him alive is a sense that he is "yet to discover something profound. Something small. That holds all big things together"; something that would allow him to say "I did not suffer for nothing" (2013, 142). For German, too, melancholic attachment to the aspirations of a revolution/ transformation is a way of regaining meaning and agency – a sense that the sacrifices, his own and of other people like him, could yield redemption.

The differences between the authors' use of a critical melancholic mode of memory relates to the contexts against which they write. Mohlele's novel counters the largely hopeful narratives of transition and in particular the narratives of 'Black' aspiration in an Afropolitan Johannesburg (Nuttall 2004, Wright 2019). In so doing, it participates in voicing the contemporary disillusionment with transition (Robbe 2018, Van der Vlies 2017, Worby and Ally 2014) in an ambiguous mode: while accentuating the pathology of Che's melancholic attachment to revolutionary desire (often with the use of irony), it also stresses the critical force of those 'futures past' in reorienting social imaginaries in the neoliberal present. In the context of melancholia's prominence in contemporary Russian culture (Kalinin 2019), Ivanov's novel does not develop a new mode, but, importantly, it shifts the focus from the Soviet to the transition period as the 'lost' object. Furthermore, the loss is represented as the failed promise of socioeconomic justice (attempted on a community level during the early transition) as opposed to the more common narratives of the loss of national/imperial belonging. The validation of transition's 'futures past' is what distinguishes these memories from state-supported trauma narratives.

Childhood memories, the everyday, and narratives of repair

While melancholic perspectives have been a common affective strategy of representing disappointment but also attachment to certain aspects of transitions, another mode of remembering – centered around autobiographical recollections of childhood and youth during this turbulent time – has emerged in both countries. These narratives may involve forms of melancholia too, but their figurations of 'repair' (as outlined above) and non-allegorical, autobiographical form is what constitutes this second mode. My reading of two novels – Daria Dimke's *Zimniaia i letniaia forma nadezhdy* [*Winter and Summer Forms of Hope*][17] and Nadia Davids' *An Imperfect Blessing*, both published in 2014 – will demonstrate how narratives of repair are developed via memories generated through an 'imperfect' childhood gaze. The childhood perspective provides a unique lens on this time: by combining contradictory impressions and weaving together the traumas and memories of different generations, it has the capacity of juxtaposing divergent contexts, temporalities and experiences, of bridging differences without foreclosing contradictions.

---

17 The book was re-published in 2019 under the title *Snegiri* [*Snowbirds*].

One of the most evident levels on which these novels intervene into the established narratives of the transitions as dramatic events (cast in a positive or negative light, framed as ultimate victory or betrayal) is the foregrounding of 'everyday' and family-centered perspectives. Davids' novel is structured as a diary of the fourteen-year-old Alia, written in the past tense, i.e., as a memory of her life in the turbulent times before the first democratic elections: the entries span the time from January 1993 to January 1994, with the two last chapters reflecting on the weeks just after the first democratic elections in April 1994. The narrative also includes flashbacks to events during the 'state of emergency' in 1986 focalized by Alia's uncle Waleed and narrating his engagement in anti-apartheid struggle. Along with the parallel narrative of 1986 that resurfaces as trauma in the present (these chapters are narrated in the present tense), the text includes flashbacks to the early 1970s, involving the trauma of the entire family and community of District Six who were forcibly removed from Cape Town city center. The novel recollects major tragic events and the overall presence of violence and anxiety (states of emergency, the assassination and commemoration of Chris Hani[18]), but, witnessed by Alia, they are woven into the narrative of ordinary life within the spaces and communities of Cape Town. Attention to local practices, conflicts, and revelations characterizing everyday life in extraordinary times renders transition as a highly ambiguous period of personal and collective (trans)formation and growth, combining grief and joy.

Dimke's novel narrates the time between 1987 and 1992 in an unnamed Siberian city, likely Irkutsk where the author grew up, through a series of stories about young Dasha and her family's everyday life.[19] The narrative entwines casual childhood memories with references to World War II, the Holocaust, and the Gulag, recalling the child's encounters with family and societal traumas. References to exact dates are rare but present at several dramatic points in the text, such as when Dasha stops receiving letters from her friend who lives on Abkhazia and hears that this must be due to a 'military conflict.' Her question "Is 'military conflict' a 'war'?" alludes to the extent of the warfare and ethnic cleansings in Georgia

---

18 Chris Hani was the head of the ANC military wing uMkhonto we Sizwe during the 1980s and General Secretary of the South African Communist Party (SACP) in 1991–1993. He was assassinated by a far-right Polish immigrant a year before the first democratic elections and at the height of his popularity.

19 The novel's title might be an allusion to the poetry volume by Vsevolod Nekrasov *Mezhdu letom i zimoj* [Between Summer and Winter] (1976), a representative of Soviet 'unofficial' literature, who practiced the intermingling the conventions of children's and adult poetry in his texts, in particular via a combination of avant-garde aesthetics and the everyday (Morse 2018). The novel's conveying of memories of World War II and Stalinist repressions via a child perspective and focus on the everyday aligns it with the practices of 'unofficial' remembering during the Soviet period.

and Abkhazia during 1992–1993, all reduced to a 'conflict' by media reports. A moment of irreparable loss, when the six-year-old Dasha learns about the passing away of her mother, is also rendered with the mentioning of a date: "During the summer of 1989 it turned out that death had the taste of wild strawberries and the eyes of our mom. The same summer, we learnt writing. The old way of defining things had appeared incomplete, and we needed to learn a new one." (Dimke 2014, 117) This laconic and striking depiction of perceiving loss casts light onto the silences and gaps in the earlier stories and interconnects the traumas of the protagonist and of her grandparents, as revealed in the chapters that surround this one.

Thus, with regard to content, style, and intonation both novels are characterized by a combination of the ordinary and exceptional, daily and historical, personal and collective within the narratives that oscillate between drama and humor. These characteristics of style and genre allow for dialoguing the traumas of different generations via memories of transition when, as depicted in both novels, moments of joint reflection and mediation became possible. Such moments take place within the family contexts; however, speaking, silences and conflicts within these 'private' contexts are rendered as refractions of public processes.

In Dimke's novel, a friend's remark that during school lessons about World War II "they [. . .] never speak about the Jews" triggers reflection which shifts from a friends' conversation to the politics of history teaching to the protagonist's family history whose grandparents – one Jew, the other German – were victims of Nazi and Soviet repressions. Since her grandparents, like the majority of victims during the (post-)Soviet time, would not speak about this past, the narrative recollects precisely these silences and the fragmented ways of telling and hearing about it. Switching between the narrator's reflection in the present and her childhood memory, the narrative engages with this topic through everyday details: the grandfather's love of Albrecht Dürer's artworks, his knowledge of German, his German surname; then the remark that "after seven years of the camps, Grandpa and Grandma were sent for eternal settlement to one of the villages of the blessed Siberian region," where "Grandma worked as an all-round doctor and Grandpa as an all-round teacher" (2014, 51). The final chapter tells a joyful but somewhat eerie story of how Dasha and her brother accompanied their Grandpa on his yearly visits to an old friend. Only when this friend dies, Dasha learns that he was her Grandpa's labor camp guard. The child's perspective places this strange friendship between a victim and a perpetrator within the context of family rituals and the times when she became socialized into the experience of reconciling. A similar way of learning indirectly about her Grandma's experience of the War as a Polish Jew is rendered through the memories of Grandma's tales about the lions and people who lived in a fairy town that was once destroyed by a war. The key to this metaphor is provided when Dasha recalls how Grandma later explained that these stories had been her only way to speak about this past: "in those stories [. . .] I could be whatever I wanted: a stone lion, a castle, a clockmaker, a cat, a knight. There was no objective, single definition, it was always possible to choose. It was always possible to break the loop, to stop living within the loop which they tied around us." (Dimke 2014, 106–107) These memories provide a framing for the ways in which the grandparents deal with their difficult experiences. Such 'reparative' framing completes, as it were, the rituals created by the grandparents through the granddaughter's mediation which interconnects those pasts with events and traumas in her own life. The transition period becomes a meeting point for those memories and a 'space' of intergenerational connection.

In Davids' novel, the 'long' transition (including the intensified anti-apartheid struggle and state-supported violence in townships during the late 1980s) is the time of both intergenerational conflict and initiated repair. The entire narrative is built around family conflicts – between two brothers (Alia's father and uncle Waleed, to whom she is very attached), between Waleed and his mother, the family matriarch, and between Waleed and his girlfriend. At the core of these conflicts is Waleed's anti-apartheid political commitment. Witnessing acts of state-incited violence and of Black people's lives sacrificed in the course of the Struggle makes him psychologically scarred and intolerant to the 'passivity' of his relatives. The 'repair' is initiated as he begins writing creatively – a process associated with his walking through the deserted spaces of District Six and recovering a sense of belonging through remembering the suffering and joy of the community. The 'colored' community is represented, throughout the narrative, as diverse and divided (along the lines of class, gender, generation, politics, religion, etc.), but also connected through multiple solidarities. Acts of memory, in several episodes, reach across and beyond communities: "the immediate, always accessible image of the wrecking ball in the District and the women gathered around it" makes Waleed feel "a heartache he could not name" (Davids 2014, 158) when he hears about demolitions in a 'Black' township. The structure of 'both/and' (two historical moments, of 1986 and 1993, different memories of displacement and the displaced, trauma and nostalgia) is central to the novel. On the eve of the transition, Alia loses her romantic interest who emigrates with his family to Australia (as many South Africans did, fearing the consequences of political change or looking for better opportunities). Her recollection of the election day and Waleed's view of the moment explicates this duality: "[h]e says you can't really be free if there is food everywhere but you are kept hungry. This is a sad place to end. I don't mean it to be. But it's always like that here, isn't it? Both things at once." (Davids 2014, 404) This is what the novel renders as the "imperfect blessing" of the transition, which involves finding and losing, hope and unabating pain.

Conclusions

This chapter began by juxtaposing theoretical observations on how the times of transition function in the Russian and South African imaginaries as *other times* – 'times out of joint,' of crystallized conflict and crisis, and of projected fears, distress, and hopes of the present. Over the past decade, we have seen how the 1980–1990s transitions have become objects of critical reassessment and *remembering* in political commentary and scholarship, and also – with a great variety, intricacy, and tenacity of interpretations – in works of fiction. The emergence of transitions as mnemonic objects seems to follow the earlier trajectories of persistent engagement with apartheid and Soviet pasts in the respective cultures. The latter enquiries continue in the present, but instead of giving way to elaborations of future-oriented imaginaries, as some critics expected, mnemonic preoccupations are developing a new focus on the periods of transition. In this chapter, I reflected on how these memories can be examined not only within but also across the postsocialist and postcolonial contexts that followed very different sociopolitical regimes. Such comparisons can elucidate the similarities and differences of engagements with anticolonial and socialist utopian visions as well as their transformations and afterlives since the time of the transitions.

As I note in the final passage of the Introduction to this volume, the full-scale invasion of Ukraine and the war waged by Russia have further antagonized and weaponized memories of transition in political and popular discourses. In this context, we might want to turn to the media of literature, film, or visual art in their capacity of developing modes of remembering that can hold together the ambivalent and differential visions and perceptions of the past, as exemplified by the narratives I discussed in this chapter. The ambiguities of mourning the loss and attempting to rekindle hope, for which these narratives provide form, can offer a path beyond the opposition between the celebratory and paranoid, disaster-oriented discourses of transitions.

My reading of South African and Russian novelistic recollections of the transitions from the 2010s focused on outlining two modes – of melancholia and repair. While I tried to show the distinctiveness of these modes, I certainly regard them as nodes on a 'melancholic-reparative' spectrum rather than separate entities. In selecting these four novels, I concentrated on the ambiguous and critical expressions which convey the traumas and violence of the transitions while evoking senses of hope and futurity. They do so in in different ways – by elaborating melancholic attachment characterized by 'weak messianism' (the novels of Alexei Ivanov and Nthikeng Mohlele) or by telling stories of reparative remembrance (by Nadia Davids and Daria Dimke) that mediate 'weak utopianism.' These modalities of memory and futurity may be related to the aspects of gender and generation foregrounded by the narrators' and focalizers' perspectives, though no conclusions can be made based on this small selection.[20]

Compared to the temporalities of dystopia and apocalyptic anticipation that have dominated post-Soviet and postapartheid fiction (and social imagination, more broadly) since the 1980s, these narratives of melancholia and repair reconfigure time by reflecting on loss in ways which, as Judith Butler once suggested in her writing on melancholia, can be "paradoxically productive" when "loss becomes condition and necessity for a certain sense of community, where community does not overcome the loss [. . .]" (2002, 467–468). To develop a perspective on melancholia that addresses the losses suffered not during the Soviet and apartheid periods but during the transition, I drew on Artemy Magun's theorization of post-Soviet transition as a "negative revolution" which turned out to be "unconscious" and "incomplete" in its negation of the preceding order – in fact, sustaining fetishist attachment to the Soviet-type authority. In this light, I found that mnemonic returns to the 1980–1990s written in the melancholic mode highlight the "incompleteness" of transformations that led to neoliberal normalization and involve a longing for more radical negation. For theorizing the second mode, I relied on Marianne Hirsch and Eve Kosowsky- Sedgewick's conceptualization of 'repair' to understand how transitions are recollected, particularly through autobiographical childhood perspectives, as the times of intergenerational and intercommunal breakup and connection. Thus, the negativity of the transitions is being represented and, at the same time, re-addressed through invoking memory of hope and new beginnings.

Along with conceptualizing recent reconfigurations of (post-)transitional time, this chapter proposed possibilities for interconnected reading of postapartheid and post-Soviet writing and began theorizing *memories of transition* as a possible nexus between postsocialist and postcolonial perspectives on transformation. While memories of state socialism and colonialism usually yield diverging stances and affects, recollections of these systems' collapse and transformation may reveal intriguing possibilities of dialogue in the present. Now, when the presence of colonial violence is increasingly being interrogated within the contexts that diverge from the 'classical' paradigms of (post)colonialism, reading postsocialist and postcolonial/postapartheid literature alongside can help us to comprehend the complexity and complicity of transition narratives in the continuing colonial practices. Exploring contemporary memories of the end of the Cold War as focalizing the missed opportunities of decolonization offers an entry point for understanding this entanglement.

---

20 Examining a larger corpus of texts from the 2010s is a project for my larger study-in-progress.

Works cited

Agamben, Giorgio. *Potentialities: Collected Essays in Philosophy*. Ed. and trans. Daniel Heller-Roazen. Stanford: Stanford University Press, 1999.

Assmann, Aleida. *Cultural Memory and Western Civilization: Arts of Memory*. Cambridge: Cambridge University Press, 2011.

Atanasoski, Neda, and Kalindi Vora. "Introduction: Postsocialist Politics and the Ends of Revolution." *Social Identities* 24.2 (2018): 139–154.

Barnard, Rita. "On Laughter, the Grotesque, and the South African Transition: Zakes Mda's *Ways of Dying*." *NOVEL: A Forum on Fiction* 37.3 (2004): 277–302.

Barnard, Rita. "Introduction." *South African Writing in Transition*. Ed. Rita Barnard and Andrew Van der Vlies. London: Bloomsbury Academic, 2019. 1–32.

Benjamin, Walter. "On the Theory of Knowledge, Theory of Progress." *The Arcades Project*. Trans. Howard Eiland and Kevin McLaughlin. Cambridge, MA: Harvard University Press, 1999. 456–488.

Boehmer, Elleke. 1998. "Endings and New Beginning: South African Fiction in Transition." *Writing South Africa*. Ed. Derek Attridge and Rosemary Jolly. Cambridge: Cambridge University Press, 1998. 43–56.

Boehmer, Elleke. "Permanent Risk: When Crisis Defines a Nation's Writing." *Trauma, Memory, and Narrative in the Contemporary South African Novel*. Ed. Ewald Mengel and Michela Borzaga. Leiden: Brill, 2012. 29–46.

Brown, Wendy. *Undoing the Demos: Neoliberalism's Stealth Revolution*. Princeton: Princeton University Press, 2015.

Buck-Morss, Susan. "The City as Dreamworld and Catastrophy." *October* 73 (1995): 3–26.

Butler, Judith. "Afterword: After Loss, What Then?" *Loss: The Politics of Mourning*. Ed. by David Eng and David Kazanjian. Berkley: University of California Press, 2002. 467–473.

Chantsev, Alexandr. "Fabrika antiutopii: distopicheskii diskurs v rossiiskoi literature serediny 2000kh" [Anti-Utopia Factory: The Dystopian Discourse in Russian Literature of the Mid-2000s]. *Novoe literaturnoe obozrenie* 4 (2007). https://magazines.gorky.media/nlo/2007/4/fabrika-antiutopij. html (Accessed April 3, 2023).

Chari, Sharad, and Katherine Verdery. "Thinking between the Posts: Postcolonialism, Postsocialism, and Ethnography after the Cold War." *Comparative Studies in Society and History* 51.1 (2009): 6–34.

Clowes, Edith W. *Russian Experimental Fiction: Resisting Ideology after Utopia*. Princeton: Princeton University Press, 1993.

Crimp, Douglas. "Mourning and Militancy." *October* 51 (Winter 1989): 3–18.

Cvetkovich, Ann. *Archive of Feelings*. Durham, Duke University Press, 2003.

Davids, Nadia. *An Imperfect Blessing*. Cape Town: Umuzi, 2014.

Demir, Danyela. *Reading Loss: Post-Apartheid Melancholia in Contemporary South African Novels*. Berlin: Logos, 2019.

Dimke, Daria. *Zimniaia i letniaia forma nadezhdy* [Winter and Summer Forms of Hope]. Moscow: Ripoll Classic, 2014.

Djagalov, Rossen. *From Internationalism to Postcolonialism: Literature and Cinema between the Second and the Third Worlds*. Montreal and Kingston: McGill-Queen's University Press, 2020.

Etkind, Alexander. *Warped Mourning: Stories of the Undead in the Land of the Unburied*. Palo Alto: Stanford University Press, 2013.

Frenkel, Ronit, and Craig McKenzie. "Conceptualizing 'Post-Transitional' South African Literature in English." *English Studies in Africa* 53.1 (2010): 1–10.

Fukuyama, Francis. *The End of History and the Last Man*. New York: Free Press, 1992.

Fukuyama, Francis. *Identity: Contemporary Identity Politics and the Struggle for Recognition*. London: Faber & Faber, 2018.

Gready, Paul. *The Era of Transitional Justice: The Aftermath of the Truth and Reconciliation Commission in South Africa and Beyond*. New York: Routledge, 2011.

Grunebaum, Heidi. *Memorializing the Past: Everyday Life in South Africa after the Truth and Reconciliation Commission*. New York: Transaction, 2011.

Hirsch, Marianne. "The Generation of Postmemory." *Poetics Today* 29.1 (2008): 103–128.

Hirsch, Marianne. "Introduction: Practicing Feminism, Practicing Memory." *Women Mobilizing Memory*. Ed. Ayşe Gül Altınay, María José Contreras, Marianne Hirsch, Jean Howard, Banu Karaca, and Alisa Solomon. New York: Columbia University Press, 2019. 1–23.

Hook, Derek. *(Post)apartheid Conditions: Psychoanalysis and Social Formation*. New York: Palgrave Macmillan, 2013.

Huntington, Samuel P. *The Third Wave: Democratization in the Late Twentieth Century*. Norman: University of Oklahoma Press, 1991.

Ivanov, Alexei. *Nenastye* [Nasty Weather]. Moscow: AST, 2014.

Kalinin, Ilya. "Soviet Atlantis: A Melancholic Fantasy of the Post-Soviet Subject." *Eurozine* 22 November, 2019.

Karkov, Nikolay, and Zhivka Valiavicharska. "Rethinking East-European Socialism: Notes towards an Anti-Capitalist Decolonial Methodology." *Interventions* 20.6 (2018): 785–813.

Khatib, Sami. "The Messianic without Messianism: Walter Benjamin's Materialist Theology." *Anthropology & Materialism* 1 (2013). http://journals.openedition.org/am/159 (Accessed April 3, 2023).

Klumbytė, Neringa, and Gulnaz Sharafutdinova. "Introduction: What Was Late Socialism?" *Soviet Society in the Era of Late Socialism, 1964–1985*. Ed. Neringa Klumbytė and Gulnaz Sharafutdinova. Plymouth: Lexington Books, 2013. 1–14.

Koselleck, Reinhart. *Futures Past: On the Semantics of Historical Time*. Trans. Keith Tribe. New York: Columbia University Press, 2004.

Kosofsky Sedgewick, Eve. "Paranoid Reading and Reparative Reading, Or You're So Paranoid, You Probably Think This Essay is about You." *Touching Feeling: Affect, Pedagogy, Performativity*. Durham: Duke University Press, 2003. 123–151.

Kruger, Loren. *The Drama of South Africa: Plays, Pageants and Publics since 1910*. London: Routledge, 1999.

Kukulin, Ilya. "Zamykanie gorizonta: ozhidanie sotsialnykh katastrof v literature sovremennoi Rossii" [The Closure of a Horizon: Anticipation of Social Catastrophes in Contempotrary Russian Literature]. *Puti Rossii: preemsvennost' i preryvistost' obschestvennogo razvitiia* [Russia's Paths: Continuities and Breaks in Social Development]. Ed. A. M. Nikulin. Moscow: MVSgSEN, 2007.

Kukulin, Ilya. "Cultural Shifts in Russia since 2010: Messianic Cynicism and Paradigms of Artistic Resistance." *Russian Literature* 96–98 (2018): 221–254.

Kunkel, Benjamin. "Dystopia and the End of Politics." *Dissent* (Fall 2008). https://www.dissentmaga zine.org/article/dystopia-and-the-end-of-politics (Accessed April 3, 2023).

Kurtović, Larisa, and Nelli Sargsyan. "After Utopia: Leftist Imaginaries and Activist Politics in the Postsocialist World." *History and Anthropology* 30.1 (2019): 1–19.

Lee, Christopher. "Decoloniality of a Special Type: Solidarity and Its Potential Meanings in South African Literature, during and after the Cold War." *Journal of Postcolonial Writing* 50. 4 (2014): 466–477.

Levinson, Alexei. "1990e i 1990i: soziologicheskie materialy" [The 1990s and 1990: Sociological Materials]. *Novoe literaturnoe obozrenie* 2 (2007). https://magazines.gorky.media/nlo/2007/2/1990-e-i-1990-j-socziologicheskie-materialy.html (Accessed April 3, 2023).

Magaziner, Daniel, and Sean Jacobs. "The End of South African Exceptionalism." *The Atlantic* (August 27, 2012). https://www.theatlantic.com/international/archive/2012/08/the-end-of-south-african-exceptionalism/261591/ (Accessed April 3, 2023).

Magun, Artemy. *Negative Revolution: Modern Political Subject and Its Fate after the Cold War*. New York: Bloomsbury, 2013.

Malinova, Olga. "Framing the Collective Memory of the 1990s as a Legitimation Tool for Putin's Regime." *Problems of Post-Communism* 68.5 (2021): 429–441.

Mamdani, Mahmood. *Citizen and Subject: Contemporary Africa and the Legacy of Late Colonialism*. Princeton: Princeton University Press, 1996.

Mark, James, and Quinn Slobodian. "Eastern Europe in the Global History of Decolonization." *The Oxford Handbook of the Ends of Empire*. Ed. Martin Thomas and Andrew S. Thompson. Oxford: Oxford University Press, 2018. 351–372.

Mbembe, Achille. "Negative Messianism Marks Our Times." *Mail & Guardian* (February 3, 2017). https://mg.co.za/article/2017-02-03-00-negative-messianism-marks-our-times/ (Accessed April 3, 2023).

Mezzadra, Sandro. "Challenging Borders: The Legacy of Postcolonial Critique in the Present Conjuncture." *Soft Power* 7.2 (2020): 21–44.

Mohlele, Nthikeng. *Small Things*. Johannesburg: Jacana Media, 2018.

Morse, Ainsley. "Between Summer and Winter: Late Soviet Children's Literature and Unofficial Poetry." *Russian Literature* 96–98 (2018): 105–135.

Nixon, Rob. *Slow Violence and the Environmentalism of the Poor*. Cambridge, MA: Harvard University Press, 2011.

Nuttall, Sarah. "City Forms and Writing the 'Now' in South Africa." *Journal of Southern African Studies* 30.4 (2004): 731–748.

O'Brian, Anthony. *Against Normalization: Writing Radical Democracy in South Africa*. Durham: Duke University Press, 2001.

O'Connell, Hugh C. "A Weak Utopianism of Postcolonial Nationalist Bildung: Re-Reading Ayi Kwei Armah's *The Beautyful Ones Are Not Yet Born*." *Journal of Postcolonial Writing* 48.4 (2012): 371–383.

Oushakine, Serguei A. *Patriotism of Despair: Nation, War and Loss in Russia*. Ithaca: Cornell University Press, 2009.

Platt, Kevin M.F. "The Post-Soviet is Over: On Reading the Ruins." *Republics of Letters: A Journal for the Study of Knowledge, Politics, and the Arts* 1 (2009): 1–26.

Platt, Kevin M.F. "Commemorating the End of History: Timelessness and Power in Contemporary Russia." *Power and Time: Temporalities in Conflict and the Making of History*. Ed. Dan Edelstein, Stefanos Geroulanos, and Natasha Wheatley. Chicago: University of Chicago Press, 2020. 400–419.

Popescu, Monica. "Translations: Lenin's Statues, Post-Communism and Post-Apartheid." *The Yale Journal of Criticism* 16.2 (2003): 406–423.

Popescu, Monica. *At Penpoint: African Literatures, Postcolonial Studies, and the Cold War*. Durham: Duke University Press, 2020.

Prozorov, Sergei. *A Time Like No Other: Russian Politics after the End of History*. DIIS Working Paper no. 2006/17. Copenhagen: Danish Institute of International Studies DIIS, 2007.

Ries, Nancy. *Russian Talk: Culture and Conversation during Perestroika*. Ithaca: Cornell University Press, 1997.

Robbe, Ksenia. "Confronting Disillusionment: On the Rediscovery of Socialist Archives in Recent South African Cultural Production." *Safundi* 19.4 (2018): 398–415.

Robbe, Ksenia. "The Moral Right to Economic Crime: Remembering the Russian 1990s in a Tragic Mode in Alexei Ivanov's *Nenast'e*." *Remembering the Neoliberal Turn: Economic Change and Collective Memory in Eastern Europe after 1989*. Ed. Veronika Pehe and Joanna Wawrzyniak. New York: Routledge, 2023 (forthcoming).

Robbe, Ksenia, and Hanneke Stuit. "Looking Sideways: Beyond the Crisis of Genre." *(Un)timely Crises: Chronotopes and Critique*. Ed. Maria Boletsi, Kasia Mika, Natashe Lemos Dekker, and Ksenia Robbe. Cham: Palgrave Macmillan, 2021. 67–76.

Roberts, Ronald Suresh. "How 'Transitional Justice' Colonized South Africa's TRC." *Modern Languages Open* 1 (2020).

Scott, David. *Conscripts of Modernity: The Tragedy of Colonial Enlightenment*. Durham: Duke University Press, 2004.

Shapiro, Ian. "On the Normalization of South African Politics." *Dissent* (Winter 1999). https://www.dissentmagazine.org/article/on-the-normalization-of-south-african-politics (Accessed April 3, 2023).

Sharafutdinova, Gulnaz. *The Red Mirror: Putin's Leadership and Russia's Insecure Identity*. Oxford: Oxford University Press, 2020.

Shevchenko, Olga. *Crisis and the Everyday in Postsocialist Moscow*. Bloomington: Indiana University Press, 2009.

Titlestad, Michael. "South African End Times: Conceiving an Apocalyptic Imaginary." *Tydskrif vir Letterkunde* 51.2 (2014): 52–70.

Tlostanova, Madina. *Postcolonialism and Postsocialism in Fiction and Art*. Basingstoke: Palgrave Macmillan, 2017.

Traverso, Enzo. *Left-Wing Melancholia: Marxism, History, and Memory*. New York: Columbia University Press, 2017.

Van der Vlies, Andrew. *Present Imperfect: Contemporary South African Writing*. Oxford: Oxford University Press, 2017.

Wentzel, Jennifer. *Bulletproof: Afterlives of Anticolonial Prophecy in South Africa and Beyond*. Chicago: University of Chicago Press, 2009.

Worby, Eric, and Shireen Ally. "The Disappointment of Nostalgia: Conceptualising Cultures of Memory in Contemporary South Africa." *Social Dynamics* 39.3 (2013): 457–480.

Wright, Timothy. "Ruined Time and Post-Revolutionary Allegory in Nthikeng Mohlele's Small Things." *Social Dynamics* 45.2 (2019): 198–212.

Yurchak, Alexei. *Everything Was Forever Until It Was No More: The Last Soviet Generation*. Princeton: Princeton University Press, 2006.

Afterword

Andrew van der Vlies

Refusing the Anti-Politics Machine: On Post-Transitional, Transitional Times

South African journalist and (now Princeton-based) historian Jacob Dlamini's ex-traordinary – and controversial – first book, *Native Nostalgia*, begins with a reflec-tion on a troubling encounter. During August of 2009, reporting for the Johannesburg newspaper *Business Day*, Dlamini visited Thandukukhanya, a settlement on the fringes of Piet Retief, a farming town in South Africa's eastern Mpumalanga province (near the border with Eswatini/Swaziland), named for a leading nineteenth-century white pioneer (*Voortrekker*) and now known as eMkhondo. Dlamini had grown up in a broadly similar space during the last years of apartheid rule, in Katlehong, an-other segregated zone from which many residents, all Black (South) Africans, had fre-quently to travel great distances to work, often for white employers in the suburbs, on farms, or in industry. Fifteen years into the post-transitional "New" South Africa (the ruling African National Congress, in power since 1994, had won the April general election with 65.9% of the vote), it might have been expected that most residents of Thandukukhanya would support the new regime. Of course, Dlamini knows better; not even he, however, expected to encounter Black South Africans, and especially women his own mother's age, reflecting nostalgically about the apartheid-era past. "The conundrum" (Dlamini writes) "is this: What does it mean for a black South Afri-can to remember life under apartheid with fondness?" (2009, 13).

Dlamini understands implicitly that this position, unthinkable for a Black citi-zen to speak a decade before, confirms both the tragedy *and* the maturity of a post-transitional dispensation. The too-easy narratives of deliverance from oppres-sion that characterize post-transition national mythography obscure the possibility that liberators might in turn become oppressors – as the massacre of striking mine-workers at the Lonmin platinum mine at Marikana would confirm for South Afri-cans only three years later (Kylie Thomas touches on this in her chapter in this volume, also addressing the failures of the new dispensation to follow through on promises of justice for those murdered by apartheid forces). Even if not actively op-pressed, the supposed beneficiaries of liberation are reduced in such post-transition narratives to homogeneity – and passivity – in state-sanctioned accounts that cast the transition as a process that is definitively finished. Transitions have jagged edges, however, and especially if, as so often the case, they do not deliver quite what was promised by those who present themselves as its driving force. South Afri-ca's ruling party, Dlamini suggests, in seeking to manage the transition as a process with an end, "created an anti-politics machine in which black people – who alleg-

https://doi.org/10.1515/9783110707793-013

edly suffered the same way, struggled the same way, and lived the same way under apartheid – feature as nothing more than objects of state policies or, worse, passive recipients of state-led service delivery" (2009, 20). Dlamini's observation here accords well with Wendy Brown's analysis of the waning of "the distinctly *political* character, meaning, and operation of democracy's constituent elements into *economic* ones" (2015, 17). (I examine this waning, and specifically the economization of political rights in a neoliberal frame, as treated in other recent work by Black South African writers, elsewhere; Van der Vlies 2017.)

What Dlamini found, in Thandukukhanya and elsewhere, was that it was in relation to the delivery of basic services to the most indigent that the ANC government was signally *failing*. General dissatisfaction about this fact is what drove at least some of the nostalgia for aspects of life under white minority rule that Dlamini observed. The emblematic encounter in which this nostalgia is voiced – and that begins *Native Nostalgia* – confirms for Dlamini that South Africans are not "agreed on the meaning of their past" (2009, 6). "It is all too often taken for granted," he writes, "that the story of black South Africa" features "a neat separation between a merry precolonial Africa, a miserable apartheid South Africa and a marvelous new South Africa in which everyone is living democratically ever after"; rather, for many, "the past, the present and the future are not discrete wholes, with clear splits between them" (Dlamini 2009, 12). As Megan Jones writes, invoking the Cameroonian-South African philosopher Achille Mbembe's ongoing engagement with the discontents of postcolonial transitions, subjectivity in such times and places is more frequently "criss-crossed with temporal currents that reach ahead and behind, horizontally and vertically" (Jones 2014, 107). Real-world examples like Dlamini's confirm such affective-temporal complexities.

Uneven temporal experiences amongst members of a community, across and within generations, in the same place or across very different spaces, is described in Darwin Tsen's study, in this collection, of the ways in which Taiwanese writer Luo Yijun's (駱以軍) work engages (in similar way to Dlamini's) with the impossibility of framing the past as being over. Instead, it is a kind of *dysrhythmia*, a being out of joint, to use a term referring to "a biological clock that's been disturbed after traveling across time zones" (Tsen, 116). This is a productive way of redescribing what David Scott suggests is the waning of an "old consoling sense of temporal *concordance*": our sense of "[t]he present as time, as a temporal frame of meaningful experiential reference, no longer appears – as it was once prominently pictured as appearing – as the tidy dialectical negation of an oppressive or otherwise unwanted past," Scott notes on the basis of his work on the aftermaths of failed revolutions in the Caribbean (2014, 5). In consequence, Scott continues, it becomes difficult "to continue imagining the present as through it were merely waiting for its own dialectical overcoming in a Hegelian-Marxist story of futurity understood as the ready horizon of Universal History" (Scott 2014, 5). Indeed, subjects find that their sense of time "has become less yielding, less promising than we have grown to expect it should be" (Scott 2014, 5). With reference to his own Taiwanese examples, and drawing on Svetlana Alexievich's *Secondhand Time* (2013, trans. 2015), a book about memories of the Soviet transition (with much to recommend a comparison with postapartheid South Africa, too), Tsen notes that "[o]ne population's hopeful socialism or market reform is another's nostalgia or nightmare[,] which they have already experienced decades earlier" (121). Indeed, the uses made of the past, and especially in narratives of transition that are mobilized for present political purpose, inform, whether or not explicitly, each of the chapters of this collection. All recognize the challenge of approaching memories of transition with the sensitivity and openness to complexity that differing sets of contexts, representations, re-appraisals, and indeed returns, demand.

Nuance and openness to complexity is, however, not always universally welcomed in societies whose rulers, or new elites, prefer more straightforward narratives of overcoming (demonstrated in this volume in Bonifacio Valdivia Milla and Pablo Valdivia Martin's discussion of Alonso de Santos's *Trampa para Pájaros*, and differently in Cara Levey's discussion of Southern-Cone exile narratives). Dlamini's book was itself the subject of very mixed responses in South Africa, including hostility from some fellow Black intellectuals. As Megan Jones observes, "journalist Andile Mngxitama [. . .] accused Dlamini of reproducing white hegemony," while the writer Eric Miyeni, misconstruing *Native Nostalgia*'s premise as being "that growing up in apartheid-designed townships was fun," refused even to read it (2014, 110). Anecdotally, a white academic who set the text on a course on postapartheid nonfiction at a leading South African university in the wake of the Fees Must Fall movement decided not to teach it after students concluded – based on its title alone – that it was objectionable. Categorical thinking returns in the strangest guises in the long post-transitional period without term.

Refusal of complexity feeds new repressive attempts to recast the past in ways that privilege ongoing (or new) injustices, as two chapters in this volume fascinatingly outline in relation to postcommunist Russia. Andrei Zavadski notes the ways in which Putin and Medvedev sought to homogenize accounts of Russians' economic hardships during the 1990s to contrast with economic stability under their increasingly authoritarian governance. Mykola Makhortykh draws on Instagram posts to analyze the range of affective attachments to the immediate post-Soviet past that linger (and are intriguingly curated) in this extraordinary social-media archive. Zavadski points to a variety of media projects that sought in response to actualize what he calls "*countermemories*" of the decade in service of the development of a "mnemonic counterpublic" (repurposing Michael Warner's term), a longed-for commons to counterpose what Dlamini calls the "anti-politics machine" (2009, 20). Of course, such counterpublics might appear more utopian to some than to others, and the nature of post-transitional neoliberalism and its attendant polarization of groups according to multiple interests means that those with the capacity – education, leisure, capital – to activate countermemories are often elites whose idea of a counterpublic can be similarly exclusive.

Similar dynamics – and pitfalls – are evident in Kostis Kornetis's contribution, which explores the resurgence of reflections on Greece, Portugal, and Spain's transitions to democratic rule during the mid-1970s that emerged in popular cultural forms during the global recession of 2008–2010. Although the stasis these counter-memories sought to replace is different from that in Russia, the uses of memory – and specifically of the responses of ordinary people to earlier if different moments of crisis – are similar. Kornetis uses the term 'memoryscapes' to designate the similar dynamics at stake and in evidence in these three countries. His invocation of Ann Rigney's work on "the possibility of re-enacting cultures of joy, hope, exaltation and anticipation, rather than just reviving memories of pain, trauma and loss," might strike the reader as a version of a 'counterpublic,' though their engagement with politics is varied. The "aesthetical (and political) reemergence of codes of the 1970s music and films" three decades or more after the transitions that are recalled involves a degree of nostalgia, Kornetis finds, though one that understands its function clearly as a coping strategy for "dealing with the disenchantment with the present-day political situation" (Kornetis, 178). (Something similar might be said of Dlamini's account of some of his interviewees in Thandukukhanya.) What Kornetis calls 'cultural nostalgia' thus serves something like the function of what Svetlana Boym memorably cast as 'reflective' rather than 'restorative' nostalgia (2001, 41). It is not that those who recall aspects of earlier moments during a repressive period (of the kind from which an earlier transition is supposed to have delivered them) wish to return to a prior state. Rather, they wish to reflect on which aspects of the earlier state might somehow be recuperable in the future. (Here we see intimations of the usefulness of Walter Benjamin's thought about the task of his brand of historical materialism – and weak messianism – to which I will return.) Jacob Dlamini invokes Boym, too, recalling her observation that "Russians are fond of saying that the past is more unpredictable than the future" and offering as instructive mirror the South African satirist Pieter-Dirk Uys's joke that "the future is the only thing about which South Africans are certain: it is the past we are not sure about" (Dlamini 2009, 143).

Uncertainties of this sort manifest in several of the postcommunist contexts discussed in some other chapters in this collection, for example in Florin Poenaru's discussion of Herta Müller and Katherine Verdery's engagements with secret police archives of surveillance (in this case of the Securitate in Romania). Poenaru's discussion of the "file-memoir" that attempts to make sense of the capacity of the archive's revelations (about friends who might have been informants, of what level of detail of one's life was not private, and so forth) to "alter the memory of the past significantly" or "to cast past memories that now gained new meaning in a different light," demonstrates this complex affective-temporal destabilization. "[W]hat Müller's and Verdery's narratives express" – Poenaru suggests – "is not the encounter with an element from the past that cannot be properly integrated, but on the contrary, an element from the present (the revelation of knowledge) that retrospectively changes the coordinates of the past" (Poenaru, 49). "What indeed was the past to us?," Dlamini asks in *Native Nostalgia*; what was "the struggle against apartheid? Was it resistance or collaboration? Was it both?" (2009, 143). The answers, as he has gone on to demonstrate in subsequent work, are seldom straightforward. Poenaru's discussion casts the experience of finding the past unsettled as methodological challenge. Indeed, one of the significant strengths of many of the preceding chapters is their engagement with theoretical frames in multiple fields that do not always transfer from the context in relation to which they have developed to another.

If one response is for a writer to offer their *own* story, this is certainly partly what Dlamini offers in *Native Nostalgia*. As is the case in several of the cases discussed in this volume, he does this less to render his own story exceptional, than to work towards a revaluing of ordinary experiences of which his own might be emblematic. "[N]ot everything we did in townships was a reaction to white oppression" (2009, 108), Dlamini observes, in the course of his critical memoir of an apartheid-era childhood in Katlehong. Reflecting on family and community life, on imaginative connections with other people and places (listening to the radio "against the grain" [40]), and on the everyday experience of the world of the township, Dlamini's book offers us (inter alia) mediations on rodents and vermin, real and metaphorical; on class stratification, education, and music in the township; on money and sociality (burial societies, lending and borrowing, mutual support); and on the township *sensorium* – sight, taste, smell, noise, shebeen (or speakeasy) culture. One of the most contentious and fascinating reflections involves Dlamini's memory of an older generation's relationship with Afrikaans, the language of the white minority government, so often cast as the tongue of the oppressor but here recast as a language Dlamini remembers in positive terms. His mother and her friends spoke it when they didn't want the children to understand; "it was also the language of colloquial expressions." Indeed, "there was more to Afrikaans than conventional political history will have us believe [. . . .], there is a deeper sense in which Afrikaans was (and is) the language of black nostalgia" (Dlamini 2009, 139–40).

Here is an important attempt to recuperate the actual experience of daily life in a pre-transitional and transitional time (and place), and one that is necessarily in conversation with earlier (polemical) calls for attention to the everyday, not least that by Njabulo Ndebele. In 1986, Ndebele argued that Black South African creative expression, and especially writing, had been constrained by its reliance on the tropes and terms of engagement dictated by the spectacle of apartheid brutality, injustice, and revolt. Everything, Ndebele wrote

> has been mind-bogglingly spectacular: the monstrous war machine developed over the years; the random massive pass raids; mass shootings and killings; mass economic exploitation [. . .]; the mass removals of people; [. . .] draconian laws [. . . .] [i]t could be said [. . .] that the most outstanding feature of South African oppression is its brazen, exhibitionist openness. It is no wonder then, that the Black writer, sometimes a direct victim, sometimes a spectator, should have his imagination almost totally engaged by the spectacle before him. (1986, 143)

To break out of this circularity, the writer – but indeed every kind of cultural worker – had, Ndebele argued, urgently to "rediscover the ordinary."

Several chapters in this collection engage with precisely the problems and difficulties of restoring a sense of the ordinary. Such a dynamic is at stake in Ioana Luca's mobilization of Ann Cvetkovich's idea of the "archive of feelings" (2003, 7) to refer to "cultural texts as repositories of feelings and emotions, which are encoded not only in the content of the texts themselves but in *the practices that surround their production and reception*" (quoted in Luca, 244, her emphasis). Form is central to the evocation of ordinary experience of disjuncture, in particular. Mónika Dánél's chapter on the Hungarian movie *Bolshe Vita* (1995) and the Romanian novel *Hotel Europa* (1996) demonstrates how formal qualities (especially the "non-hierarchical juxtaposition" of different temporalities) give the texture of the disruption of the ordinary (or ordinary disruption) (Dánél, 110). Fragment might be said to be key to Dlamini's book, too; he describes it as emphatically *not* "an ethnography" of Katlehong, not a "conventional retelling" of the history, "neither a memoir nor indeed a cultural history" but rather "a gathering of fragments of memory, souvenirs of the imagination" (2009, 107). This might strike a reader as Benjaminian, and indeed Dlamini invokes the German writer's invocation to "brush history against the grain," to mobilize memories of the past (even the past under an oppressive regime) in a present that might integrate uncomfortable complexity in a renewed commitment to the commons (Dlamini 2009, 109).

Benjamin's sense that it is the task of the historical materialist, who seeks to refuse the homogenizing impulse of official (and ideologically conservative) versions of the past, to reach back and reanimate the latent energies of past utopian moments as they might be constellated (as if in a flash) with the present, in a present now-time, *Jetztzeit*, full of renewed potential (Benjamin 2006, 395–396), is invoked (appropriately) fleetingly in a number of chapters in this volume. Kornetis observes that his study of Southern European cultural nostalgia engages with phenomena that might be understood as a Benjaminian recuperative projects, a collective attunement to fragments of past modes that are reconstellated (in Benjamin's terms) in the present (178). The nature of the counter-hegemonic memory projects outlined by Zavadski is also very Benjaminian: what flashes up from the past might produce counterpublics to challenge the hegemon (188). Kylie Thomas quotes Benjamin as epigraph and subheading and redescribes *Jetztzeit* (perhaps inadvertently) as "transitional time" from which a new "political time" might be activated (139). And in the final chapter, Ksenia Robbe quotes my own reconfiguration of the stasis of postapartheid disappointment as a "Benjaminian 'now time' which suggests a non-progressivist historicity and 'weak messianic' hope (Van der Vlies 2017, 6–9)" (Robbe, 286). Robbe notes too that "identifying and theorizing the 'weak messianic,' in turn, can allow for conceptualizing critical possibilities also in the representations that invoke revolutionary 'unfailure' (here she is invoking Jennifer Wenzel [2009, 153]) "to point at the emancipatory desires and potentialities behind and beyond [. . .] transition processes" (Robbe, 296).

In her book on Benjamin's *Arcades Project*, Susan Buck-Morss poses a fascinating question: "Is unfulfilled utopian potential a psychological category (a wish of the collective unconscious) or a metaphysical one (the very essence of the objective world)?" (Buck-Morss 1989, 243). Perhaps, she continues, Benjamin is referring to both.

> Contemporary psychoanalytic theory might argue that the desire for immediate presence can never be fulfilled. Perhaps Benjamin would respond that it makes no difference. The point is, rather, that this utopian desire can and must be trusted as the motivation of political action (even as this action unavoidably mediates the desire) – can, because every experience of happiness or despair that was ours teaches us that the present course of events does not exhaust reality's potential; and must, because revolution is understood as a Messianic break from history's course and not its culmination. (Buck-Morss 1989, 243)

How to restore the political, to refuse the anti-politics machine (which now feeds in many places in Europe and elsewhere on the fuel of populism, both of the left and the right), is perhaps the chief challenge of our strangely transitional age, our "continuous present," in terms offered in Thomas's chapter, "in which time is on endless repeat and the possibility of addressing the challenges bequeathed to us by the past have come to seem insurmountable, their enormity even serving as a useful excuse for inaction in the present" (151). In the face of despondency, indeed of political depression, Ann Cvetkovich reminds us that "there are no magic bullet solutions, whether medical or political, just the slow steady work of resilient survival, utopian dreaming, and other affective tools for transformation" (2012, 2). Amongst the most powerful such tools – exemplified by the intellectual labor testified to in this collection – is remembering (or rememory-ing) transitions past, recognizing their ongoing resonances *and* revolutionary promise, as well as their inevitable, immeasurable, losses. This remains our most powerful prescription against the forces of forgetfulness unleashed anew all around us as we send this collection to print. What transitions will we be tasked with remembering in the future in relation to Ukraine, the West Bank and Gaza, or Myanmar? How will we measure our complicities in accepting processes of memorializing trauma that is ongoing in these places and elsewere as we type, teach, research, read – and close the book?

February 2022, rev. January 2023

Works cited

Benjamin, Walter. "On the Concept of History." Trans. Harry Zohn et al. *Selected Writings, Volume 4 (1938–1940)*. Ed. Howard Eiland and Michael W. Jennings. Cambridge MA: Harvard University Press, 2006. 389–400.

Boym, Svetlana. *The Future of Nostalgia*. New York: Basic Books, 2001.

Brown, Wendy. *Undoing the Demos: Neoliberalism's Stealth Revolution*. New York: Zone Books, 2015.

Buck-Morss, Susan. *The Dialectics of Seeing: Walter Benjamin and the Arcades Project*. Cambridge MA: MIT Press, 1989.

Cvetkovich, Ann. *Depression: A Public Feeling*. Durham, NC: Duke University Press, 2012.

Dlamini, Jacob. *Native Nostalgia*. Auckland Park: Jacana, 2009.

Jones, Megan. "Fracture and Selfhood in Jacob Dlamini's *Native Nostlagia*." *African Studies* 73.1 (2014), 107–123.

Ndebele, Njabulo S. "The Rediscovery of the Ordinary: Some New Writings in South Africa." *Journal of Southern African Studies* 12.2 (1986), 143–157.

Scott, David. *Omens of Adversity: Tragedy, Time, Memory, Justice*. Durham, NC: Duke University Press, 2014.

Van der Vlies, Andrew. *Present Imperfect: Contemporary South African Writing*. Oxford: Oxford University Press, 2017.

Wenzel, Jennifer. *Bulletproof: Afterlives of Anticolonial Prophecy in South Africa and Beyond*. Chicago: University of Chicago Press, 2009.

About the Authors

Mónika Dánél is an Assistant Professor at Eötvös Loránd University, Budapest, and was a Postdoctoral Researcher at the University of Oslo (2018-2021). Her research interests lie in contemporary Eastern European Studies (in particular, Hungarian and Romanian Literature and Film), theory of intermediality, multilingualism, space and body theory, memory and gender studies connected to postsocialist societies. She led the international project *Space-ing Otherness. Cultural Images of Space, Contact Zones in Contemporary Hungarian and Romanian Film and Literature* (see: http://contactzones.elte.hu/). She co-edited *Event-Trauma-Publicity* (2012) and *Space – Theory – Culture. An Interdisciplinary Handbook of the Space* (2019), and published two monographs in Hungarian: *Transparent Frames: The Intimacy of Reading* (2013) and *Language-Carnival: The Poetics of Hungarian Neo-Avant-Garde Artworks* (2016).

Kostis Kornetis is an Assistant Professor of Contemporary History at the Universidad Autónoma de Madrid. He has taught at Brown University, New York University, the University of Sheffield, and has been CONEX-Marie Curie Experienced Fellow at the Universidad Carlos III and Santander Fellow in Iberian Studies at St Antony's College, Oxford. He has published *Children of the Dictatorship. Student Resistance, Cultural Politics and the "Long 1960s" in Greece* (Berghahn Books, 2013) and co-edited *Consumption and Gender in Southern Europe since the Long 1960s* (Bloomsbury 2016) and *Rethinking Democratisation in Southern Europe* (Palgrave Macmillan, 2019). His new book *Transitional Generations: Memory, Conflict and Democratization in Southern Europe* since the 1970s is forthcoming with Oxford University Press.

Cara Levey is a Lecturer in Latin America Studies at University College Cork, Ireland. Her work generally focuses on the politics of memory in the Southern Cone. She is the author of *Fragile Memory, Shifting Impunity: Commemoration and Contestation in Post-dictatorship Argentina and Uruguay* (Peter Lang, 2016) and articles on commemoration and intergenerational memory in *ACME, History and Memory, Journal of Latin American Cultural Studies* and *Journal of Romance Studies*. She is also interested in post-crisis culture in Argentina and is co-editor (along with Daniel Ozarow and Christopher Wylde) of *Argentina since the 2001 Crisis: Recovering the Past, Reclaiming the Future* (Palgrave Macmillan, 2014), which was published in Spanish translation in Argentina in 2016. Her current book project considers the manifold ways in which the past is treated and 'worked through' by second generation and will be published with University of Wales Press in 2023.

Ioana Luca is a Professor in the Department of English at National Taiwan Normal University. She has published on life writing, exiles' literature, and transnational American studies. Her publications include articles in *Social Text, Rethinking History, Prose Studies, Biography: An Interdisciplinary Quarterly, European Journal of Life Writing, Slavic and East European Journal, Journal of American Studies*, and in several edited volumes, including *Cultures of Mobility and Alterity: Crossing the Balkans and Beyond* (2022). She also co-edited several special issues, most recently *Postsocialist Literatures in the US* in *Twentieth Century Literature* (2019) and *The Cultures of Global Post/Socialisms* in *Comparative Literature Studies* (with Claudia Sadowski-Smith, 2022).

Mykola Makhortykh is a Postdoctoral Researcher at the Institute of Communication and Media Science, where he studies politics- and history-centered information behavior in online environments and how it is affected by digital platforms and their affordances. To achieve this goal, he combines traditional social science methods (e.g., content analysis and focus groups) with novel computational approaches (e.g., deep learning and agent-based testing). His other research interests include

https://doi.org/10.1515/9783110707793-014

armed conflict reporting, disinformation and computational propaganda research, cybersecurity and critical security studies, and bias in information retrieval systems. Recently, he published on the impact of platforms and digital affordances on memory practices in journals such as *Memory Studies, Media, Culture & Society, First Monday* and *Visual Communication*.

Florin Poenaru is a Lecturer in Sociology and Anthropology in the Department of Sociology and Social Work, University of Bucharest. He has a PhD in social anthropology from Central European University and was a Fulbright Visiting Scholar at the City University of New York. He works on issues related to class, postsocialism and global history of Eastern Europe and teaches classes on contemporary theories in sociology and anthropology. He is a co-editor of CriticAtac, founding member of LeftEast and regular contributor to Bilten. His latest book is *Locuri comune: clasă, anti-comunism, stânga, Tact, 2017*. He also took part in over a dozen of election monitoring missions across Eastern Europe, the Balkans and the Middle East.

Ksenia Robbe is a Senior Lecturer in European Culture and Literature at the University of Groningen. She works at the interfaces of postcolonial and postsocialist, memory and time, and gender and feminist studies. She is the author of *Conversations of Motherhood: South African Women's Writing Across Traditions* (University of KwaZulu-Natal Press, 2015) and co-editor of *(Un)timely Crises: Chronotopes and Critique* (Palgrave, 2021) and *Post-Soviet Nostalgia: Confronting the Empire's Legacies* (Routledge, 2019). Her current research engages with memories of the 1980-90s 'transitions' in Russophone and South African literatures. She is leading the collaborative project "Reconstituting Publics through Remembering Transitions: Facilitating Critical Engagement with the 1980-90s on Local and Transnational Scales," supported by the NETIAS programme (2021-24).

Kylie Thomas is a Senior Lecturer in Art History at the Radical Humanities Laboratory at University College Cork and a Senior Researcher at NIOD Institute for War, Holocaust and Genocide Studies in Amsterdam. She is the author of *Impossible Mourning: HIV/AIDS and Visuality after apartheid* (Wits University Press & Bucknell University Press, 2014) and co-editor of *Photography in and out of Africa: Iterations with Difference* (Routledge, 2016) and *Women and Photography in Africa: Creative Practices and Feminist Challenges* (Routledge, 2020).

Darwin Tsen is an Assistant Teaching Professor and coordinator of the Chinese language minor at Syracuse University. He received his Ph.D. in Comparative Literature and Asian Studies from the Pennsylvania State University. Darwin's fields include modern and contemporary Chinese and Japanese literature and culture, critical theory and literary theory, film, Asian and Eastern European postsocialism, as well as Asian American literature. His book project, *Collectivity after Socialism in Fictions of the Transpacific* will be forthcoming from De Gruyter's Transnational Approaches to Culture series. The book examines how collectivity is imagined in the novels, films, television, documentaries, and comics of China, Taiwan, Malaysia, Japan and the U.S., five disparate geographical origins tied together by the recession of Chinese socialism and the rise of neoliberal globalization. His work has appeared in *Modern Chinese Literature and Culture, Teaching Anthropology, Comparative Literature Studies*, and *Verge: Global Asias*.

Pablo Valdivia Martin is a Chair-Full Professor of European Culture and Literature (University of Groningen), Accredited Full Professor [Catedrático Universidad] of Arts and Humanities (ANECA, Spain), Associate in Applied Physics at Harvard Paulson School of Engineering and Applied Sciences (Harvard University) and Academic Director of the Netherlands Research School for Literary Studies

(OSL). Before joining the University of Groningen in 2016, he worked at the University of Amsterdam, The Cambridge Foundation Villiers Park and the University of Nottingham. His research deals primarily with the 'Humanities,' 'Social Sciences,' 'Communication,' 'Computational Literary Studies,' 'Cultural Analytics' and 'Technology,' and the notions of 'Culture, Literature and Crisis' from a multidisciplinary transnational perspective. He is an expert on 'Cultural Narratives' and 'Conceptual Metaphors.' He carries out multidisciplinary research with particular emphasis on Digital Humanities, Artificial Intelligence, University Innovation, Data Science, Applied Physics, Social Sciences and Cognitive Sciences.

Bonifacio Valdivia Milla is a Spanish Literature and Language Professor at the School of Arts (Granada, Spain). Currently, Professor Valdivia Milla is the Director of the Reading Hub at Teatro Alhambra embedded in the Andalusian Research Center for the Study of the Performing Arts (Seville, Spain). He is an expert in performing arts with a long-standing trajectory as a theater critic collaborating with public institutions and Andalusian media (2004-2008). He was an expert advisor to the Andalusian Government Theater Program "Abecedaria" (2011-2018). Furthermore, he coordinated for several years the *Festin* Program of Theater in partnership with the University of Granada (Spain).

Andrew van der Vlies is a Professor in the Department of English, Creative Writing, and Film, at the University of Adelaide in Australia, and an Extraordinary Professor in the Department of English at the University of the Western Cape in South Africa. A graduate of Oxford and Rhodes universities, he is author of *South African Textual Cultures* (2007) and *Present Imperfect: Contemporary South African Writing* (2017), as well as editor or co-editor of a number of volumes, including *The Bloomsbury Handbook to J. M. Coetzee* and *Olive Schreiner: Writing Networks and Global Contexts* (both 2023).

Andrei Zavadski works at intersections of memory studies, public history, media studies, and museum studies. After receiving his PhD from Freie Universität Berlin in 2020, he was a Postdoctoral Researcher at the Centre for Anthropological Research on Museums and Heritage (CARMAH), Humboldt-Universität zu Berlin, and a fellow at the Centre for Contemporary History (ZZF), University of Potsdam. He is currently a Research Associate at the Institute of Art and Material Culture, TU Dortmund University. He is a co-editor of *Politika affekta: Muzei kak prostranstvo publichnoi istorii* [Politics of Affect: The Museum as a Public History Space] (2019) and of *Vse v proshlom: teoriya i praktika publichnoi istorii* [All Things Past: Theory and Practice of Public History] (2021). His work has appeared in *Europe-Asia Studies, Problems of Post-Communism, Media, Culture & Society, Novoe Literaturnoe Obozrenie*, and other journals.

Index

https://doi.org/10.1515/9783110707793-015

www.ingramcontent.com/pod-product-compliance
Lightning Source LLC
Chambersburg PA
CBHW050643270326
41927CB00012B/2856